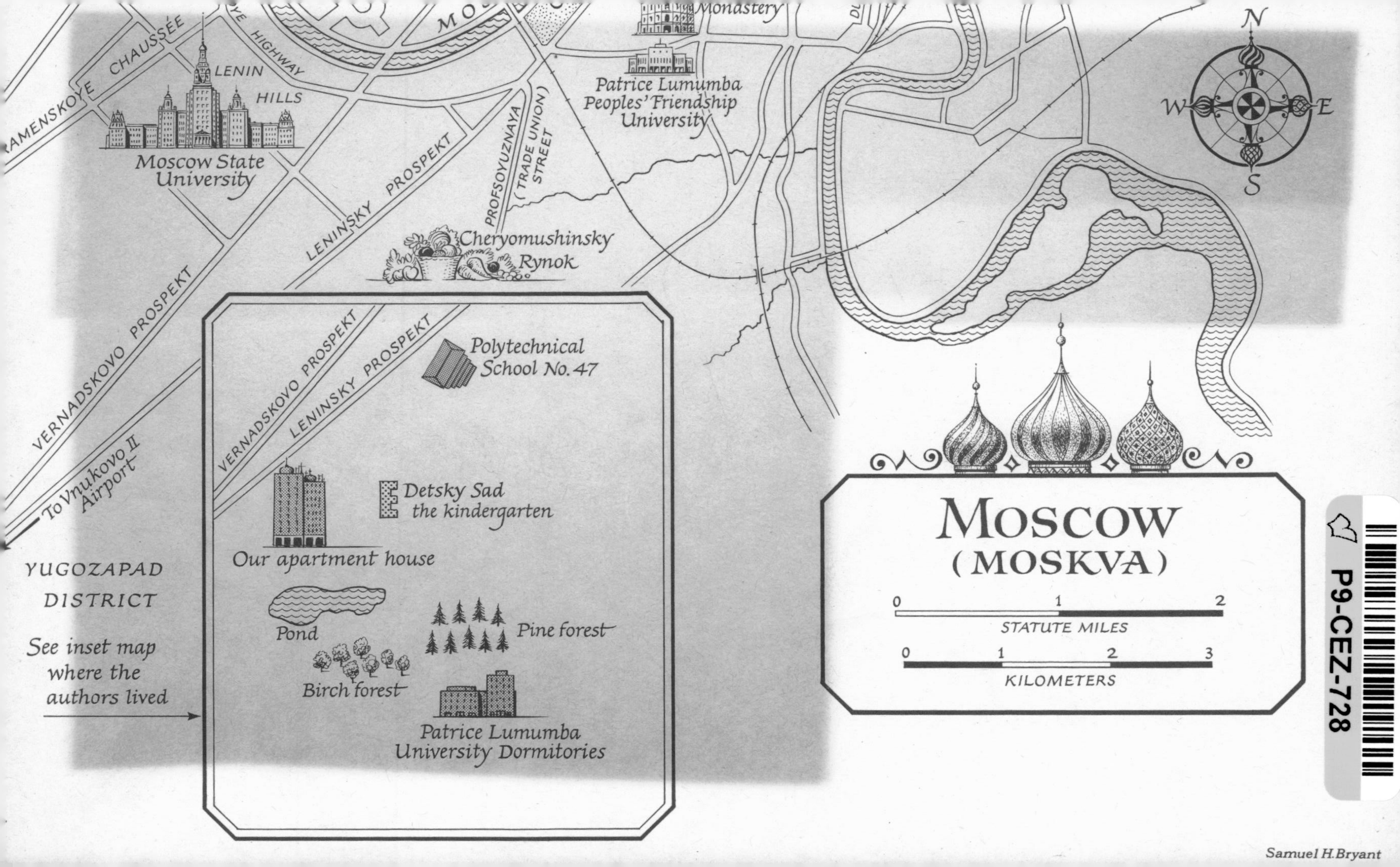

Monastery
Patrice Lumumba Peoples' Friendship University
LENIN HILLS
CHAUSSÉE
HIGHWAY
Moscow State University
LENINSKY PROSPEKT
PROFSOYUZNAYA (TRADE UNION STREET)
Cheryomushinsky Rynok
VERNADSKOVO PROSPEKT
To Vnukovo II Airport
N
W
E
S
VERNADSKOVO PROSPEKT
LENINSKY PROSPEKT
Polytechnical School No. 47
Detsky Sad the kindergarten
Our apartment house
Pond
Pine forest
Birch forest
Patrice Lumumba University Dormitories
YUGOZAPAD DISTRICT
See inset map where the authors lived
MOSCOW
(MOSKVA)
0
1
2
STATUTE MILES
0
1
2
3
KILOMETERS
Samuel H. Bryant

An
American Family
in Moscow

By Jerrold Schecter

The New Face of Buddha

An
American Family
in Moscow

Leona and Jerrold Schecter
and Evelind, Steven, Kate
Doveen and Barnet

Little, Brown and Company
Boston / Toronto

FIRST EDITION

T 11/75

The photograph on page 15 is by Martha Pearson, the one on page 33 by Strobe Talbott. The remaining photographs are by Jerrold L. Schecter.

The authors are grateful to the Washington *Post* for permission to reprint material from the articles "The Two Lives of Ivy Litvinov" (August 15, 1971) and "An Uneasy Passover in Moscow" (April 11, 1971) in Chapters 13 and 14. Copyright © 1971 by the Washington *Post*.

LIBRARY OF CONGRESS CATALOGING IN PUBLICATION DATA

Schecter, Jerrold.
  An American family in Moscow.

  1. Russia — Politics and government — 1953–
  2. Russia — Social conditions — 1945–   3. Russia
  — Social life and customs — 1917–   4. Moscow —
  Description.   5. Schecter family. I. Schecter,
  Leona, joint author. II. Title.
  DK274.S342   947.085′092′2   75-20307
  ISBN 0-316-77301-8

Designed by Susan Windheim

*Published simultaneously in Canada
by Little, Brown & Company (Canada) Limited*

PRINTED IN THE UNITED STATES OF AMERICA

*To our mothers and grandmothers, Belle Rubens Protas
and Miriam Goshen Schecter, and to the memory of our
fathers and grandfathers, Barnet Protas and Edward Schecter,
whose spirited storytelling links us to our past*

Preface

This book grew out of the laughing, remembering, storytelling and competitive interrupting that took place around the family dinner table in Washington whenever a visiting friend, politely trying to draw out the children, asked, "What was it like living in Moscow?" After that, all we needed was a referee.

When we began our life in Moscow, Evelind was thirteen, Stevo eleven, Katie nine, Doveen seven and Barney five. When we left there in 1970 they were two years older, and now, when this book goes to press in 1975, their ages range from twenty to twelve. The two eldest were born in Kobe, Japan, while Jerry was serving there as a U.S. Navy officer; Evelind is still often called Evachan (Little Eve), Steven is still Stevo, from Stebochan (Little Boy Steven). Katie was born in Montclair, New Jersey, during the three years when Jerry reported for the *Wall Street Journal*, then was a writer at *Time* in New York. Doveen and Barney were born in Hong Kong, which Jerry used as home base while he covered all of Southeast Asia and reported on China for *Time* from September of 1960 through the summer of 1963. We spent the academic year 1963–1964 in Cambridge, Massachusetts, when Jerry was a Nieman Fellow at Harvard. Then we returned to the Far East, where Jerry was Tokyo bureau chief of *Time* for four years before we went to Moscow.

After a few noisy sessions in which the children told about their experiences in Moscow we decided their memories ought to be preserved. We tried a tape recorder but the children were intimidated by the sound of their own voices. Writing was more satisfying and it eliminated the effort of interviewing and transcribing. Laziness bred brevity — wanting to get done with their writing chores they learned to tell their stories succinctly and therefore, we think, better. We have not changed their writing at all, except to reduce it where they repeated themselves or each other. Looking now at what they wrote earlier, they are sometimes embarrassed by their own brutal honesty at a younger age. Doveen read over her geographical summary at the end of chapter 9 and demanded, "Be sure you make it clear I was eight when I wrote it."

Evelind is a Russian studies major at Yale, Stevo is taking advanced Russian and studying Soviet film makers at Harvard, Katie, Doveen and Barney are at the Georgetown Day School in Washington, where the two girls are studying Russian and Barney will start it again in ninth grade. They all look forward to returning to the Soviet Union someday, perhaps for study, or because their careers require it, or just for the pleasure of visiting old friends and favorite places.

We sometimes think it strange that the two years in Moscow should have shaped their future interests. They spent three years in Hong Kong and four years in Tokyo, during which they were also avidly engaged in their surroundings. They spoke Japanese and were beginning to read it. Nevertheless, Moscow was such an intense experience that for a while it blotted out all the immediacy of the previous years. Even dreams, they told us, began to take place in Japan again only after they had left Moscow.

We have tried to describe the special quality of the Russian years and the human relationships that left their imprint on us. In the repressive and ideologically stringent Russian society there is always the threat of potential punishment for giving vent to natural emotions. Curiosity about the outside world, inventiveness, experimentation and impulse are dangerous in the Soviet Union. Stopped at the borders both physically and intellectually, rigidly directed from the center, citizens are caught in the narrow limits in between. Friendships take on an added dimension of risk, passion and commitment. In describing them, we felt it necessary to change most people's names and in a few instances to give a composite personality rather than a singular, identifiable one. In every other way, this is as it was for us in Moscow.

Acknowledgments

Our thanks go to all those who made our two years in the Soviet Union a rich and intense experience. They are friends, named and unnamed, whose strength of character was an inspiration, whose humor and perseverance in the simple pleasures and amenities of daily life made Moscow our home.

In the course of writing our experiences we relied heavily on the friendship, editorial skills and critical talents of Gregory Freidin, John Nathan, Strobe Talbott, Pamela Sanders, John Shaw and Stanley Cloud. They helped us to blend our voices and to clarify them. There was always the quiet pleasure of sharing with them.

We are grateful to Judy Protas for her detailed review of the manuscript and to Lynn and Harold Mayer for their editorial suggestions.

The descriptions of censorship of news stories in chapter 8 draws in detail from the accounts of former Moscow correspondents which appeared in the July 1968 issue of *Survey*.

Henry Anatole Grunwald and Murray J. Gart of *Time* offered their personal support while we were in Moscow and throughout the writing of the book.

Ned Bradford, senior editor of Little, Brown, sustained our idea for a family book in the Soviet Union with his gracious encouragement and astute editorial suggestions. Jean Whitnack's devoted attention to detail and sense of style were invaluable in the final editing of the manuscript.

Contents

Illustrations

An
American Family
in Moscow

1

Arrival in Red Square

JERRY AND I STOOD outside the National Hotel in the bright May sunlight looking across to the Kremlin. The yellow and white walls of the Kremlin armory glistened, and even the dour red brick of the Lenin Museum seemed fresh. The young Intourist guide who accompanied us was taken aback by my first incautious remark. All I said was, "How clean the air is in Moscow! You can take a deep breath and not fill your lungs with smog, unlike Tokyo or New York." He cut me short in mid-breath.

"Of course we have smog. What do you think? We have as much smog as any other great city of the world."

We had come on a reconnaissance trip from Tokyo to see if the family could join Jerry on a two-year assignment as the Moscow bureau chief for *Time*. For four years there had been no *Time* man in Moscow. The last correspondent, Israel Shenker, was expelled in 1964 after *Time* ran a cover story on Lenin which the Russians considered disrespectful and insulting. In Moscow, Lenin was sacrosanct. In a society where religion was ridiculed the cult of Lenin had become the source of moral and philosophical certainty. The story said that Lenin, his wife Krupskaya and a young Frenchwoman, Inessa Armand, lived together in a *ménage à trois* that lasted, with interruptions, for ten years.

"We never wrote about George Washington's mistress," a Russian official told Jerry by way of explanation and warning on the ground rules. This "offense" of referring to Lenin's private life followed by only two months a cover portrait of Leonid Brezhnev framed by a chipped sickle, broken blades of wheat and a slash line that read, "Breadlines in Utopia."

Time had made no promises to change its coverage of the Soviet Union, except to assure that Jerry would not be "anti-Soviet." In Tokyo we had met Vsevolod Ovchinikov, the correspondent for *Pravda,* the Communist Party newspaper. His judgment about us, we knew, would play an influential role in our acceptance or rejection by Moscow. In late-night dinners at our home and his we discussed Communism, Buddhism and the American work ethic without resorting to cold-war slogans.

Upon what conditions had the Russians relented and accepted our application for accreditation? Would we have an apartment or would we and our five children have to live in two hotel rooms? Shenker, his wife and two children lived in the Sovyetskaya Hotel for fourteen months. Would we live under the cloud of past recriminations or would we be allowed to start afresh?

We took it as an indication that *Time* was welcome in Moscow again when we were shown to a two-room corner suite in the Natsional Hotel, with its own balcony overlooking Red Square.

Jerry scheduled the trip so that we would be in Moscow for the annual military parade on May Day. The week started with cold rain on a gray, wintry landscape, but within a few days we watched the bare trees turn green and the air become warm. May Day was sunny and the still-wet streets had been washed down for the parade.

In the morning we walked among the crowds of people out enjoying spring and the holiday on the wide boulevards. I wondered aloud to Jerry why the streets were so wide. Barricades would be hard to mount across these huge expanses of macadam. Were they designed with the security of the state in mind? The access to Red Square is narrower, and here it was necessary to have a press pass to enter and review the parade. Jerry's pass didn't admit me, so I returned to the hotel and watched from the small, iron-fretwork balcony attached to our suite. From my perch I saw a stream of tanks and missiles draw up to the gates of the Kremlin, pause and wait their turn to enter the stage where they would impress with their bulk and devastating promise. We had been drawn to taking the Moscow assignment because we wanted to understand Communist power, and here it was before our eyes.

What Jerry saw in Red Square on May Day morning dispelled any doubts he had: it was going to be a worthwhile two years.

Jerry: The clock on the Spassky Gate struck 10 A.M. and Marshal Grechko, the defense minister, raised his sword to a salute position. Standing in a ceremonial Zil open limousine, he was slowly driven from the Lenin Museum at the end of Red Square to the reviewing stand for the Politburo atop the maroon marble Lenin Mausoleum in the middle of the square. There he received a salute from the commander of the Moscow garrison and the parade began in earnest: First the regular infantry in calf-length black boots marching in a modified goose step on the heavy cobblestones. Then army paratroopers, special forces with pink berets, navy and air force. Next the motorized artillery, tanks, amphibious vehicles small, medium and large. Finally the missiles: first the small surface-to-air missiles, SAM-1's and SAM-2's; then the medium-range ballistic missiles, followed by underwater missiles; then the giant surface-to-surface missiles, the SS-11's and SS-13's. The intercontinental ballistic missiles with red-tipped warheads rumbled across the square on half-tracked diesel engine carriers.

As the procession of carriers gathered momentum crossing the square, the whining and clanking crescendoed, then held steady in a deafening roar that blotted out everything but the power of the passing weapons. For a moment I thought they could not be real. Perhaps they were dummies, like Disneyland replicas. These were the missiles that could destroy America.

Along with threatening the West, the Politburo was showing its own people what they were sacrificing for. Shoddy plumbing, lack of trucks to distribute food, shortages of housewares and automobiles, all were supposed to be compensated for by the roar of the missile trailers and the naked display of military might in Red Square. As the missile carriers disappeared below the domes of St. Basil's Cathedral, swarms of workers paraded across the square and were followed by floats and balloon-bearing youths. Some grotesque floats showing bloated Uncle Sams squeezing the oppressed of the world with wringers made of dollars and bombs, and condemnations of the Vietnam war, passed in blurred streams to the blare of martial music.

The day was soft and warm but the missiles had stirred a chill in my innards. Never have I seen such a massed display of power. Can I ever fathom the sources of strength that produced this war machine? The force of Red Square and the Kremlin behind its red-brick walls was no longer symbolic, but real.

Leona. Jerry and I were forced to contrast this dazzling show of nuclear weapons with the rest of what we saw around us. Even in our first brief visit we found that Russia is still the backwater of Europe that it was in tsarist times. As the Intourist guide demonstrated in his defense of the Moscow smog, the Russians suffer from a sense of inferiority in style and productivity to the world's other power centers. The fruits of peace have been subordinated to building for war. This contradiction gnaws at the Russians and makes them crave elegance and efficiency.

Young Russians asked us why their country must always be second-class in everything but armaments. Military technology has not been carried over into modernization of everyday living, as in the West where, for instance, electronic miniaturization developed for weaponry gave us a new sophisticated range of consumer appliances. In Moscow, when we wanted to change our airline reservations, it took the clerk two days of angry shuffling through piles of tickets before she could confirm our new reservations. There was no computer. Russian consumers don't use personal checks or credit cards.

After we made our way around the city, visiting the site of the new apartment house where we might be given rooms, Jerry was ready for his meeting at the Press Department of the Ministry of Foreign Affairs. His first encounter with Soviet officials was painful but promising.

Jerry. Monday, May 6, 1968. A bright warm morning with a soft breeze. The sun shines on the golden onion domes of the Kremlin churches. Our breakfast of Algerian orange juice, yoghurt, dark toast, ham, eggs and coffee, ordered the night before from the hall *dezhurnaya* (woman on duty), arrived at the room. I chose my formal blue pin-striped suit with a white shirt and a bright striped Dior tie, kissed Leona goodbye as she lingered over coffee and *The Forsyte Saga*. I asked why she wasn't reading Lenin instead of Galsworthy in Moscow. "This is a great anticapitalist tract," she said.

I set off down the great staircase. Taking the steps two at a time requires concentration because they are so wide and the carpet is loose.

The circular Art Nouveau wrought-iron banister, left over from a by-gone era, is the last touch of elegance in the hotel. The stained-glass windows behind the stairs add to the pre-Revolutionary look.

Felix Rosenthal, the Russian interpreter for *Life*, was waiting for me in the lobby, carrying a giant briefcase of python skin that a friend had brought him from Mali. Although *Time* had been banned *Life* maintained its bureau. Felix was friendly and helpful. The Ministry of Foreign Affairs, Ministerstvo Inostranykh Del (or MID) is one of the wedding cake landmarks of Moscow that were dropped upon the broad boulevards by Stalin to commemorate his reign. From a distance the architecture is solid but ugly, with the heavy rectangular lines that strive to impress with power, but on close scrutiny reveal a lack of imagi-nation. Two huge doors that appear to be the main entrance are closed; all traffic is controlled through a small revolving door to the right. Inside, we were halted by a policeman in a red and blue uniform. Felix explained that we had an appointment.

At two minutes after ten an attractive, brown-haired girl with a full figure and a pleasant manner conducted us to the office of Fyodor Matveyevich Simonov and a younger man with a brush haircut named Voznikov, who was in charge of American journalists. Simonov had the Kremlin pallor of a washed-out war-horse who has spent twenty-five years in bureaucratic servitude. Yet he retained his smile and a genial sense of accepting the system which he tried to convey.

We talked about cable cards, press cards and visas. Simonov ex-pressed sympathy about the housing problem and said, "We will do all we can to help you." He indicated we would get an apartment on Leninsky Prospekt when the apartment building, still under construc-tion, was completed. There was no mention of *Time*'s expulsion. Simonov casually added that an Italian television correspondent had been living with his wife and child in a single hotel room for four years, and working there as well. Later, Felix explained that this was a way of warning me that if the Press Department decided not to help me I would not receive an apartment. In Moscow there was no such thing as renting an apartment through a real estate agent. As we neared the end of our conversation Simonov said Mr. Zamyatin would like to receive me for a few minutes.

Leonid Zamyatin (now director general of TASS, the official Soviet news agency) was government spokesman and head of the Press Depart-ment. Of medium height, he had a full head of wavy gray hair and the brisk air of a young executive. The walls of his office were barren except for a portrait of Lenin. We shook hands warmly and sat down on straight-backed chairs with tatty rose-colored cushions, around a worn table with a glass top that was off kilter. He began by asking me how I liked Moscow and if this was my first visit. Tea in glasses and cookies were served. Then slowly he worked into a lecture. "It is important for correspondents to better relations between our two countries," he said. "I do not expect you to write for your editors like a *Pravda* writer does. That would not be fruitful." By this he meant that the *Pravda* man follows the Communist Party line but I was expected to free my copy of cold war preconceptions. Unspoken, but reassuring to me, was the knowledge that a new *Pravda* man would be permitted to come to New York when I was admitted to Moscow. My acceptance in Moscow had been carefully used by the Russians. Zamyatin lashed out at my predecessor as a man "who came here with bitterness in his heart," and warned me "that there was no sense having a man in Moscow who will write things that could be written in New York or Washington." The Press Department would try and help me, but "it is easier to ask questions than to answer them, as I found out when I was a student taking exams." He told me that the Soviet Union was following a policy of peaceful coexistence but that while there could be economic cooperation and trade, it did not mean ideological convergence.

I knew that *Time* had been rehabilitated when Zamyatin took out a pile of photographs of Hedley Donovan, editor in chief of Time Inc., and George Hunt, managing editor of *Life,* and their wives muffled in furs riding on a sledge pulled by a troika of snorting horses through the snow. Zamyatin asked me to take the photographs back to New York. They suggested traditional Russia, a landscape upon which we could savor the pleasures of Russian life without ideological differences.

Leona. We came to Moscow hoping to understand a part of ourselves that had been abandoned sixty years before by our grandparents. Our parents' generation, like most first children born in America, wanted no part of their Russian and East European heritage; they wanted to shed their parents' immigrant ways and fit into a Yankee mold. The next generation, ours, typically looked for its roots. We were born Americans, we had no doubt who we were, but we looked back in time for our ethnic distinctiveness, which we thought would add richness to our lives within the American experience. When we wanted to name our first son Samuel we met stiff family opposition: "We've spent our lives getting rid of names like Sol, Sam, and Max. That was our rebellion."

My father, like many sons of Russian Jews, left Byelorussia when he was thirteen, after his Bar Mitzvah. If he had stayed behind he would have been drafted into the Russian army where he would have been forced to eat unkosher food and give up his religion. It was 1906, a year after the abortive uprising of 1905, in which he had taken part. As a young tailor's apprentice he attended a workers' meeting in the forest near Pinsk. The tsar's cossacks came on horseback to break up the meeting and barely missed my father, who hid himself in a roadside ditch. A year later he joined a group that fled over the Carpathian Mountains and found their way to Amsterdam. From there he sailed in steerage to New York, where his older brother had preceded him. Forty years later he could still remember his seasickness on his first voyage across the Atlantic. We asked if he would ever like to go back to Russia for a visit. He answered by describing a dream he often had in which he walked back to his birthplace on a long bridge, but after he visited and wanted to return to America, the bridge had disappeared. He remained a celebrator of American freedom and opportunity to the end of his life.

When my father arrived in New York he went to work as a tailor, the trade he was trained for in Pinsk. After fourteen years in the garment district sweatshops, he bought a farm in Sullivan County which he immediately converted into a summer hotel. The clientele were "landsmen" from his corner of Russia. The next year my father married my mother, an American daughter of Russian Jews who came from the area around Kiev. The hotel grew each year with guesthouses built by my father and local carpenters; not until he needed steel beams did my father employ an architect. The hotel work was a hard change for my mother from her profession as a legal stenographer but she had some knowledge of the hotel business from helping her Russian parents run a lunch restaurant on the edge of the garment district.

Her father, who was only a legend to me because he died before I was born, had been a doctor in the Russian army and later the doctor for a rural area, in the employ of the tsar's government. He found his

medical domain difficult to cover and was called to account for allow-
ing my grandmother to dispense medicine. He was given the choice of
sending away my grandmother or losing the job; he left for America,
promising to send money for her and the children to follow. After
years of waiting and working as a governess and seamstress, she borrowed money from a relative to go to America, where she intended to
divorce my grandfather. She found him unable to cope with the economic demands of the New World, but as attractive as ever. She
opened a restaurant to support the family, which in time included
three more children, my mother among them. He never contributed
very much work to the restaurant but he took loving care of the children, spoke seven languages, and was learned in the Torah, which he
treated as literature, not as religion. He was an iconoclast and a non-
believer in God, and spent many afternoons arguing his point of view
with his friends as they filled and refilled their tea glasses from the brass
samovar my grandmother had brought with her.

When we left for our first look at Moscow, my mother stayed with
our children in Tokyo. I asked if she remembered any Russian from her
childhood but she could only dredge up the words for dog, bread,
and gentleman. Her parents spoke Russian when they didn't want her
to understand. When I began to study Russian I recognized many
words that had been incorporated into Yiddish, which my parents spoke
to each other when they didn't want me to understand.

In Moscow that first week, the Intourist guide took me to see Tolstoy's house in the city. As I entered the long bungalow with its floors
painted brown, I had a sense that I'd been there before, but I couldn't
recall what I was reminded of. Later, when I was back in Tokyo, my
mother listened to me describe the moment and knew immediately what
I had sensed. "Years ago, when you were still a young child, all the
floors in the hotel were painted that way. Then it was considered old-
fashioned so we scraped and varnished them all." Tolstoy's house
looked to me like the guesthouses my father built, long cottages with
rows of windows on both sides, a country style of architecture he unconsciously carried with him. The other hotelkeepers in the Catskills, many
of them Russian Jews, built the same way.

After we had been in Moscow a few days we went to the Hippodrome to see the trotting horses race. I never watched the horses because I couldn't take my eyes off the stands. The faces, the mannerisms,

the accents, the way of walking and wearing clothes took me back in time to a home I had left years before. The spectators at the Hippodrome in Moscow made me feel as if I were at the Monticello racetrack back in Sullivan County, New York. The faces were as familiar as the waiters, bellhops, taxi drivers, sportswriters and the hotel guests of the Catskills where I was born.

As I watched these familiar figures at the racetrack and on the streets of Moscow I came to a sudden awareness that changed my perception of myself. For all at once I realized that the mannerisms, the mental habits, the view of life, the shoes and hats and coats and even the walk of old ladies, which I had looked upon in New York as being separately and distinctively Jewish, were indeed Russian or East European. The way my father and his brothers laughed, the cruel delight they took in cutting down their victims with ridicule, the uncontrolled frenzied shouting that took place when they disagreed with one another, all of which I looked upon as Jewish family traits, were straight out of the pages of Maxim Gorky's *Childhood*.

Finding more of myself than I anticipated made me smile. It also made me more ready to accept my grandparents' ways, because for the first time I could visualize them in context. I brought with me also an open-minded attitude toward the great Revolution that was perhaps conditioned by my maternal grandfather's religious skepticism, my father's participation in the uprising of 1905, and their expectations that change in Russia would bring progress.

We had not yet visited the Anglo-American school when we met its American principal at a cocktail party. He warned me that his school had no obligation to accept all our children; there might not be room for all five. The school was a convenience to the diplomatic corps and a favor for which newsmen should be thankful. We were not to look upon places in the school as a legal right, as we might expect of a neighborhood public school in the United States. The seventh grade, which Stevo was due to enter, had only two other members. The Anglo-American school ended with the eighth grade, so Evelind, who was ready for ninth, would either have to be sent abroad or attend a Russian school.

We returned to our suite in the Natsional Hotel and talked about the problem. As far as I was concerned, we weren't coming to the Soviet Union if we had to send our daughter away to boarding school. For me, the time when children leave home of their own will comes soon enough; I wasn't about to push them out before then. Jerry calmed me with a simple decision that was to enrich our lives in Moscow and have a permanent effect on the children's approach to learning: "We won't send her away from us. She'll go to Russian school. They'll all go to Russian school."

In Tokyo and in Hong Kong before that, we had wanted to send the children to Japanese and Chinese schools, but it was nearly impossible. Written Japanese and Chinese are so difficult that a student cannot easily enter it after first grade. Returning Japanese businessmen who had lived abroad for years found that their children had missed so much of their native education that they had to enter the American school with foreigners. Second, the racial difference that set our children apart from Asian children could not be overcome. Although they spoke Japanese fluently and played at ease with Japanese children, no amount of adaptation could change what the eye could plainly see.

For a few months in Hong Kong, when Katie was turning four, she attended a Chinese kindergarten in Aberdeen, a fishing port a few miles from our house in Shouson Hill. Each morning she and the daughter of our Chinese cook, dressed in clean pinafores with ribbons in their neatly combed hair, climbed into the school bus at the gate of our crumbling colonial mansion. The Chinese school demanded homework of their four-year-old students, so in the evening the cook sat Katie on his lap and led her hand through practice sheets of Chinese characters. Her behavior at home, which was increasingly rambunctious, masked some unhappiness, but she insisted she loved school. The bubble burst after two months, when Evelind had a day off from the British school she attended and went with the two little girls to see what it was like. Evelind came to report that Katie spent most of the day crying, sometimes from having her blond curls pulled by curious, laughing Chinese playmates, sometimes from being knocked down by classroom bullies who resented a foreign child's attracting so much attention. Katie was unwilling to admit how much she suffered because she loved getting dressed up and going off with the cook's little girl every day. Just then she came down with chicken pox, which provided an excuse to stay away from school, and she never returned.

In Moscow there was a chance that we might don the skin of the Russian bear and read his heart. Our racial memories stemmed from this soil. Dressed like Russians, our children would look like their class-mates. The language, though difficult, was, in some ways, structurally similar to Western languages, and like English, it was reduced to an alphabet that could be learned quickly. I noticed with satisfaction that in a week I could read street signs; in the Far East I had been function-ally illiterate for nearly ten years of my life. Whereas our children were a burden to the teacher in a Chinese school, and the Japanese flatly refused to accept them, the Russian educators we soon met greeted us warmly and indicated a willingness to go out of their way to help our children learn Russian.

From Moscow we flew to Paris and Copenhagen to outfit the re-established office. We ordered double-decker children's beds, and a washer and dryer that would work on Moscow's 220-volt, 50-cycle cur-rent. We were warned that imitation furs would not sustain us through a Moscow winter. Nor would I stay warm in the fashionable but short-haired seals and curly lamb coats paraded before me in the fur shops of Copenhagen's Østergade. I tried on full-length chinchillas and crisply cut minks, just to see how they would look, enjoying the choosing as much as the buying of my first and only fur coat. I had to keep in mind that the coat would have to go shopping in the farmers' market in the morning and attend diplomatic balls in the evening. When Jerry pulled a flamboyant long-haired red fox coat from the rack and beckoned me to try it on, I could see by his smile that he hoped it would fit. Its full-ness and flowing auburns would hardly melt into the population un-noticed, but it fitted and kept me warm through two long Moscow winters.

Then to London to take the polar flight back to Tokyo. At Heath-row Airport we waited in a large room filled with Japanese who would take the same flight. The lounge was alive with a peculiar excitement. The Japanese travelers bowed and smiled more broadly than at home in Tokyo, noisy in their delight in talking to their countrymen again. They seemed genuinely relieved to be finished with Europe and on their way back to a civilization where they understood the rules, where they could expect to get what they gave. I found myself sharing their relief, and I knew I would miss Tokyo.

First we would have to learn Russian. We chose a summer course at the Monterey Institute for Foreign Studies in Monterey, California, a small liberal arts college started by former teachers of the army language school there. The institute promised two years of college Russian in ten weeks. Jerry, the two oldest children, then thirteen and eleven, and I enrolled in the regular course, six days a week. To tutor the three younger children at home, the institute hired a young graduate student who had emigrated from the Soviet Union as a child and who still spoke fluent Russian.

We began each morning in a large general class of about forty students to whom Mrs. Elischer, an aged but stalwart lady of the old regime, explained the rudiments of grammar. After a short break for a stroll in the sunshine and a snack from the candy machine to feed Stevo and Evelind's hungry brain cells, we returned for an hour of drill in a smaller class of twenty. Then back to Mrs. Elischer for another hour of explanation, followed by another hour of drill. After a pause for lunch we settled down each day for an hour in the language lab, listening to tape recordings of properly pronounced oral drills which we were to repeat in unison. On Friday Mrs. Elischer had us take a short dictation; I knew from my nervous perspiration that it had been too long since I had taken a written examination. The pace was a chapter a day and we had to race to keep up. During the first week we had not recovered from the trip across the Pacific; we no sooner donned earphones in the language lab than we fell asleep. But by the start of the second week we all knew how to read and write the Russian alphabet, a modest accomplishment but enough to spur us on.

The three younger children, at home with Mara Stein, their tutor, clipped pictures from magazines and labeled them in Russian to use as flash cards. Barney, who was five, complained that Mara always gave him the hardest words; he would rather catch fiddler crabs along the Point Lobos beach than sit still for her word games. The girls, too, thought it was a game about a made-up language. They could not imagine a real country in which people talked this way. Mara ate with us and conducted our mealtime conversations in Russian. She helped us prepare the next day's lesson in after-dinner sessions that lasted late into the night. *Roditelny padezh* (which means genitive case) became a family swear word. We kept working by reminding ourselves that this ordeal would be over in ten weeks and learning to speak Russian in Moscow would be at a more leisurely pace.

Our fellow students were college juniors and seniors, graduate students and teachers. The inclusion of Evelind and Stevo in a group of this caliber was an experiment for the school and a worry both to

Evelind and Leona studying in California, August 1968. (Photo by Martha Pearson)

the teachers and to us. We tried to slow them down, get them to relax and skip some of the homework, but the specter of Russian school, the gaping unknown that lay before them, drove them to absorb as much Russian as they could.

About the first week in August Mrs. Elischer sent them to the blackboard to take a dictation, assuring them that she didn't expect perfection. They performed on a par with the best in the class. This wonderful old woman kissed them both and smiled with joy, the special happiness felt only by a teacher who has given her best and begins to see results of her efforts.

They had met an enormous challenge. Classes in Russian school with children their own age couldn't be as difficult as this summer had been. Some of the terror of entering Russian school "without a tongue" had been blunted, but they still faced the uncertainty of how they and Russian kids would take to one another. They still had before them the task of making friends with schoolmates who not only spoke a different language but whose mentality and upbringing were totally different from their own. Who would change, our kids or the Russians? Could they attend Russian school for two years and not become indoctrinated with Communist ideas?

The white-haired, heavy-set old White Russian army sergeant who drilled us in grammar at the institute also did his best to instill fear into the children and us. He spent time that should have gone to imperfect verbs and noun case endings on romanticized memories of life in tsarist St. Petersburg and his days in General Kolchak's security guard in the war between the Whites and the Reds. Curling his handsome lips over lifeless dentures, he regaled us with stories of orphan children left homeless after the Civil War and how they were rounded up by Stalin and never heard from again. He interrupted Evelind, then thirteen, from her note taking to ask what she would do if left with the responsibility for her four siblings. As we ate our sandwiches between classes in the school's outdoor cafeteria, he stopped by to tell us the story of the Soviet folk hero, Pavel Morozov, a teenager who turned his father over to the Bolsheviks for shielding landowning peasants during the collectivization drive by Stalin. Enraged neighbors lynched Pavel but the Communists made him a martyr to the cause. Would Steven, then eleven, remain his father's son after being hammered by Communist propaganda in school every day?

The profound and reassuring voice came from our petite and wrinkled, proudly straight-spined, eighty-year-old Russian teacher. Vera Aleksandrovna Elischer told us not to worry. Despite the tsarist double-headed eagle she wore on her collar every day, she said life in Moscow would give the children a firsthand experience that few Americans could duplicate and provide them with a depth of understanding and an ability to judge the differences between Soviet and American cultures that would never leave them. She told us not to be concerned about their growing away from us ideologically, because in a close-knit family such as ours the primary and final influence would be from the home. "Remember," she added, "Soviet or tsarist, Russians are still Russians. They love children."

2

After Czechoslovakia– Limbo

THE DAY AFTER our grueling ten-week effort to learn Russian ended, Leona and I, and all the children, were enjoying the quiet hour before dinner in the stone house we had rented on the edge of Point Lobos Park overlooking the Pacific Ocean. We held our breath as we watched a deer nibble leaves in our rose garden. The ringing telephone jangled and broke the mood. Evelind answered. "The Russians have invaded Czechoslovakia!" she proclaimed through the calm of the California dusk. We could hear waves breaking on the rocks of the point and seals barking. Our idyll in California was over before it began.

The daily four-hour classes in Russian, the endless laboratory sessions listening to tape recordings and the long nights of learning case endings were suddenly relevant. We surrounded the radio to hear details of giant Soviet transports flying into Prague to disgorge tanks and troops. It was still only 3 P.M. in New York and I called Dick Clurman, chief of correspondents. "Can you leave tonight?" Clurman asked. "I'd like you to be in Moscow now, barring that I want you to leave immediately." I wondered how soon it would take me to file my first story from Moscow.

We both checked schedules and within minutes were back on the telephone again. With luck and the time difference I could be in Moscow the next afternoon.

Clurman came to the airport in New York to bid me farewell between flights. Along with cash and traveler's checks he provided instructions: "See if you can file for this week. We want to know what the mood is in Moscow, what people are thinking and saying." It was the kind of moment that delighted Clurman. He envisioned himself as a commander deploying his troops for war. He had a heroic sense of adventure and a willingness to spend heavily on the big story to achieve results. He believed in purposeful journalism that when possible was also elegant and gracious. He was the delight of his correspondents and the bane of the accountants.

Clurman gave me two sleeping pills and told me they should guarantee five or six hours of sleep. The potion worked and it was early morning in Copenhagen when I awoke. Three hours later, the only first-class passenger on a Boeing 707, I saw the white birches and green fields around Sheremyetevo, the Moscow airport. There were only a few buildings in the midst of green, rich woods. It hardly seemed as if I were landing in the capital of a nuclear power that had just sent her armies into Czechoslovakia.

Felix Rosenthal, the *Life* interpreter, and Volodya, the *Life* driver, greeted me as I emerged from immigration. There was no customs inspection and we quickly drove from the airport past the signs for the Czechoslovak Airline and the wooden country houses on the edge of the city, across the bridge being built over the Moscow River. Felix had little news to offer except that *Pravda* had run an eight-section, 13,000-word editorial on two complete pages that detailed the Soviet case against Alexander Dubcek, the secretary of the Czechoslovak Communist Party, and his economic and political reforms.

The *Pravda* piece made the reasons for the invasion brutally plain. The Czechs, it said, were pursuing one aim: "to undermine the ideological-theoretical basis of Communism." At the office I devoured the *Pravda* editorial and digested it into a seven-page file, which I sent off to reach New York just before the deadline. Then, exhausted, I had a ham sandwich and a Czech beer and slept. (It was one of the ironies of the invasion that the supply of Czech beer in Moscow continued to be prized and that the Russians preferred it to their own soapy brew.) With the eight-hour time difference between New York and Moscow I had caught up with the clock in a physical sense but felt terribly alone and depressed.

I still had no inkling of what Muscovites felt about their role in this historical event. Here it was three days after the invasion of Czechoslovakia and the Russians were ready to welcome the captive Czech president, Ludvik Svoboda, with full state honors. We had no idea where Dubcek was being held or what status he had.

Western foreign correspondents were barred from the official airport, Vnukovo II, where Leonid Brezhnev and the defense minister Marshal Grechko, complete with honor guards, hugged and kissed President Svoboda and Defense Minister Martin Dzur. When the Czech national anthem was played the wives of the Czech correspondents wept openly. Standing on Leninsky Prospekt watching Svoboda drive to the Kremlin in an open car I felt like an extra in a film extravaganza. Crowds lined both sides of the street in the bright sunshine, waving paper Soviet and Czech flags that read, "Welcome Czechoslovak friends." The arrival of Svoboda was highlighted on the television news and he was praised as "an outstanding statesman and military leader who made a great contribution to the joint struggle against a common enemy — German fascism.'

The American press corps gathered for its regular Friday afternoon meeting at 3 P.M. in the chancery that had the air of a memory hole in Alice in Wonderland. The floor plan seemed to have no order. Corridors twisted and turned like a maze, sometimes dead-ending for no reason. Embassy officers appeared and disappeared behind corners and in alcoves. The military attachés had their own floor complete with built-in recorded music to foil bugging devices. This was the chancery where a bug had been found in the American eagle on the national seal in 1956 and the embassy was ever ready for violations of its security. The windows of the ambassador's office were closed to prevent any sensitive Soviet listening devices that might be installed in an apartment house across the street from picking up conversations. For critical security matters there was a quiet room, a clear plastic igloo inside a secure area of the chancery where the ambassador could meet with the senior staff to discuss policy. A video camera behind the Marine guard's desk surveyed the entrance and courtyard, and his logbook kept a record of visitors.

I had expected a more official setting for the chancery of the United States Embassy in Moscow, not a run-down, yellow stucco, converted apartment house with creaky elevators and a grimy clutter. The camp chairs in the ambassador's office and the government-issue furniture were shabby like the rest of Moscow. The air conditioner was so noisy it had to be turned off if we were to hear each other.

Ambassador Llewellyn Thompson was out of the country, having returned to Washington for "consultations" on August 22. Attendance was limited to American citizens working for American publications, and of the twenty-five accredited American correspondents, half were there. It was my first look at most of them. Emory Swank, the chargé d'affaires, would offer an analysis of the situation. The group included Henry Shapiro of United Press International, who shared seniority with Edmund Stevens of the London *Sunday Times* and *Newsday*. John Dornberg of *Newsweek* and Jack Bausman, bureau chief of the Associated Press, were there. The office was cramped and hot. Swank sat behind the ambassador's oversized desk with an American flag at his left.

There were two big overstuffed chairs and a couch in the ambassador's office. Henry Shapiro and Ed Stevens usually sat in the big chairs, a privilege accorded to their seniority by their colleagues. I was not aware of it the first day and got sharp looks as I sat in one of the comfortable black chairs. Then, realizing it was Shapiro's place of honor, I shifted seats. He smiled and sat down.

My colleagues were wary of each other, an attitude peculiar to Moscow. In other capitals there was no need to visit with the American ambassador as a group. Japanese and Russian correspondents got the line from their ambassadors around the world, but no self-respecting American newsman would rely on embassy handouts. A courtesy call and a chat with the ambassador, or lunch or dinner with him, was quite correct, but a weekly briefing and exchange of views were unseemly and unprofessional. Yet Moscow was a special case. American correspondents could not pick up the telephone and call government officials without getting clearance from the Press Department of the Ministry of Foreign Affairs. Telephones were tapped and all overseas calls monitored. Only on rare occasions would the Ministry of Foreign Affairs issue a statement or hold a press conference. The Press Department considered what was reported in *Pravda* and *Izvestia* and on the TASS wire as news enough for foreign correspondents.* The weekly

---

* *Pravda (Truth)* is the newspaper of the Central Committee of the Communist Party and has its central offices in Moscow. It is also published in other major cities

meeting with the ambassador was a measure of desperation. Since none of us wanted to give away his carefully nurtured sources or his special insights, there was no real give-and-take between us.

As we sat in the ambassador's office Svoboda entered the Kremlin, where the Czech flag flew over the guest quarters. Still nobody knew where Dubcek was.

"The saddest thing," Swank began, "it that it shows the complete unwillingness of the Soviet Union to make an adjustment to change." Nobody knew how the vote to invade was cast, but speculation was that Brezhnev sought to spread responsibility among the eleven Politburo members. He was the centrist who forged the consensus to invade. Pyotr Shelest and Nikolai Podgorny, the hard-liners, probably urged the invasion. Kosygin, considered more rational and intelligent, was presumed to be against it. But Swank warned, "This is sheer speculation." Embassy briefings rarely provided news; they were good summary and review sessions.

I wanted to meet Russians and talk to them about the invasion. A friend of Felix's from Novosti, the government news and feature agency, stopped by the office briefly and told me that the new government would be formed in Prague by Monday. He rattled off the names of those who had accompanied Svoboda to Moscow. "We expect a new government over the weekend," he said. It was rumored that Svoboda would finish his talks the same day and return to Prague. On the surface all was in order and under control. There was little to indicate the struggle actually taking place as Svoboda insisted that Alexander Dubcek, the head of the Czech Party, Premier Oldrich Cernik, and Josef Smrkovsky, the president of the Czech parliament, be included in the talks.

I checked with the UPI office. Nobody had hard details; all anyone knew was that the talks were continuing. I filed to New York on the Svoboda arrival and TASS's description of it as "a friendly official visit to discuss questions of mutual interest."

---

like Leningrad and by Regional Party organizations. These editions of *Pravda* contain both material from the central offices in Moscow and locally originated stories. *Izvestia (News)* is the official government newspaper of the Council of Ministers. All these newspapers, plus two other newspapers of wide circulation — *Komsomolskaya Pravda* and *Trud (Work)*, the organs respectively of the Young Communist League and the trade union organizations — carry news from TASS, the telegraphic agency of the Soviet Union, and from Novosti, another government-sponsored news and feature agency, as well as from their own correspondents.

Bitter, black humor was beginning to emerge. "How do the Russians go to visit their friends?" asks one Czech of another. "In tanks," was the reply.

If I were a Russian who read only *Pravda* and *Izvestia* and watched Soviet television, I would have seen the events in Czechoslovakia as a counterrevolution aided by West Germany and U.S. intelligence agents. "German revanchism" was a slogan used to raise the specter of World War II, in which twenty million Soviet citizens were killed; it was an emotional trip wire that brought back to millions memories of the suffering of the Great Patriotic War. The image was of West Germany rising again as a military power to conquer Russia. If this seemed far-fetched to me as an American, it was real enough to any Russian old enough to remember the war. Every family had lost a relative or a loved one; they still lived with scarred psyches and broken lives. Felix told me about his uncle, who lived through the siege of Leningrad, the terrible nine hundred days when the Germans cut off all supplies of food and fuel, so that half the population of three million perished. Even in 1968, twenty-five years later, he still could not stand to see crumbs left on the table. After a meal he would meticulously sweep them together in a pile and eat them.

I asked Felix to join me for dinner in a restaurant where there might be ordinary workers. Given the Soviet method of seating strangers at the same table to fill empty spaces, we might have an interview. I was anxious to practice my Russian. We walked across Kutuzovsky Prospekt to the Crystal Café, two blocks from the office. The restaurant was crowded on Friday night. We walked up the wide staircase to the second floor amidst the heavy smell of cabbage soup and the sound of a five-piece dance band reminiscent of the 1950's.

We were seated with a young couple who said they didn't mind if we joined them. I struggled away in Russian with Felix helping. There was no caviar so we ordered smoked sturgeon for an hors d'oeuvre. The girl's blond curls had a stiff beauty-parlor finish. She wore a simple gray suit of shapeless cut, but she had soft, gentle skin that gave her a glow despite the plainness of her dress. Her husband, Anatoly, in slacks and a white shirt open at the neck, was an engineer in a factory. She was an office worker. They were recently married. I asked what they thought about the events of the past week. Anatoly said, "I read about it in *Pravda*." He explained that Soviet troops had been called in to crush a counterrevolution. "It is too bad this had to happen. We have given much to Czechoslovakia and our people died to save the Czechs in the war. Why should the Czechs trade with the West when we made sacrifices for them?" he asked.

There was no way to check on what was happening inside the Kremlin except to see if the talks were continuing. On Saturday afternoon the Kremlin was closed to tourists. A crowd carrying Czech and Soviet flags gathered near the Borovitsky Gate, but at 3:30 P.M. the crowd was told that it could go home and troops waiting in the side streets were sent away. The meetings continued in the Council of Ministers building. We waited for news of a new Czech government but none was announced. Svoboda's continued presence in Moscow on Saturday night indicated that he had won his demand that Dubcek, Cernik and Smrkovsky join the talks.

The only signs were the Czech flag flying over Svoboda's quarters and a cluster of waiting black limousines. Outside the red-brick Kremlin walls young couples sat under the linden trees on this warm summer evening and boys whistled at girls from passing cars.

Czech journalists passed the word that Dubcek had joined the talks. Dubcek and Smrkovsky had been flown to Moscow on Thursday, two days after the invasion, and had been held under house arrest. By Saturday evening it was obvious that the plan for a quick take-over and change of government in Prague had failed. The waiting group of Soviet citizens directed to cheer Svoboda's arrival and departure, dubbed the "rent-a-crowd" by Moscow foreign correspondents, was ordered to cease its vigil. This was the signal that Svoboda remained in the Kremlin.

I drove around Red Square, which was deceptively normal. A brief rainfall had broken the dryness and dust of late August. The Borovitsky Gate, through which the Czech delegation had entered and would come out, was open to foot traffic. Near St. Basil's Cathedral tourist buses were lined up. In the Moscow River below the Kremlin wall, excursion boats passed in the cool dusk.

That evening I was invited to Peredelkino for dinner at the home of Victor Louis. Although he is a Russian, Louis is a correspondent for the London *Evening News*. He is said to have links to the KGB (Committee for State Security) and high-ranking Soviet officials. In my first week on the job I was curious to hear the line he would take on Czechoslovakia.

Poster that reminds the Russian people: "Don't forget the lessons of history!
Revanchism, Diversionary Tactics, Espionage, Anti-Communism"

Peredelkino is a fifteen-minute ride west of Moscow down Kutuzov-sky Prospekt, past the victory arch for the Napoleonic war and the circular museum that re-creates the Battle of Borodino, in which Marshal Kutuzov turned the tide against the French. The wide boulevard with its seven-story apartment houses (Brezhnev lives in six rooms at Number 26) has a middle-class look that reminded me of the Grand Concourse in the Bronx, except for the occasional giant portraits of Lenin. The stolid apartment houses give way to new workers' housing and a single motel. Then the white birches begin. Huge trees shadow the roadway and there is a quiet sense of being in Turgenev's countryside.

Peredelkino is where the privileged people in the supposedly class-less society live. Here are *dachas* (country villas), with ponds, gardens, streams, and privacy for writers, generals and ministers. The dry, pervading summer dust of Moscow and the heavy dank body odors of people pressed in lines waiting for food or buses disappear.

In Peredelkino tall wooden slat fences, painted forest green to blend into the landscape, demarcate the enclaves of the elite. There are no nameplates or identifying signs of individuals, no brightly painted letter boxes. There are only small, discreetly placed numbers, the mark of anonymity and fear, a carry-over from the purge years. In all of Moscow there was no telephone directory publicly available, no name directories in the lobbies of apartment houses. All inquiries had to be directed to special information offices. Vigilance against spies and foreigners is a habit from Stalin's time. Suspicion still dominates Russians when they meet someone outside their group or collective; toward foreigners suspicion is a duty. The Czech invasion scratched this dormant nerve of the purge years and a sharp shiver ran through the body politic. I was warned by my colleagues to expect a freeze. I was surprised to receive the invitation to dinner and wondered how the Russians there would respond to me.

Victor Louis's house is at the end of a gravel road with high trees and high fences. A double gate bars the entrance. Onto the original wooden frame dacha with its angular peaked roof he had added two concrete wings with picture windows. The lawn was carefully mowed and the guests were gathered on the patio in the rear, which faced a formal English flower garden with roses, gladioli, asters and nasturtiums.

Louis insisted that I take a swim in his pool, by all accounts the only privately owned swimming pool in the Soviet Union. It is a round prefabricated plastic tank five feet deep and forty feet in diameter on the edge of the garden. The water is cool and pleasant. Below the pool is a clay tennis court and small changing-house designed to resemble a Swiss chalet. In Moscow, where the change-over from communal living to one-bedroom apartments is still under way, Louis's ostentatious affluence is calculated to impress and puzzle foreigners and fellow Russians alike. Nobody else comes near to living this way except Politburo and some Central Committee members. Beyond the tennis court is a small public park and a river with a waterfall, a seeming extension of his dacha garden.

Victor Louis speaks English with only a trace of a Russian accent, the English of Russians trained by British-educated teachers. As we shook hands he said: "You do not look like a man who has just been rehabilitated." It was an opening with a double meaning and I sensed I was being tested. He wanted to tell me he knew of *Time*'s recent troubled past, at the same time alluding ironically to his own past and what it was like to be rehabilitated. He had been arrested on charges of black-marketeering in 1947 and was imprisoned in labor camps for nine years, until 1956. Some fellow survivors accused him of being a *stukach* (stool pigeon) — a camp informer.

Everything about him seemed layered with double meanings and complex motives. He has an alert, intelligent face with smooth skin and high color. His smile was calculated, not spontaneous. His eyes seemed hidden behind wide steel-rimmed glasses. When he took them off I had to look hard to see what was hidden within. When he laughs his eyes do not join in, and they quickly become cold and challenging. Despite his slouched shoulders and slight potbelly on a slim frame he is not a relaxed person. He has a veiled intensity, a wariness, perhaps the mark of the prison-camp survivor.

Louis exploits the isolation of Western correspondents and diplomats. (Travel by foreign correspondents without written permission is limited to forty kilometers or twenty-five miles around Moscow; the artists' and writers' colony of Peredelkino, only fifteen miles away, is officially off limits.) An invitation to Louis's dacha, therefore, conjures the air of a clandestine undertaking, a partaking of the forbidden fruit. Actually, if one drives out to Peredelkino in a taxi, as I did that evening, or with a Russian in a car with Moscow license plates, there is no problem, but given the mood of Moscow there is always the fear that a visit to a forbidden zone without official permission could be used to fuel a provocation.

The other guests included a West German correspondent and his wife, the builder of the new wings of the house, a Russian journalist, and a foreign-trade official named Gennady with his flirtatious wife, Mira. A tall, soft-skinned blonde with a vibrant face and passionate nostrils that crinkled with suggestion, Mira insisted on reading my palm when we were introduced on the veranda. She grasped my hand and placed it close to her full breast so that it grazed the soft white cotton of her blouse. "You are very far from your parents. You have had and will have many love affairs," she said in halting English, lifting her eyes to mine. We both laughed.

Louis was busy playing host, offering what he called "reactionary Czech beer" in frosted, heavy mugs. It was the kind of arrogant touch he seemed to enjoy. He showed me the grounds with a sweep of the hand and said that his English-born wife, Jennifer, was responsible for the gardens. Unsolicited, he mentioned that he had in the garage a Mercedes 450 SL, a peach-colored Porsche, the only one in the Soviet Union owned by a Russian, and a Landrover. His gardening tools came from Abercrombie and Fitch in New York, he said. When complete the house would have its own sauna and he planned to build a small ski tow on the hillside nearby.

As we entered the house for dinner I was stunned by the ikon collection spread over two walls. The faces of Christ, the Virgin Mary and Saint George, painted in glowing reds, ochers and browns, stared out through ornate gold and silver frames. On the floor was a white polar bear rug. Nailed to the wall over the fireplace was a collection of porcelain plates inscribed with *khleb i sol* (bread and salt), the blessing representing the body of Christ and the salt of the earth. The plates are a traditional wedding gift. The collection ranged from the most primitive to the most elaborate, highly glazed platters in blues, pinks and yellows.

In contrast to the art of traditional Russia there was a painting by Oskar Rabin, the "unofficial" artist whose dark samovars and grim street scenes offered a bitterly satirical comment on the lack of vodka, food and freedom of ideas, characteristic of the mood of Moscow intellectuals in the 1960's. An abstract impressionist work by Vladimir Nemukhin hung on the opposite wall. Here was a flash of the soaring spirit of Kandinsky, still the mainstream of inspiration for abstract impressionists in Moscow even though he left the Soviet Union shortly after the Revolution. Neither Rabin nor Nemukhin is permitted to join the Union of Artists. Louis's display of their "disapproved" work in his house was a calculated effort to show that his taste in art did not conform to the dictates of the Soviet state. It was another of his carefully constructed contrasts to the norms of Soviet life that he took pride in emphasizing.

The supper table was laden with caviar, salads of chopped. green onions, coleslaw, tomatoes with fresh dill, chopped chicken livers, a whole fresh-water pike in jelly, sausage, smoked salmon and heaping platters of dark bread and butter.

The first course was a summer soup made of cold kvass, chopped cucumber and diced sausage, a Russian version of gazpacho. Kvass is the national soft drink of the Soviet Union, an uncarbonated brew dark amber in color and with a mild tang that emanates from fermented rye bread. The Russians say it is their Coca-Cola and stand in line to buy it by the glass, quart or pail. Unlike other soft drinks, kvass is not bottled, but is dispensed by spigot from tanks mounted on trailers that are parked on street corners. I found kvass soup, served with dollops of sour cream, a refreshing new taste. I wondered if the children would like it.

There was vodka to accompany the caviar and provide a toast of welcome. A simple but smooth Georgian red wine enhanced the supper. Everybody but our host quaffed it in quantity. He only sipped from his glass but joined the conversation to expound on Soviet policy or discuss the pleasures of buying old ikons and furniture in the secondhand stores of Moscow. People were getting rid of old chests, desks and chairs for new machine-made furniture. If one knew the staff and rewarded them they would call to announce new acquisitions, Louis said. "This is a better method than Western advertising," he added sardonically. Later I learned that word of mouth was the way Muscovites learned where and when hard-to-find suitcases or good cuts of meat were available. Newspapers carry no consumer-product advertising.

Louis was clearly proud of the way Jennifer had organized the meal. Jennifer came to the Soviet Union as a nanny for a British military attaché. The Louises' three boys were in Russian schools but they all had learned English at home and Jennifer read them Dr. Dolittle stories. Jennifer's Russian was passable, but she deliberately maintained her English accent and mannerisms. There was a whipped cream–covered trifle for dessert that gave the meal an English touch and the watermelon was served with knife and fork.

Over strong black coffee, brandy and Cuban cigars I joined Gennady, who is responsible for negotiating the purchase of chemical plants from Western Europe. He was confused and upset by the invasion. He knew how badly the Czechs needed to trade with the West and enter into new economic arrangements, but he avoided a detailed answer by saying only, "I do not understand."

Louis invited me to see his study and office on the second floor. Purple jacquard silk woven in a floral pattern covered the walls, an anomalous backdrop for the jumble of portable typewriters, tape recorders and six shortwave radios lined up on the floor. He pointed to them proudly and said he bought new ones on his trips abroad. "I always like to have the latest model," he explained. The telephone on the desk had a new Swedish combination receiver and concealed dial. A copy of an antique telephone stood in its box, waiting to be installed in the new wing of the house when it was completed. On the desk were an Abercrombie and Fitch catalogue, a cigar cutter made of deer antler, and a new device for automatically dialing telephone calls. From a bookshelf filled with the latest works on the Soviet Union and China he pulled out two thick leather-bound scrapbooks and began leafing through them, pointing to newspaper and magazine articles on his exploits and the scoops he had achieved over the years.

In 1959 he had translated *My Fair Lady* into Russian and arranged for it to be staged in the Soviet Union, never bothering to obtain permission from the authors because the Soviet Union did not belong to the international copyright convention.

He had had a worldwide exclusive on Nikita Khrushchev's ouster from power in 1964. There were stories on how he had befriended the unorthodox writer Valery Tarsis, who was allowed to leave the Soviet Union in 1966 after his exposé of life in a Soviet insane asylum, *Ward Seven*, appeared in the West. The move to send Tarsis out rather than arrest him was clearly an effort to counteract the unfavorable impact of the trial of Andrei Sinyavsky and Yuly Daniel, who in 1966 were sentenced to hard labor for their writings that "slandered" the Soviet Union. Louis had accompanied Tarsis in London and served as his interpreter. His relationship to the Soviet government and to the KGB were speculated on in the articles he showed me. Most of the clippings were from 1967 and told of his role in offering an alternate manuscript of Svetlana Alliluyeva's memoirs and family photographs to newspapers and magazines in Europe. He flipped to March 1968 and his exclusive account of the death of Yury Gagarin, the Soviet Union's first man in space. His sources had provided him with details of the crash of the jet trainer which Gagarin was flying. He also showed me stories that said he had tried to sell an unauthorized version of Aleksandr Solzhenitsyn's *Cancer Ward* in the West, but this he denied. In a dispatch to the London *Evening News* the week before the invasion of Czechoslovakia, he insisted that the Soviet Union would have to deal firmly with the Czechs.

I asked how the Politburo would justify the invasion and if there would be any protests like those in the United States against the Vietnam war.

"We fought for Czechoslovakia and we supplied them with the raw materials and credits to rebuild. For twenty years we have given the Czechs the best we have and provided their military security. They have no right to seek more and better in the West. They cannot just walk out. Our people feel they have sacrificed for the Czechs," he said emphatically.

"But how do you and your friends feel about the invasion?" I asked.

"Of course intellectuals are opposed to oppression and regret the need to send Soviet troops, but there was no alternative," Louis said.

"What do you mean no alternative?" I asked heatedly. "You know there was no Western intelligence plot to foment a 'counterrevolution.' Crying 'German remilitarization' is just a cover-up for the loss of Soviet control in Prague and Eastern Europe."

"Of course," Louis replied with a shrug. "Our interests were at stake and we had to defend them. The Czechs have an obligation. We tried. Our leadership traveled there twice to find a way out. Can you think of any other time in history when the Soviet leadership traveled to a country and said, 'Now be good boys, we mean business.' It's as if the entire cabinet of the United States traveled to Guatemala or Nicaragua to try and resolve your difficulties there. In Stalin's day Dubcek would have been brought to Moscow in two hours, dead or alive.

"Dubcek simply could not control the situation," Louis went on to explain. "Look around the Communist bloc — the Romanians conform internally, although they are more independent in foreign policy. The Poles have their own domestic system but they back us down the line in foreign policy. You can have leeway in foreign affairs or in domestic policy but not both. Dubcek couldn't keep his promises and he tried to move too fast.

"Why should the Czechs be allowed to have a convertible currency and not the other Communist countries in Eastern Europe? Why should Czechs be allowed to travel to West Germany and other Western countries when Russians cannot? The Czechs must be part of the Communist bloc and make the same sacrifices as the Russians and the other allies. The Soviet Union does not have enough gold or foreign trade to support a currency that can be convertible into dollars; therefore nobody else in the bloc can have a convertible currency."

Then to lighten the mood he told the story about Dubcek taking Brezhnev and Lyndon Johnson for a ride in his car. "Let's drive to the left," says Brezhnev. "Let's drive to the right," counters Johnson. Dubcek flicks the turn indicator to the left and steers the car to the right.

I had left Victor Louis's dacha with the same uneasy feelings I had had when discussing the Vietnam war with American officials. The pattern of rationalization was disturbingly familiar.

The next morning I received a telephone call from a colleague who told me there had been a demonstration by a group of six people in Red Square against the invasion of Czechoslovakia. Among the demonstrators was Pavel Litvinov, the grandson of Maxim Litvinov, who had been Soviet foreign minister from 1930 to 1939 and ambassador to Washington during World War II. The group unfurled a banner that read: "Hands Off Czechoslovakia," and shouted the slogan "For Your Freedom and Ours," which was used by the Polish-Russian democratic movement in the nineteenth century. The banners were ripped from their hands and the demonstrators were punched and pushed into police cars. I confirmed the details from other correspondents and diplomats. What could such a protest mean, I wondered. How many people were these demonstrators speaking for? How would the regime treat their protest? If there were an open trial to make an example of them

Jerry in Red Square. (Photo by Strobe Talbott)

the dissenters would have an opportunity to challenge the invasion, much as American protestors challenged the government policy in Vietnam.

Throughout September it was rumored that an open trial would be held. Litvinov and his friends were being held in jail and Soviet law required that they be tried. There was a freeze on public discussion of the invasion as their fate was being decided. Would it be a show trial in which Litvinov and the others were forced to confess their "error"? Would it be a trial like that of the writers Andrei Sinyavsky and Yuly Daniel, who in 1966 were sentenced to hard labor for their writings that "slandered" the Soviet Union? Their trial led to a series of protests that formed the basis for the dissident movement and the publication of appeals for human rights. The arrest and trial of Pavel Litvinov and his fellow protestors continued the development of dissent and marked a new turning point in Soviet intellectual opposition. The democratic movement became better organized and reached more people.

In the hot, dry September days that followed the invasion I sought to reestablish the *Time* office and rebuild files that had not been touched for four years. *Time* scheduled its first cover story on Aleksandr Solzhenitsyn, timed to the publication in the West of his novels *Cancer Ward* and *The First Circle*. I tried to interview him by requesting a formal meeting through the Press Department of the Ministry of Foreign Affairs.

Solzhenitsyn was living in a small dacha outside the twenty-five-mile travel limit. Special permission was needed to make the trip but I could not obtain it. Thus the usual practice of going to his house and waiting for him to open the door in hopes of gaining an interview could not be followed. I also applied for interviews with the heads of the Writers' Union and the leading literary magazines. After half promises the Press Department said the interviews could not be arranged. Everybody was either sick or on vacation. There would be no official cooperation.

Still, I was able to gather fresh glimpses of how Solzhenitsyn was living, writing, and building his role as Russia's conscience. My colleagues introduced me to Russians who knew Solzhenitsyn. They told me he was being harassed by the KGB and would not meet foreign journalists. He wanted only to continue his writing. Meanwhile the prospects for obtaining an apartment in a new building brightened and we were assigned rooms in the Ukraine Hotel until it was ready. I returned to New York briefly to work on the closing of the Solzhenitsyn cover and to bring the family back to Moscow.

3

Trials, Public and Private

I ARRIVED IN MOSCOW with Jerry and the children on October 3, a clear but sunless autumn day. Rudy Chelminski, the *Life* correspondent, and his wife Brien welcomed us at Sheremyetevo Airport. As we rode together between the flat bare winter fields on the way into the city, they pointed out the huge stylized tank trap that stands as a monument and a marker showing how close German troops advanced on Moscow before they were repulsed in World War II.

The edge of the city was a disarray of earth-digging and construction equipment, as if the city were growing in rings like a tree. The outer ring was made up of postwar apartment houses of tan brick with glass storefronts on the street level. The streets were without distinction, with no thought of beauty or planning for a community, but they were remarkably clean. As we came toward the center the structures were older, from grandiose castles of the Stalin era back in time to nineteenth-century yellow stucco row houses. After we lived in Moscow for a while I came to love both the monstrosities and the streets of old houses; they were particularly appealing at sunset, when the gargantuan edifices became romantic fortresses in silhouette and the yellow houses absorbed the sun's light and glowed with golden fire.

Later I would confirm my first impression of the city's spanning out in concentric circles. At the center is the Kremlin, whose walls and towers enclose the ancient city. We visited the Kremlin often, sometimes to look at its cathedrals or museums. The ornate collections of tsarist jewels, robes and gilded carriages are a mute but eloquent testimony to the Revolution that swept away their living reality and petrified them in display cases for bemused posterity to gaze upon. We visited Lenin's austere apartment, now a museum. We often walked the cobblestone road under the Kutafya Tower and through the Trinity Gate to the Palace of Congresses, the Lincoln Center of Moscow, where we saw lavish ballets and operas or listened to speeches extolling the next goal of the central planners.

Around the Kremlin are the graceful avenues of what were once the commercial quarter and the most fashionable residences. Once-proud mansions of yellow or pale green with sculptured plaster eaves and lintels, in brave but inadequate repair, now bear name plaques of city or government agencies. Scattered among them are the main hotels, all within view of the Kremlin. The old university buildings across from the Kremlin still house some of the faculties, even though a new main campus has been constructed in the Lenin Hills in the new city beyond the Moscow River that winds swiftly through the city like a snapped whip.

The next ring of buildings, formerly comprising the suburbs for poorer Muscovites, are streets of attached yellow stucco houses, the repeated patterns of windows and doorsteps punctuating their humble sameness. They are encircled by Sadovoye Koltso, the old garden ring road. The new avenues of apartment buildings fan out from it, beginning with post-Revolutionary construction, much of it in gray sandstone, with square, heavy proportions, and ending with the white prefabricated boxes of the present. The newest apartments, only twenty minutes' drive from the center, are on the edge of the city near the birch forests that surround Moscow.

Growth, the persistent eater of woods and open spaces, seems to have been gentle with Moscow, leaving untouched many parks, formerly imperial gardens, the zoo, the racecourse and a number of open squares as it spread outward. Old factory and working-class areas on the eastern side of old Moscow have remained in place. In the old city, in fields between the apartment buildings, and in the new suburbs are still to be found wooden houses with carved and sagging window frames, and with their old tile-covered stoves still puffing smoke and warmth.

Once while walking from the zoo to Kalinin Prospekt, a street also known as Moscow's "golden mile" because of its modern construction and one skyscraper, I passed the site being cleared for the new American Embassy along the western bend of the Moscow River. The bulldozers had been through once, but they hadn't finished; in one swipe they had torn off half of each of a row of houses, leaving a panorama of another era. In each house, stripped of the privacy of its façade, I could see the central stoves and chimneys still standing, most of them of white tile without decoration. Pale wallpaper still covered plaster walls where broken wood laths poked through like splintered bones. The next time the bulldozer came it carried away centuries in its path.

On that first day the office drivers delivered us to our suite of rooms in the Ukraine Hotel, with Kutuzovsky Prospekt on one side and the Moscow River on the other. The hotel is a mass of stone, tall as well as wide, with spires reaching up from the roof — one of the monuments to Stalin's taste. Since we were on the ninth floor and the elevators were very slow, we had to avoid too many trips up and down in a day. Our suite consisted of a bedroom, a separate bath and toilet, and a large sitting room with two couches, some stuffed chairs and a large round table with enough wooden chairs for all of us. Next to the suite we had two small rooms with bathrooms. The interior spaces of the hotel, the lobby and halls, were as broad and massive and dull-colored as the stone exterior. The spaces and maze of halls were awesome to the children, and the four who slept in the two small rooms felt they were vulnerable to the traffic of drunks and strangers outside their doors. Evelind slept on a sofa in the sitting room.

For the first two days we took our meals in the hotel dining room, but except for the chicken noodle soup the cuisine did not appeal to the children. They were not the only ones to find the Russian sauces heavy with fat and unpalatable. There seemed to be almost a hundred Japanese staying at the Ukraine Hotel. Having moved so recently from Tokyo, the children immediately began chattering in Japanese and making friends. These Japanese businessmen and designers had spent months waiting for the ministries to sign contracts, many of which had been initiated on previous trips that had taken similar amounts of patience and intestinal fortitude.

A pretty young Japanese woman who represented a dress company in Nagoya attached herself to us at our first dinner and implored Jerry to order her a dish of plain rice. She spoke no Russian and could not convey this simple request to the waiter. It was inconceivable to him that anyone should want to eat unseasoned rice, but he brought it to her.

"Isn't there anything good to eat in this country?" Stevo cried after two days of the hotel fare.

We quickly overcame the problem of unfamiliar diet. The next morning I walked to the Gastronom, a food store that accepts only Soviet coupons purchased with foreign hard currencies. I came back with cold fingers aching from the straps of the plastic bags that were filled with cheeses, grapes and pears, onions and potatoes, brussels sprouts on the stem, canned tomatoes and strange cuts of meat. We had veal parmesan and spaghetti cooked on a two-burner hot plate that belonged to the office, with boiling water from an electric samovar supplied by the hotel. There is nothing like a good meal to draw a family together, make them sit back and relax and even smile a little under conditions that test all their resources. We used the space between the double windows as a refrigerator, which worked well until there was a sudden rise in the temperature. We washed dishes in the bathroom sink with the hotel's harsh face soap, which was as hard to get off the dishes as the food was, since we had no brush or gritcloth. Jerry came back from a trip to Paris with liquid detergent and dishwashing cloths, luxuries in Moscow. We never did get over the awkwardness of draining the washed dishes in the bathtub.

The Japanese woman from Nagoya, whose hotel room was next to ours, kept her eye on us, and it did not escape her notice that I had set up a hot plate and had begun cooking our meals in our bedroom. With a wide-eyed *"Ah so desuka!"* she followed suit and soon had a regular procession of countrymen in her room sharing the rice, seaweed and dried fish soup she produced mysteriously from her baggage.

The first couple of days I cooked with the hot plate on the floor. Then one of the maids took pity on me and brought me a table. The maids took our dirty clothes every morning and brought them back the next day, beautifully finished by the hotel laundry. They received a weekly tip from us and didn't hint for bonuses, even though they gave more than the required services. One day Stevo came in from outdoors with a cinder in his eye and I wasn't there. The chambermaid, tall, flaxen-haired and efficient, knew what to do. She grabbed his head, pulled him toward her and cleaned his eyeball with her tongue. This old-fashioned method worked quickly and painlessly. He admitted later that she scared him but it felt good.

Each floor of the hotel had its own small buffet, a canteen where we often bought sweet buns, bread or hot tea when we didn't want to wait for our own samovar to boil up. The children liked to drink tea in the buffet so they could have it in the old Russian filigree glass holders. Also, you never knew whom you'd meet. One day a noisy, openhearted group of Georgians were eating at the next table, which they had spread with peaches and apples brought from home. It didn't take long for them to invite the children to join their party and share their fruit.

When this had happened to our children before, as it often did in Japanese trains and restaurants, we thought it was the Japanese attraction to the light-haired and exotic; when it continued to happen in Russia we realized it was the curiosity in their big wondering eyes that made strangers want to feed them. One night at the Moscow circus a blond Russian woman who had her own child in tow offered Doveen an apple and candy. Doveen was embarrassed, having been teased for so long by her brothers and sisters about the way the Japanese doted on her. She hoped that in Russia she could melt into the crowd.

All of the children suffered from a feeling of not belonging in those first months; each of them wanted to look Russian and be treated like any Russian child at school. It took a while.

On our first visit to school, the five children, Jerry and I sat on straight-backed chairs against the wall of the directress's office. She sat at her big desk, facing us. Barney would go to kindergarten but she had to find places for all the other four at her school. She was a tall woman, substantial but not fat in the way Russian women often are, with a handsome but stony face. Her hair was short and brushed back in a neat, uncomplicated hairdo with a frizz of little curls at the nape of her neck. She spoke no English, so Nadezhda Aleksandrovna, head of the English Department, sat with us along the wall, leaning forward to translate. We had met Nadezhda Aleksandrovna when we first looked at the school the previous May; she told us that the children of Professor James Billington of Princeton had attended their school with success and our children would do well there too. "Don't worry," she had said with a warm and reassuring smile, "we love children."

From left to right: Katie, Barney and Doveen in Red Square. (Photo by Jerrold Schecter)

This was a "special polytechnical school" that concentrated on the teaching of English. We thought that half the classes would be in English, but when we entered the children, we learned that the school offered one course in the English language every day. The rest of the subjects were taught in Russian.

The directress, who taught Russian and Soviet history, bore the responsibility for the political correctness of the school. She found it a burden to have foreign children in her school because they brought with them, even unconsciously, the ideologies of competing systems. A poor child from Calcutta whose father had been brought to Moscow to beam back broadcasts in Hindi extolling Soviet life was no problem. But Americans or Canadians or upper-class Peruvians, their pockets bulging with ballpoint pens and bubble gum, their apartments replete with shiny consumer goods and appliances, were a living negation of the superiority of Communism, which she must drive firmly into the impressionable minds in her care. Our children were brought up differently; they might cause distractions by their lack of discipline. If they came for only a year they might be unwilling to put forth the effort necessary to participate; why should they strain to learn Russian when they would "never use it again." But even if they sat by quietly, their idleness in itself would be an unsettling example for the Russian children, and boredom soon leads to mischief.

The directress sat listening to Nadezhda Aleksandrovna, but the teacher's words were not as important to her as what she read in the children's faces, in their eyes, in their bearing. She searched them with large, intelligent, worried eyes. Did she accept the children? Was she amused at the bold colors they wore? Did she sympathize with the strain of being scrutinized? She gave nothing, only the air of authority.

Finally she spoke. Decisively and with no room for bargaining she ruled that Doveen would be in the first grade with other seven-year-olds. In an American school Doveen would have been in second grade, but since Russian children start a year later, this did not present a problem. Katie went to second grade, with children a year younger than herself. Stevo and Evelind were assigned to the fourth and fifth grades, where the age gap widened to two years for Evelind; in maturity the gap was even wider since Stevo was ready for American seventh grade and Evelind for ninth grade.

The directress said they could wear their usual clothes for a few days until they could buy school uniforms, but with an eye on Katie's pink and green stripes, she suggested they choose something with quieter colors. We laughed at that, relieved that she had finally spoken. We didn't reflect much more on where she placed the children; in the tension of the moment we were happy she hadn't put them all in the first grade. Just as we rose to leave, she pointed her finger at Stevo and he jumped with nervousness. He must cut his hair, she commanded, at a Soviet barbershop. The girls should wear their hair tied back or in braids. The children answered *"Da"* to everything — anything to get out of her office. For Jerry and me that ended the session, but for the children it was just the beginning.

Stevo. The first time I went to Special School Number 47 off Leninsky Prospekt my hair seemed ridiculously long because everyone else's was so short. I was wearing a white Italian fisherman's sweater. My whole family stuck out in the middle of the gray and white uniforms dotted with red scarves. The directress of our school looked very stern, but the head of the English Department who came to translate was pleasant. We were told we would have to go to school six days a week. This was a blow because we had heard the day before that there were American movies at the embassy on Saturdays.

The next day Nadezhda Aleksandrovna brought me to the front of my class and made an introduction. She left, and my teacher stood up and said something about finding me a seat. By her gestures I thought she was offering me hers, so I sat down there. Everyone laughed very loudly, and I turned a little red. The teacher's grim face cracked a smile for a minute, and she quickly showed me to a desk.

She dictated some sentences and I tried to keep up, copying, but the sweat soon began to pour. The lesson was finally over, and a whole group of kids gathered around my desk. They kept asking me, *"Otkuda ty? Otkuda?"* but I didn't understand. An Indian girl in our class was brought forward to translate. "Where are you from?" she asked. I answered that and a few more questions before the next class.

I was getting very tired toward the end of the day, and our class had gym. Our teacher had been yelling all day long at kids for minute disobediences or mistakes. Each of her tirades cut right into me, and I was feeling weak from them. The girl who sat next to me explained to the gym teacher that I didn't have any shorts, but he said I should stay and watch anyway. I went down underground to the smelly bare dressing rooms where the shower was broken. Some kids got into a fight which was soon stopped. Everyone got into lines and came marching upstairs, pushing and shoving. I had had enough violence. There were a couple more kids who had forgotten their shorts, and we had to sit and watch the others march around the room with sticks on their shoulders, splitting and converging in set patterns. When the marching was over, a separate leader from the boys and the girls landed in front of the teacher and barked off something about "This is Class 4A of Special School Number 47 ready to carry out their exercises for the day. Hup!" The teacher barked something back, and then they got on with the class. They climbed ropes, threw balls, vaulted over sawhorses, and were finished, at last.

I went out to look for my mother, exhausted and upset after contemplating what I had seen and heard. When I saw her smiling face, it was too much of a contrast, and I burst into sobbing tears.

I cried almost every night for three months whenever I thought about going to school the next day. I realized and admitted to myself that it was never that bad when I actually got there. That was when we were living in the hotel, and Tolya the driver took us to school every morning. After the first week, we asked him to drop us a block away because our Volvo station wagon was so conspicuous. What we really wanted was to fit in. I used to get a horrible feeling in my stomach whenever I was out of school and thought about it. Even a year later, when we were all quite comfortable, I went down to the floor of the lower grades and a kid pointed at me, telling his friends that I was an *inostranets*, a foreigner.

Leona. During the two months we lived in the Ukraine Hotel, Barney went each day to the *detsky sad* (kindergarten) near the older children's school. The first time I left him there, he kicked and screamed, "You're leaving me here and I can't speak Russian." I started down the stairs while the teacher held him; I was full of pain, hesitant, helpless with indecision. Was this the cold-water treatment that makes men out of five-year-old boys, or would this maim him permanently?

It was one of the moments in our years of living overseas when I was angry with our whole way of life. We ripped the children out of environments not once but over and over, each time just as they had managed to adjust, to become comfortable in an alien atmosphere. It was one of the times when I was sick and tired of being an outsider, when I wanted to go "home" and put down roots in an ordinary, tree-shaded, American plot of ground.

The Russian children gawked at the confrontation between Barney and me. Neither the teachers nor the children said a word. They found us a curious phenomenon, and a dangerous one, the teachers let me know. Any hint that the child could win out in this contest would destroy the naturalness of the way they themselves played it. Russian children grow up watching their mothers go off to work every day, and they expect it. They stayed until five o'clock every day, but I picked up Barney at one, before they lay down for their naps, at the same time our older children finished school.

While I waited for him to put his coat on I had a look at his classroom. It was clean and the toys were attractive. The older teachers were both firm and warm, but the younger girls recently out of Infant Pedagogy had not yet learned how to express affection. I wondered how much physical loving they had received in their long school life, which had begun in a crèche run by the state.

The process of learning Russian was not as terrible as Barney expected.

Barney. I started kindergarten, the detsky sad, when we moved to Moscow. On the first day, my mother went with me. I did not want to go and I kept saying to her, "Do I have to go?"

My mother left me at the classroom and I was frightened. It was new and scary and I screamed and tried to get out. I banged at the door, but the teacher locked the door and then calmed me down. Nobody understood me. I couldn't speak any Russian, so she picked up things like dolls and toy trees and named them in Russian and then made me say the names. One of the things she picked up was a toy car. It was not like the ones in America. It was hollow and made of cheap plastic.

The teacher was a middle-aged woman with brown hair. She was very strict. In a few days there was a change of teachers. We got a tall blond-haired lady who was strict too. The two switched back and forth.

A girl had gotten in trouble so the teacher pulled down her tights and spanked her. The teacher then turned to me and she saw I was horrified. She said if I was good that would never happen to me. Another time the teacher and the maid locked two boys in the closet.

After a while I began to like the detsky sad. The kids were not mean and I became friendly with some of the boys in my class. They helped me learn to speak Russian and helped me to read the books on the shelf. One time the class went for a walk in the woods and we saw a big brown cow. I learned a lot of new words on the walk, how to say cow, tree, field, flowers and rabbit. We had a playground at the school where there was a hut and equipment to play on.

At the end of the school day when I went home, all the other children slept on cots in the classroom because their mothers worked. One time I slept there too and the little mischief-maker, Kaarina, talked all the time and wouldn't let anyone sleep. After the nap we had a snack of warm milk. It had lumps of fat in it and they stuck to my lips and made me feel sick to my stomach.

Leona. After we left the children at their first day in Soviet school, I went back to the hotel, Jerry to his office. In our suite on the ninth floor, I gathered the laundry and then my thoughts. I felt a little guilty over those few pleasant hours of privacy before I had to pick up the children. I had a little time to hide but they were pushed directly onto the stage of their new life.

In the car when I returned for them at one o'clock I had buns and fruit to hold off *obed,* the big midday lunch, until after we shopped for uniforms. The children all greeted me with undisguised relief. To be able to chatter in English again was like taking off stiff corsets; they could drop their apprehensive smiles, wiggle out of the roles they had played all day in which they weren't ever sure of the rules.

The easiest step to looking Russian was to wear a school uniform. Evelind's first impression of school was the sight of so many students all dressed alike.

Evelind. All the students were in uniforms and struck me as being very neat. The boys wore gray trousers with a white shirt and gray jackets. The girls wore brown dresses with waists and a full gathered skirt, plain bodice, and long, slightly puffy sleeves. Over their dresses they wore black aprons with two front patch pockets. All the girls had white cuffs and collars, which added to their spritely look. Most of the boys and girls wore triangular red scarves around their necks. I was a little awed at so many kids bustling around talking to each other, knowing their way about, all with neatly braided or closely cropped hair and erect posture. I was further impressed by a girl who pushed past me into the office with a message in her hand. She seemed impeccable: her hair was cut close to her head in a plain, functional haircut and the fitted bodice of her dress showed her full figure and posture to advantage. She barely noticed me, quickly handed over her message, and left when dismissed by the secretary. At that moment she lived up to my image of a well-trained, loyal young Communist, sure of her beliefs and herself. I began to wonder how I would survive among these young Soviets with their military bearing. The first day we came to school in our usual clothes, but afterward we would go to buy uniforms.

Leona. When Tolya came to pick me up at the hotel he brought an envelope with fifteen ten-ruble bills, a reminder to me that I would need rubles to buy clothes in Detsky Mir (Children's World), a regular Soviet store open to ordinary Russians. Until this time I had shopped only at the Gastronom for food and at a branch of the Beriozka (Birch Tree — a hard-currency specialty shop), where we bought the children Bulgarian sheepskin coats. There are ten special stores where one can pay only in coupons which represented dollars or other hard foreign currency, purchased from a state bank; most of my expenditures were in coupons. Therefore it was easy for me to forget to keep a supply of rubles on hand. As time went on, the problem and annoyance never diminished: I had to remind myself to carry cash in two idioms, rubles and coupons. I would never, as long as I lived in Moscow, have the carefree security of a checkbook and credit cards, without which I never leave the house in the United States. How often, on entering a taxi, I would scramble in panic to make sure I had "real rubles" in my handbag. At the official exchange rate in 1968 one ruble equaled $1.11. There are 100 kopecks in one ruble. (In 1973, after the devaluation of the dollar, one ruble equaled $1.32.) Considering how little the rubles were worth on the black market or on international exchanges where they fetched only one fifth to one eighth of their legal exchange rate, and how useless they were in the "dollar stores" (where the best goods were sold), perhaps the word "real" should have been reserved for describing the coupons — those little pastel pieces of paper.

To attempt to stand still in Detsky Mir on a busy day is to invite a storm of elbows and shoulders buffeting you on all sides. Russians learn from an early age to push and shove for survival. One would have connected this urge with the individualism needed to get ahead in a capitalist society, and yet in the New York jungle there is an effective taboo against physically touching other shoppers in a department store. In crowded Tokyo where, as in Moscow, the group counts for more than the individual, we learned to beware of the elbows of little old ladies carrying umbrellas; otherwise we felt insulated from the abrasive touch of strangers in a museum or crowded store. But in Moscow arms are as much a propellant as feet in moving through streets, restaurants, theaters and stores.

Evelind. Elvina, the office translator, accompanied us to Detsky Mir. When we got there Tolya easily found a parking space on the street next to the building. He was to come with us, explained Elvina, and after a few minutes I understood why. As soon as we entered the door I was introduced to the "big push" — the Soviets' way of getting around a large crowd. No one bothered to say "Excuse me," they all just pushed straight ahead, pulling you along in the vacuum they created. As one person moved on, another pushed you into the empty spot. Once inside the door the boys went off with Tolya, and the girls, together with Elvina, moved up on the escalator through economically lit sections of baby clothes, hats, and dark-colored heavy coats to the uniform section.

A couple of racks of brown school dresses, curtained-off dressing rooms and a counter formed a self-enclosed rectangle behind a rope barrier. Elvina started to explain the system while we stood in line along the side of the rectangular area. The "three-line" system was used in every store. First we had to wait in line to look at the sizes and styles of uniforms. Once in the rectangle we were handed a couple of uniforms to try on. When we found the right size we would give it to the salesgirl to hold while we got in a second line waiting to pay the cashier. Then there was a line to another counter where we presented the cashier's receipt and picked up the dress. The first line, we could see, would be at least an hour's wait. Elvina sent us off to look around while she held our place.

Looking around was easier said than done because of the engulfing currents of humanity. I managed to get to the next section, which turned out to be men's suits; the only colors displayed were a dull gray and black. All four styles available were on headless mannequins that stood in a row on a raised platform about two feet above the floor. I headed back to the line for school uniforms, hoping to pick up an ice cream cone from a small stand I had seen near an exit. The only kind of ice cream they had was vanilla, but it was refreshing after all the contact of bulky bodies in scratchy, rough clothing. This was a good day for ice cream; sometimes Moscow ice cream had a slight taste of turpentine. On my way back to the uniform section I noticed the section for school aprons. The line there was short because no one bought their aprons until after they'd bought their dresses. When I got back to the dress line Elvina had progressed only a quarter of the way but she thought it unwise to give up our place to go after aprons. I stood in line while she went to have ice cream.

The people in line were mothers and daughters with a few grandmothers substituting since it was a weekday and most women were at work. They all wore bulky shawls and sweaters against the raw weather. Some of the girls were slender, even skinny, but none of the older women were less than stout. All of the girls and women wore their brown or straw-colored hair in buns or braids. No matter how sloppy the bun looked by that time of day no one let their hair down, as it was considered *nekulturny* (uncultured). All the women carried shopping bags. They would be lucky to get a piece of brown paper wrapped around their purchase; certainly no bag would be supplied.

After an hour we made it into the rectangle and the salesgirl asked me what style I wanted while she measured me with her eye for size. Style? Did they have styles in brown wool dresses? There were three: one with three buttons down to the waist in front; another with buttons down the back to the waist with a high collar and tucks in front; and a straight style with no waist. They all had side plackets, which my mother said disappeared in America about 1950.

They had no time to waste on my indecision. The salesgirl informed me that the straight tent style only came in small sizes and a motherly saleswoman assured me that the high-collared style was *modno* (modish), what all the girls my age were wearing. She handed me two different sizes and showed me into a dressing room, a partitioned area with a curtain. On the permanent wall was a full-length mirror. The uniform was enormous and I burst into giggles at the sight of myself.

I looked like Little Orphan Annie; the hem came down to my ankles, the sleeves hung to my knuckles (a rare occurrence for me because I usually can't find them long enough), the waist was only a bit low. The next smaller size was my size. The dress fitted snugly around my waist and the puffy peasant sleeves were comfortably loose. The length was still exaggerated, but the hem could be taken up and then let down as I grew. I left the dress with the salesgirl and went to get the apron so we could pay for them both at the same time. It took only a few minutes to pick out the black wool apron with slightly frilled shoulder straps (which the saleslady told me was modno) and a thin white cotton one for special occasions. Katie bought the tent style and Doveen took one that buttoned down the front. We all bought the same kind of apron. After a ten-minute wait at the cashier's and a five-minute wait at the two counters where we'd left purchases, we met the boys. Stevo was a bit upset about having to wear the ill-fitting gray wool uniform jacket. He was lucky to have brought gray pants from New York. We were tired and wanted to get back to the hotel, so we left the shopping for school supplies for another day.

The next morning I started school relieved to be in uniform. I was glad not to stick out like a sore thumb. There had not been time to get our uniforms ironed by the hotel laundry and we had no iron, so I wore it with its store wrinkles. The hem was an uncomfortably conservative length in the era of the miniskirt, but later in the day as my self-consciousness wore off I noticed that a few of the skirts were as long as mine. I nearly tripped on the full skirt going upstairs, and resolved to take up the hem that night. As time went on I adjusted to the uniforms and the prudish appearance that accompanied them. I was soon wearing my hair pulled back, and hiding my stylish fishnet American pantyhose under a plain black pair.

My one uniform was washed once every three months on vacations because the dry cleaners were unreliable, took too long, and required that all the buttons be taken off before they would take the clothing. I had duplicates of the white collars and cuffs, which I changed every few days and basted back on. If I forgot to use deodorant and wash under my arms every day I began to smell like a Russian, and as my uniform shrank a little with each washing I began to look like a Russian. I soon understood why no one's dress fitted exactly right and the value of the apron which covered the front so that my increasingly

"Empire" waist didn't show. I lost my awe of the girl who came to the office with the message our first day when I noticed that her uniform fitted as well, or as poorly, as mine did.

In the morning I left my coat, with my scarf, two pairs of gloves that I wore one inside the other, and my fur hat tucked into a sleeve, hanging on the open racks in the school basement. I hoped I would remember the spot in the afternoon. When we arrived at school we changed our outdoor boots for a light pair of indoor shoes — I carried mine in my bookbag — and left the boots under our coats. On some days a prankster mixed up the boots and then it took a half hour of confused yelling to sort them out again.

In one way I couldn't look Russian: I didn't have a triangular red scarf around my neck to signify that I was a member of the Young Pioneers. Everyone wore them, and a serious humiliation was to have your Pioneer scarf taken away as punishment for bad behavior. These scarves also provided a good means of letting out tension because the wearer could chew the tip of one corner.

Leona. From the beginning, Evelind went to school each day with a dedication born of the knowledge that her only alternative was boarding school in a faraway country where she would have fewer certainties to cling to than she had in Moscow. When her brothers and sisters annoyed her she threatened that she would leave for boarding school; no sooner was the dreaded word uttered than they began to hug and kiss her and beg her not to leave. She needed them as much as they needed her. We depended on each other like a primeval ring around the cave fire, all strangers on a foreign strand.

Katie and Doveen, the younger girls, came and went cheerfully, little caring that they didn't know what was going on in their classes. They laughed and played and felt no pressure to learn Russian in a hurry. Jerry and I told them they would come to understand and they believed us. After six months they could do their homework and could chatter with their friends in broken Russian. It took Barney a little less time to operate in Russian because his kindergarten vocabulary was more limited. They had to learn Russian, not only for school but because it was the lingua franca of the ghetto; it was the only communication among children of Pakistanis, Hungarians, Poles, the Cameroons.

During the first weeks, Stevo held a tenuous attitude toward Russian school. He had worked long hours with torturous concentration in Monterey, so by the time he arrived in Moscow he had a heavy investment in learning Russian. It was too late to take on the flippant attitude of some American and Canadian teenagers he would meet later, who felt they wouldn't learn enough in their one year in Russia to use it again and therefore didn't bother to study. But starting school was not the pleasure it had been in Tokyo: the happy return to old friends, talking over the adventures of the summer, facing an academic challenge that was a natural progression from what he had finished the year before. Starting Russian school was all uphill and he couldn't be sure he'd ever reach the level at the top where he could walk without straining all the time. Was it worth the effort to succeed at this tremendous task?

"If it doesn't work out," he asked, hesitating to admit how uncomfortable he was in Russian school, "can I change to the Anglo-American school?"

"Sure," I answered, "but give it a few months."

"Ha," he muttered with a wry smile, "by that time I'll be used to it."

He wondered if he wanted to be different from the American and British boys his age who attended the Anglo-American school. He was a little jealous, those first weeks, over their easy life. Their only anguish was boredom and their inability to comprehend their Russian environment.

One day the son of another American newsman who lived in the foreign compound on Kutuzovsky Prospekt came to play with Stevo at the Ukraine Hotel. He was Stevo's age, plump and fair-haired, with a pleasant disposition. He told Stevo and me that school was easy enough — no problems — but there was nothing to do after he came home.

"Sometimes another American kid and I take the bus down to the Kremlin. We climb around on the cannons until somebody kicks us off." Then he told us of his unsuccessful adventure in lemonade-stand capitalism in the Soviet Union.

A part of his daily routine when he returned from school was to stop at the Dom Igrushky (House of the Toy), Moscow's largest toy store, which was across Kutuzovsky Prospekt from his apartment house complex. He and his friend soon noticed that the shelves of oversized

Barney, Stevo, Doveen, Evelind and Katie on the steps in front of Polytechnical School 47. Katie is not in uniform because she had to wear a dark skirt and white blouse for a special program that day. (Photo by Jerrold Schecter)

crude plastic dolls, poorly molded cars and soldiers, flimsy beach balls and doll carriages remained stagnant, but a few better toys were always in short supply. Kaleidoscopes, imported British car models, baby blocks, metal dump trucks, standing models of Tatar horsemen, miniature doll household utensils were quickly bought up and did not appear in stock again for many months, if at all. The two boys conceived of a plan to buy toys to resell at a profit when the store supply was exhausted.

During the long winter they bought and stored a cache of the best toys that appeared on the shelves of Dom Igrushky. When spring came they set up shop in a large packing crate, placing it on the grassy mall between the apartment houses. They offered not only toys that were no longer available in the Russian toy store, but lemonade as well. They drew a sizable crowd of customers, mostly foreign children from their housing compound, and a few curious Russians. They also drew the attention of the Soviet authorities, who were outraged by this exercise in "speculation."

When they received the first warning, they laughed it off. What harm, they thought, could there be in setting up a lemonade stand and selling some toys? They responded to the second warning with annoyance — what right did anyone have to stop them? Isn't this a free country? "Well," the amiable storyteller said, laughing, "that's what we forgot. It isn't a free country."

There were no more warnings before the Soviet mechanism for dealing with "profiteering" took matters in its own hands. Early the next morning some teenage Russian boys were dispatched to douse the lemonade stand with gasoline. Within minutes it was destroyed in a roaring fire. A Russian policeman stood by to see that the fire didn't spread.

When the fire burned out, so had the taste for free enterprise.

Forced into clandestine operations, the foreign boys found Stevo's knowledge of Russian useful.

Stevo. At three o'clock I met my friends in the boiler room of the American Embassy. There were three of us: Mike, Andrew and me. Mike was the son of a diplomat and Andrew's father worked for an American newspaper. They both went to the Anglo-American school; I was an outsider because I went to Russian school.

They wanted me to translate for a deal they were going to make. Andrew and Mike were good friends, and they had a Russian contact who wanted chewing gum in large quantities. Andrew couldn't get any himself because correspondents aren't allowed to use the American Embassy commissary, and that is the only place gum is sold in Moscow, except on the black market. He contributed two dollars and Mike bought a hundred packs of Wrigley's. We were supposed to meet Grisha (the Russian contact) at four, but we left at ten after three just to make sure we weren't late. It only took about ten minutes by bus to get over to Andrew's foreigners' ghetto so we were taking our time.

When we got on the bus, we didn't pay because it's an honor system. I had never been caught, but we just happened to be on one of those buses with a checker. We didn't see her coming and when she asked for our tickets we didn't have any. At the next stop she took us off the bus and gave us a long spiel about how we foreigners were "spoiling the glorious Soviet Motherland" by being dishonest. Finally she let us go. I always paid after that.

When we got on the next bus and paid our lousy five kopecks each, I noticed it was two minutes to four. We ran all the way from the bus stop to the meeting place, a quiet little park behind the fences of the ghetto, but we were still a little late. Grisha was there with his friend Misha. They handed the gum to Grisha and he handed it to Misha. As Misha counted, Gisha pulled a bill, a single bill, out of his pocket and handed it to them. It was a hundred rubles! This was wilder than our wildest expectations, but we tried not to show it. Misha finally finished counting, and they made up a meeting time for the following week. We left and headed for Dom Knigi (House of the Book) to get the money changed.

The bus ride down was uneventful, and when we got there Andrew and I went in while Mike waited outside. I pretended to look at some books while Andrew went to the cashier. He came back very agitated and asked, "What does *nedistvitelny* mean?"

I didn't want to create a scene in the store, so I waited till we were out on the street again with Mike before I told him that it means "fake" or "not real."

The next time I saw Andrew, he told me how he got even with the Russians. In place of foreign currency, he had traded Monopoly money for rubles.

Leona. When an American correspondent arrives in Moscow, as in other foreign capitals, there is a ready-made community of American and foreign journalists who are eager to get to know him and his family. It is a solidarity of outsiders, and helps to reduce the sense of being a beleaguered minority. I was appreciative, therefore, when Joan Weyland, wife of an AP correspondent who had been there five years, one of whose children went to Russian school, gave a morning coffee party in my honor.

She asked me to come a half hour before the rest because she wanted to prepare me for what I would hear. The conversation would probably be negative toward Moscow: "All the bad things they'll tell you about living here are true, but whether you have an interesting, fulfilling time in Moscow or you spend all your life here complaining depends on the attitude you start with."

At the coffee party that morning I kept quiet and listened. Except for the hostess, every woman there expressed the attitude that she was doing time, bearing it, looking forward to the day when her husband would be assigned elsewhere.

Moscow intensifies the best and the worst in people's characters. Those who broke under the strain were bent toward failure before they came. Emotional problems worsen because there are few diversions. The propensity to drink is heightened by boredom and the cold, dark winters. Years before, Seymour Topping of the New York *Times* cautioned us: "You need maturity to go to Moscow. Don't go until you're ready for it." An assignment to Moscow is a challenge to a marriage; if the marriage is not doing well it's likely to break up there, but a well-founded relationship will grow closer and stronger. The normal outlets for tension, like shopping or a spontaneous weekend in the country, are missing. There is nothing to buy and no place you're allowed to go, without tedious paperwork and permissions. It is a pressure cooker life, where all your equilibrium must come from within you. For the Russians around us the pressures were different and more intense.

We began to understand these pressures and be pulled into them by the trial of Pavel Litvinov and Larisa Bogoraz-Daniel.* On October 9, 1968, they and three other dissenters were brought to trial.

---

* Larisa Bogoraz-Daniel is now Larisa Bogoraz-Marchenko. She divorced Daniel and married Marchenko, the author of *My Testimony*. In April 1975 he was arrested and sent into exile for allegedly failing to follow the terms of his parole.

Jerry. The trial was a turning point in our lives in Moscow. Until then the invasion of Czechoslovakia had cast a pall over the city's intellectual life. Fear and uncertainty dominated. Nobody knew how far the government would exert pressure to maintain its position that Soviet troops had been invited into Prague to provide "fraternal aid" and to crush "German revanchism." The tension was felt in numerous and pointed ways. The most obvious was that Russians would not see or be seen with foreigners, especially foreign correspondents who in times of trouble are branded as spies. Phone calls to poets, writers and journalists were not answered. People normally available pleaded sickness or too much work at the office. The black humor got more bitter and began to make the rounds. A favorite story was of two comrades meeting and one asking the other: "How's the situation in the socialist camp?" The reply: "Oh, the situation is all the same in the camp, except the fences and the barracks are different."

The atmosphere was so distorted that when William Styron and his wife Rose stopped off in Moscow after attending an international writers' meeting in Central Asia, even they refused to discuss openly whether the poet Yevgeny Yevtushenko had actually sent a telegram to General Secretary Brezhnev and Premier Kosygin protesting the invasion. Over a scotch in his room at the Ukraine Hotel Styron spoke in elliptical terms, implying that Yevtushenko had protested. At one point, however, Rose Styron, who had not been in on the conversation, rejoined us and blurted out innocently that she'd heard the text at the writers' meeting. I promised not to involve Yevtushenko in the details of how the telegram had gotten to the West. This was a critical point, because had he sent it or released it himself he could have been accused of anti-Soviet behavior. Yevtushenko refused to answer his telephone or to comment on the story in the London *Sunday Times* that quoted his telegram. He told Henry Shapiro, the UPI bureau chief, that he had not sent the telegram to London. When Shapiro asked Yevtushenko if a telegram from the poet to Brezhnev and Kosygin existed, the poet complained of a poor telephone connection and advised Shapiro to call back. Shapiro was not able to reach Yevtushenko again and wrote a story saying that the poet had denied sending the telegram.

Yevtushenko was trying to protect himself. He had sent the telegram to Brezhnev and Kosygin and it had reached London via a foreign writer friend who had memorized the text. Technically, Yevtushenko had not sent it abroad. Had he allowed his name to be linked directly to the protest and acknowledged it, he would have been accused of the serious charge of defaming the Soviet Union by collaborating with the Western press.

The trial cleared the air by bringing the issues into the open. Not since the trial of Andrei Sinyavsky and Yuly Daniel in February 1966 had there been an open confrontation between intellectuals and the regime within the Soviet legal framework. Although the supporters of Sinyavsky and Daniel paid a heavy price in arrests and intimidations, they gained unity, purpose and a dignity that sustained them.

Friends of the demonstrators' families passed the word in early October that the trial would start in a small courthouse on Silversmith Quay. Located in the old working-class district of Moscow, Silversmith Quay is in a section of the city where the streets are named for the craftsmen who lived and worked on them in tsarist times. The craftsmen are gone, but the houses, made of logs, with crooked windows, remain. They are shabby now, weather-worn and heavily painted over with layers of peeling browns and yellows. But their character is still strong thanks to the hand-carved wooden fretwork that frames the windows with traditional artistry and grace.

The October morning light was golden and full on the first day of the trial. I asked Tolya to stop the car three blocks from the courthouse so I could walk past the old log houses, lined up like a village of peasant *izbas* (log huts) along the canal. By walking I became part of the scene and eliminated the stares that followed my Volvo station wagon with its white K-04 license plates, the black numbers identifying me as an American correspondent. (K is for foreign *korrespondent;* 04 is the number for Americans. Russians have black license plates with white numbers.) Elm leaves rustled underfoot along the quiet embankment. The side streets beyond the canal were narrow and the trees still thick with foliage, giving the sense of a long-established neighborhood. The wide boulevards and sprawling high-rise apartment houses of postwar Moscow were hidden from view. Coming to the trial was like stepping back into the past, to the Russia of the nineteenth century with its struggles for conscience and its intellectual ferment.

On October 9, the demonstrators were brought to trial, charged with violating article 190.1 and 190.3 of the Russian Federation Criminal Code. Article 190.1 prohibits "deliberately spreading false fabrications or systematic defamations which are detrimental to the Soviet state and social order." Article 190.3 prohibits "organizing or actively participating in group actions which disturb public order." Penalties range from a fine of one hundred rubles to three years of "corrective labor."

Since the courtroom was ostensibly open to the public the trial carried with it the unspoken but assumed right to discuss openly the issues of Soviet law and politics that the court was to judge. The genie of dissent was again out of the bottle. While the trial would serve as an example of the punishment in store for others who dared to criticize government policy, it would also be an open rallying point for criticism of the invasion of Czechoslovakia. Each person who appeared on the tree-lined streets outside the courtroom knew that he or she would be subject to harassment and risked jeopardizing a position at an institute, office or university.

The first battle was to enter the courtroom in the three-story yellow-stucco people's court. Only by attending the trial and passing on the testimony and debate could the full impact of the protest be passed to the outside world. I joined the crowd pushing and shoving against the high wooden doors. Policemen in blue overcoats with red shoulder boards barred the door. There was the heavy smell of stale, unwashed sweat, garlic and tobacco in the crush around the entrance-way. It was the characteristic smell of Moscow, lighter or heavier depending on the season of the year, but always prevalent. People eyed each other with the intensity of animals at bay, searching for friend or enemy. Members of the defendants' families and their close friends were at the head of the line. The trial was scheduled to open at 10 A.M. but the courtroom, designed to hold forty people, had been filled by the authorities by 9:30 A.M. Only four members from the families of each of the five defendants were permitted through the heavy brown doors after showing their internal passports, required of all Soviet citizens.

I pressed closer to the entrance and finally broke through the crush against a policeman who examined my blue leather-covered press card from the Ministry of Foreign Affairs and waved me away. According to Soviet law the trial was open to the public and foreign correspondents, but how could we enter if the courtroom was full? We were told that nearly a hundred people were pressed into the narrow benches and along the sides of the simple, high-ceilinged room. Among those admitted were Pavel Litvinov's wife and his cousins Vera and

Masha, also grandchildren of Maxim and Ivy Litvinov. I had read Ivy Litvinov's short stories in *The New Yorker* and had heard that she was still living in Moscow.

The turning-away of friends continued until there was a common realization that further efforts to enter would be futile. I studied the faces around me. I had never seen Russians like these before. The friends of the defendants were the intellectuals, young and old. Their clothes had that distinguishing rumpled look that clearly marked them off from the conservatively attired conformists. Their faces were vital, marked with passion and intelligence, some fresh and unlined, others worn and etched with memories of pain and suffering in labor camps and more recently in mental institutions.

Pyotr Yakir was pacing back and forth along the sidewalk. He is the surviving son of General Iona Yakir, commander in charge of the Kiev military district, whom Stalin ordered executed in 1937 along with the best of the Soviet high command. Yakir is burly and intense with a strong-featured face that seems to rise from his powerful shoulders. His thick black hair and beard are flecked with gray and his eyes burn with fervor. When his father was murdered, Yakir was thirteen years old. He was sent off to a labor camp and spent the next seventeen years in camps. His only crime was that his father was a victim of the Stalinist terror. Finally, in 1954 a year after Stalin's death, Yakir was released. He became a central figure among the dissidents and they looked to him for leadership and strength. Surviving in the camps had ingrained in Yakir an instinctive sense of how far it was possible to press or embarrass the KGB within the framework of Soviet law. During the years of Khrushchev's power (1954–1964) Yakir came into his own as a historian. Khrushchev's speech at the Twentieth Party Congress in 1956 decrying Stalin's terror led to mass rehabilitations of victims, including Yakir. He even became friendly with the Khrushchev family. Yakir grew to understand the power of foreign press reporting on life and events in the Soviet Union and the magic of the transistor radio, which could beam reports back to the Soviet Union within three or four hours.

I will always remember my first look at him. I stared hard at his eyes trying to measure the man. I saw in his face suppressed pain, bitterness, cunning and a questing for life. I had heard that Yakir was drinking heavily and there was a trace of red in his eyes that heightened their anguish. Squat and powerfully built, he moved with a strong yet furtive gait, watching carefully those who were close to him or those who might be observing him from a hidden recess or trying to overhear his conversation. I introduced myself to him as the *Time* correspondent in Moscow. He shook my hand, scrutinized me carefully, smiled politely but declined conversation.*

I glanced across the crowd and found former Major General Pyotr Grigorenko. A head taller than everybody else, Grigorenko was easy to spot. He wore a battered blue felt derby and carried a heavy wooden cane. He seemed an unlikely dissenter with his proud military bearing accentuated by the aged dignity of the heavy jowls. He still had the posture and clear blue eyes of a commander. Born in the Ukraine, Grigorenko possessed the open bluff manner characteristic of that area and he resembled in some ways Nikita Khrushchev in his straightforwardness and combative manner. Grigorenko had publicly criticized "a growing cult of personality" around Khrushchev in 1961. He was quickly transferred from his post as an instructor at Frunze Military Academy to the Far East. But he persisted in his criticism of Khrushchev and in 1964 he was forced out of the army and arrested. Since there were no specific charges against him he was declared insane and held in an asylum, where the state psychiatrists certified that he was a schizophrenic. After two years Grigorenko was released but only with the warning that he would be recalled to the asylum if his activities were again declared to be "insane" by the authorities. Grigorenko was not cowed by such threats and he appeared at trials, supported the Crimean Tatars in their struggle to return to their lands, and freely gave his support to those still seeking to win reduced sentences for Sinyavsky and Daniel. He worked quietly as a construction foreman and in his spare hours wrote his own history of the effects of Stalin on the Soviet military in World War II.†

* Yakir was arrested for disseminating anti-Soviet propaganda to Western correspondents and tried in September 1973 after being imprisoned for one year and four months. He was subjected to continued interrogation and harassment during his confinement. At his trial, reminiscent of the purge trials of the 1930's, Yakir turned state's evidence, denouncing former friends and implicating them. He was sentenced to three years in prison and three years in exile but the jail sentence was waived and his exile period reduced. He is now reported to be living quietly in Moscow, working as a historical researcher.

† In 1969 Grigorenko was again arrested, this time for his efforts on behalf of the Crimean Tatars. He was detained in a mental hospital for five years — until June 1974. He now lives on a pension of $60 a month because he was reduced to the rank of private. As a major general his pension would normally be between $268 and $408 a month.

The crowd itself was a cross section of Soviet life: bureaucrats, engineers, students, and workers in blue overalls, khaki jackets and battered hats. Dumpy, plump women in worn cloth coats; intense, long-haired blond girls hanging on the arms of poets; fine-faced youth with glasses; rugged, red-bearded scientists; and distinguished-looking teachers, mathematicians and critics. Their arguments were impassioned, urgent, giving vent to long-suppressed feelings. They seemed evenly divided for and against the defendants. A woman in worker's clothes shouted: "The defendants should be shot." Quickly a policeman led her away. The open debate was to have limits and there was no violence. The respectables in the crowd turned on the friends of the accused, derisively calling them dollar speculators and *tunyadtsy* (loafers). The friends of the defendants were equally spirited in defense. They called their taunters *stukachi* (informers) and asked them if they really believed that the Soviet troops in Prague were providing fraternal aid.

Such public expression of views is rare in the Soviet Union, and come only at moments of climax and crisis; otherwise opinions are held within, where they fester and molder. But now the Russians were arguing openly over freedom of speech, Vietnam, Czechoslovakia and how men should live and behave.

My own role and that of my colleagues covering the trial was clearly defined. By reporting on the trial and the street debate it engendered, the protest would have a life of its own beyond the simple act of defiance in Red Square. The intellectuals of Moscow were placing the Soviet leadership on trial before the court of world opinion. They were appealing to their own people and to the world to understand the meaning of the invasion. The Czechoslovakian experiment had gone too far for the Politburo in Moscow but the Prague ideals of a more open press, less Party control and more individual initiative and freedom were being endorsed by Moscow intellectuals as examples that the Soviet Union might follow.

The arguments rose in volume and there was shoving and pushing. Quickly the police ordered the crowd from the front of the courtroom and off the street. Everybody moved to a small, tree-filled park with an open-air, lattice-framed shelter in which there were benches to sit on. A white sign said it was a "library reading room." The friends of the defendants had gathered around Grigorenko and were signing a petition urging that they be admitted to the trial. The petition was addressed to the Soviet leaders Leonid Brezhnev, Aleksei Kosygin and Nikolai Podgorny. The small courtroom, charged the signers, had been deliberately chosen for the trial and "the audience was selected by the Committee for State Security (KGB) in the first place" and "there is no doubt that it has been done in order to turn the trial announced as open, into a closed one." The petition requested that the trial be transferred to a larger courtroom and that "all agents of the KGB be cleared from the courtroom and the approaches to it." Grigorenko had signed along with the friends and relatives of those on trial. Suddenly, a well-dressed young man wearing a black cap and a red scarf grabbed the petition from Grigorenko's hands and started to rip it apart. There was a brief scuffle and the intruder was shoved roughly against the thin wall of the reading room. The wall buckled. Grigorenko raised his cane as if to strike, but Yakir grabbed his arm and eased him away. "Provocateur. This is hooliganism," shouted Grigorenko, his face red with anger. "Who are you?" When the man refused to show his internal passport, Grigorenko insisted that they both go to the local police station.

Off they marched followed by a group of foreign correspondents and a group of witnesses, some friendly and some hostile to Grigorenko. The walk along Silversmith Quay to the police station climaxed the opening of the trial and the street forum that had developed. Mixed into the marchers were *druzhinniky* (vigilantes or volunteer police in civilian clothes), KGB agents, workers and students, including one with a camera who insisted he was taking pictures of the crowd for his student newspaper. It was the classic informer's pose. In small knots they argued. Workers in blue faded jackets shouted that the intellectuals wore beards and dirty clothes, had no jobs and were parasites. The intellectuals responded with humor. An attractive young woman reminded an accuser that both Marx and Lenin were bearded.

Two students argued fiercely over Czechoslovakia. "The decision to aid the Czechs was taken by collective leadership," explained the youth. "Don't tell me about collective leadership," countered the other. "Collective leadership means that separately each one is against the invasion but together all are in favor of the invasion."

There was always the sense that this free exchange of ideas and emotions was under surveillance. As we neared the police station I noticed a bearded youth carefully listening to a conversation between two students. At that moment one of the students sensed he was being watched and turned to confront the suspected informer, crying out: "How much did you sell your soul for?" But the bearded youth held his ground and answered arrogantly: "My soul belongs to the Party."

At the police station Grigorenko sought to have the man who tried to tear up the petition identify himself. A cluster of potential witnesses milled around the entrance, but a plainclothes official stepped forward and warned the group not to loiter in front of the station. Angrily, they told him they were witnesses waiting to be called. But the police officer insisted they leave and shouted at them: "I don't need any people here." A neatly dressed young student trudged away, then turned bitterly to shout at the police station entrance: "What's the need for the people?"

Grigorenko never did find out the name of the agent provocateur, yet by bringing him to the police station he had at least satisfied his own staunch belief in Soviet law and the rule of law which he and the others who supported him felt could be made impartial and just. Grigorenko and other dissidents never argued against the Soviet system. They insisted that the constitution was not being followed and that if only it were observed the Soviet Union would be an example for the world.

Again that afternoon I returned to the trial and stood on the street listening to arguments, meeting friends of the defendants and trying to learn what had happened inside the courtroom. The families emerged at the end of the first day and it was questionable whether any of them would meet with the press. Briefly they told us what happened in the courtroom as we walked through the twilight.

In this way I met Pavel Litvinov's friends. As the group waiting outside the courtroom walked away from the trial, two young bearded men chatted cautiously with me. One had a dark brown beard that made him look like Christ on an ikon. The other had a red beard that covered his strong youthful face. Christlike Anton, the shorter and more introspective of the two, led a small dog on a leash that added a strangely social note to the street forum. Fedya, the taller one, spoke excellent English and together they explained in detail how the trial had gone and the gloomy prospects for sentencing.

I met them every evening that week at the trial. They were curious about the United States and the West; they had a sophistication about their own country and the U.S. that was refreshing. Both had studied English in school and at the university and they listened to the BBC and the Voice of America. Like most Russians I came to know, they spurned the propaganda of Radio Liberty and preferred the more detailed news broadcasts of the BBC to the Voice of America. They found the Voice of America too concerned with air crashes and disasters rather than with the kind of political news they listened for. They saw the BBC as a more credible reporter of news on the Soviet Union. I was impressed by the breadth of their knowledge of affairs in the United States and their concern over the Vietnam war. They were troubled by American activities in Laos and Cambodia. They managed to get copies of the *International Herald Tribune, Time, Newsweek* and the British Sunday papers. They had a keen sense of the character and tactics of all the foreign correspondents in Moscow.

Our friendship began slowly because of the suspicion that is endemic in Moscow. I wondered if they were really friends of Litvinov or if perhaps they were plants, agents designed to trap me in a violation of Soviet law, some embarrassment that could be used to expel me and my family from Moscow. Later I learned that they were indeed taking my measure, seeking to make a firm test of my discretion and sensitivity, trying to discover whether or not I could be trusted. While the system forced impersonality in public life and complete conformity in political behavior, in private lives and in friendships in Moscow there was an intensity of honesty, emotional expression and intellectual forthrightness unlike anything I had experienced in America or Asia. Private friendships with foreigners, perhaps because of the dangers involved, took on a resonance and richness that contrasted completely with the dullness and drabness of life around us.

Foreign correspondents were briefed on the trial by Lev Yevgenevich Almazov, deputy chairman of the Moscow City Court.* We sat in a small room with yellow walls on the street-level floor of the courthouse and listened to Mr. Almazov blandly explain that the testimony

---

* The Moscow City Court is actually a Regional court because Moscow is drawn on the government organization chart as a Region and therefore has a court of its own. Regional courts are comparable to county courts in the United States. The deputy chairman of the Moscow City Court handles administrative and procedural matters and is not a judge. Judges are not elected but are chosen by the Moscow City Soviet for five-year terms.

at the second day of the trial was from witnesses who "told what they saw from far and near and the side in Red Square." Their testimony, he said, dealt with the blocking of traffic in Red Square and with disturbances. When we asked him about Czechoslovakia and the political aspects of the trial Mr. Almazov explained firmly that "this is not a political trial. It is a criminal trial under article 190. There has been evidence presented to prove that the defendants disturbed public order." The evidence to prove that the defendants deliberately spread false fabrications or systematically defamed the Soviet state and social order presumably would come later.

The tactics of the trial were of constant concern to the friends of the accused and their families. After every session they quietly passed word to the press of what had occurred. The wire services sent it to London and Paris, and a few hours later it was heard in Moscow on the BBC and then the Voice of America.

After each session I looked for Fedya and we talked about the day's events. We gave each other the latest news we had heard on Czechoslovakia. Fedya was deeply concerned about how long the Soviet occupation would last and how the political impact of the invasion would filter down to affect life in Moscow.

The trial was an insight into the pervasive fear and suspicion that is a part of Soviet life. The loss of life during the Stalin terror created a style and pattern of relationships that exist even to this day, just as the Depression in America left permanent scars on many of us. Beginning with the assassination of the Leningrad party leader Sergei M. Kirov on December 1, 1934, life in the Soviet Union became a constant watch of fear and dread. Over the next seven years an estimated ten million people were sent to labor camps. After the war Stalin's paranoia grew and an estimated ten million more were sent to camps. Only in 1956, after Stalin's death, was the brutality unmasked at the Twentieth Party Congress.

Fifteen years after Stalin's death the Soviet people still had not absorbed the shock of de-Stalinization nor focused on a confident path for the future, when the collective leadership of Brezhnev, Kosygin and Podgorny thrust the invasion of Czechoslovakia on the nation. The leadership, in an effort to justify its actions in Prague, felt compelled to crush dissent at home. Those who had seen the toll of the purges hoped to forestall a return to the bloody past. The trial of

Litvinov and Mrs. Bogoraz-Daniel brought this apprehension to the surface and began what was to be a lively and continuing struggle.

On Thursday, the second day of the trial, the prosecution submitted as evidence the placards protesting the invasion that had been displayed in Red Square and the slogans shouted by the demonstrators. At the end of the day we gathered to hear the news. We were told that the prosecution had asked the court to change the penalty for Litvinov, Mrs. Bogoraz-Daniel and Konstantin Babitsky, a literary critic, from the maximum of three years in a labor camp to exile, a lesser sentence. The state prosecutor asked a five-year exile for Litvinov, four years for Mrs. Bogoraz-Daniel, and three years for Babitsky. For the two other defendants, Vladimir Dremliuga and Vadim Delone, the court asked the maximum of three years in a labor camp. When the family appeared they said the verdict would probably come on Friday.

"Exile," my friend Fedya said, "will be much better than labor camp." In exile Litvinov and Mrs. Bogoraz-Daniel would be free to live and work in a remote area of the Soviet Union. Even if the work was hard, the climate and living conditions severe, they could at least have their families with them. They could not return to Moscow but they could have visitors. Fedya reminded me, "The tradition of being exiled from the capital was a noble one in Russian history. In tsarist days political exiles included Dostoevsky, Trotsky, and of course, Lenin."

On Friday afternoon Silversmith Quay was crowded with more than two hundred people awaiting the verdict, most of them friends and relatives of the defendants. The mathematician Aleksandr Yesenin-Volpin, son of the poet Sergei Yesenin, stood in the cold, his fine features glistening above a luxuriant black beard and below a dark beret. The tiny poet Natalya Gorbanevskaya, with close-cut red hair, conversed with one group of friends and then another. An unmarked green bread truck stood parked at the side of the court building. This was the vehicle in which the five would be transferred back to prison after the trial. When the doors of the courthouse opened and the family members emerged, they were surrounded by well-wishing friends who embraced them with tears. The defense attorneys received bouquets of gladioli and roses. The three-judge court deliberated for two hours on the verdict, which was exactly what the prosecution asked: exile of five years for Litvinov, four years for Mrs. Bogoraz-

Daniel and three years for Babitsky. Delone and Dremliuga were sentenced to three years in a labor camp.

Foreign correspondents received a final briefing on the verdict by Mr. Almazov. He duly explained that the trial was about the violation of public order; witnesses testified that the accused had blocked traffic in Red Square, shouted slogans, and carried signs. He refused to discuss the substance of the protest or disclose the text of the signs, which we already knew read "Shame on the Occupiers," "Hands Off Czechoslovakia," and "Long Live Free and Independent Czechoslovakia." The court held that there was a criminal conspiracy to disturb public order and the defendants held "false views," since they disagreed that the Soviet Union gave "fraternal aid" to Czechoslovakia.

In the farewells outside the courtroom one of the friends of the defendants beckoned me toward him with a swift nod. We walked toward the end of Silversmith Quay quietly, as if leaving the courthouse. Only when he was certain that we were not being followed did he tell me that the defendants' concluding statements to the court had been transcribed and they would be ready for distribution that evening. I was to meet him in front of the concert hall near Pushkin Square at 8 P.M.

As the hour neared, I left my car at the office and took a taxi to the theater. There, as the evening crowd gathered for the performance, I waited for the trial transcripts.

This was my first experience in receiving *samizdat,* or self-published news, essays, literary works and proclamations. Hand-typed copies are covertly distributed in Moscow, Leningrad and other major cities of the Soviet Union by young intellectuals, students and workers seeking a free exchange of information and ideas. Samizdat materials included statements by famous writers like Solzhenitsyn, records of trials, or the essays of the physicist Andrei Sakharov. None of the ideas they expressed were officially sanctioned and any Soviet citizen caught carrying the material on the street, possessing it in his home or giving it to a foreigner risked being arrested and tried for defaming the Soviet Union. Over the next two years I became familiar with its importance in Soviet political life. Searching the faces of the passersby in front of the theater, I tried to look relaxed and Russian, as if waiting for my date to arrive for the performance. It all seemed like a bad spy movie, except that this was the only means to obtain an expression of the conflict of ideas in the Soviet Union.

My friend came with his wife at five after eight and we greeted each other openly and warmly. Then we walked down the street, still crowded with theatergoers, to a small park alongside the theater. There we sat down on a bench and chatted about the trial while the transcripts were swiftly passed into my hands. We sat a bit longer speculating about exile. Mrs. Bogoroz-Daniel would leave her son behind. Because of her activities he was having difficulty being accepted by a university. Yuly Daniel was still in jail. Pavel Litvinov could take his wife into exile with him, and although their life would be arduous it would be infinitely better than being in a labor camp, where the chances of survival were unpredictable.

I saw these friends often during the next two years and spent many hours listening to their aspirations for their country. We were around the same age and they loved our children, so our friendship soon grew beyond political discussions. They had a strong respect for the law that they believed was contained in the constitution of the USSR and the legal codes of the Republics. It was adherence to the rule of law that they were struggling for; they believed that the leadership of the country, not the protestors, violated their own constitution.

Alone back in my office at 14 Kutuzovsky Prospekt, I turned on the lights, locked the door, and read the transcript of the trial. It was in English, which was unusual. Samizdat almost always came in Russian and required rapid translation of often difficult ideas in order to meet deadlines.

Mrs. Bogoraz-Daniel was allowed by the court to be her own defense attorney. From the beginning of the trial she disagreed with the formulation of the indictment and denied that there was a conspiracy, that public order was disturbed, and that the meaning of the slogans was "slanderous."

"My point," she told the court, "is that we did not render fraternal aid to Czechoslovakia. What we need is a clear formulation of the entry of armed forces." Then she asked, "What does 'gross disturbance of public order' mean? Different people may understand this differently. I saw in Insurrection Square a massive protest demonstration against the usual aggression of the United States. A huge crowd with self-made banners walked up the garden ring road, overflowing onto bridges and sidewalks; the movement of transport was held up. The demonstrators shouted and threw bottles of ink at the American Embassy. The disturbance of the normal functioning of traffic was far greater than any disruption our little demonstration might have caused. The action of the participants in that demonstration was also extremely crude. We in our protest were only a few people sitting quietly on the parapet holding up our placards. I consider that the demonstration at the American Embassy was a far grosser disturbance to public order. Nevertheless, not one of the participants was brought to criminal responsibility."

Mrs. Bogoraz-Daniel also tried to defend herself and the others against the charges under Article 190 of spreading "false fabrications which are detrimental to the Soviet state and social order."

Mrs. Bogoraz-Daniel: "The slogan 'Down with the Occupiers' does not contain anything false, anything deliberately false, and there is nothing slanderous about it. If the very fact of the entry of troops is not slanderous then the slogan is no more slanderous."

The judge, very agitated, insisted: "You are not being tried for your convictions. They are clear enough to us."

Mrs. Bogoraz-Daniel responded: "I am talking about how I understand the word occupation."

As they argued, the judge interrupted her to say: "There was an entry of troops but this was not an occupation. Do not speak about your convictions but about the acts of which you are accused."

The transcript of the trial read like a piece of theater. It lacked only suspense, because I knew from the beginning that the final act would be a verdict of guilty and a sentence of exile. I had now seen the Soviet legal system at work in a political trial and found it in reality quite different from the elaborate explanations I had heard from Russian legal experts visiting Harvard University during my year there as a Nieman Fellow in 1964. Here was an aspect of Soviet law that was governed by arbitrary political power. The government on the highest levels had determined to make a test case and an example of the protestors. Foreign policy is an area of Soviet life in which dissent is not permitted; "fraternal aid" was not to be criticized.

During the week of the trial I met and talked with more Russians than I had in the two months I had been in Moscow. The friendships I made at the trial lasted and enriched our stay in Moscow. These Russians were alive with ideas that went far beyond the stale formulas of *Pravda* and TASS. Moscow was beginning to show us the human complexity and warmth that lived within the high walls of the fortress-like apartment buildings. In these homes I often sensed an initial suspicion of foreigners, the heavy risk taken in meeting with me, a foreign correspondent. Even when it was purely social, each meeting included an uninvited ghost — the ingrained fear of the purge years and the warning that such a meeting might once again be used as grounds for incrimination. A cup of tea, a few glasses of vodka, heavy bread and sausage shared with us could form the basis for an anti-Soviet act, and this thought was always with us.

Henry Shapiro, the UPI bureau chief, described the extreme paranoia of the Stalin years: a bathtub overflowed in the apartment of his upstairs neighbor, a famous writer, so Shapiro went up to tell him that water was seeping through the floor. The neighbor refused to open the door because he feared any contact with an American journalist. Czechoslovakia brought these memories back.

Moscow in the autumn season was at its best. The hot dry dust of summer was gone and the evenings were cool. Watermelons were still on sale on open-air fruit stands; vendors sold Hungarian apples straight from the crates. In the dark rooms of old wooden houses we saw precious collections of ikons salvaged from ruined country churches; the same collectors cherished abstract paintings and a photograph of Aleksandr Solzhenitsyn, the moral exemplar for Soviet intellectuals. The Czech invasion hung in the air but politics did not dominate all emotions. Life for most Russians and even for foreign journalists was filled with day-to-day concerns and simple delights.

Our circle of Russian friends grew. We brought them to our apartment carefully, picking them up at a Metro station and driving them past the *militsioner,* the policeman who guarded the entrance to our building, so they would not be stopped, questioned and humiliated. Each building where foreigners live is controlled by Soviet policemen who are on twenty-four-hour duty in a guardbox at the entrance. Soviet citizens who want to enter must work there or have written invitations unless they are accompanied by their foreign hosts. Ostensibly the police are there to protect foreigners, but in practice they serve as spies who keep a record of comings and goings and the names of any visitors.

Inside our closed doors we played the phonograph and talked under the "jamming" roar of the Beatles and the classics. We learned to be wary of listening devices we supposed were hidden in our walls and telephones, but we also realized that unless we could remain open with our friends and true to ourselves, our assignment in Moscow would be wasted.

Leona. In Moscow we seemed to have entered a preindustrial society with its own sense of time. Our friends never appeared to be compelled by a deadline. They could drink and talk for endless hours. The workday, we soon noted, was like the workday we had seen in Southeast Asia. Measured by American standards, no one did more than half a day's work in a full day. The lack of individualism was evident everywhere; the avid competitiveness of young professionals in the West was nowhere to be seen. In Japan we had seen the competitive spirit directed toward the success of the group rather than the individual; in Russia this drive was missing altogether.

The lack of individualism manifests itself in the day-to-day conversations of ordinary people. Unlike Americans, Russians talk very little about making money, paying for their children's education, or saving for their old age. These expenses of life, which form the incentives for American financial planning, are organized for Soviet citizens by the state. Therefore, when they plan their annual vacation it's not to escape on their own but rather to go to a resort, rest home or sanitorium sponsored by their trade union, political group, ministry or other collective where they work. Russians never think it odd that they spend their time away from work with the same people they work with every day.

Russians have less to buy with their money than Americans do. The Japanese, who were no less ravaged by the Second World War, have risen from the ashes to challenge the United States in consumerism, but the Russians, despite their sacrifices and hardships, are still standing in line to buy meat and potatoes. There is no private housing on sale, with the exception of cooperative apartments only accessible to an elite. Country dachas sell for about 5,000 rubles — three and a half years' wages for a worker who earns, on the average, 120 rubles a month, and there is no system of real estate mortgages. The land continues to be the property of the state, which charges an annual rent or tax.

On the face of it, buying on time is easier in the Soviet Union than in the West because there are no interest charges, but in fact it is a limited benefit. In order to buy an apartment the householder must put down 40 percent of the purchase price and pay the rest monthly, without interest. But the down payment, usually 2,500 to 3,000 rubles, is out of the reach of most. Those who pay it do so by borrowing from their friends, who are usually willing to lend some of their savings (about 500 rubles) because the money does not earn more than 1½ percent interest if it is left in the bank. Since custom decrees that no interest be charged on personal loans, the only consideration is whether the borrower can be trusted to pay the money back. Many people belong to credit unions, but the loan the borrower can get from them is normally not more than 200 rubles. For the apartment buyer, this may be just the amount he needs after he has borrowed from every other possible source. Thus, the individual act of purchasing an apartment often represents the cooperative effort of the buyer's friends.

Even if he has enough for a down payment, the buyer faces the expense of bribing an official to give him an apartment in a desirable location. The scarcity of new housing near the center of the city or in a pleasant district creates a pressure to pay for favors. Once in the new apartment, the need to bribe continues, for the installation of a telephone may require the delivery of a gift of ten cans of instant coffee, on sale at the hard-currency Gastronom but rare in ordinary Moscow foodstores.

Cars are often privately owned, but again, only by a privileged few. Soviet citizens who work abroad and have access to foreign currency can buy a car in New York or Paris and take delivery in Moscow. One of our friends, a journalist, paid $1,000 through the Russian consulate in New York for a small Russian-made car which would have cost him 5,000 rubles if he had purchased it in Moscow.

Russians permitted to travel abroad are shocked at how high living standards are in the East European countries, for whom Russians feel they sacrificed lives and treasure in the war against the Germans. A Soviet journalist told us that even the lifestyle in dour East Germany makes it appear, by comparison, that Russia lost World War II.

Part of the reason for the Soviet Union's low productivity lies in the Russian fear that Western methods of success will dilute their Slavic heritage and their Communist ideology. Fear of losing their identity and beliefs keeps Soviet life static. We came to see power at work and instead found a country physically and spiritually at world's end, run like a monastery, shut off tight from the international flow of ideas, styles, experiments, comforts, the simplifications of work and the complications of life created by technology in the rest of the world.

The frame of reference which Russians share when they talk to each other is socialism. According to Marxist ideology, socialism is an intermediate stage of revolutionary development that comes after capitalism but before the ultimate stage, which is Communism. Under socialism the society is ruled by the dictatorship of the proletariat (working class), which in reality means the Communist Party acting on behalf of the proletariat through the Central Committee and the Politburo. In the final stage, Communism, the entire society, working together as a collective, rules itself.

The Soviet Union today considers itself a socialist society moving toward Communism, and claims it is a classless society that has eliminated the profit motive. In reality, privilege and material perquisites, summer homes, special shopping privileges, and clubs organized on a group basis have replaced individual gain. The Soviet Union is a classless society with privileged people. Privilege is extended not to individuals per se but through the group they belong to. For instance, the *Pravda* journalists as a group have their own summer rest homes on the Black Sea or Baltic coast, the Russian equivalent of a company-run resort in the West. There are, of course, no private resorts.

For the solution of day-to-day problems the Soviet Union has rejected the capitalist framework of the expediter, middleman and management consultant. Russians are unfamiliar with the choices and flexibility — as well as the problems — of a market economy.

The prejudice against the middleman limits the transfer of food from farm to market. Twenty miles from Moscow apples rot, unharvested, because the grower has no truck, and no bureaucrat cares enough to make the connection between the orchard and the city market. There's no profit in it. Instead, apples are imported from Hungary. Muscovites travel south in summer not only in search of sun but to eat fruit from the trees, which is often given away because the grower has no hope of selling it before it spoils.

The majority of Russians accept the low quality of consumer goods, the time-wasting methods of doing business through central planners, and the inefficient arrangements for shopping as part of socialism. They do not openly protest these shortcomings but they ridicule the system privately with biting humor. They usually accept a baffling change or arbitrary government action as being for their own good. The historical authoritarianism of the tsars has been replaced by voluntary collectivism, a continuity that still accepts direction from above. Their vocabulary is sprinkled with phrases from the lexicon of socialism and they are proud of their collective spirit.

One day I called a number listed in the foreign telephone directory and asked for "Gaspozha Heatherington" (Mrs. Heatherington, a formal manner of address usually reserved for foreigners). It was a wrong number. I dialed again, only to get the same voice on the line. I asked, "Isn't this Mrs. Heatherington's number?" The man laughed and said, "We don't have any mistresses or masters here, only comrades."

The handful of individualists are misfits. They are the frustrated and alienated critics of the regime. As in many Asian societies, "the nail that sticks up is quickly hammered back into place."

We were still living in the hotel the first week in November, when the children had a week's holiday from school for the anniversary of the Great October Revolution. Jerry and I were particularly glad that we had decided to send the children to Russian schools, so that we were on the same calendar as the rest of the country and could take part in the celebration.

With the help of Elvina and Tolya, Jerry arranged sleeping compartments for all of us on the night train to Leningrad. He also got press passes for us to get into Victory Square, in front of the Winter Palace, to see the military parade. Reservations at the Baltic, a small hotel near the train station, were made for us. Not only would the city be overcrowded for the holiday, making it necessary to have hotel reservations, but our whereabouts had to be accounted for whenever we left Moscow.

Tolya saw us off at the Leningrad station on the Krasnaya Strelya (Red Arrow), that leaves Moscow at midnight and arrives at Leningrad at 8 A.M. We brought fruit, cheese and biscuits for breakfast, which we supplemented with glasses of hot strong tea served in filigree holders by the conductor at seven. We all slept well on the rolling train so that when we stepped out on the platform everyone was rested, fed and bright-eyed, ready to embrace Leningrad.

The Intourist car that was supposed to meet us was nowhere in sight. A line of taxis standing at the station couldn't help us because Nevsky Prospekt, where the Baltic Hotel is situated, was closed to all traffic because of the parade. Jerry ran back and forth between taximen and policemen, trying to explain our difficulty, worried that the parade would be over before we could get out of the train station. Just when it seemed that one of the policemen might be convinced, the Intourist car showed up. The official-looking black limousine had no trouble getting us onto Nevsky Prospekt and to the hotel, where we stopped only long enough to drop our luggage, but the driver couldn't take us any further. We would have to catch up to the parade on foot.

We had never been to Leningrad before, but we needed only to be set off in the right direction down Nevsky Prospekt. This great avenue is lined with shops, museums, and grand buildings from tsarist days. Lovely bridges cross the numerous canals that intersect the avenue. Peter the Great built them as part of his "northern Venice" in the early eighteenth century. At the end of Nevsky Prospekt we would find the Winter Palace, facing the historic square in which the statue of Victory celebrates the defeat of Napoleon's armies. It was from this square in 1917 that Tsar Nicholas's soldiers turned upon him and stormed the Winter Palace, sealing the fate of the old order.

The entrances to Victory Square had been cleared of traffic and pedestrians for the parade, so that down the length of Nevsky Prospekt all we could see were parked troop carriers and soldiers on guard at each corner. Only passholders could enter the square, and except for us they were all there already. We started off, running. At the end of the first block the sentry stopped us and demanded to see our pass. He wasn't sure the pass included the children and me. Jerry explained that the Press Department of the Foreign Ministry in Moscow said we could all go on his pass. The sentry then conferred with his superior, who let us through. We started running again. The cold Baltic air bit into my lungs as we ran, laughing, half carrying, half pulling the younger children along. We were stopped at every corner, and at each corner Jerry talked us through the sentry post. Midway down the avenue we increased from seven to eight as a wrinkled old woman, her head wrapped in a babushka, cheerfully decided to become the children's grandmother so she could see the parade, too. Her great bulk waddled as she ran with us, pulling Barney along by his other arm, but she failed to fool even one sentry. The young soldier refused her with a good-natured smile, and she flashed him hers, which lacked three or four front teeth. She went back down a side street with no hard feelings.

When we finally reached the square we found it so filled with spectators that we couldn't see the marchers. We could hear their goose step, and the children small enough to be lifted onto our shoulders caught a glimpse of the Soviet military display over the heads of the crowd. After the effort of getting down Nevsky Prospekt, it was frustrating to reach our goal only to be caught in a limbo where we could see nothing. There was no place else to go until the parade was over. A Russian standing next to us spoke English and started a conversation. He was a scientist working on cancer research. He said he rarely had a chance to practice English, so we responded by asking him questions about his work — on a simple level, of course, since we have no special knowledge of cancer research. We told him our names and asked him his. Suddenly he took on the smirk of a chess player who has figured out your game and he refused to answer. The last thing he wanted was for us to get to know him. The chance to practice English wasn't worth being associated with foreigners.

Then the crowd cleared and we could see how grandly the Winter Palace is situated, the open square before it magnifying its splendor. We walked around the palace to the Neva riverfront, where the battleship *Aurora* was bedecked with bunting for the occasion. Later, when the children saw the film *Ten Days That Shook the World,* they remembered the day in Leningrad when we stood by the river and told them how the crew of the *Aurora* mutinied against the tsar and sailed up the river to support the rebelling soldiers and workers in the Revolution. For the moment we were caught up in the excitement of their history and their legends, in the thrill of standing on the spot where fifty-three years before, a Russian might have stood watching the *Aurora* approach and not known the momentous change the battleship had taken in its course.

We returned to our hotel for lunch and to meet our Intourist guide who would take us on a tour of the city and of the Hermitage Museum, housed in the Winter Palace. A year earlier I attended an art history course in Tokyo given by Professor Kidder of International Christian University. He had explained that the stylized gold animal ornaments of the Scythians, who inhabited the ancient Ukraine, were the root and seed of the artistic tradition from which much of the medieval animal motifs of Western Europe took their impetus. The Scythian animal art, which reached Ireland in the West and Japan in the East, is preserved and on display in the Hermitage Museum. For me, much of the enthusiasm for the trip to Leningrad was centered in the chance to set my eyes on Scythian gold.

When we arrived at the Hermitage after lunch, in the company of Nadezhda, an attractive Intourist guide in her late twenties, I asked her to lead us to the Scythian gold collection. She explained that we would need a special guide to see it because it was housed in the Treasure Room, where only a limited number of people were admitted at a time. We had to pay five rubles extra for the special guide. We agreed to this arrangement and she went off to pay the fee. She returned in a few minutes to inform us that it would be impossible to get into the Treasure Room for three days — it was all booked up. I stared at her in disbelief. "That's not possible. We must see it today. I came half the world to see it." Jerry tried to calm me, promising that we would be in Leningrad again and we would reserve in advance. "But the children . . . ," I stammered. "Who knows when we'll get here again with all the children." Evelind looked at me compassionately; she thought I was going to cry.

"It's all right, it's all right," she said.

Nadezhda looked at me helplessly. "Come," she said, taking Evelind by the arm. "You come with me and explain it to the lady in the office. Perhaps a child will have more influence than I have."

The pleas of a child worked. Evelind and Nadezhda returned with a museum curator who would take us through. She was a tall woman with luxurious golden hair pulled back in a bun and with a dowager's buxom fullness. In her British-accented English she let us know that we were overworking her. She began her forced tour on a tired note, with a haughty disdain for this pack of children who couldn't possibly be interested in what she, an art historian, could offer. As for the children themselves, from the moment they entered the Treasure Room they tuned out her prepared explanation. They pressed their noses to the glass cases and pointed out to each other motifs they recognized from prehistoric Japanese pottery they had seen in Tokyo. They interrupted her monotone with questions about where particular pieces came from, what they were used for originally, how old they were, or by what stamping process chains of repeated patterns were produced. To keep up with them she found herself answering their questions avidly. She forgot Jerry and me and addressed herself to the children, catching their enthusiasm. They had awakened a tired heart. By the end of the tour she had become their affectionate friend. She hugged them and made them promise to come back again. The Russian in her won out over British training. As we left she turned to Jerry and me. "I've always thought I could never give up my work to stay home and have children. But for five like these maybe even I could stay at home." Her eyes glistened and her smile was sad as she said goodbye to us.

We went through the rest of the Hermitage but the only thing that interested the children was the trapdoor in the parquet floor where the hermit tsarina had food sent up on a little dumbwaiter because she really wanted to be alone.

4

Moving In, Getting Mugged, Making Do

WHEN THE CALL CAME from UpDK (Upravlenie po Obsluzhivanyu Diplomaticheskogo Korpusa — the Administration for Servicing the Diplomatic Corps) that our apartment was ready, Jerry and I found the news that we had waited a month to hear a jolt to our now peaceful hum of life in the Ukraine Hotel. It meant moving again, more adjustments, new arrangements for getting to school in the morning, a new kindergarten for Barney, a new pattern of housekeeping habits to be formed, the fourth change in four months.

Before the housing engineer was ready to go out to Yugozapad (Southwest district) for our first glimpse of the new apartment, it was midafternoon. It would not be the last delay we experienced in our dealings with UpDK, which supplies foreigners with all their needs from maids, interpreters, and Russian language teachers to repairs, hotel and travel reservations, and theater tickets. There are no help-wanted ads in Moscow. Only people from UpDK can be hired to work in the offices and apartments of foreigners. UpDK sets the prices for rents, supplies, telephones and electricians. Without it you cannot function and if you could you would be outside Soviet law. With UpDK you are under total control. The control does not originate at UpDK, but at the Ministry of Foreign Affairs and at the KGB.

The November light was pale; there was a threat of snow in the air. It was only a twenty-minute drive from the *Time* office on Kutuzovsky Prospekt to our apartment house in Yugozapad, but the change from the dense center to the open woodlands at the edge of the city made it seem longer. Along Leninsky Prospekt rows of apartment houses, all of yellow brick, all set at the same forty-five-degree angle to the avenue, looked like a residential street in Queens, New York. Then the city ended abruptly and there were wide fields of grass and weeds, with only Dom Mebeli, a furniture store the size of an airplane hangar, set among them on the left, a few tall apartment buildings rising starkly from the fields on the right. Away from the avenue, behind Dom Mebeli, stood a new growth of apartment buildings, white, still being built, a different generation from the ones we had passed on Leninsky Prospekt. At the roof level, across three or four buildings, large red block letters spelled out the only kind of advertising to be seen in Moscow: "Workers of All Countries Unite."

The housing engineer had tried to get the elevators operating for our visit but the electricity was not yet working, so we walked up the emergency stairs to see the apartment on the sixteenth floor. The cement staircases were at the rear of the building and had large picture windows with a view of the grassy slope and woods that were interrupted only by the artificial pond just completed in the ravine below the house. The stairwells were cold and musty, with the special chill of freshly set cement that hasn't lost its dampness; the air was kept stagnant by the sealed firedoors and immovable windows. I tried to run upstairs, at least for a stretch, but the cold quickly set into my lungs and I had to stop on each landing for a long breath.

By the time we got to the sixteenth floor and into the apartment it was getting dark and we had to rely on the light coming in from outdoors. The apartment was not as cold as the stairwells but the damp smell of wallpaper glue and new plaster was overwhelming. The apartment did not even have the warmth and intimacy of poverty — only gray, pasty, soft linoleum laid over bare cement and just-hung pale-green wallpaper that was already peeling loose from the gritty cement walls.

They had given us two apartments, one with two rooms, one with four, plus the kitchens. This was an experimental, luxury apartment house, a departure from the precast, instant slums they were putting up around it. It was a building for diplomatic personnel, yet there was not a dining room large enough to seat twelve people with any comfort.

In contrast to the roomy kitchens of Russian families, ours had no eating space and would barely give us room to walk from refrigerator to stove once the cabinets were in. The apartment was a rabbit warren of tiny rooms, with closets not deep enough for a normal clothes hanger and with toilet cubicles in which a tall man's knees hit the door. As in old Russian houses, the apartment had dropped ceilings in the hallways to provide overhead storage space. One water faucet served both sink and bathtub, on a swivel, and the cast-iron sides of the bathtubs showed their bare, claw-footed legs. But then we had not come to the Soviet Union expecting luxury.

The two redeeming features were the extravagant and huge windows of double thickness that faced east and west, and the balconies. For the two apartments there were three large balconies. From this great height we could look out over woods and fields, a tiny church in the distance, Patrice Lumumba University dormitories beyond the trees, and other apartment houses, hundreds of apartment houses recently constructed or still unfinished.

The south wall of the apartment was solid, with only a narrow window from floor to ceiling. I pushed it to see if it moved and found that it opened at an angle, so that a child could easily trip over its low sill and fall sixteen floors to the ground. I locked it then and never opened it again. When we moved in we barricaded it with a table full of houseplants.

This graceless labyrinth of cement boxes stung me momentarily, dropped me, yet made me reach for that resourcefulness we had mustered over and over in our moves from one country to another, when we had to create a home, take it apart, move on, and do it again. Instead of dejection, Jerry felt anger and resolution. Without a moment's hesitation he ordered the interpreter to tell the building engineers, "Take out this wall of closets," leaving free access from east to west, balcony to balcony, light to light. "Take out this wall," making a long, L-shaped living room, now with three large picture windows. "Cut a door between the apartments, from one children's room to another. Seal the kitchen wall of the second apartment," making another bedroom. The soft, primitive Russian linoleum (linoleum of good quality was imported from East Germany), which already showed imprints of the workmen's machinery, had to be ripped up in the foyer and living room and replaced with parquet flooring. One bathtub would be removed to make way for a clothes washer and dryer. The voltage provided for each apartment would be insufficient for automatic machinery; more had to be added. Jerry held up a limp piece of wallpaper that had come unglued. "Rip this off and finish the walls with a sealer that at least can be painted over."

Yes, they could do all this, but even with pressure to hurry the work it would take another month. By this time the threat of living in hotel rooms another month had lost its fangs. I could readily accept it rather than move into this wretched cage in its present state.

The next day the list of changes was drawn up and UpDK set prices on the work, $2,000, which included the cost of restoring the walls in case any future tenant wanted them put back. After some negotiations Jerry signed the agreement and they began pulling out the closet wall, which was only composition board, and chopping down the cement wall to open the third room of the L. The largest single expense was for additional voltage. It seemed rather curious that the structural changes, the plastering of walls and the parquet flooring, which would have been exorbitant in any American city, were quite reasonable.

We soon gleaned from conversations with foreign neighbors and diplomats from foreign embassies, that the Soviets have a sliding scale of charges, depending on who you are. Newsmen pay less than diplomats for the same work, but more than representatives of Third World countries. You pay the least if you are from a socialist country. A month later, when the wooden container which brought our household goods was emptied and I tried to sell it to a Pakistani who was leaving, he patiently explained to me that he could get a new one from the Soviets for $120 and I was asking $200. When we asked the Soviets to build us one the same size when we left, the bill was $500. A Canadian diplomat who had the twin of our apartment at the other end of the building was given an estimate of double the amount we paid to get the same work done.

In the weeks that followed, we continued our regimen in the Ukraine Hotel, the children trying to cope with school lessons in Russian, and our teacher, Tamara, appearing at nine in the morning three days a week to teach Jerry and me "active" Russian.

Tolya arrived at the hotel one day with Lyuba, a housemaid sent to us by UpDK, and Elvina to translate the interview. The meeting proceeded with greater ease than I had ever experienced in hiring household help. Lyuba had had sixteen years of experience in diplomatic houses and was bored with my questions about her capabilities in this or that aspect of housework. Since her husband didn't work and was at home, she was willing to work afternoons and evenings instead of mornings. She had only one question: When could she start? She wanted to come to the hotel to help me, but I didn't have enough work to keep her busy and she would only be a burden to me. As the weeks of renovation of the apartment wore on she became impatient, but fortunately she waited for us and didn't take another job. Perhaps UpDK gave her no choice.

Tolya and I visited the hard-currency furniture shop to buy kitchen cabinets. Walking into the dimly lit furniture showroom was like entering a movie set for a film in the 1930's. The overstuffed chairs with wooden arms, the highly lacquered veneer buffets and dressers recalled the earliest *moderne,* which in America had by then been discarded or put into children's converted attic rooms. Here it was all new and just imported from Poland and East Germany, available to Russians only for foreign currency. Most Russians hankered after it.

Tolya and I went straight for the kitchen department and it took no time at all to choose a set of table, chairs and cabinets because it was the only one that looked more modern than the one my grandmother had discarded about 1940. It was painted white and the table top was of a yellow figured formica, not for a *House and Garden* display but pleasant and workable enough. The hitch was that the set on display was already sold and I would have to wait for another shipment from Poland. "Perhaps ten days" — we were advised to leave our address on a form. Tolya encouraged me to choose a bird-in-hand, but I was hopeful that another shipment was on its way. A year later we had to get cabinets sent from Finland; the promised Polish furniture never did arrive.

Our apartment began to take on quite a different personality from the depressing one we had met on our first visit. The removal of walls let in light and gave an attractive feeling of space, a roomy aerie on a mountain peak. We now had so much light that a pure white paint on the walls would have been blinding. Instead we chose off-white tones that contained gray and green pigments to absorb some of the sun's rays. We were about to call Helsinki for paint, but the housing engineer, who exuded an air of experience, assured us that the Soviet Union now could supply paint up to international standards, at less cost and trouble than ordering it from abroad.

One day when I arrived a little before three in the afternoon to see how the work was going on, all was quiet. The six or seven painters and plasterers, all ruddy-cheeked women dressed in stained white coveralls, their hair tucked under white cloth turbans, lay about the floor resting after their two o'clock meal. One had her palms pressed together to form a pillow under her cheek and another lay with a pile of brushes under her neck for support. The motionless forms, in graceful relation to one another, were like white swimmers in an impressionistic tableau. Both friendly and proud of their careful craftsmanship, they seemed to care about leaving me a well-finished apartment. They were knit together as a group in self-protection against the leering jokes of the men. They had only disdain for the men's hidden bottles of vodka on the job and their shabby work. The women rebuffed any attempts to rush them in their tasks. Their pride and high standards were an anachronism in Moscow, where the turnover of construction workers prevented the building up of a skilled corps of artisans.

A Soviet friend who is a building engineer explained to us that willingness to work in construction is one of the few ways that a farm worker can gain permission to live in Moscow. The foreman barely has a few weeks to teach the new men how to use unfamiliar tools before they learn their way around the city and find less strenuous, higher-paying jobs. "There won't be any more experimental buildings such as this one," our friend said grimly. "It takes too much time and skill to do all this hand finishing. I for one wouldn't undertake anything but a prefabricated, mass-produced building where the least-skilled workmen are needed and where the process of putting it together is simple and repetitious."

The men workers were happy to see me so they could begin bargaining on how many bottles of vodka I would supply when the job was done. When the parquet was nearly finished they informed me that unless they worked overtime they would have to leave the wood unpolished because they were being called off this job for another job the next morning. Moreover, if I wanted wax instead of the varnish they provided, I would have to find it myself. We came to an agreement on the price of overtime and the number of fifths of vodka I would supply. Then Tolya and I set off to find the wax, which we were able to buy after trying four or five stores that normally carried it but hadn't had any in stock for months.

The workmen had sealed the wrong kitchen door but didn't take long to open it again. They thickened the wall of the kitchen that would now be a bedroom with composition board from the torn-down closets, which served well as a noise insulator.

When the work was finished we could only marvel at how attractive the apartment had become. The matte, off-white walls and expanses of glass and the waxed yellow-oak parquet floor welcomed us to move in. They were luxurious, not only for Moscow, but for anywhere in the world. The sense of spaciousness afforded by making one large room out of three small ones compensated for many deficiencies.

We still had no cabinets in the kitchen and only a few shallow closets without hanging rods in the rest of the apartment. And we were still faced with a sickening stench of stale urine whenever we opened the second bathroom door. No amount of disinfectant and scrubbing seemed to help. It was finally traced to a fault in the exhaust system of the central airshaft that served the whole line of eighteen floors of toilets, one above the other. It was remedied, but for weeks afterward we played host to classes of engineers from the Air Exhaust Institute, who brought what looked like toy wind spinners to scientifically meter the rate of the air current in the exhaust duct.

This building had no gas supply, so we had to sell our two-oven American range and make do with the small Soviet electric stove supplied to us. We kept the extra stove from the second kitchen that had now become a bedroom, so in effect we could have two small ovens going at different temperatures at the same time. The first soufflé I made never formed a crust, but once we accustomed ourselves to the idiosyncrasies of the Russian ovens they served us well.

On a cold gray afternoon in the first days of December, Lyuba and I stood shivering and stamping our feet to keep warm on the bedroom balcony and looked out over Yugozapad. We were there to watch the movers, to see that they did not scratch gashes into the new parquet floor and to show them where to deposit the boxes, furniture and barrels they unloaded from the room-size wooden container in the parking lot below. Our household goods had come from Tokyo around the Cape of Good Hope, through the Baltic Sea to Helsinki (where they were thoroughly drenched when the container was left out on the docks in a rainstorm), and then to Moscow.

The men were nearly finished and Lyuba stood with me as I tried to count all the apartment houses in view, beginning with those nearest to us, prefabricated five-story walkups called *Khrushchovy,* a pun meaning Khrushchev's Slums. Past the muddy double road up a steep slope across the way began a complex of buildings that was a small city in itself: a small shopping center and white rectangular boxes of various heights, most at right angles to each other but some at a slant to the others. There were walkways and gardens between them, but in December the natural landscape was bleak and the pale thin trees emphasized the raw newness of the community. When I reached a count of 120 I stopped because some buildings hid others behind them and I wasn't sure which ones I was counting twice and which ones I couldn't see at all. Besides, Lyuba thought the point was made: "There are a lot of new buildings here and all the Muscovites crowded into old apartments would love to move out here, but it's hard to get these new flats. You have to be high in the Academy of Sciences, or the police, or have money. Some of them are cooperative apartments, but you have to be a professor at Moscow University or a high official to have the price they're asking per square meter."

Lyuba was more impatient than I for us to move in. I offered to pay her for the waiting time while we were in the hotel, but what she really wanted was an outlet for her enormous talent and energy, which rarely flagged in the time she worked for us. She had shrewd, twinkling blue eyes, and a long thin nose that turned up at the end. Her graying blond hair was pulled back in a bun. She looked exactly as I expected a Ukrainian peasant woman to look. Her wages of $154 per month were set by the agency, but the hours were to be agreed on between us. I was pleased that she was willing to work the hours most convenient to me, from two to nine every day but Sunday.

Although Lyuba and I had only met a couple of weeks before, she was already introducing me to her special brand of realism. She believed what she read in *Pravda* about the world beyond the one she could see with her own eyes, but no ideological training could distort what she could perceive with her own clear intelligence. There was no contradiction in her own mind when one day she told me that before the Revolution everyone in Russia was a slave, "just like in America where everyone works for someone else. All the workers in factories are capitalist slaves." The next day she complained that there was a shortage of foods in the Soviet markets and all the crab, caviar and chicken was saved for the Gastronom so it could be sold for dollars. "Why shouldn't we Soviet workers eat the best? We are a rich country and the people aren't getting the riches. When there was really nothing to eat during the war we kept on working anyway. I was taken from the Ukraine and sent to work in a factory in the Urals. We had a little hard bread and some soup, hardly enough to stay alive, but we kept working day and night. I'm not lazy, I work hard and I have enough money to pay. Why am I not as good as a foreigner who can walk in and buy what he wants?"

I listened and laughed. "It's just the opposite in America, Lyuba. There the stores are full of good things and everyone complains that they don't have enough money to buy what they want."

"You mean," she turned to me incredulously, "you don't have two kinds of stores in America? Anyone can walk into any store and buy anything he sees?"

"Yes," I answered, "but you have to have the money."

This problem was hard for her to understand because the Soviet Union has the highest saving rate in the world. Even with low salaries and high prices for food and clothing, the average citizen saves money. Lyuba and her husband had a combined income of over two hundred rubles a month. They paid eleven rubles a month for one room plus a large kitchen and a bathroom, including utilities. They spent up to three rubles a day for food. They owned half a share, with her husband's brother, of a dacha reachable by electric train from Moscow. Never having driven a car in their lives (they were in their fifties), they did not think of buying one now.

As we stood huddled in our winter coats in the gray December chill, Lyuba remarked that she didn't like this damp, dispirited weather — she looked forward to the real freeze. When the temperature dropped and snow fell the air would clear and we wouldn't feel the cold so much. I soon learned that all Muscovites felt the same: they welcomed the real winter, no matter how cold, and complained that reservoirs built around Moscow had tempered the weather, causing the winter to come later than it did in former years. We shivered

and talked about our families with an immediate intimacy that was all
the more strange because she spoke only Russian and a few words of
German, and understood only a little English. It was not quite six
months since I tremulously opened the grammar book to Lesson One
in my first Russian class in California. She told me that she had never
had children because her husband was ill and she had to work. He was
shot in the head in the war and had never been able to work since
then. He was a good man and theirs was a happy marriage; she willingly accepted the reversal of roles. He tried from time to time to take
a job, but immediately his blood pressure would go up and she would
receive an emergency call. Then she would have to take time off from
work to nurse him. She asked me to buy her unground buckwheat
groats — *grechnaya kasha* — in the dollar Gastronom because the doctor prescribed it for her husband and it was often unavailable in the
Soviet markets.

She talked of one sister who lived on a *kolkhoz* (collective farm)
in the Ukraine and another who lived in Odessa.

"I would love to visit a kolkhoz," I said. "Maybe we can all go
visit your sister. Is it a good life? They must have plenty to eat in the
Ukraine."

"Yes," she agreed. "We'll all go to visit her. She would love to see
us, especially in summer when the fruit is pulling the trees down,
there's so much of it. My husband and I like to go there for vacation
— we store up enough health for the whole year. It's nothing to me,
because I saw it all as a young girl, but my husband likes to go in the
fall when they butcher hogs. They catch the blood from the jugular
vein and make blood sausage." She made a face to show her disgust.
"He's a city boy, he gets a big thrill out of it." Then her face grew
mysteriously dark to indicate travail and hardship beyond my imagination. "My sister works very hard. No, it's not a good life, but there's
no way to get out of it."

Even though our apartment building was occupied entirely by foreigners, we didn't feel as separated from the Soviet community around
us as the foreigners did who lived in the larger ghettos composed of
whole complexes of buildings, closer to the center of the city. Our
neighborhood seemed to be made up of Academy of Sciences members,
lower-level workers for the KGB, and teenagers from the government-
owned farm near us — they were attracted to our woods and pond.
(This farm, a *sovkhoz,* had salaried workers, in contrast to the kolkhoz,

which is run by share members.) Because we foreigners were so few we lived closer to the realities of Soviet life, as well as to its dangers.

Stevo. Across the concrete-lined lake from our apartment building was a man-made forest. Its rows were neatly planted, but it was large and dense, not hard to get lost in. On the other side of it was one of the campuses of Lumumba University. The students were almost exclusively black, from African countries. There were many gruesome stories about the woods told by African students and Russians. One African student was said to have been hanged by some *khuligany* (hooligans) in the woods. One fall a girl was missing, and they could not find her all winter. In the spring, when the drifts melted, they found her in the woods in the melting muck with a knife in her back.

My first encounter with hooligans occurred when I was eleven in our first year. It was a very gray day, and I had just entered the soggy dark woods. When I looked up from the ground, I saw a tall boy about eighteen years old with long blond hair and a Soviet sailor's anchor belt buckle, letting himself down out of a tree. Some of his hair hung in his face, and one of his eyes peered off distractedly to the side. He said, "Hey." I returned the greeting and he asked me a question: "*Dyengi yest?*" I looked at him dazedly, unaware of what he wanted. He repeated the question a few more times before my mind fell into gear and comprehended that he was asking me for money.

"*Nyet,*" I snapped back automatically. Adrenalin had started to flow and my body tingled.

"And what are you going to do if you've got some, eh?"

I did not understand that either, and he repeated it a few times, becoming more insistent. As I stood there, looking dumb, he reached for my pockets. I moved back from him and pulled out the thirty kopecks' change that was in my jeans. I handed it to him and turned away, walking quickly.

"Hey, you! Hold up over there!"

I continued.

"Hold on, or I'll give it to you, you jerk!" He came running after me, swinging his arm around in an arc gathering momentum for his fist. I stopped, and he gave all my pockets a thorough search. I was shaking a little by then, but he couldn't find anything. I think he had finally realized that I might be a foreigner because of my clothes and my incredulity, so he asked me my address. I wouldn't answer and he said, "Good boy, thanks a lot. You're a good little kid." He had missed the trolley pass in an inside pocket of my coat.

Leona. Stevo returned from the woods angry, humiliated and shaken. Lyuba suggested we immediately notify the militsioner on duty in front of our building, to see if he could catch the young hooligan. Stevo and I promptly rode down in the elevator, found the militsioner, and walked with him to the edge of the flat plateau on which the apartment house stood and looked down the ravine that dropped sharply from where we stood to the lake and woods below. Stevo described the younger mugger and the anchor belt buckle he wore. The policeman glanced at the woods where Stevo pointed and nodded his head to indicate he understood. "You watch out for him," the policeman advised, "and when you see him again call me." He smiled helplessly and walked off to his guardbox.

We had been in the apartment only a few weeks when it was time to light the first candles for Hanukkah, the Feast of Lights, which commemorates the return of the Jews to their temple in Jerusalem after its desecration by the Romans. Then, only enough oil was left to burn the holy altar lamp for one day, but by a miracle it burned for eight days. Hanukkah is now mainly a children's holiday. Families light an additional candle every night for eight nights, say a prayer together, and present gifts to each other. Both Lyuba and Tolya understood that we were celebrating a children's festival, but since they had never seen it before, they assumed it was an American holiday. I tried to explain that it was Jewish, but didn't know the word for "Jewish" in Russian. So night after night Lyuba watched and listened, a stranger at a pagan custom, and shared the children's pleasure at the gifts they received. Then late in the week of Hanukkah I took the children to the Pushkin Gallery. There on the wall hung a blue of the bluest Picassos, from the museum's permanent collection: *Stari Yevrai S Malchikom* (Old Jew with a Boy). A knot of frustration untied before my eyes. When we arrived back at the apartment I told Lyuba with great pleasure that we were *Yevrei* and that the candles were for a Jewish holiday. She took in my news with decent friendliness, but without her usual warmth.

In that first year, three mornings a week were taken up with Russian lessons, and two disappeared in the small chores of setting up a new home. We managed to get two moonlighters, maintenance men from another building, to put up the closet and curtain rods we had been forewarned to bring from America. They sold us a used kitchen cabinet that would serve until the promised furniture arrived from Poland. It was the Russian equivalent of a cabinet with sliding doors, but since the necessary runners weren't available, the doors were hung on a wire pulley that ran off its reel and stuck every day, virtually reducing Lyuba and me to tears. In the process of hanging this monstrosity on the wall, the moonlighters drilled directly into a hidden sheathed cable, causing a frightening display of electrical fireworks and a short circuit eighteen floors long. Lyuba managed to find the building electrician, a patient and gentle craftsman, who came to repair the damage and explain the danger they had caused. There was a hushed exchange between Lyuba and the electrician, after which he smiled amiably and assured her he would not report that two men from another building were illegally picking up extra cash at the time they fouled the cable. Smiles of relief and appreciation on the faces of the two nervous bunglers.

Eventually Lyuba and I papered the homely bathroom walls with bright pink striped wallpaper from Helsinki, and replaced the uncomfortable toilet seats with better plastic ones. The appearance of new toilet seats was a notable neighborhood event at the household store across the road; as I and others emerged from the store, people walking by saw what we had under our arms and rushed in to buy the last ones before the store ran out of them again. In the two years we lived there, that was the only time I saw toilet seats for sale.

Although we bought most of our food at the hard-currency Gastronom, either the children or I walked each day across the muddy road and up the log steps set into the steep hillside that led to the household store and the Russian food market. Mainly we went for fresh bread, but the children often stopped at the open stands outside the market for fresh éclairs, ice cream, a drink of kvass, or a pack of frozen *pelmeny* (a Siberian version of ravioli) to boil at home and eat with sour cream. At another stand there was a shoe repair man, and a man who mended any kind of metal object. The children were afraid, at first, of the clusters of drunken workmen sharing bottles of vodka and cheap wine outside the market, but it was a busy, well-lit place and it soon became apparent that the rough-looking drunks were noisier than they were dangerous.

As I came down the hillside one evening in early December I found a drunk asleep on the cold soggy ground next to the path. When I arrived back at the apartment I suggested to Lyuba that we call the police because the man would surely have pneumonia before morning. "Then let him die," Lyuba said mercilessly. "He'll be more of a help to his wife when he's dead and she receives his pension than now, when he drinks up the money and there's nothing left to feed the children. Don't worry, the police will pick him up soon and send him home tomorrow. It won't help. He'll get drunk and fall down someplace else two days from now.'

Her lack of compassion was shared by everyone we knew. The problem of drunkenness is enormous in the Soviet Union, both personally and economically. It was common to see crowds of workmen drunk before the factory doors opened at 7 A.M. If a worker couldn't pay the high price of a bottle of vodka, deliberately made expensive by the state, he would customarily look for two fellow workers to share a bottle with him. There was a popular joke about an American spy who parachuted into a Russian forest with two other spies. The other two were quickly detected and shot, but the third got away. He changed into Russian workers' clothes and at the first light of day wandered into a town. He saw a line of people and joined it; it turned out to be a line at a liquor store. As he reached the head of the line the last man in front of him turned around and asked, "Are you the third?" The spy threw his arms in the air and asked, "How did you know?" The Russians who heard the story laughed heartily, for they knew that "Are you the third?" was an invitation to share a bottle of vodka.

When I went to buy bread I usually looked around the market to see if there were food products we could use that weren't sold in the Gastronom. At the meat counter the butcher used an ax to hack at unidentifiable parts of beef laid on a tree stump. Occasionally I found old-fashioned, long-cooking oatmeal, sometimes cornmeal, once or twice cornflakes. One day I found a Russian cake mix, which intrigued and delighted Lyuba; she had never seen one before. We tried and liked it, but it never appeared in the store again. There was little variety and even a supply of staples couldn't be relied on.

On the way home I often stopped for a look at the household

store, but the stock of colorless, poorly made kitchen and bath utensils was usually disappointing. Now and then there were yellow and green molded pottery items from Georgia decorated with profuse, Near Eastern ornamentation. Sometimes there were kitchen pans of brightly colored enamel over cast iron, crude copies of Czechoslovakian and Scandinavian wares. But the one factory in Leningrad that produced them couldn't keep the stores supplied, and the pans were often chipped in shipping. Printed oilcloth sold out the day it arrived at the store. When our iron broke, the only one we could get weighed eleven pounds.

When I passed the household store one day, there were lines of people waiting for boxes of laundry detergent. From a distance the design on the boxes looked like the familiar orange and yellow one printed on Tide boxes. I came closer — I couldn't believe that the Russians had imported laundry detergent from the United States. But it was Tide, printed in Russian letters. I examined the box closely and saw that it came from Iran. The clerks had to limit the amount per customer because the appearance of powdered laundry detergent was so rare that it excited the shoppers to buy as much as they could carry. Some of them had traveled for two hours on the Metro (subway), equipped with heavy twine to tie the boxes together for easier carrying. I told Jerry about the "Tayud" that night and he learned at the office that the Iranian government had a franchise from Procter and Gamble to produce it in Iran. The Iranians supplied it to the Russians as part of the payment for a steel mill that the Russians had built for them.

We thought we would never miss a billboard or a commercial, but when we lived without any commercial advertising, we found we missed its colorfulness and the information it gave about new products, new styles and the availability of consumer goods — all aspects of life missing in Moscow. When we finished the contents of boxes of American dry cereal, the children took the empty cartons to their beds and clutched the familiar packages as they fell asleep.

At home in America we bemoaned the waste of excess packaging, but in Moscow we saw its opposite: the waste of man-hours when people stood in line waiting to sell back empty jars at the collection points. We had been warned to bring with us screw-top jars for storing leftovers because Russian jar tops must be removed with a can opener and cannot be replaced firmly on the jar for reuse. Since we always had so many jars to resell, Tolya made an arrangement with the man at the recycling center to receive less than the value of the jars in exchange for not waiting in line. Together they agreed on a rough estimate, rather than counting out how many there were of various sizes and computing the exact amount due us. Later the collection man profited from the excess value of our jars.

Shopping in the neighborhood was only for bread and curiosity, not for filling the larder day by day. About three times a fortnight Tolya picked me up in the office station wagon to go shopping at the Gastronom. He always reminded me to take our collection of airline carry-on bags, string carry-alls and plastic bags — the Gastronom did not supply paper bags.

As in other hard-currency stores, a sharp-eyed bouncer stood near the door to pick out the unlikely customers who tried to enter the privileged sanctum. He had no trouble telling a Russian from a foreigner; he then had to distinguish the gate-crashers and the curious peasants from the maids, drivers and other Russians who had access to foreign money and therefore could justify their presence there. These privileged Russians included high-ranking officials of the Party and army, members of the KGB, Russian wives of foreigners, and writers and journalists who earned foreign royalties and salaries. They had to transfer their funds from abroad through the state bank, which first discounted a heavy tax, then issued them coupons.

Inside the door, the arrays of fish and meat, cheese and butter, candies, liquor, wine, cigarettes, canned and fresh fruits and vegetables were grand by Russian standards. The ships that unloaded munitions in Haiphong harbor brought back a steady supply of fresh pineapples and bananas. Cuban catsup was thin and sweet, but better than no catsup at all. Algerian orange juice in cans, like any canned orange juice, doesn't give the pleasure of frozen orange juice, but that technology hadn't reached Algeria or the Soviet Union.

We accustomed our palates to the new sensations of preserved lampreys and pickled flower squash, and learned to butcher rumps of veal at home because the Gastronom butcher's handsaw left splinters of bone where he cut through the center of the leg. The range of food was limited but the quality was excellent. It changed only to include seasonal fresh fruits and vegetables.

It was no hardship to eat tenderloin of beef at a ruble a pound ($1.11), but it required ingenuity to think of new ways to prepare it because it was the only cut of beef they sold. Occasionally the butcher would grind it for me, but most of the time the electric grinder was out of order and in summer they refused to use it because they said the bits left in the machine after each use made it unsanitary in warm weather. Fresh chickens were only a little over a pound each, emaciated but tender. We had to be ready to clean them as soon as we got them home because they came with all their insides except the gall bladder.

I asked Lyuba why the Soviets didn't have poultry cleaning plants. "We have always been at war," she sighed. "We haven't had time since the last war. If you could have seen how terrible it was, you'd know how much we've done since then. We can't have everything we want right away." I forbore to remind her that "right away" had now gone on for twenty-five years.

Woodcock, grouse and pheasant were almost always available frozen, but in addition to gutting them and removing gullets full of pine seeds, we had to pluck them as well. Lyuba didn't mind; she saved the down for pillows. Ducklings came from Eastern Europe, frozen and cleaned.

We drank Château Montrose 1961 for a ruble, twenty-five kopecks ($1.38), and Château Giscours 1962 for two rubles, fifty kopecks ($2.76). Johnny Walker Black or Red Label, Napoleon cognac, liqueurs and gin were plentiful and inexpensive. Russian vodka was a ruble a bottle.

At the next counter were large bars of Swiss chocolate and many kinds of small individually wrapped Russian candies, sold by weight, each type named for a Russian fairy tale or spacecraft, and boxes with standard assortments of cookies and crackers. We tried them all. From the same clerk you could buy long-grain and short-grain rice, unground buckwheat groats and a white cereal that looked like farina. She sold one kind of flour, two kinds of noodles, both of which became a glutinous mass if even slightly overcooked. She offered a few spices — nutmeg, cardamom, pepper and salt — but no cinnamon and no vanilla. She had never heard of brown sugar. There were no quick-cooking or instant breakfast cereals on sale; perhaps the closest the Gastronom came to convenience foods were packets of dried soup imported from Switzerland and canned Bulgarian eggplant. Both olive oil and plain vegetable oil were usually in stock. The white granulated sugar was too coarse to go through the cake sifter, but tasted like any other.

The dairy counter required a reeducation in eating. "Warmed butter" was clarified butter, sold in jars; I learned that it made wonderful cakes with little beating because the milk solids were removed. At first we missed cream cheese, but an American friend taught us to substitute *lyubitelskaya smetana* (amateur sour cream), a little too soft but delicious without the usual gum arabic. In place of yoghurt we ate clabbered milk with the canned Bulgarian raspberries we all loved for breakfast. *Kefir* was close to buttermilk in acidity, but lumpy instead of smooth. There was no creamed cottage cheese — the curds were stiff and dry, just right for puddings and cheesecake. Next came a wide variety of cheddar cheeses, sausages and ham, all made to European rather than American taste, all very good. There is no resemblance between an American hot dog and veal *kolbasa;* the latter is paler in color, less sweet and less spiced. It has a smoked flavor. At the next counter, an old-fashioned delicatessen showcase, was an assortment of smoked fish that intimidated the uninitiated and delighted its devotees — eel, salmon, sturgeon, whitefish, Baltic herrings, lampreys in season.

At the far end of the store was the counter for canned and fresh fruits and vegetables. The clerks there had a reputation for haughtiness and short tempers; if you were a newcomer they looked you over carefully for stylishness and potential favors before they decided whether they would take you first or leave you till last on a busy day. One American woman assured me it was necessary to bring them gifts of mascara, lipstick and eyeliner pencils, but I declined her advice. The clerks weren't friendly at first and were even less so after I complained one day that they had charged me for tomatoes but had not put them in my order. After a couple of months, though, perhaps with the aid of Tolya's flirtatious joking, we reached an easy rapport and they greeted me pleasantly.

The East European canned fruits, vegetables and jams were not oversweetened and overstandardized; a speckled peach remained with its blemishes and enhanced the natural flavor of the fruits. In the fall the Gastronom had cucumbers and tomatoes long after they had disappeared on the Russian market, but once the season was over we didn't get any for months. Occasionally they would have boxes of lettuce no bigger than seedlings, heavy with black lumps of soil. It took such excruciating patience to clean the leaves that it wasn't worth the effort. During the winter we ate cabbage, onions, potatoes, carrots and beets, the root-cellar vegetables. We could buy fresh mushrooms, flat-leafed parsley from the south, and oranges and lemons from Morocco all winter in the Gastronom, but the regular Russian markets didn't have them. In the fall we enjoyed the harvests of fresh green beans, pumpkin, brussels sprouts, fresh dill, cauliflower, pears, apples and grapes; in the spring, lavish baskets of cherries and strawberries. The best of everything came from Bulgaria. Some fruits and vegetables — corn on the cob, artichokes, asparagus, avocados, grapefruit and endive — never appeared.

Those who yearned for a head of iceberg lettuce in winter or for a ripe French Brie cheese, certainly had to adjust to living in Moscow, but the quality and variety of food satisfied every nutritional need and most of our tastes. We thought we missed American convenience foods, but the only taste that didn't pale within a few weeks after we were back in America was the luxury of frozen orange juice.

After getting past the bouncer and feasting hungry eyes on the display of foods that could not be seen anywhere else in Moscow, it was necessary to get down to the work of shopping. First you had to stand in a line for meat, then in another for fish, sausage and dairy products, then in another for dry staples and sweets, in yet another for spirits and cigarettes, and in still another for fruits and vegetables. When your turn came in each line you had to be prepared to reel off the products and quantities you wanted for the clerk to write on an invoice: "Two hundred grams of ham, sliced please, not too much fat please; a half kilo of *tvorog* (pot cheese); a smoked whitefish — yes, the one on top will do; two packets of *lyubitelskaya smetana* (sour cream)." What I bought and how I liked it were always exposed to the people in line behind me, waiting and listening, and I always felt rushed by them to get on with my order, not waste time on deliberation or mind-changing. My Russian improved rapidly under the pressure; I always imagined their feet tapping impatiently.

For each item I called out the clerk had to list the price in two columns, one referring to the amount in coupons, the other giving the comparable value in rubles. There were different degrees of privilege; some Russians had another kind of coupons and had to pay the ruble price, usually three times the hard-currency price. The clerk kept one copy of the invoice, which her assistant referred to while gathering your order, and gave you a copy.

With your invoices you queued twice: once for the cashier who received coupons for fresh produce, liquor and staples; a second time for the cashier who charged you for meat, fish and dairy products. The cashiers scanned each invoice for obvious mistakes, then took your coupons and marked your invoices paid. With these in hand you had to get back in four more lines to pick up the orders the clerks had put together for you. This might go quickly if there were only a few people shopping, or it might take hours on a busy day. The only way to shorten it was for Tolya and me to stand in different lines at the same time.

A couple of months before we left the Soviet Union the Gastronom moved to a new location. The new Gastronom had Italian display counters for frozen and refrigerated foods. It also had check-out lines past a cashier's cash register where you paid for your purchases all at once, rather than in separate lines. Customers could pick up canned goods and boxes of dry staples from open counters and consider them for as long as they liked before either putting them back or dropping them into their imported shopping carts. The clerks, once overworked, stood around smiling, checking to see that shelves were well stocked. There was an illusion created of buying in an American or European supermarket until the customers reached into their purses to pay the tab on the shiny new calculator. We still had to tear coupons out of the same clipped-together booklets, riffling among the different pastels for five, ten, twenty kopecks, and one-, five- and ten-ruble pieces of scrip. And the same bouncer stood at the door welcoming his regular customers, checking the unfamiliar faces.

5

Caviar for Breakfast

AFTER WE MOVED INTO OUR APARTMENT in Yugozapad, Jerry and I entered Barney in the detsky sad that curled like a sleeping cat in the shadow of our apartment house, and he felt more secure. By this time he could repeat in perfect, resonant Russian the slurs from the little Soviet chauvinists: "Here comes the foreigner."

This detsky sad was the model kindergarten run by the Academy of Sciences, primarily for the children of their own members. The twin experimental apartment building next to ours was assigned to the Academy and families of the Soviet scientific elite lived in most of the apartments. The kindergarten had a doctor in full-time attendance who had a tired, sour but essentially handsome face and who was warm and humorous but strict. She checked each child as he arrived in flu weather, and if his nails weren't cut and clean, home he went. She seemed less surprised than other Soviet citizens at the size of our family and told me she would be insulted if I didn't give Moscow equal time with Japan and Hong Kong and have at least one baby while I was there. She was only half-joking: the Russians are seriously disturbed at their own low birthrate, which at its present crawl will have them enveloped by the other Soviet nationalities by the year 2000. When not in her office she wandered around the school, lending support to the teachers when they needed her. She was also on duty during weekends because some of the Academy people boarded their children at the kindergarten and worked on special projects outside the city. The school had to be ready to keep the children if the parents were unable to take them for the regular weekend break. The dormitories where the children slept, as well as the cribs in them, were clean, airy, well kept and sterile. Even the doctor felt compassion for these children, who were hungry for affection and latched themselves onto any visitor.

Barney's teacher, who when you looked closely was no more than thirty, seemed ten years older because she was always harassed, her hair in disarray. She had charge of up to thirty children from nine in the morning until five, and those whose parents worked late stayed until 7:30 P.M. She was supposed to have two assistants, but they were often absent, leaving her with only the help of a cleaning woman to get through the day. She had to pull out a cot for each child at one o'clock and put them all away at three. She also fed the children three meals from a hot plate, with food sent up from the central kitchen. In hot weather she had to give them showers.

Barney. In kindergarten for breakfast they give you starchy juice called *kesir* that is like paste. Also they give you a slice of bread with a big chunk of butter on it. You can't spread it unless you use the back of your spoon because they don't have knives. They give you soft-boiled eggs, too. For lunch they give you potato soup with a piece of black bread and a section of garlic. Other times they give you fried fish with mashed potatoes, which is very good. When we got oranges it was a big treat because the oranges came from Morocco.

Leona. Since the full day was inconvenient for us, I picked up Barney at one o'clock every day. If I left him to nap from one until three he would be up until midnight at home, which might be all right for a mother who wasn't with her child all day, but was difficult for us. The working mothers told me it was hard for them, too, because they were tired when they got home from work and still had housekeeping chores to do. A few times Barney went back after naptime, especially in winter when the teacher built an ice slide in the yard and let them play in the snow for hours. Usually, when I came to get him I wore my red fox coat, and while I waited for him to put on his boots and coat the other children stroked my coat and asked me how did I do in English, over and over again, laughing, running away, coming back to touch my coat and ask me how I did. The teacher, full of affection for the children but always rushing past, told them it was *nekulturny* to stroke my coat. Once she stopped, put her hands on her hips, and said to me in an appealing voice, "I not only feed them, teach them letters and numbers, bed them down for naps, I also have to give them *vospitaniye,*" the wonderful word for "nurturing upward."

I did my best to keep smiling at her and at the children as I waited for Barney to put on his outer clothes each day, but it wasn't easy. In that overheated, airless room I could hardly bear the mingled odors of thirty bodies and the leftover food that had not yet been returned to the kitchen. The Russians have always been and still are afraid of drafts, so they don't open windows in winter except when a room is empty. The stretch of the day when Barney's classroom was full was too long without fresh air. The room had a sour, sickening stench.

Perhaps the room was worse than usual that first winter; after the November snows, which were all pleasure, beckoning the children out into the yard for hours to build snow castles, the heavy frost came and kept everyone in for six weeks. We loved November that year. Barney's teacher showed him, as if he were some underprivileged child who had never seen snow before, how to start with a snowball and roll it in powder, then keep rolling it until it was half his height. The other boys rolled these into a wall of snow and then used it as a fort from which to throw snowballs at the others.

Skating was Barney's favorite lesson of the week.

Barney. At detsky sad in the winter we were given figure-skating lessons on the skating rinks. They poured water on one spot on the sidewalks between the apartment houses and in a few minutes it turned to ice. The skating teacher came one day when Mom was there; she brought me to school. He came in with a big sack on his back and put it on the floor. He asked Mommy if I wanted skating lessons. I said yes, so he looked at me and then in his sack and pulled out a pair of secondhand brown figure skates. They fitted perfectly so they were to be my skates to own. Mom agreed to pay seventeen rubles for them. The lessons were free. The teacher came once a week. The first lesson he showed me how to position my feet and said, "I could make a good skater of him." He showed how to push off and then left me in the corner of the rink to try it out while he skated with the other children. I fell a few times but gradually I got it. By the fourth lesson I was skating as well as any of the other kids.

Leona. Then the temperature dropped to fifteen below zero.* It was too cold to go out except to and from school, the children's faces wrapped in scarves with only a slit left for their eyes. During the frost the only time the children got out of the schoolroom was to trek downstairs to the music room where they practiced songs and dances for the New Year's program, when parents and grandparents would come to see them perform. For the musical show the girls wore new ribbons in their hair and everyone wore white blouses with blue shorts.

When the heavy cold came I was unprepared for it. The thermometer registered in the twenties when the children came from school, ate, and went out to ski on the slope behind our building. A little later when I came out, I found them coming in. They said the temperature had dropped suddenly and it was too cold. I thought they were giving up too quickly. Barney was at the foot of the slope crying, so I skied down to him, thinking I would encourage him back up the slope and we'd try it again together. By the time I reached him a moment later I knew what they meant, but I knew I couldn't carry Barney up, so we began to climb, sidestepping. He was so cold he couldn't concentrate. I screamed at him to stop crying and listen to me. He tried: sidestep, skis together, sidestep, skis together, but we were both in pain and he couldn't stop crying. With me tugging and pulling to help him move faster, we eventually made it to the top and into the building. That was the end of winter sport, from the first week in December for six frozen weeks with only brief respites. When the temperature rose to five above zero Stevo was off with **Canadian** and Russian friends to play ice hockey on the frozen-over basketball court at Patrice Lumumba University, just past the woods. Around Christmas it got warm enough to go out, well bundled, for a sleigh ride.

The morning after the dreadful climb up the cold slope, I put on some step-in shoes and a fur coat to take Barney to school, just across the parking lot. I had on slacks but no stockings. I ran with him and

* The temperatures given in the book are Fahrenheit.

it was bearable, though it was much colder than I thought it would be. Just as we were about to go in the school door, a red-haired Russian lady who might have been a young grandmother bringing her grandchild to kindergarten stopped to harangue me about the way I was dressed. I told her I didn't want to get Barney into the building late so she let me go, but she was waiting when I came out. She yelled at me that I was stupid to come out without boots. She warned that I would get very sick if I didn't dress properly. I stood listening to her lecture, freezing, wanting nothing so much as to run home and warm my feet. She believed she was doing her socialist duty.

When the deep frost came we slept later because it didn't get light until about 8:30 and our bodies required more sleep. Nature, apparently, created its own balance: our bones and muscles knew from the temperature and the short days that it was time to hibernate, like bears. The children couldn't sleep late except on Sunday.

Stevo. I woke up to the scraping of snow shovels at six o'clock and shivered under two layers of blankets. I looked out of the window and saw the snow swirling sixteen stories below. I washed myself and limped back to my room. My brother had just awakened, and he was grouching already. I dressed in three layers of clothes and went to have breakfast. At least that was enjoyable: leftover red caviar mousse on black bread. After breakfast, I put on my monstrous fur coat and went out into the hall to try and catch the elevator, a flimsy wooden crate that still had a late-night smell of ladies' perfume and cigarette smoke. As usual it wasn't working. I trudged down the sixteen flights of stairs, and my coat seemed to become heavier and heavier. When I finally reached the ground floor and looked through the window at the cold hell outside, for an instant I almost had the strength to walk back upstairs. I plunged out into the flurries of snow. I groped through the snow for a few yards, and then I saw my Norwegian friend, Morton, walking a bit farther ahead of me. I shouted to him several times before he heard me. He waited for me, and we walked together along the icy path.

By the time we reached the bus stop, our toes, fingers and noses were numb. There was the usual crowd of about twenty people, and the buses only came every ten minutes. We walked up and down waiting for the bus. Fifteen minutes later the bus arrived. Although ours was

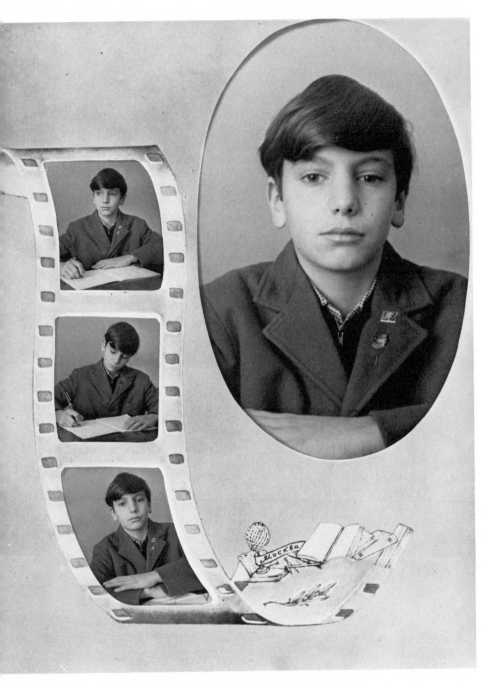

Stevo in his Soviet school album

only the second stop on the line, the bus was already full. We were almost carried on to the bus in the torrent of people, and after paying the fare of five kopecks we tried to find a bar to hang onto. As the bus started to move, there were still people trying to get on, and the doors closed only when we were well under way. At the next stop there were even more people and as they piled on, one man behind me shouted, *"My ne spryatki zdes!"* (We're not sardines in here!). This time, when the bus started, there was no room to get inside so the men just hung out the doors. The next stop was mine, so I tried to move to the door. I was like a piece of metal trying to break away from a strong magnet. I don't know how I did it, but somehow, inch by inch, I reached the door. Morton was right behind me, so when we got to it, I thought our troubles were over. When the bus stopped, I started to step down, but just as at the other stops there was a crowd of people trying to get on. I tried to get off, but the crowd kept pushing me back on. I finally managed to shove through them, but my bag was still stuck in a mass of bodies. I heaved and tugged until it came out. Then it was Morton's turn. He pushed his way out but the people trying to get on knocked him over. I bent to pick him up from the sidewalk, and noticed that my coat was almost torn off my back.

When we walked up the school steps, twenty minutes late, I saw the directress waiting for us, and I felt as if I had already done a whole day's work.

Leona. Fortunately, by the time the children were forced indoors by the cold they had begun to make friends. During the long afternoons they played Monopoly on the living room floor. After Doveen explained the capitalist rules in broken Russian, the Soviet children bought and sold public utilities, boardwalks and apartment houses with gusto. In a very short time they thus became excellent players. Barney was busy trading stamps or chewing gum for old Stalin medals, lead soldiers and stamps he couldn't find elsewhere. Stevo traded Jerry's leftover coins from trips abroad for a fortune in old Russian money.

Barney. Doveen and Stevo both had stamp collections so I wanted to start one too. They gave me five stamps and I started spending my allowance at the stamp store on the bottom of the apartment building across Leninsky Prospekt. One time I was walking out of the stamp store and there were some boys fourteen or fifteen years old selling stamps out of their albums at high prices. Some were Communist Chinese stamps and some were of Mao shaking hands with Stalin. Some were Czechoslovakian; only four were Russian. They knew selling stamps was illegal so they quietly called me over to the side and asked me if I wanted to buy some rare stamps. I looked through one or two albums and I bought a Mao stamp for twenty kopecks.

One day I was walking around our building when two Russian boys walked up to me and asked if I would trade them some gum for stamps. I said I would if I liked the stamps. They took some papers from their pockets folded to the size of stamps and unfolded them. They had some beautiful old animal stamps. I ran up to the apartment and got some gum Daddy brought from America and ran down with it and gave it to them and got the stamps. They asked me how much gum cost in America and I told them a dollar was worth a hundred pieces of bubble gum. The next day they tried to buy a hundred pieces of gum from me. They brought me a dollar but before I took it I read what it said on it. I was so used to Russian money I had to look carefully. Then I saw it was fake so I wouldn't sell them the gum.

In a few days I went back to the stamp store and they had three American stamps for sale. There was the Statue of Liberty, Lincoln and the Freedom Bell. The whole set was selling for three rubles ($3.33). It seemed strange to me because I knew I could get them cheaply in America.

Stevo. I had friends in school who collected stamps and coins. Stamps from Western countries were occasionally available in philatelic shops, but they were quite expensive. Modern foreign coins were only available through the trading network between collectors. I was a prime source of these foreign commodities for a bunch of my classmates. They were hungry for the everyday common currency and postage of England, France and America. I, in turn, received what was exotic to me, but commonplace for them.

I traded pennies, pence, nickels, shillings, francs, pfennigs and dimes for heavy three- and five-kopeck pieces from the eighteenth and nineteenth centuries. The passage of time shows in the transition from a simple stick outline of a double-headed bird to a complex and ornate crested eagle that was the mark of the tsars. They also brought paper money from the old days. I have a big long and wide one-hundred-ruble bill from the reign of Elizabeth II. It is beige with an intricate precise-lined portrait of her on one side and a watermark that can be seen by holding the bill up to the light. Alexander III used this technique on his bright red and green one-thousand-ruble notes. I also acquired some rare "Kerensky money" issued at the time of the Provisional government. These bills are dated 1918 with the crest of the tsarist eagle. One friend traded me a 100,000-ruble bill from 1919. At one point the Soviet government changed the currency from rubles to chervontsy. I have a few of these bills, which were printed in 1937, each with the same stern portrait of Lenin.

Some of my trading partners at school became good friends outside of the sphere of stamps and coins.

Doveen. When I went to Special School 47 in Moscow I had a classmate whose name was Lyena. She was very thin, kind and gentle, and I liked her very much. She had only one dress and her uniform, and her family was very poor.

One day Lyena invited me to her house after school. I said, "I don't know if I can, but let me call my mother." It was the first time a Russian girl asked me to her home.

At twelve o'clock I ran down to the school office and asked if I could use the telephone. The lady in the office didn't scold me about using the phone because I was a foreigner. My mother said I could go to Lyena's house, so I ran upstairs to tell Lyena, who was waiting for me. We ran downstairs to the school buffet and bought poppy-seed buns to eat along the way.

Lyena lived in a five-story apartment building not far from school. Nobody in Moscow lived in a house. When we went into the building it was dark and gloomy in the hallway. Lyena's apartment was shared with another family. The bathroom was unusual for a Russian apartment — it was big. The toilet was small and separate from the bathroom. The kitchen was tiny. There was a kitchen, a toilet and a bathroom which the two families shared, and one medium-sized room for each family. I didn't see the other family's room because the baby was asleep there, but Lyena said it was exactly the same as theirs. In Lyena's family's room there was an armchair that folded out into a bed where Lyena slept and there was a couch that folded out into a double bed which was where her mother and father slept. The couch was covered with a kind of grayish-brown bumpy material. There were a couple of old-fashioned family pictures on the wall and some plants on the windowsill. A few books on a shelf and the best china were inside a glass cabinet. It was very peaceful and pleasant in that apartment.

I did not meet Lyena's mother and father because they were working, but her *babushka* (grandmother) was there hanging up clothes in the bathroom. Lyena and I talked and played and had a nice time. All the time I was there that afternoon I felt like any other Russian friend of Lyena's.

Katie. In Russian school recess is very different from America. Instead of going outside (since it's so cold) they have a big hall the size of two rooms with posters on the walls. The kids link arms and go around in pairs or triplets, in a big circle, talking. Everyone is trying to play tag and have a good time so they have older kids act as monitors.

Katya, a fat girl who was my friend for practically only one reason, to get gum from me, came over and we walked around. Soon Kaarina, my best friend, came over and we walked, all three of us. One of the boys started playing tag and in a few seconds our nice trio was running in all directions. A monitor soon caught us and in the amount of time it took to break us apart we were back together. We talked some more and Katya invited Kaarina and me to come over the next day. We said we'd better ask. It was nice to know Kaarina liked me better. The bell rang and we all went back to our classrooms.

The next day Kaarina and I went to Katya's house. We went home after school and then at two o'clock we met outside Kaarina's building, which was next to ours, and walked to Katya's together.

We walked through the snow until we came to the main road; we crossed it and climbed up a hill. We passed the bread store and saw the men hauling in big cartons of bread, fresh and unwrapped. The doors were open and we could smell the sweet and sour smell of the store. We walked down a few alleys and streets and came to Katya's house. Katya was taking care of her little sister outside when we came and she left her sister with a girlfriend to show us in.

Katya's apartment house was four stories high, of red brick, with five entrances in the front because it was very long. Each entrance had a little garden.

Katie and her friend Kaarina in their classroom. (Photo by Jerrold Schecter)

There was no elevator so we climbed the steps to her apartment on the top floor and went in. There were two big rooms, a kitchen and a tiny bathroom. Katya, her little sister and her parents lived there. Her grandmother lived in a lower floor in another small apartment. Katya explained that she and her sister slept in one room and her parents slept in the living room. We talked about school, looked at some pictures of Russian paintings and then went outside to play hopscotch and jump rope, but it was too cold to play. Then we went in for some tea.

We sat down at a little kitchen table and Katya's grandmother poured us some tea and placed some cookies on the table. Then she left. As soon as her grandmother was gone Katya climbed up to reach a high shelf and got down a bottle of rum. Kaarina gladly accepted some in her tea and Katya took a lot but I said I didn't want any. Katya poured some in anyway. She said it was her grandmother's so she had to be careful. She quickly put it back. The tea tasted much better and warmed our stomachs. After tea we said we had to leave. As we were putting on our coats we met Katya's mother, who had just come home from work. It was five o'clock and getting dark.

We climbed down the dark steps and into the street. Kaarina and I started walking home across a field that Katya said was a shortcut. The moon was coming out and we could see a few stars. The wind pushed against us and made us walk a bit faster. We passed the bread store and the kvass stand with some drunks around it. We talked and hurried home, each wishing we were safe at home instead of out on the cold dark street. Giggling and laughing we were soon at Kaarina's house. I said goodbye and started home. A light snow began to fall but I still felt warm from the tea.

Evelind. Olya, my deskmate at school, lived with two other families in a four-room apartment with a communal kitchen, bath and toilet. She occupied one room with her parents, a divorcee had one room, and a couple, their young boy and the grandmother had the other two rooms. As Olya and I walked up the five flights to her apartment on the top floor she filled me in on all the occupants of the apartment. Olya's family had the largest room and she saw nothing strange in sleeping in the same room as her parents. The single woman was moving out soon into a newer apartment, even though she had quite a bit of room in this one, since her husband had left after a stormy divorce. The authorities were trying to ease living conditions and people were moving out of these five-story buildings to the new high-rises as they went up. This was a slow process, however, because there was such a housing shortage anyway, without people moving out of their cramped quarters.

I sympathetically asked, "Wouldn't you like to move out of this apartment into a larger, more modern one?"

She quickly retorted, "No. Then I would have no little brother or grandmother to live with." Olya happily told me how she loved Anton, the three-year-old who stayed home all day with "Grandma," and how she got to take him out to play on nice days. She added that Antosha had been sick in bed for a few days, but should be out of bed by now and perhaps Grandma would be making him a treat that we could taste.

Both of us were huffing for breath when we finally reached her door. She led me through a short hallway and into a sunny kitchen where an old woman was standing at a heavy iron stove and a little boy sat on the floor playing with a large green plastic dump truck. On Olya's entrance he jumped up to give her a hug and receive a loud kiss. Beaming, Olya presented me to Antosha, pushing him forward to shake my hand. He smiled but stuck to Olya for protection. The grandmother greeted me with a welcoming smile — Olya had talked about me before so she knew I was a foreigner going to Soviet school, and a friend of Olya's. After she had tested my Russian to see if I would understand the lesson she was giving Olya about making cabbage soup, she was willing to accept me with no further ado. She showed Olya the pan of stewed meat her mother had left her and told her to give me a chair at the kitchen table. Olya said we would be eating in her apartment and put the pan on to heat while she handed me dishes from the shelf.

Balancing our plates, we went across the hall to her family's room. I could hardly contain my surprise at the orderliness of the apartment compared to the cluttered, crowded ones I had seen when I visited other friends. The others were chopped up into two or three tiny rooms plus a kitchen, a toilet chamber with just enough space to sit in, and a bath. The rooms I had seen were scarcely large enough to hold the furniture, much less all the plastic and porcelain souvenirs of

Moscow's sights, the plastic dolls and the artless paintings. Olya's apartment was one long bright room which comfortably held the sofa bed, two bureaus, a china closet, a desk and her armchair-bed. Along the windowsill, hanging from the walls, and on the floor were potted plants that gave a freshness to the room. There was an oddly shaped chair in one corner — it was Olya's bed, with three layers of cushions that gave the chair its strange shape.

A brown cotton curtain that hung from a pole set in the walls a few inches from the ceiling covered the coats, stored books, and boxes of things seldom used. Carelessly stacked among old newspapers that had piled up over the years were volumes of the collected works of great Russian writers. (Printing was so inexpensive in the Soviet Union that most people had whole sets of gilt-edged classics of approved Russian and Soviet literature.) Nothing was neatly arranged; one cardboard box sat on another at an angle and all the books were out of order. On the coat rack hung about six coats. It was a surprising number by my standards because Olya's father was a truck driver and her mother was a department store clerk, but in the Soviet Union that did not mean that they lived at a lower level than anyone else. Their pay was average for a Moscow citizen, and they had the advantage of her father's bringing home fresh produce from his trips during the winter, when prices were exorbitant and everything was scarce. Also, her mother was on the spot when long-awaited goods arrived. (Goods came in spurts, and the successful inhabitant of the city had to keep up on which stationery store had toilet paper so that she could stock enough to keep the family off newspaper for a few months, or when a dairy store got in fish after a long, almost meatless winter.)

Olya gave me a dab of her mother's East German face cream, and put a sample in an empty jar for me to take home and try. (I have never had such a bad allergic reaction to anything I ever put on my skin.) She opened one of the drawers in the glossy light-brown cabinet and showed me a delicately knitted, baby-blue sweater that her grandmother had made for her. She explained that she got to wear it whenever she went out to a party or did not have to wear her school uniform to a function. I noticed the printed sweater that I had seen her wear with a plaid skirt on school outings. We moved over to the desk and flipped through the bright flowers and animals on the stamps she had collected from East European bloc countries. She gave me a few for my little brother with the promise that I would bring her some American stamps. She parted with a wire-legged yellow fuzz chicken for me to remember her by, making me promise not to crush it. She had quite a collection of postcards, some given her on holidays, some bought in sets — poets, Lenin in various poses and at different stages of his life from six years old upwards, and intricate scenes of revolutionary battles done in the style of illustrated Russian fairy tales: bright reds, blues and greens, with pictures that look like fiery dragons until you look closely and find the Red star and tanks.

The sun shone in through the large windows onto the parquet floor and we gossiped and giggled until Grandma came in to tell us to taste her finished soup.

Leona. One day during the last week in December Katie and Barney took advantage of a slight letup in the cold spell to go sledding. Barney perched his sled on the hill on which our apartment house stood, took off down the slope and crashed into a large cement cylinder that rose up out of the ice of the artificial lake below. Katie, whose turn on the sled was next, looked on in horror. She ran to him and saw that he was badly hurt. She struggled back up the hill and called the militsioner, then came up to tell me. When she and I came down in the elevator, we could see through its small windows that the policeman was waiting with Barney in his arms. I took Barney from him and we rode back up.

He couldn't walk, he was slightly nauseated, and he had the most vivid purple eye I've ever seen. After taking an X ray, the American Embassy doctor decided that the leg wasn't broken, but rather was indented, as from the blow of a ball hammer. Barney could walk on it as soon as he felt ready.

The next week we left Moscow for a winter vacation. We had to carry Barney around London and he saw the collection at the Tate Gallery from a wheelchair. Ten days after the accident he began to walk, and a few days later he went skiing in Gstaad. He fell and cried a lot, but insisted that he had no pain.

For the next two months he left my side only under duress; he was hesitant to leave the house to go to detsky sad each morning and sometimes, fully dressed and halfway to school, he turned around and came home. I pried into his days at school, searching for the cause of his unnaturally bad temper and his insecurity. Then one day he had his weekly figure-skating lesson at school and we learned the reason for his disturbing behavior. He was skating in a line of children when the girl in front of him fell backward and knocked him down. Instead of bouncing back up with her he lay there unable to move his leg, and when I arrived to pick him up he was seated in a low chair and crying with pain. The school doctor thought it wasn't broken, but suggested an X ray to make sure. There was no one at the *Time* office who could come for us so the doctor asked the young man who delivered supplies to the detsky sad to take Barney and me in his truck and to wait and bring us back.

The young delivery man took us to the Morozovsky Children's Hospital and carried Barney into the X-ray room. There were several large big-bosomed women who looked like peasants but were dressed all in white like hospital attendants; each held a baby swaddled tightly in white wrappings, waiting their turn to be X-rayed. These women looked too old to be the mothers of the babies, but their woeful clucking and mournful concern seemed more personal than that of nurses. When the technician came out of her laboratory waving Barney's leg X ray, still wet, to show me that his leg had been broken months before, these old women shared her excitement and dismay as if he were one of their own charges. I had seen an angry citizen drag an eleven-year-old boy by the ear over to a policeman because the boy was smoking; the attitude in the waiting room was just the same. Every child was everybody's business. Children were a collective concern. The technician showed me that the bone had broken straight across and now had a fuzzy area on both sides of the break, which indicated healing tissue.

Next, a doctor examined Barney and ordered a half-cast for two weeks, which wouldn't keep the leg rigid but would keep him off his feet. By the end of the two weeks we had a new problem: Barney's cheeks began to hurt. I could hardly believe that the doctor would visit him at home for what seemed an obvious case, but the clinic assured me that a sick child is safer at home. The nurse on the phone said to wait, the doctor would be there within two hours. A visit from a busy doctor in her white Medical Aid car confirmed that Barney had the mumps. My Russian teacher, Tamara, explained that this was not unusual care accorded a foreigner; all medical services in the Soviet Union go out of their way for children. The birthrate is so low that children are considered precious and privileged; they would not risk taking a feverish child out of his home to be examined in a clinic.

Later a pediatric orthopedic specialist examined Barney's leg and pored over the original X rays taken at the American Embassy. "Do not be too critical of the American doctor's performance," she told me. "The quality of his X ray is so poor that no one could tell that the leg was broken. At best, a break in a child's bone is often hard to detect. Adult orthopedics is different from children's; that is why it is a separate field of study and that is why I am here."

This professional generosity was surprising because there was no cooperation between the American Embassy doctors and the Soviet medical service, only suspicion. Rather than consult a Soviet specialist, the American doctor sent his difficult cases abroad for treatment and advised women to have their babies in Helsinki or elsewhere in Europe. A British diplomat told me that he and his fellow diplomats were not allowed to use Soviet medical services because of an incident some years before. A foreign service officer, requiring minor surgery, had been given sodium pentothal as an anesthetic by Soviet doctors and was then interrogated for professional secrets while he was under its influence.

The bone specialist measured the girth of Barney's two legs and showed me that the broken one was now thinner by a couple of centimeters than the other. She thought he didn't need massage, but prescribed a series of visits with the muscle therapist to restore the strength of his leg through exercise. Before we left the doctor's I asked her to examine another of the children for an orthopedic problem. She looked the child over and after a series of X rays prescribed the same course with the therapist.

We began our thrice-weekly sessions with Maria Gregorovna in her carpeted exercise room in the basement of the clinic. A third child came along to watch, but she didn't allow either of us to wait passively while the other two stretched and pulled at the wall ladders and walked a slanted plank. She made us all strip to our underwear and learn her precise regimen for a strong and flexible spine. "You are as old as your back," she warned me in her humorless, prissy manner. The charge, when she remembered to charge us, was seventy kopecks for each child for her hour of remonstrance, exhortation and expertise.

In the middle of February a little new snow fell and the sun softened the sting in the air. Friends from the embassy came with their children to ski. At the end of the afternoon, when we tried to account for eleven pairs of skis, we found we were missing one small pair. They were the skis Doveen wore that day, a blue pair with a Japanese television cartoon character painted on the toes. Doveen had gone in before the others, but Katie was sure she had brought the skis up and stood them in the corridor to dry. We concluded that some Russian child had walked off with them but I wasn't terribly upset; they were a small starter pair that would be too small for Doveen or Barney by the next season.

I had long forgotten the blue Japanese skis by the following winter, when Stevo spotted them on a child coming down the slope behind our apartment building. I stood on the flat of the parking lot at the top of the hill when Stevo herringboned up, excited, eager to tell me he had seen Doveen's skis. Stevo glided down the hill in an easy traverse and asked the child where he'd gotten his skis. *"Iz ruk"* (secondhand), the little boy replied.

"Who sold them to you and how much did you pay?" Stevo asked.

The child pointed with his ski pole to a boy about Stevo's age, nearly thirteen, who had already perceived that the accusing finger was pointed at him, and was scampering up the rolling slopes that led to his apartment house on the other side of the forest. From my vantage point on the hill the scene lay before me like a morality play. Stevo, the victim, recognizing who wronged him, gets evidence from the witness, who points to the robber. The guilty one stumbles across the snow on foot, looking back, his eyes dark with fear, dreading what Stevo, fleet-footed on his skis, will do when he catches him. Stevo climbed back up the hill and stood beside me. "I know that boy who stole the skis. He belongs to the same gang as the guy who mugged me in the woods last year," Stevo said, watching with delight the frantic efforts of the sub-teenage gangster to escape.

"What will you do about it?" I asked.

"Nothing," he said. "He knows that I know he took the skis. That's enough. If I go after him his friends will have to defend him; then my friends will have to fight on my side. It isn't worth it. We don't need the skis anymore."

Stevo and I returned to the apartment triumphant with the mystery of the missing skis solved. But it wasn't enough for Lyuba. She did not share our satisfaction, first because we had disproved her constant avowal that Soviet children don't steal, second because our response went contrary to official pedagogical theory on how to treat such situations. "You mustn't let him get away with it," she insisted.

I protested, "But the little boy paid ten rubles for the skis. I don't want to take them away from him. They only cost five rubles when they were new. By now they're too small for Barney, anyhow."

She blushed with anger and embarrassment. "Naturally, we don't like to think that our children steal in a socialist country, but these children are different from their parents' generation. They are not getting proper guidance from their parents." I was sympathetic and assured her that American children also steal. Since she felt personally ashamed every time some festering sore of socialist society came to view, I felt obliged to perform the ritual of matching that social illness with one of ours. A wrong in Russia didn't always equate with a wrong in the West, but there were enough rights and wrongs in both societies to give anyone pause from playing holy.

"The problems with this generation are so widespread," Lyuba said, "that the government finds it necessary to instruct us how to deal with them. We must go to the apartment of the boy who stole the skis and wait there for his parents to come home. We must tell them what he has done. They will punish him. How can they correct him if they don't know he is learning to be a thief?"

"How do you know they care?" Stevo asked.

"If the mother is away at work how can she control him?" I asked, recalling the self-defense of the young mothers at school who were accused of not sufficiently disciplining their children. Both Lyuba and socialist theory — liberated mothers with children raised by the state to uphold socialist ideals — were defeated that day.

Lyuba was even more deeply stung the next week, when a young hooligan ripped the fur hat off her husband's head on a windy street and ran away with it. It happened so quickly that her husband could not even get a look at the thief. She implored me to buy him another hat in the Beriozka, a dollar store, because there were no fur hats available on the Soviet market. This time she was philosophical about the theft. "How can you blame a boy for stealing, if he is cold, too? If he could buy his own hat and also stole my husband's, then I would be angry." Once again, money was not the issue. I wondered if she would have been less forgiving if she hadn't had me to replace the hat for her.

Lyuba wasn't due until two o'clock but she often came earlier. Even with all the housework she had to do, Lyuba was never short of time for talking. From the beginning we delved into our most heartfelt values and the concerns of women. As we talked she constantly corrected my Russian; she was precise about grammar as one could only be who had learned Russian as a second language. She couldn't throw off her Ukrainian accent, but I never noticed. I had a hard enough time learning vocabulary to keep up with the depth of our conversations and trying to get the forms right. Tamara, my Russian teacher, was afraid I would latch on to Lyuba's Ukrainian accent; even worse, she feared that I would absorb inelegant expressions during my long afternoons with Lyuba. Usually they didn't cross paths; Tamara left by twelve, and even on her early days Lyuba didn't arrive before one. But one day by some mischance Tamara, Lyuba and Tolya found themselves in the apartment at once. Tamara, the urbane Muscovite, tried not to show her disdain to Lyuba, the former peasant, as she beseeched her to teach me only the best Russian. Tolya watched with suppressed laughter as Lyuba twisted her mouth and tried to pull her tongue out of her teeth, ready to counterattack. "You've no need to worry, Tamara Aleksandrovna," Tolya assured her, now rocking with laughter, "Gospozha Schecter talks like a Tatar. We can hardly understand her."

In the two months we lived in Moscow before we moved into our apartment, I learned from other foreign women that it was the custom to pay maids a part of their salary in hard-currency coupons, which could be used to buy the best food and imported clothing. To pay in coupons was illegal, but everyone did it. It was hard to be so stiff-necked with someone who worked in your home every day. The custom was universal and the authorities knew it, yet the workers found it humiliating to take as a clandestine favor from their foreign employers what they felt should have been their right. The question of the coupons was raised at a union meeting. UpDK's answer was a farcical solution that institutionalized the existing practice. Each employer would sign a form letter prepared by his office in English, authorizing the worker to receive and spend a limited number of rubles in coupons. The worker would carry this letter on his person; if challenged in the dollar store to prove his right to be there, he would be armed with the proper identification. The letter warned the workers that the purpose of the plan was to allow them to dress properly for work, not to buy privileged items for their husbands or wives. Lyuba handed me the letter to sign and sneered at its hypocrisy.

The bureaucratic double-dealing of UpDK later came between Lyuba and me, and caused a brief misunderstanding. The service agency mandated a pay increase of twenty rubles a month for all house-maids, but was unwilling to announce the increase to its foreign clients directly. Instead, each maid had to ask for it individually. Lyuba declined to ask me for it; instead she went to the *Time* office and asked Elvina to tell me she wanted twenty rubles more a month. Since we were already paying twenty rubles more than the average rate, I thought the demand a bit steep. Through Elvina, Lyuba defended the increase on the grounds that we are a large family and she had so much work to do. My feelings were hurt: why hadn't she come directly to me to negotiate the raise? Was she implying that I mistreated her? I called some other women and learned that the decree had come from UpDK; everyone was affected by it, not just Lyuba and myself. Later, when I asked why she hadn't come straight to me, she wept with embarrassment. "It wasn't my idea, it was UpDK," she explained, which didn't account for her indirection. It took me a little while to get over my hurt and a longer time to reconstruct her motive. If she had confronted me with the demand from UpDK, I might have protested or at least betrayed a flicker of disbelief in my face. Most assuredly, I would check with my foreign friends. Apparently Lyuba decided it would be less mortifying to our friendly relationship if before we saw each other again, I found out for myself that it was UpDK, not she, who asked for the raise. Of course, if UpDK had openly announced the increase, as it got around to doing at a later date, we would have been spared the whole charade.

During an afternoon busy with housekeeping a few months after we had moved into Yugozapad, Lyuba remarked that the children's progress in Russian was outstanding. I agreed with her, and for a moment we indulged in the self-congratulation of a grandmother and mother. Then, without warning, her role changed and she reverted to her Ukrainian peasant origins. "Yes, it's always the same with the Jews.

They've always pushed their children to do well. It was always that way here and it's the same with you. At least you don't push food into your children to make them fat, like the Russian Jews do. In Odessa every Jewish child knew two or three languages and could play on at least two musical instruments. It paid off — they have the easy jobs, they are the intelligentsia with all the privileges. You never see a Jew in a factory or on a collective farm," she finished bitterly.

I was stunned but there was nothing I could contradict in what she said. In those few words she stated the position of the average Soviet worker who is not a virulent anti-Semite but who sees an irreconcilable difference between himself and his Jewish countrymen. This residue of jealousy and resentment is always there, ready to be played on by Kremlin propagandists when a scapegoat or distraction is needed.

Later she asked me to save the children's outgrown clothes for her sister's grandchildren in Odessa. One day a long time later she showed me the address on a package to her sister's daughter, who was married to a man with an obviously Jewish name. I asked if her niece had married a Jew. She grimaced with displeasure and nodded sadly. She knew I was Jewish; still, she counted on my understanding her feelings. She accepted intermarriage but didn't like it.

Evelind had a friend at school, a girl named Vera, who was Jewish. In her description of her friendship with Vera, Evelind indicates that being Jewish made Vera different from her classmates, in some of the ways Lyuba said Jews are different. Vera knew she had to excel.

Evelind. As I wormed my way out of the crowded Moscow synagogue into the throng on the street, I bumped into Vera. She smiled slightly, recognizing me as the American from school, but did not stop to greet me.

The next day I pulled her aside on the stairs and asked her why she had been at synagogue the day before. Was she a Jew also? She blushed and nodded yes. We grinned and continued down the hall, knowing that we each had a new friend.

After that she often asked me to check her English homework and I was surprised to find no mistakes. All my other friends had little interest in learning English and only just passed the course. English was supposed to be the specialty of the school; they were supposed to become proficient at it. But how could they keep interested with a teacher who had never heard English spoken, except on scratchy British tapes, and asked me, "Are your friend ill today?" Somehow Vera had got a lot out of seven years of work and I understood why after she spent an afternoon at my apartment.

We planned to meet at the bus stop because she was afraid that the militsioner who "protected" my diplomatic apartment building would stop her. I arrived at exactly four o'clock but waited for a few buses to let off people until I distinguished her face among all the other women who got off, all dressed in shapeless coats and printed kerchiefs. Vera was dressed up for the afternoon in a blue raincoat, a printed silk scarf tied under her chin, thick nylon stockings and an awkward black plastic handbag that she held on her arm.

Once next to me she tucked her arm into mine and we started to walk. Vera tugged me at a jerky gait, leaning slightly forward. It was just her nervous way of walking, but it made me very uncomfortable. I never got used to the Russian custom of linking arms, no matter if you were a boy or a girl.

She slowed down as we drew nearer to the building and held my arm still tighter. She was relieved that the militsioner smiled when we passed. Going up in the rattling, shaking elevator to our double apartment she still held my arm, but smiled.

We took a tray of steaming tea and a plate of cookies to my room. She smiled when she saw my cubbyhole, saying she had her own room, but it doubled as the living room. She took off her raincoat and folded up her scarf, fluffing up her wavy, thick brown hair that lay loose on her shoulders, not tied up as it had been in school. Pulling at her jersey dress, she explained proudly how she had made it and asked me if it was too long. The dress was a bit long and oddly shaped, but what could you expect from those cheap Soviet patterns that made sixty different sizes? I showed her my crocheting and we gossiped about school.

I soon discovered that Vera thought the way any fourteen-year-old does about clothes, love, boys, the future — something that had not occurred to me because all of my classmates were a year younger than myself. Afterward, I couldn't remember whether we spoke in English or Russian, but it was probably Russian because Vera's English was not up to chatter level. We were wary of what we said because we assumed the room was bugged, but I pulled little bits and pieces out of her about what it was like to be a Soviet teenager, and also a Jew.

Kids seldom dated, but birthday parties were often coed — a rare occurrence in my grade. She thought some boys were nice, but generally immature, still knocking her schoolbag out of her hand and pulling her hair. All of the kids loved music and I promised her a tape of our new records.

She did not want to speak out about anti-Semitism, but she made it clear that she felt it in school among teachers and students. She was particularly bitter about a couple of teachers who blatantly spoke against Jews in front of her class. She could deal with the kids, she explained with an impish smile that I readily understood. Being taller than most of them, she and I could easily cow them when it came to avenging something they said or did. As a friendly older oddity I was given some respect. As an academically outstanding member of her class she got respect by helping others. She was not timid, put up with no guff, and was aggressive in her competition for good grades. She tried for perfection because that was what would get her on to college and a career. Above all, she was a kind, good-natured classmate to the kids she had grown up with.

She told me her mother was a French translator and her father was an engineer who worked on German equipment. With her accomplishments in English she hoped to become as fluent bilingually as her mother, and although she didn't say it, get the same privilege of traveling abroad. Her father got to travel to Germany on business and her mother to France and Egypt — each at separate times. They were Jews striving to get ahead in a society that did not welcome them, and working for the best in spite of it.

6

Schoolchildren of the Revolution

FOR THE CHILDREN school life was all-embracing. They attended school six days a week.

Katie. All five of us walked single file to the bus stop slipping, complaining and laughing. The field we had to cross was about half a mile long but in the middle of winter it seemed miles long. I was carrying cross-country skis but soon gave up and let Stevo carry them for me. We kept walking along the hard packed snow but I kept slipping until I was wet and much colder. Doveen whined about having an earache. At last we got to the end of the field and as everyone climbed down the snowbank to the street I looked back at the huge white blanket with one brown streak in it, the path.

At the trolley bus stop we met Mandit, Doveen's Indian friend; Morton, Stevo's Norwegian friend; and Kaarina, my Russian friend. A bus came along but it was too crowded; we watched it pull away with people's arms and legs sticking out the doors. We got on the next trolleybus that came along. It was very crowded so we didn't bother to pay. We got off the hot, smelly bus. It was very cold and we had to walk carefully because the wind was pushing us so hard.

We walked up the steps of the school and some boys threw snowballs at us but it was getting late so we didn't fight back. We rushed to take off our coats, stuffed our gloves, scarfs and hats down the sleeves, and tried to find a hanger where our class hung their things. There were rows and rows of racks from one end of the wide hallway to the other where each class hung their coats. We pulled off each other's boots and placed them under our coats, then put on our shoes. Kaarina wore slippers like most of the Russian kids. We ran up the steps to our classroom, had our hands and fingernails inspected, and sat down.

The teacher walked in and we all stood up until she instructed us to be seated. She was a stout woman of about thirty-five with short curly rust-colored hair. She often yelled at the other children but never at me. There was another foreign girl in my class from Yugoslavia who had a twin brother in the same class. Her brother was yelled at quite often but she never was.

Our first class was grammar and we were going to have a dictation. We took out our *tetrad,* a small notebook used for any kind of writing in school. The dictation was about rabbits but I was so busy trying to get everything down on time I never figured out what the story was about. The teacher rattled on, stopping after each sentence, but I was already a sentence behind. So I copied from my friend Katya, who sat next to me. After a while I was doing fine, just copying from Katya's paper whenever I got a chance, or else trying on my own. Soon it was over and my wrist was aching from having to write so fast. Then we put our tetrads back in our desks and took out our math tetrad, which had graph paper sheets in it. The teacher gave me separate problems because it was too hard for me to figure out the word problems. I worked for half an hour on long division while the rest of the class worked on story problems. She gave us our homework, then we lined up to go down to the buffet for breakfast.

Since everyone had to be in school at 8:30 the school gave us breakfast. If you were younger, in first and second grade, you had to eat it and your parents paid a few rubles a month for it. Bigger kids could decide not to have the breakfast, and buy a bun instead.

The breakfast was different every day. Sometimes they served boiled eggs with mashed potatoes or else a kind of Cream of Wheat with a raw egg in the middle and compote in a glass with dried fruit and cooked apples. Most of the food was very unappetizing and the dishes were always wet because they didn't have time to dry them.

I got in line and bought a bun for two kopecks. When our class was finished eating we went back to the classroom.

One day in history class my teacher told us that the Russians invented the light bulb and the locomotive. She had pictures and explanations of the first light bulb and there was a picture of some tsar riding in the first locomotive.

Another time the teacher was telling us about how the Americans fought against the Russians in some war. She kept looking at me and getting more and more excited about how terrible the Americans were. She came to her senses and continued the lesson but her accusations stayed with me and I felt terrible during recess.

The Russian children I knew envied the Americans for chewing gum, felt-tipped pens and comic books but otherwise were quite satisfied with where they lived. Many American children don't know much about Russia except that it is a Communist country and many Russian children don't know much about America except that it is capitalist.

Next was English, in a classroom one floor up from my homeroom. English was very boring for me. The only thing I was interested in was when the teacher made a mistake and I had to argue with her, or when she tried to teach the class a song. I got straight A's in English.

After English was recess. I only went to the bathroom in school about twice in two years. The bathroom stank something terrible. The toilets had no seats, there was no toilet paper and no doors. They were just separated by wooden walls.

Our next class was reading. The teacher assigned each child a poem to memorize so by the end of the week everyone in the class recited a poem. I was to recite a poem and I was getting very nervous as my turn approached. Then the teacher called me up. I did fine at the beginning but I got stuck and someone had to tell me a few words and then it all came back to me and I finished the poem. Some other poems were recited but I hardly heard them because I was still getting over having to recite mine.

After reading we all rushed downstairs to get our skis for P.E. Everyone was very excited as we pulled on our ski clothes and boots and took our skis and poles outside.

The teacher led our class of thirty kids to an apple orchard and there we put our skis on. When everyone was ready we started out at a slow pace because we were still in the orchard, but as we got into the open fields people started passing each other and everyone tried to make his cross-country skis go as fast as possible. After about half a mile of going pretty fast we came to a forest and the teacher led us to a small hill that had a sharp curve in it. Here he taught each person to go down the hill. He left the people who had trouble there to practice while he took the better skiers to a higher hill with a little jump a few yards away. I stayed behind to practice because I was pretty bad on cross-country skis. This was my first time on them. We practiced for about half an hour but each person only got to go down about five times because there were so many of us. Then we all got in single file and went home, much slower than coming there because everyone was tired out. We skied through the apple orchard with small scrawny trees all bare for the winter and came to the street. We took off our skis and hurried back to school to get our books.

It was one o'clock and school was over for our grade. Barney and Doveen had already gone home at twelve and Evelind and Stevo might not get out until two.

I met Kaarina at the coatrack with my books and we started home.

Evelind. The sky was a cloudless blue and the sun looked brilliant and warm from my large sealed window, but our American thermometer read ten below zero. I put on an extra pair of wool tights and a red thermal undershirt under my uniform. It was almost eight o'clock and I hurried to put on my fur hat, wrap a scarf around my neck and nose, and fit my schoolbag handle over two pairs of gloves. I had a ten-minute walk over a treacherously icy path to get to the 8:10 trolley. Between trolleys there were only small buses, so crowded they only stopped to let people off. The people waiting at the stop would charge the open door and the bus would take off tilted to one side with people hanging out the doors.

Once out of our building the clearness of the day was exhilarating but I knew not to inhale too deeply or my lungs would start to ache. I made it to the stop in time, got onto the two-car red and white trolley, and worked my way to the front over the accordion-like partition just in time to get off at school. I walked through the double doors that kept the heat in, past the white plaster bust of Lenin and down to the basement to the rows of racks where the upper grades hung their wraps. As I peeled off my layers, Olya came in. She gave me a warm hello and I showed her my new shoes that my father had just brought back from a trip to the States. They were a simple brown-leather pair of modern design and I had not gotten used to them yet, but Olya assured me they were very nice even if they did have a strange shape. I slipped her a piece of red licorice and we walked up the stone steps to our Russian class on the third floor. She thought the licorice was very strange, but she liked it and told me to save some for her and not give it all to the other kids.

As we walked into the classroom a spitball landed on my arm and I started for the giggling boy who had blown it at me. Another of his victims reached him first and was hitting him over the head with a book. Instead of revenge I went over to the windowsill and pulled a dead leaf from one of the plants. On one wall the leaves of a hanging plant had been draped around a bulletin board showing a picture of the poet Yesenin, a drawing of a pond covered with ice and surrounded by birch trees, and a poem about winter by the poet.

On my half of the wooden faded-turquoise desk I set my pencils, leaky fountain pen, Russian grammar book and daybook. No ballpoint pens were allowed and my Parker soon joined the crowd of leaky Soviet fountain pens. The students used rag blotters they bought in a stationery store or their aprons, the inside of a jacket pocket, sometimes their red neckerchiefs. My daybook contained a list of my teachers, a page for quarterly grades, and two pages for possible commendations by the directress. It had a daily schedule, with room for the homework assignment and space for the grade on a test, an answer in class, or for discipline. The daybook went up to the front of the room when a student answered a question, and the teacher marked down a grade when he finished. If a student got in trouble the teacher could ask for his daybook and write in a "two" (D) which also went down in her gradebook. After a while these two's had little effect because students got them so often, both for slight infractions of the rules as well as for more serious offenses. At the bottom of each two facing pages, which represented a week, was a space for a weekly behavior grade and a grade given for the neatness of the daybook, from the homeroom teacher. If there was no parent's signature at the bottom of the page on Monday morning the student could be sent to the directress.

Just as I finished writing my schedule in my daybook the Russian teacher came in. I rose to stand next to my desk until everyone was quiet and he nodded to us to sit down. This didn't take long because Aleksei Leonidovich was well liked and respected; the students gave him little trouble. When someone had not done his homework or the side conversations became too audible, he dealt with the offenders firmly, without the loud screaming that most of the teachers indulged in. He was a handsome man in his early thirties, tall, trim and blond, with a warm smile that never failed to charm. He was assistant director of the school and his quiet, relaxed manner was the right contrast to the gruff and stern directress. We loved to hear anecdotes about his experiences. While I was in his class he went to Hanoi for six weeks with a group of Soviet teachers. When he came back he spent a class period telling about schoolchildren in camouflaged bamboo schoolhouses among the ruins of American bombing. He was trying to explain to this generation that had not experienced war the atmosphere that fills a country when all its resources go to one use — war. He told us how the schoolchildren had to reuse what scraps of paper they could find by erasing them after each assignment. He made each of us feel guilty, not just me, the American, when he said, "You're all bourgeois compared with those children in North Vietnam." After that class we all felt subdued. No one condemned me personally as an American.

Later, as I was chatting with a friend from the other homeroom, she started to talk about American capitalist imperialists who owned factories and used slaves to run them. "But there are no more slaves in America," I protested.

"How do you know?" she challenged me.

"I'm an American capitalist, you know," I reminded her.

"But you don't own factories."

Perversely, I replied that I might someday, but she refused to believe I could ever be that evil.

Aleksei Leonidovich said good morning and proceeded to take roll call, calling students by their last name or patronymic.* He couldn't use first names because in each homeroom (two per grade, each with thirty-five to forty students who took all their classes together except English) there were at least three or four first names duplicated, even triplicated. Whenever I forgot someone's name I could go far with a

---

* The common form of address among Russians is the name and patronymic, or father's name. Thus, Maria Ivanovna is Maria, daughter of Ivan, and Ivan Ivanovitch is Ivan, son of Ivan.

Fifth grade, Polytechnical School No. 47. Evelind is seated at far left in the first row

guess because everyone seemed to be Lena, Olya, Natasha, Andrei, Volodya or Sasha. Once he had taken roll he started to correct homework by calling two people to the blackboard (which was more brown than black because it was only a large piece of linoleum covered with a few coats of shellac) to write out the assignment. As I sat up from my writing position on the bench Olya and I shared, my eyes would glide to the spot on the wall where I was used to seeing a clock in other schools I had been to. Only the friendly picture of Lenin stared back. As the time approached for the class to end, the students slid their belongings into their uniform schoolbags to wait for the bell. When it rang everyone tensed, waiting for dismissal. Aleksei Leonidovich smiled impishly at the anxious faces watching him and hesitated for a second before waving his hand and saying "Begone!" With that everyone rushed for the small doorway at once, rushing to get out of the room for a ten-minute break.

I wasn't quite so anxious to go out into the chilly hallway, but I knew that we would be pushed out of the room soon enough by the teacher on duty, so I fortified Olya and myself with another piece of licorice and moved on. We walked past the long open room that had been built off the hallways on three floors for recreation space, and into the drafty stairwell. During this short break we walked arm in arm in a circle around the big open room — the only recreation allowed. Games of tag were soon squelched and the kids had to be content with stepping on the heels of the boys walking in procession in front of them; even sitting on the windowsills or huddling over the radiator was not condoned. The worn stone steps could be slippery for my smooth-soled indoor shoes and so we walked up the two flights of steps to the biology class on the fifth floor mindful of the steps and the boys charging down them.

We stood outside the locked classroom door near the recreation area that had been closed off to form the auditorium. Holiday assemblies and Pioneer meetings were held there. Marya Illyinichna, the biology teacher, did not like the students bumbling among all her costly treasures, which she used to show us the structure of life, so she seldom let us into her room until the bell rang for class. Then she would tell everyone to hurry up and be quiet so that she could start class. She would not start until she had everyone standing like statues beside his or her desk. This sometimes took quite a while because the students were not as eager as Marya Illyinichna to start the detailed lecture for the day. All she could do was scream or demand the class discipline book that had to be signed after every class and give us a low grade so that we would get a lecture (that had little effect) from our homeroom teacher when she saw the booklet at the end of the week. Marya Illyinichna loved her subject and wanted us to love it — which often meant keeping us overtime. She sometimes seemed on the verge of tears when we insisted that it was time to go. Some of her enthusiasm did rub off and the students learned large amounts of biology, zoology and anatomy during their three years with her. We all loved to peek into her back room and get a quick glimpse of her treasure trove: endless rolls of charts, delicate, bleached skeletons, colorful stuffed animals, and a plastic chart with models of human embryo growth that she used for anatomy class.

We were working on basic zoology and the definitions of the embryo, placenta and womb. She was near the end of the roll and suddenly she called, "Schecter?" I started and answered "Da," as I moved out of my seat to stand next to my desk. Olya had quickly opened the textbook to the page we were studying and held it in her lap. There was complete silence in the room as Marya Illyinichna asked me to define a placenta. I knew what a placenta was, but forgot the exact definition, word for word, from the textbook that would have been the best answer. Marya Illyinichna was pleased with my answer, however, and gave me a five without any more questions. As I sat down I received congratulations from Olya and the kids in front of me. Although I had little trouble with my written work I was seldom asked to answer aloud in class; when I was I always had the support of the whole class and answers were whispered to me whenever I had trouble. I paid my friends back when they needed help on a test in physics or some other class I happened to understand well enough to give them the answer.

The school worked on a European system in which the students took from nine to eleven courses. I took English, Russian language, Russian literature, ancient Russian history, zoology, chemistry, geography of the continents, physical education, home economics, and technical drawing. This schedule was workable because English was the only class we had more than two or three times a week — it was taught every day. The heavier subjects, such as physics, chemistry, and history, were broken up, to be taught over a two- or three-year period; for example, Russian history took three years, starting with cavemen through the first half of the eighteenth century, the last half of the eighteenth century to the Revolution of 1917, and finishing with Soviet history. The textbooks had to be updated and reissued every time there was a major change in historical perspective, such as when Stalin was no longer lauded as a great hero; any book that mentioned the Lenin-Stalin Mausoleum had to be changed to remove Stalin's name. When it came to America, no effort was made to update the pictures of the 1929 Depression breadlines; a typical American schoolhouse was a dilapidated one-room wooden building. Homework assignments consisted of one or two written exercises or three to five pages of reading. The textbook chapters were broken into subheadings just long enough for an assignment, but not long enough to swamp a student.

If a student did not manage to get everything finished he could often slide by as long as there was no written test. The teacher called on the students alphabetically, so each of us could tell when we had to be prepared. Also, cheating was widely accepted among the students. If the teacher ever left the room during class, discipline immediately broke down and notes and answers flew across the room. Everyone helped each other so that there were very few kids who did not give answers as well as accept them. The students knew how far they could go with each teacher — how good their hearing, eyesight, and tolerance were — and were seldom caught. When a person was caught the punishment depended on the mood of the teacher and the importance of the work; punishments ranged from being moved to another seat to automatic failure; in the background always lurked the loss of the Pioneer scarf.

After zoology Olya and I dropped our bookbags in the next class and went down to push through the crowded lunchroom to buy a bun to tide us over until we had finished classes for the day. Today we had six classes, the minimum being four, and we would not go home for lunch until we were finished with classes for the day at two-fifteen.

Leona. The children were all home by two-thirty. They left school when their classes for the day were over, which might be noon, one o'clock or two-fifteen. At two they ate a hearty meal of soup, sausages, smoked fish, cheese and thick bread. Usually, by the time they had finished eating, there was a Russian friend at the door dressed for skiing down the slope behind the apartment house and through the birchwoods just beyond, or skating on the artificial pond in clear view of our balcony. By five o'clock it was dark, time to sit down to homework.

Evelind spent the afternoons of the first months translating history and geography, word by word. One afternoon she explained to me why the Mongols have slanted eyes: "It comes from the thousands of years of protecting themselves from sandstorms in the desert."

I opened my eyes with alarm and exclaimed, "That's Lysenkoism!"

"You mean I'm working so hard and learning the wrong things?" she wailed. We had our first long, hard conversation about ideology and evolution.

From the 1930's until the early 1960's, the Soviet government accepted the theories of Trofim D. Lysenko, who believed that characteristics could be altered by the environment and then inherited by succeeding generations. His ideas, though scientifically unsound, were considered "progressive," in contrast to "bourgeois genetics," which hold that hereditary information is printed into the reproductive cells from the outset of life and cannot be changed except by mutation. Mutations may be helpful or harmful to the individual. If harmful, they are eliminated by the principle of the survival of the fittest; if helpful, they become part of the process of evolution.

Lysenko's genetics were suited to the basic Marxist principle of dialectical materialism and the goal of changing man through Communism. But his dominance kept the Soviet Union out of the world community of modern genetics and held back for more than twenty-five years much-needed advances in agriculture. In the 1950's voices began to be heard against Lysenko but he was not dismissed from his post as head of the Institute of Genetics until 1964. As late as 1969 it was apparent from what Evelind was learning at school that wrong ideas, especially when wedded to ideology, die hard.

Doveen took her first exposure to ideology lightheartedly, and seemed to enjoy being included among Lenin's grandchildren. The threats endured by the Russian children of what might happen if they did not live up to their vows as Communists did not weigh heavily on her.

Doveen. A few weeks after I started school in Moscow, all the first-graders were told to wear their white aprons the next day because there would be a special ceremony. The newcomers would be given their Oktyabryata pins.

An Oktyabryata was a child of the Revolution, a child of October, since Lenin's Revolution took place in October. The Oktyabryatas were the grandchildren of Lenin.

The next day all the children were whispering excitedly. The classroom smelled of freshly starched white aprons. We were taken to the auditorium and lined up side by side. On the opposite side of the room stood the first-grade teachers and the directress, facing us. The directress gave a speech about our duties as the grandchildren of Lenin. She told us to obey our elders, help wherever possible, and be good citizens. She told us that if we followed rules and behaved civilly we could become Pioneers. It was the goal of all the first-graders to become Pioneers.

When the directress stopped speaking a group of Pioneers filed in. A patriotic song blared on the phonograph. Each Pioneer was given a pin to put on one Oktyabryata. The pins were either plastic or metal. They were in the shape of a red star with a picture of Lenin as a young boy in the middle. The plastic ones had a small photograph encased in them and the metal ones were embossed with the picture. We wore our pins every day.

After you have been an Oktyabryata you become a Pioneer in third grade. Then you are given a red kerchief to wear around your neck every day. To become a Pioneer you take a pledge similar to the Oktyabryata pledge. After being a good Pioneer you can join Komsomol when you are fourteen. You must be recommended by your teachers and learn some Communist Party rules. During the time you are a member of Komsomol, until you are twenty-eight, you study Communist Party philosophy. Then some become Party members and some do not. It is very difficult to become a Party member because only a few are chosen. As you go through these stages you are constantly threatened by teachers telling you that you may lose your pin, your kerchief, or your privileges if you don't behave.

One day during recess my friend Maxim was caught hitting Boris, though Boris had hit him first. The teacher came over to Maxim and grabbed him by the collar. She told him to stand against the wall until recess was over. When recess was over and everyone else was in their classrooms, she grabbed him again and dragged him into our classroom. She shoved him in the corner and started yelling at him about how he could not be a child of Lenin if he misbehaved. She tore off his Oktyabryata pin and his uniform jacket. She told him he could not wear the uniform of an Oktyabryata if he did not live up to his pledge to be a good citizen.

Stevo. It was during the first year that I had my first political argument. I was on *dezhurstvo* (cleanup) duty with my deskmate. It was our turn to clean up the classroom after school. We picked up the trash on the floor, mopped it, emptied the trash, washed the board, and watered the flowers. The girl doing it with me called me a "little capitalist" because I wasn't very good at sweeping and mopping. She said that I had always had maids to do the work for me. She was right, but I argued violently that it wasn't true. I became very able with a broom and mop from that day on. She talked on and on, citing America's outstanding faults: the Vietnam war, racism, poverty, and class differences. "JFK was the only good American president you ever had," she said. I told her he was a very rich capitalist and exploited a lot of workers, but she wouldn't believe me. We were both eleven years old.

Evelind. In the Soviet Union the students in elementary and secondary schools clean their own classrooms, shovel snow around the school, and pick worms off the school's cherry trees. This is part of the communal way of life. As a new member of the student body of P.S. 47, I joined in and did my share.* Only the boys' bathroom had hot water to mop the floor. Olya and I would choose to see who would suffer the trauma of making sure no one was in the boys' room. Sometimes we burned ourselves with the scalding water in the effort to rush out of there quickly. There was no washing soap in the school, so we used bicarbonate of soda or chalk to wash the desk tops. (The chalk was almost as good as soap. Unlike American chalk it crumbled easily into abrasive grains. It crumbled whenever I had to answer at the blackboard, and I usually returned to my seat with my hands covered with chalk, trying to resist the urge to wipe them on my black apron.) Before vacation the whole class pitched in to scrub the walls, windows, and floors with rags.

---

* Unlike P.S. 47 (Public School 47) in the Bronx, which, coincidentally, Jerry attended, P.S. 47 in Moscow stands for Polytechnical School 47. The children also referred to it simply as "Special School 47."

ВСЕГДА ГОТОВ!

"Always Prepared!" In the background is the Solemn Oath of a Pioneer of the Soviet Union: "I (surname, first name) joining the ranks of the Vladimir Ilyich Lenin All-Union Pioneer Organization, solemnly swear before my comrades to love my Motherland passionately, to live, learn and struggle as the great Lenin showed us and as the Communist Party teaches, to always carry out the laws of the Pioneers of the Soviet Union"

Another form of dezhurstvo was when my whole homeroom had to keep the school in order for one or two weeks in every six. We had to arrive punctually at eight in the morning for a line-up reviewed by the directress. (It was hard enough to get to school at eight-thirty in sub-zero weather while it was dark, but arriving half an hour earlier was excruciating.) The directress would take roll and check to see that our uniforms and hair were in place. She would tug on the neck of a boy to indicate that he needed a haircut. Once, when my hair was not pulled all the way back in a full pony-tail she grabbed my hair, exclaiming, "Schecter, *po-russky!*" ("Schecter, the Russian way!"). As soon as she took roll everyone went to his post.

One job was helping the younger kids take off their street clothes. Peeling off the layers of mufflers, coats, sweaters, boots, and socks gave us plenty to do. This was the best job because we could say hello to our friends as they arrived and discovered whose brother and sister was whose. There was a special excitement in this because so few students had brothers or sisters that those who did were considered lucky to have each other even if they fought a lot. During recess, we had to monitor the cafeteria to make sure that the noise level stayed down and that no one left the room with any food. It was easy to buy a quick bite to eat and be on duty at the same time. The stone steps on the stairwell landings were icy cold, and the hallways were chilly because the radiators could not fully counter the cold that came in through the many cracked and broken windows that would not be replaced until spring.

The students also kept the school grounds clean. If there was a snowstorm the class on duty was responsible for keeping the walks cleared.

From the first grade boys and girls alike share in the cleaning of the school. Some skip, but if they do it too often they run the risk of losing their Pioneer scarves.

7

Pleasures and Fears
of Friendship

FOR JERRY AND ME, three days in the week began with a ring of the doorbell promptly at 9 A.M. Our Russian teacher, Tamara, always arrived full of energy and dedication, ready to drill us through two hours of slow, painful reading and translation with frequent leafings back to the Russian-English glossary.

We often began by wading through an article written in the stilted, official journalese of *Pravda*. Even after the length of time it took us to read a piece of literature suitable for junior high school students, and the dutiful patience it required of her to hear us through it, she still had enough emotion left for a repressed tear over the death of Bela, Lermontov's Caucasian tribal heroine. At the end of the lesson the ashtray next to her copy was filled with cigarette butts ringed with bright lipstick. Like many Russians we knew, she smoked incessantly.

We worked hard at learning Russian, as if the secrets of roots, stems and case endings, once discovered, would be the key to something more meaningful than just the language in our effort to understand Russia.

At first Tamara traveled an hour by Metro from the center of the city. But after a few months the new cooperative apartment for which she and her husband had been waiting was finished and they moved into it, only a short bus ride from our apartment house. The move, Tamara told me with relief, ended twenty years of living in a small apartment with her mother. She would no longer have to listen to her mother's daily list of aches and pains, nor shush her husband's complaints about cooking smells when her mother boiled fish and onion soup.

Tamara was a stereotype of the model Soviet citizen but she could not erase in herself the lingering image of the dignified, upper-class Russian of pre-Revolutionary Moscow. Her hair was not lavishly thick, but she kept it tinted to its original strawberry blond and pushed it back in a rim of short curls. She had high full cheeks with strong Great Russian coloring, and shapely lips that she never neglected to cover with bright shiny lipstick. She had delicate eye-lashes and lively blue eyes. Her figure was matronly but well formed, and she carried to good advantage the foreign clothes her husband Vadim brought her from his trips abroad.

The first thing that struck us about Tamara was her jewel collection, which already adorned her ears and fingers by the time she arrived at nine in the morning. Most of the emeralds, rubies, diamonds and opals she wore had been acquired during the three years she and Vadim worked in India. Under his direction, the Soviet Union successfully set up a Russian studies institute in New Delhi, many of whose graduates Tamara and Vadim later welcomed to Moscow as scholars and diplomats. Tamara worked long hours as an instructor and assistant to Vadim in India, and she was rewarded with whatever jewel pleased her eye. Vadim was rewarded with a chair in Indian languages at Moscow University. He was later offered the chance to repeat his triumphs in Cairo, but declined humbly but cleverly, asserting that he didn't have a good enough understanding of Arab culture.

As a member of the linguistic faculty, Vadim was considered politically dependable. No one who had not proved his orthodoxy could belong, since faculty members had access to foreign literature and publications. This meant that he could take vacation trips on a Soviet liner to Egypt and the Canary Islands. It also meant that he received a salary of about 1,000 rubles a month, which made him one of a wealthy minority. No wonder price was never an object for him and Tamara. She complained not about the money he lent his friends — so they could leave their savings to draw interest — but about the inconvenience: when they ran out of cash it was she who had to be bothered going to the bank for more. Why didn't they borrow from their credit cooperatives where they worked, she wondered peevishly.

Tamara longed for a child, and her eyes glazed with tears when she talked about adopting one. But she was in her mid-forties; she worried that it was too late to change the pattern of their lives by adopting a child. Her freedom to work and move about as she pleased was too important a habit to give up. Tamara told me that all Soviet women grow up knowing they will work when they finish their education. "Motherhood," she said, "is an interruption, a professional sacrifice. Working is a right," she said.

Perhaps she would have been calmer with her own child, but she scared Barney one day when she arrived for my lesson and found him home with a cold. She frenziedly wrapped his legs in blankets and made sure he was not sitting in a draft. On other occasions she demanded such perfection from our children in their Russian pronunciation, making them repeat her example until they were blue with frustration, that I wondered how she would have handled imperfection in her own offspring.

She had an old socialist's faith in the powers of pedagogy; she believed it was through the proper training of children that society would achieve its Communist goals. She was constantly disappointed in the Soviet children she knew. They had lost the Revolutionary drive that had been instilled in her as a child, they had forgotten the hardships of World War II and the effort it had taken the country to recover from its devastation, and as a generation they got by with as little work as possible.

She felt at her wits' end with her niece, who refused to work for high marks in school. "I warned her that with her grades she'll have to become a hairdresser. Do you know what she answered me? 'That's fine, then I'll be a hairdresser.' " For Tamara and her sister, the girl's mother, who are both graduates of the prestigious Foreign Language Institute, the girl's underachievement was an outrage.

Tamara demanded exact and exhaustive work from herself, but in this she was more like the best of the pre-Revolutionary aristocrats I have met than like other Soviet citizens. In a classless society she enjoyed privileges that were not enjoyed by the masses, and she couldn't escape some of the attitudes that go with being set apart from the majority. She was shocked to hear that I had abandoned the formal, polite form of "you" in my conversation with Lyuba and was addressing her with the familiar *ty*. She insisted that it was improper, that I should immediately return to a form more suitable for use with a servant. She never seemed aware that her jewel collection, her new cooperative apartment, her newly acquired dacha and her new car were in open contradiction to her socialist ideals. She could afford to be a socialist!

For her the streets of socialism were paved with gold. She read *Pravda* before she arrived at our apartment and spouted its political didactics as if they were her own. After the invasion of Czechoslovakia and the rumblings of independence in Eastern Europe, she arrived one day and pronounced: "We have always given up the chance for more consumer goods in the Soviet Union for the sake of socialist solidarity. Now look at the gratitude we get in return for our sacrifices!"

She wished she were more sensual. One morning she found in our living room a Yugoslavian magazine filled with photographs of nude women. She leafed slowly backwards and forwards through the magazine, staring intently at each pose. Since pornography and even *Playboy* magazine are barred from the Soviet Union, I thought she would be critical of this aberration from within the socialist camp, but she neither giggled nor sneered in disdain. I asked her if she liked the magazine, suggesting by my tone that I thought it a waste of time. "I'm very interested in the human body," she answered solemnly, never lifting her eyes from the page.

Although she considered the liberation of women already accomplished in the Soviet Union, Tamara betrayed a streak of feminism in the stories she repeated to me from the films she saw. One heroine was a lawyer. Another was the first woman ambassador to a foreign country, Madame Kollontai, who not only represented the USSR in Norway, but was also an early promoter of freedom for women in sexual mores and marriage.

Tamara was extremely "feminine" in her bearing and interests. She loved to cook and entertain at home, to arrange her new apartment, to redecorate the dacha they bought soon afterward. She wanted a really good mink coat, and kept watch on the fur *komissionnyi magazin* (a state-run secondhand store), where used furs were sold. She didn't care how much it would cost; the problem was to find a fur of good quality. Those produced by the Soviet Union were exported. She waited for the odd chance that someone would leave a good coat on consignment. I offered to buy her one when I went abroad, but she conscientiously refused.

During the two months we lived in the Ukraine Hotel, and for about a month after we moved into the apartment in Yugozapad, "going out'" in the evenings consisted of informal dinners with friends. This was the time for meeting other journalists, the beginnings of enduring friendships with Russians whom Jerry met outside the Litvinov-Daniel courtroom. We took visiting Americans to the Aragvy, a famed Georgian restaurant, or to the Baku, an Azerbaidzhani restaurant with a unique band and dance floor. Only once during these early months were we invited to one of those full-dress evenings that form the routine of life in the foreign diplomatic service.

The menu at the Aragvy was always the same but never disappointing. The round flatbreads were served fresh and hot and the waiter held them with a damask napkin while you pulled them apart. The Georgian specialties were cold pieces of chicken smothered in a sauce of pulverized walnuts and garlic, a *solyanka* of fried cabbage in a rich gravy that contained chunks of beef, sausage, olives, kidney and liver, and *solguni,* smoked cheese cut in overlapping slices and melted together in a hot oven. The food was heavy but it went down well with a little vodka and successive bottles of Mukuzany, a pleasant, dry undistinctive red wine from the sunny vineyards of the southern Republic.

At the Baku restaurant we reserved in advance and arrived to find the table laden decoratively with cabbage roses tinted in beet juice, plates of smoked sturgeon, caviar and dark bread. It wasn't the food we came for, though. We came to hear the band, a trio of swarthy Near Easterners who plinged away at stringed instruments resembling banjos. They played rapid folk dances so familiar to them that one of the three slept while he performed. The crowd was part of the show — two short, dark, muscular Azerbaidzhani workers, their arms linked around each other's waists sideways, following the music with fast footwork, pounding the floor in a wild, rhythmic beat. The Baku was the Moscow home for Azerbaidzhanis who longed for the music, food and company of their spirited countrymen. We became part of the show, too, when we got up to dance, following their beat as best we could. The "regulars" threw five-ruble bills at our feet and brought chocolate bars to our table, demanding to know if we were Russians or Azerbaidzhanis. We scooped up the bills and gave them to the band, who never failed to recognize and welcome us ever afterward.

After our first year in Moscow the Baku closed for renovations, but when it reopened it had moved to a suburban area. We tried the new Baku once. The smoke-dimmed walls with their faded tapestries had been replaced by chrome and glass and the band was missing.

The privacy that comes with being new in town didn't last long. By the end of January we found ourselves caught up in a round of diplomatic dinners that closed in on itself. The guests were exclusively foreigners, and the conversation was always a variant on "we," the Europeans, Americans, and a few East Asians, against "them," the Soviets. The pool of guests to choose from was limited by its qualifications, so that the participants turned to almost the same dinner partners week after week, and their boredom showed. Being new, we were in demand. The wife of a French diplomat told me, "There are so few *suitable* young couples to invite." I wondered what made us suitable when most of the press corps and American Embassy officers were not. Had we achieved that perfect blend of entertaining with stories of other foreign posts but not upsetting with startling ideas or insisting on probing too deeply into a subject? Were we so bland that we fitted into the well-modulated mood of these dinners that could have taken place in any capital?

The high-ceilinged dining rooms of these foreign embassies, which would have seemed elegant elsewhere, in Moscow added to the aura of isolation. I realized how much the diplomats were cut off from the world when I ventured to tell a story about a Canadian boy who was beaten by a gang of hooligans in Yugozapad. He fended off a wooden plank aimed at his head, but his arm took the blow, and he required three months of therapy to regain use of it. The host, a young Canadian diplomat, gently chided me for breaking the code. "Come on, Leona," he said, indicating by his familiarity that he didn't really mean to criticize me. "How do you know these stories are true? How come none of the rest of us here have heard them?" I retorted that I knew the victim personally, and if he didn't know about it he should, since the boy who was beaten up was a Canadian. He spent his days reading the Russian press, which didn't report crimes of violence.

There were exceptions to the boredom of diplomatic dinners. The Japanese ambassador, Toru Nakagawa, brought with him an excellent Japanese cook and the tableware necessary for the serving of his country's haute cuisine. What a delight to sit down to a *sashimi* of perfectly fresh raw tuna delivered each week from Helsinki, enormous fresh shrimp and strawberries that arrived regularly on the Japan Air Lines flight direct from Tokyo. The pleasure was largely in the artistry of the cook, who pressed chunks of walnuts into bite-size bits of roast duckling, or fried chestnuts in a batter of broken noodles to imitate sea urchins, scooped out the pulp of lemons to use the skins as little baskets for sweetened gingko nuts and bits of piquant grilled fish. These morsels were served on hand-painted plates decorated with traditional fan and flower designs, and we ate them with polished hardwood chopsticks.

At the Canadian Embassy we enjoyed a lobster soufflé which Mrs. Ford proudly said she copied from her favorite Parisian restaurant. Served in a gold-glazed dish it set the tone of excitement and elegance. The ambassador, Robert A. D. Ford, is a distinguished poet and translator of Russian poets. The poet Andrei Voznesensky and his wife were frequent guests, as were Yevgeny Yevtushenko and the most knowledgeable diplomats, such as the Austrian ambassador, Walter Wodek.

The conversation at the ambassador's end of the table was quietly good-humored and ranged widely over literature and politics; at the other end Brazilian-born Mrs. Ford fed her guests outrageous anecdotes in a raucous Portuguese accent that consciously rebelled against the behavior codes of the diplomatic corps. About the wife of a Russian friend she explained, "I bring her presents from abroad to pacify her. I know she is really a police agent, watching not so much us as her own husband."

The excellent dinners and the stimulating repartee at the Fords' were noted not only by the invited guests but by the KGB as well. It was said that the ambassador's chauffeur was a colonel and the waiters were majors or above. At midnight at a New Year's Eve ball given by the Fords I turned to the black-coated Russian waiter standing near me to drink a toast to friendship and peace between our countries. With a droll smile he returned the toast and complimented my gown, in perfect English.

The physical difficulty of life in Moscow is a matter of doing without lettuce, shrimp and avocado, but it is the deficiency of nutrients for the spirit that takes its toll on the human organism.

An American Embassy wife told me that when she was briefed before she came she was told, "The one thing you will never have in Moscow is a friend. I don't mean Russians. I mean not even an American friend." She brushed aside the warning in disbelief, but after a year in Moscow she found it true. "Why is it so?" she asked.

The reason is complex, but the foremost aspect of our lives that separated us from each other was the mystique of secrecy. We all knew we were being watched and listened to — our telephones were tapped, outgoing overseas calls monitored. On holidays two of the three office telephones would continually be busy, then resume normal service on regular workdays. We couldn't be sure, but we suspected that the walls had listening devices. Where were they? Was there a special bug to record the pillow talk of husbands and wives? Did it help to whisper or turn up the hi-fi? We often scribbled notes back and forth to Russian friends or used the children's magic slate, a piece of celluloid on carbon paper that erases when lifted. Our awareness of watching eyes and listening ears created a vicious circle: we couldn't confirm the physical reality of the bugs, so we imposed a restraint on ourselves that surely went beyond the police's ability to keep track of us.

Everyone lived with the fear that a careless word might be distorted and exploited to harm someone else. Undisciplined talk might get you thrown out, ruin your friend's career, or at least cause you mortification. Every wife shared the responsibility for protecting her husband's sources. If she talked too much she might give away a professional secret, or tell things about friends that might be used against them.

We were not only suspicious of the Russians. We were suspicious of each other. Journalists always wanted to know how colleagues got stories they didn't get. A wife would ingenuously ask another journalist's wife, "Who was that Russian I saw you with? How did you meet him?" She got no answer, and she should have know better; she was asking the woman for the bread and butter of her husband's existence. If someone asked you how many Russian friends you had, the proper answer was "It's none of your business."

Once I casually told an American Embassy wife a curious story about a Russian friend, and worried for weeks afterward how her husband would use the information. The Russian, who had gotten very drunk, said he was the bastard son of an American military attaché. I supposed he was making it up and thought it funny, but after I told it to the American woman I imagined her husband tracking down the story and trying to enlist my young friend as an American spy. What sounds like a wild fantasy becomes, in the atmosphere of Moscow, within the stretch of possibility.

I was furious with an American cultural attaché who invited our children to enjoy pizza and Cokes and watch an American film in his apartment, and then questioned them about our Russian friends. Stevo, feeling mellow and safe in the company of Americans, began to answer honestly. Evelind on one side and I on the other kicked him simultaneously and pointed to the walls of the Russian-built embassy apartments.

The American Embassy families faced restrictions and enjoyed privileges that we didn't share, and neither they nor we were generous toward one another. (An American diplomat's wife told me after we had been in Moscow three months, "The gossip around the embassy is that you've gone native. The American kids think your kids are like Russians." I gasped at the news, but in the months that followed we learned that her report was accurate. Every attempt by our teenagers to befriend American kids their own age was rebuffed.) We didn't envy them their PX privileges, except in one instance. A group of journalists asked the embassy to order additional fresh milk from Helsinki because our children were getting sick on Russian milk. Fermented milk products caused no trouble, so it was not a matter of necessity, only the pleasure of fresh homogenized milk that wouldn't cause diarrhea. After a protracted argument that carried into the ambassador's weekly press briefings, that tested the loyalty of colleagues, provoked letters to senators, and left a trail of distrust, the embassy gave in to the "administrative nuisance" of increasing the weekly milk order by a couple of dozen cartons.

We didn't have as many favors to bestow as the embassy personnel did, but what little we had we kept to ourselves. They were so closed in on themselves that they found it practically impossible to make friends with Russians. In addition, when they met Russians at our house they were required by the American Embassy to identify themselves as members of the embassy. Most Russians were understandably chilled by this approach and refused to talk any more. Since their presence put a damper on an evening with Russian friends, we stopped inviting Americans.

Most American diplomats in Moscow were reluctant to take the initiative in meeting and getting to know unofficial Russians because of the danger to their careers. Cautious diplomats did not visit unofficial artists or dissidents and always traveled in a buddy system. One young American Embassy officer who spoke excellent Russian became friendly with a number of actors and actresses, dancers, poets and theater directors. Through them he achieved an unusual understanding of the current cultural scene. The Russian authorities labeled him a CIA agent and he became the next candidate for a "ding dong." This meant he would be the first man to be designated persona non grata in retaliation when a Soviet spy was thrown out of New York or Washington. One couple always brought four tickets when they went to the theater: two for themselves and two to give away to Russians looking to buy last-minute cancellations at the entrance to the theater. Seated together they would start a conversation and in this way they built up a large circle of Russian friends. It didn't take long for the Foreign Ministry to perceive their technique and expel them.

The charges against the people the Russians wanted to get rid of bore little resemblance to their offenses: it didn't do much good to deny the orgiastic tales, the allegations that they had exchanged liquor, records and foreign clothes for marijuana and works of underground painters, or had bought cheap rubles on the black market. Their friends and superiors might not believe, or might only partly believe, the whispering campaign started by the Russians. The main problem was far more practical. They had aborted the terms of their assignment so that the posts they were due to move to in a year or more were still filled. What to do with them became an administrative problem.

Americans in Moscow with few exceptions were a competitive, save-yourself-first noncommunity. The Russians helped make it that way. Life there was more frustrating for the women than for the men because they couldn't work at jobs, participate in politics, or contribute their time to charity. A talent for living was their only form of expression, but if you were lucky that could consume all your energies.

The lack of emotional reserve in Russian culture made our Russian friendships more satisfying than those with our compatriots. When Russians decided to accept us, warmth, directness, affection came more quickly than they would have in friendships of the same duration anywhere else. The frustration and lack of satisfaction in official life seemed to make private relationships more intense.

But underneath the spontaneous lovingness of these relationships there were distrusts and ambivalences, and these kept a distance between us and them, reminding us that we were in Moscow. Since Russians are discouraged from mingling with foreigners, why were they our friends, when we could cause them trouble? Are they really friends, or are they police plants watching us? A psychic fence stood between us; if we didn't hear from them for a while we wondered if they had been told not to call us. If we first met them in public places like the lobby of the Metropol Hotel or the synagogue, which are known to be sown with provocateurs, our suspicion of them stayed with us no matter how close we seemed to draw to each other.

The Russians we knew had plenty to fear in befriending us. Their political reliability could be doubted, which would keep them out of graduate school or prevent them from getting job promotions. They also had to fear themselves. Our Western ideas of freedom, which went beyond any liberal tendencies of their own, our pragmatic approach to economic growth, their own growing consumer desires which they saw so casually fulfilled in our home — all of this could contaminate them to the extent that they would no longer be suited to the rigidity of Russian life. They came and shared our access to records, caviar, and steak, but to offer them any of these to take home would have been to corrupt them. The embarrassment of riches could be misconstrued. We also had to protect our friends from themselves, to prevent them from exposing themselves to danger from the police on our account.

No matter how close some of our friendships became, no matter how much it seemed we were perceiving normal Russian life, we were always foreigners. We caught glimpses of the pressure that was building beneath the repression, but we couldn't really share its agony. We never got over the frustration of being outsiders looking in.

Russians with whom we had professional relationships wanted to be friends. They promised to show us the glories of cross-country ski trips in the woods, where we would drink vodka and roast shashlik over a campfire in the snow; they promised to show us how to pick wild mushrooms in the fall. But these plans never materialized. To carry them through would have been to stretch the written laws governing how far we could travel outside Moscow and the unwritten laws governing how far they could safely go beyond their professional duties toward us.

One Soviet journalist confided to Jerry that he would not accept a dinner invitation to our apartment for himself and his wife because he would have to report on the conversation. Only invitations to large official receptions in public restaurants or hotels were acceptable.

Yet there is a human dimension that cannot be completely controlled by ideology and by fear. It blunts clearcut hate or distrust. We lived our life in Moscow never fully trusting the Russians we knew, yet never being sure of our right to distrust them either.

Whenever we invited Russian friends to our home in Moscow, two strange but ironclad rules applied: The first, which we were told to observe by experienced friends before we went to Moscow, was the more important and never breached. We were warned never to introduce one set of friends to another group, even if we thought they would like each other. All the suspicions, the spying and denunciations of the Stalin years had left their imprint; a friend from one group would ask himself what this other Russian was doing befriending a foreigner. Was he sincere or had he been planted to meet the foreigner's Soviet friends and report them? They always called before they came and relied on us not to break this rule. Once an American friend with his Russian wife dropped in unannounced while some Russian friends were visiting. She tried to be friendly but they became tight-lipped and sulky.

The second rule, which I unconsciously broke once, causing anguish to my friends, had never been articulated but grew quite naturally out of the circumstances. The constant presence of the militsioner standing guard in front of our building made our Soviet friends uneasy. They assumed he was there to see which Soviet citizens were visiting foreigners. Therefore they always arranged a meeting place in front of a Metro station where we would pick them up in our car and drive them to the third entrance of the apartment building, which led to our apartment, at the end of the parking lot far from the policeman's box. We knew he wouldn't come the length of the apartment house to have a good look. We might complain; he was ostensibly there to protect us from undesirables and robbers, not from our friends. There was an unwritten rule that he would not stop anybody with us.

Later, we took them back to the Metro station by car. Once I forgot and invited some friends to come straight to our apartment. They agreed, but they were uneasy when they arrived, and later the husband said, "It was torture, physical torture, to walk past the militsioner. The fear that he would stop me, humiliate me, ask me for my identification, which he has no right to ask me for, created such knots in my stomach that I was in physical pain."

I knew that our Russian friends might call at any time and drop in for dinner, either late or on weekends when they knew they would not encounter the maid. These friends were not dissidents, but they often made remarks critical of Kremlin policy and they didn't want to have to worry that Lyuba might overhear. Nor did they want her recounting how many times she had seen the same faces at our house. They assumed that since she was supplied to us by a state agency, she would be trained and required to report whom she had heard and seen.

Anticipation of the unexpected guest became routine: I always kept an assortment of smoked fish — whitefish, sturgeon, salmon, lampreys — plus a few kinds of sausage and cheese. I usually had a strip of beef tenderloin in the refrigerator for anyone who came to dinner on short notice. For the rest, I could always manage from the three overhead foyer closets that held a year's supply of imported canned goods.

This casual entertaining of close friends was always a pleasure. One friend, a sensuous, curvaceous blonde who was a flutist in an orchestra, always brought her guitar and sang love songs. Her voice tore your heart, even when you couldn't understand the words: *"Ya tebya lyublyu. Ya tebya lyublyu"* (I love you. I love you). Anya sang it first in a throaty whisper, then with open honesty, then belted it out in a loud and broad finale, her guitar ringing in enthusiastic support. Other times she sang ballads or Siberian folksongs. Her husband Nikolai, a quiet engineer, always listened adoringly, but never sang with her. Once when he broke through his shyness, he had everyone at the party laughing and cheering as he danced a bandy-legged Charlie Chaplin routine to American rock 'n' roll on the phonograph. Neither Anya nor Nikolai spoke English, but they were generous and forbearing with our Russian, and were among the few friends with whom we came to converse in the familiar *ty* instead of the polite *vy*. Because of her flirtatiousness at parties and because she was often away on tour with her orchestra, I wondered if Anya was more sexually liberated than most Russian women I knew. She must have known she gave that impression because she made a point of telling me that she was always true to Nikolai and disapproved of women who were promiscuous.

Other friends collected the latest underground jokes to tell us. Our favorite was about the worker who was investigated by the KGB because he accumulated savings of 80,000 rubles on a salary of 80 rubles a month. He was visited by a KGB colonel, who demanded an explanation. "I made all the money on bets," the worker claimed. "Are you a betting man?" he asked the colonel. The colonel expressed disbelief, so the worker offered, for a bet of five rubles, to bite his own left eye. The colonel agreed to the bet, and the worker promptly took out his left glass eye and bit it. The colonel laughed testily, but insisted that the worker couldn't collect 80,000 rubles with a trick like that. "All right," said the worker, "I'll bet you twenty rubles I can bite my right eye." Since he obviously wasn't blind, he couldn't have two glass eyes, the colonel reasoned. He had no sooner taken the bet than the worker removed his false teeth and bit his right eye. The colonel was becoming exasperated. The worker followed this up with another offer: "I'll bet you a hundred rubles I can pee in your boots and it will smell like French perfume." Now he's gone too far, thought the colonel, and demanded that the worker show his hundred rubles while the colonel removed his boots. The worker urinated in the boots and the colonel leaned over to test the bet.

"That certainly doesn't smell like French perfume," he said triumphantly as he collected his hundred rubles.

"That's all right," grinned the worker. "I bet my neighbor a thousand rubles I could pee in a KGB colonel's boots and get away with it."

These evenings always included our children, whose Russian was

good enough to put at ease those guests who spoke no English. Russians express their affections physically; often they sat through long
philosophical discussions with our younger children clutched comfortably in their laps. The sad aspect of these friends was that with the
exception of one couple, they had no children. (The child who was the
exception never came because he was always away at a child care center
when we exchanged visits. In the six months during which we were
close friends, I never once saw him.) To have a child or two would
crowd the already limited living space in a Moscow apartment of one
room plus kitchen and bath. It was a bit easier for those with two
rooms, but even for them there was little privacy. We visited a family
with two teenaged boys; four people in two rooms lived in difficult
proximity. Another reason for the delay in starting families was a
growing dissatisfaction with the state as a surrogate parent while both
mother and father worked at full-time jobs. The alternative was for
the mother to stay home with her babies, but for two reasons Russian
women found this a hard choice to make. First, the pay scale was generally so low that a couple could not get along without two salaries.
But even if the husband made enough to support a wife and family at
home, the woman felt cheated of her right to work if she stayed home
with children.

The socialist ideal of the equality of men and women never
achieved reality. Even though Russian women grow up assuming they
can hold any job a man can, rarely does a man help with housework,
so that most women end up doing both. Friends, doctors at the clinic,
mothers waiting with me to pick up children at school, all complained
of the same things: after returning from work they had to wait in line to
shop for food, feed their families, and wash clothes until late at night.
No one had a washing machine, dryer or dishwasher. Those who had
read Solzhenitsyn's *Cancer Ward* remarked how true to Soviet life is
the scene in which the doctor comes home from a long, discouraging
day in the hospital to find her husband and son relaxing while a sink
of dirty dishes and a tubful of family laundry await her attentions.
All the women I knew had begun to question the socialist myth of the
liberated mother free to pursue her professional goals while the state
takes care of her children. The women found minimal satisfaction both
in this part-time motherhood and in often-humdrum jobs. There was
a growing attitude among educated women that they could fulfill a

more important function by raising their own children than by working.

There was never any strain to these gatherings. We managed with whatever language skills we had; we all sang and shared the warmth of friendship. Our friends were appreciative of whatever food I offered and took an interest in the recipes for Chinese dishes and in the often unfamiliar tastes. One group called, forgivingly, to tell me how much they loved the curried chicken but how unhappily the spices had affected their unaccustomed stomachs. They were surprised and delighted to discover how familiar Russian dishes had changed in the process of emigrating to America. A favorite was cottage cheese pudding sweetened with chocolate or raspberries; Russians make the same pudding but without flavoring or sugar, so it is considered healthful but not tasty. Beet borscht, which I had always thought was Russian, comes from Eastern Europe and Russians have rarely seen it. They loved any kind of *quiche,* and were amazed that they too could make one without English custard powder. The only cookbook I ever saw in the Soviet Union was for Siberian Tatar dishes; they have nothing like our homemaking magazines. Both the men and the women I knew were fascinated with cooking, which is limited for them by the narrow range of foods they can buy.

In contrast to these easygoing meals with close friends there was the dinner party to which we invited Soviet officials. One. such was in honor of a visit to Moscow by Murray Gart (who had replaced Clurman as chief of correspondents for *Time*). Jerry and his interpreter drew up the guest list: Leonid Zamyatin, head of the Press Department of the Ministry of Foreign Affairs (later, director general of TASS and official spokesman for the USSR); Fyodor Simonov, a deputy head of the Press Department; and Georgi Arbatov, director of the U.S.A. Institute; and their wives. I had met all the men before, at dinners and cocktail parties, and I had met Mrs. Zamyatin and Mrs. Arbatov at a small formal dinner given for Hedley Donovan, the editor in chief of *Time,* and for Henry Grunwald, the managing editor, and Mrs. Grunwald at the Reception House of the Ministry of Foreign Affairs earlier in the year.

Lyuba put a little extra polish on the floors that week, in anticipation of official Soviet guests. Perhaps she felt that her own countrymen would search the corners with a sharper eye and place the blame for any shortcoming on her, as if she hadn't fulfilled her norm. Lola, another maid who moonlighted as a second at dinners like this, agreed to help serve. A tall stately woman with serious blue eyes and a quick smile, Lola went around the table before dinner correcting what she thought Lyuba had out of place, the first time she came. I was about to defend Lyuba's professional expertise when Lyuba herself checked me with a smile and pointed out how beautifully Lola folded the napkins. When Lola came again I no longer felt threatened by her perfectionism and formal reserve; by this time I knew her to be a warm and caring person who only wanted to do a good job. Each time she came to help with a party we greeted each other with respect and a growing affection.

Then one time we called her for a party and she told Lyuba that she couldn't come. Was she engaged? No, she was ill and couldn't work. About a week later I saw her at the Gastronom, and as we walked toward each other I could see that the fine features of her handsome face, usually alert, looked haggard. Without hesitation she explained that she had been in the hospital to have an abortion. She said she was forty-two years old and decided it was too late to have another child. I knew that her husband was crippled and received a stipend for the disabled because he couldn't work. I agreed with her self-justification and told her I hoped she would be feeling well again soon.

A few days after our chance meeting in the Gastronom, I read a report in the *International Herald Tribune* that the Soviets, while still rejecting birth control pills because they are unpredictable in their effect on a woman's health over a period of years, had tested and accepted an intrauterine device. The Soviets had gone into production with a model of their own which was now available.

When I knew that Lola was coming to work with Lyuba again, I considered and reconsidered asking her if she knew what an IUD was and if she knew it was possible to get one in Moscow. I wondered if she would think I was talking down to her, or if she would think it an invasion of her privacy, since most Russians I knew were hesitant to talk about sex in the intimate terms Americans find permissible. At last I consulted Lyuba, who assured me I should go ahead and tell Lola what I had read.

Then I had the problem of describing it in Russian. After consultation with Lyuba again, I described the IUD as a "plastic screw." By her serious attention to what I was telling her, I could see that the humor of it didn't translate into Russian. Lola said she never heard of it; the clinic never suggested it. She would certainly inquire, she said.

By midday on the day of the dinner the house was gleaming, food was ready for the last stages of preparation, and I had placed the final rose, leaning just so, in the Japanese flower arrangement.

Lyuba and I each breathed a deep sigh and turned to the biggest annoyance we faced every time we prepared to have guests. We stood facing each other at opposite ends of our solid oak dining table that had been left in the rain somewhere along the way to Moscow from Tokyo, and had never recovered from the chill. I let go the handle that released the two halves of the table from one another, and we both began to pull. It stopped, it started again, it screeched, and when we had it open to the length we would need, the two halves of the pedestal sagged toward each other like the legs on a rag doll. The table listed toward the center of the room, with visible inches of difference in the height of the two ends. We were past worrying about the warped top — the table-cloth would cover that as best it could. The children began to arrive home for lunch. Evelind came into the room and asked why we both looked so glum.

"Look, look at it!" Lyuba shrieked, throwing her hands into the air.

Evelind ran into her room and brought out the huge Webster's dictionary and put it under one half of the leaning pedestal. Lyuba's face brightened. "Go," she said, "Get some more dictionaries." She and Evelind placed the Russian-English and the English-Russian under the other half of the table and we felt we had done all we could.

Lyuba opened the refrigerator to see if the gelatin was getting firm in the pumpkin-rum chiffon pies I had made in the morning. She chuckled at the thought of the Russian guests eating pumpkin pie. "I can't wait to hear what they say when you tell them it's pumpkin. In the Ukraine we have to throw most of it away — no one will eat it. Even when there are food shortages in Moscow, it's hard to get anyone to eat pumpkin. The reason is, nobody ever thought of putting sugar on it. They bake it with a little butter and eat it with kasha on the side. Of course nobody wants it." Another Russian friend told me that no self-respecting, up-and-coming bureaucrat will eat pumpkin because it is considered peasant food.

The guests were due at seven-thirty. At six o'clock Simonov called to say his wife couldn't come beause she was ill. I told Lyuba to take off one place and she nodded with a sour expression.

After the younger children had finished their dinner, they ran down the sixteen flights; Lyuba had warned them not to tie up the elevators. They came back with excited reports of chauffeured Zils and Sims, large sleek black sedans which brought the official guests. Lyuba shooed the children back to their rooms.

It wasn't until all the guests had arrived that someone asked when Mrs. Zamyatin would come. She couldn't come, her husband informed us, as if it had just occurred to him. Again I went to the kitchen to tell Lyuba to remove another place setting. Her face was set and angry. She shook her head resentfully.

I returned to the living room and joined Mrs. Arbatov as she eagerly examined our Japanese woodblock prints, Korean furniture and Chinese pottery. Even the rugs, similar to Central Asian carpets available in Moscow (for hard currencies and foreign coupons), fascinated her. We used them on the floor; Russians usually hung them on the wall.

When we were seated around the dinner table, Mr. Zamyatin dropped his empty bombshell. "I'm sorry your wife couldn't come," I said. "Is she ill?"

"No," he replied. "She didn't come because I didn't tell her there was anything happening tonight."

Was he really unaware that his answer was a serious breach of etiquette? Or was he playing a game of one-upmanship with the other Soviets at the table, showing how rude he could be to foreigners?

The men blanched, and Mrs. Arbatov's smooth olive cheeks turned a deep rose. She said in a low voice that controlled its anger, "You should have brought your wife. She would have enjoyed seeing a foreign home, especially such an interesting one."

I turned to him in the pose of a cowboy with two guns ready. "Pow, pow," I said. The subject was then closed.

I thought the conversation couldn't possibly get more strained, but I was too optimistic. It went from bad to worse.

Zamyatin then remarked that this quarter of Moscow, where our apartment was located, was growing so fast that the telephone exchanges couldn't keep up with the demand. We would often wait five minutes for a dial tone. Jerry and I chuckled to ourselves. We assumed his explanation was a cover-up for lapses in service caused by tapping rather than a shortage of equipment and lines. He seemed to be saying, "You think it's because of bugging, but the bad phone connections are really just what they seem to be." Everyone else at the table took him quite seriously, since what he said fitted into the standard Soviet line: "Look how fast our country is growing and progressing. What a miracle we have achieved since 1945. Of course we have to put up with inconveniences in the process." The standard line worked well, of course, on Soviets who had no chance to see what the rest of the world has done since 1945.

Seated just beyond Murray Gart on my left was Arbatov, who had been abroad often and whose job it is to know what the United States is doing. As head of the U.S.A. Institute, he directs a belated counterpart to the centers for Russian studies in American universities. Wasn't it reasonable to assume that, as an attentive student of American culture and mores, and as intelligent as he was reputed to be, he would be aware of the youth trends in the States during the sixties? This was the fall of 1969, and it wasn't for another two years that I would hear a Russian use the expression "dropout." Arbatov obviously had never heard the term when he turned to those around him and said, "I don't know why you Americans have trouble with your youth. When my son got restless I sent him to the Virgin Lands for a summer to dig ditches. He learned to respect hard work and came back ready for school."

"Yes, but now that he's done that, what can you offer him next time?" I asked. Arbatov looked at me blankly and acted as if he didn't understand the question.

Nothing improved when I announced that the rum-flavored dessert we had all devoured was made of pumpkin. I got only looks of disbelief. But as Lyuba gathered the empty plates she smiled with satisfaction.

It was in the kitchen later that she amplified her embarrassment. "Don't think, madame, that this was anything personal, the two wives not showing up. You know that I've worked in diplomatic houses for sixteen years, and it's always been the same. Our Soviet officials don't seem to learn any manners. Sometimes they just don't show up without even calling. How much expensive food I've seen left uneaten over the years because only half the party came! I'm not the only one. We signed a petition asking our officials not to shame us this way. It's a national disgrace," she said, the heat rising in her face. I must have smiled skeptically. "Yes, we Soviet workers have a right to send petitions to higher officials," she assured me; then added, "but it was the last we ever heard of it."

Lyuba went on: "If they'd listen to me I'd tell them how much hard work goes into a dinner like this one — all those courses and each one the most elegant recipe, the house, linens, the flowers, opening the table. We didn't even need to open it the whole way," she said wearily. "I bet they never stop to think what it means to open a table the whole way."

But the occasional rudeness we encountered from Soviet bureaucrats was only a puff of smoke in our faces compared with what other foreigners suffered every day because of the color of their skin.

Soon after we moved into Yugozapad, two African students from Patrice Lumumba University pushed their way into our lives and never left. Students from the dormitories beyond the birch forest took meandering walks around the artificial pond on our side of the woods, trying to strike up conversations with the foreign children. It didn't take long for shrewd, laughing, English-speaking Samuel to get our children to invite him for a mug of hot tea late in the afternoon. "I'm Samuel from Ghana," he said aggressively, flashed his white teeth in a large smile, and shot out his hand to shake mine. "Are you de mama? I'm happy to meet you, Mama." He drank tea and for two hours talked about his home in Africa. For the next year and a half he behaved as if I were *his* mama. I invited him later the same week for the first of many dinners. He brought with him Pierre from the Ivory Coast, tall, handsome and shy, who spoke French and halting Russian, but not English.

They were far from home and far from happy in Moscow, but they believed the free education they were receiving was worth the trials they endured. One was studying international law, the other economics. Some of the foreign students struggled for years learning Russian, but Samuel and Pierre managed within a few months to function in graduate classes. They both came from wealthy families tied into the political power structures of their countries, and both had received a good educational start at home.

The Moscow winters are harshly different from the equatorial climates they had left. They learned to cope by dressing warmly and by drinking vodka, but they were always cold. They said there were two winters in Moscow: a white one and a green one. What made life difficult was the racism both of the Soviet government and of the average Russian. Blacks were tolerated but made to feel unwelcome. If the Soviet government hoped to create loyal friends in a future African elite, to which it was giving a free education and which it was supporting with modest monthly stipends, it had made a bad investment.

Russians with progressive views on freedom and democracy for their own country often told us that they sympathized with America's race problems. They said they knew it was hard to control blacks. Others repeated a story, sometimes as a joke, sometimes believing it to be fact: An African student was standing in the aisle of a bus and wouldn't move to the center even though a crowd of people were trying to push on. A Russian addressed him politely, "Comrade, won't you move a little to the center and let more people get on the bus?"

"I am not your comrade," he is reported to have answered. "If you wish to address me call me *Gospodin*" (*Gospodin,* meaning master, is an old form of address now used only for foreigners in formal situations).

These same well-meaning Russians sorely resented marriages between Africans and Russians and told us, "They are the cause of the rising syphilis rate in Moscow." When an African student in Kiev married a blond Russian the couple was stoned, Samuel told us.

At the end of the first winter in our apartment, the wife of an Indian diplomat, who lived in our building but whom I hadn't seen in months, came by for coffee and a chat one morning. "Did you know," she told me in a frightened voice, "that when the snow melted the police found a number of bodies that had been beneath the snow in the woods for months. They think the African students murdered them. You shouldn't let the children go into the woods. And it is well known that only this week seven African students killed a Russian policeman when he came to the aid of a Russian girl they were trying to rape."

A few days later Samuel visited us and I asked him about the story she had told me. He had heard no such story, but he rubbed his chin and mused over it. "Seven?" he ruminated over the number. "That must be the seven students I know who were asked to leave. Yes, they did get into a fight with a policeman. Two are from Ghana, so I heard it straight from them. One of the seven is engaged to a Russian girl.

He was walking on campus with her and six other boys when a policeman in plain clothes came up to them and began calling her a prosti-
tute for going with these boys. Her fiancé explained they were engaged
to marry and told the Russian to be silent. The policeman kept revil-
ing her, telling her to leave the campus. I don't know who pushed
whom first, but they had a big fist fight and the Russian was knocked
to the ground. The police took him away and a few days later we
heard that the plainclothes policeman had died in the hospital. The
Soviets gave notice to the ambassadors of their countries that the seven
students were expelled. One ambassador asked to see the body of the
dead policeman but he was told it was impossible, the man was already buried. The ambassador said that the Soviets shouldn't let those
boys off so easily — if they killed a man, criminal charges should be
brought against them. No, no, the Soviets said, that wasn't necessary.
About three months later, the same policeman, the dead one, was back
on the campus looking for trouble again." Samuel laughed gleefully
as he finished the story.

Some of our Soviet friends, who would be horrified to think of
themselves as prejudiced because of color, said they didn't object to
African students as such. They did, however, resent "these sons of chiefs
coming here and looking down on us." Samuel never seemed to look
down on anyone, but he did behave like the spoiled son of an indul-
gent mother. He came by one spring day with a whine in his voice to
ask my help. His raincoat had been stolen from his room and the only
one he could find to replace it on the Soviet market was a plastic coat
of poor quality. Would I exchange some dollar coupons for his rubles
so he could buy an imported coat in the Beriozka dollar store?

"No, Samuel," I told him. "You'll only get yourself and me into
trouble. If we are thrown out of the Soviet Union, I want it to be
because Jerry has told some truth they couldn't stand to read, not for
a currency violation."

"But no one will know," he pleaded. I looked sideways toward the
kitchen, where Lyuba was ironing, letting him know that she saw and
heard everything.

On another occasion he wanted coupons to buy liquor for a little
party he planned to give his professors. I was outraged that he would
ask me, and told him so. Near the end of the school year he asked if
I could exchange some rubles for dollars; he was going to England for

the summer to visit his brother, and needed money for the trip. I had no green money to give him. The only way to get it was to apply to the Soviet bank to bring some in, and that would be approved only if we were about to go abroad ourselves. When he returned from England after the summer he came to tea. "Well, Samuel, how was your summer? How did you manage until your brother met you?"

Samuel then described the painful scene on the SS *Pushkin,* on which he had sailed from Leningrad to London. Since it was a Soviet ship he had been able to pay for his passage in rubles, and he had hidden some dollars that he had saved for such an emergency from the time he came to the USSR. The other foreign students had done the same. After they boarded the ship a customs officer came around to each student and demanded to know if they had any dollars. The students naïvely thought he was checking to see that they had enough to cover their expenses abroad. Instead he took their dollars, exclaiming that it was illegal for them to be in possession of foreign currency. When he reached Samuel, the wily Ghanaian said he had no dollars. Then how did he expect to manage when he got off the ship in London? "My brother, who is studying in England, will meet me and take care of my needs." The other students were by now in tears. Some took the chance that their embassies in London would come to their aid, others left the ship and returned to their universities.

Samuel's friend Pierre, from the "Coast of the Elephant's Bone," as Ivory Coast translates into Russian, was as tall, handsome and reticent as Samuel was stubby and aggressive. At dinner he explained to us the problems of development his country faced, and fondly described its variety of tribes and dialects. When his Russian became fairly fluent he would telephone Evelind from his dormitory and assuage his loneliness in hour-long conversations. We introduced him to his countryman on the floor above us, a dashingly handsome diplomat who had spent most of his adult life in Paris. There was a joyous flash of recognition in Pierre's smile when the two men met, a coming together of shared values, a love of French style and manners, and happy memories of a home they had become too worldly to live in again. The diplomat and his beautiful Polish wife, together with their three small boys, took over the care and feeding of Pierre until they were suddenly forced to leave. His wife was away visiting her family in Poland when the young aide received word from his government that there had been a falling-out with the Soviets, and he was ordered to leave within twenty-four hours. He packed all night, filling cartons and tying bureaus with rope so their drawers wouldn't slide. In the morning a truck he had ordered from Helsinki appeared and loaded his household goods for Paris. He didn't seem too upset as he thanked me for the breakfast tray I brought him, but their going was a loss to us. Their special beauty, vivacity and style were rare in Moscow.

Perhaps Samuel tried to use us badly at times, but in the end he did us an unusual service. After we bought an abstract painting from an unofficial Soviet artist, we wondered how we would get it out when we left the USSR. All paintings required a certificate of sale from an authorized official source. Other newsmen had their large collections detained for scrutiny by an official of the Ministry of Culture. At some undetermined future date, after they left, the ministry would decide whether a given painting was abstract, in which case it would be illegal and couldn't be taken out. Samuel, having finished tea on a late May afternoon, paced back and forth in front of our swirling abstract painting. I had not told him of my concern over it. A smile of pleasure lit his eyes as he studied it, and then he burst out. "What a marvelous painting," he exclaimed. "It's the map of Ghana."

Our first contact with Moscow's underground of unofficial painters came while we were still living in the Ukraine Hotel. We had a call from a man named Tyuman. He knew of us through a mutual friend, and hoped we would spend an evening at his home. He arranged with Jerry to come to our hotel and then go with us in our car to his apartment in a residential area about fifteen minutes' drive away.

Tyuman had a trim blond beard and cold blue eyes. His exceedingly jovial greeting, I realized when I knew him better, was a salesman's approach to a new client. The exterior of his apartment building was contemporary yellow brick, but the apartment itself, with its unpolished gray plank floors, its primitive kitchen with a wooden dish rack over the sink, gave the impression of rustic simplicity. It was roomy by Russian standards: two rooms, each about twelve by fifteen feet, an entrance hall, small kitchen and bath. The furnishings were sparse — a couple of single beds with colorful covers, some chairs and a desk, a few small tables.

There was only one lamp in each room, so that to show us his art collection he had to carry the one electric lamp like a torch, tilting it at a row of ikons hung at the level of the wainscoting, and at large abstract paintings on the white plaster walls above them. He had examples of the best known of those painters whose works were not considered sufficiently realistic or optimistic by the Ministry of Culture for them to be invited to join the Soviet Union of Artists. The only way these painters could sell their paintings was directly to a buyer, without the sanction of the state. Such a private transaction is illegal in the Soviet Union. Although a busy "underground" trade of this kind existed, the strict letter of the law required an artist to sell his work to the state first. The state would then resell it to the individual buyer, at prices fixed by the official agency handling it, or with a prohibitive tax reputed to be anywhere from 100 to 300 percent of the artist's price.

Tyuman was an illegal middleman in the unofficial art trade. He took paintings on consignment from artists to sell to foreigners, or arranged art showings at the studios of artists, to which he would invite his list of clients. He cultivated his trade at the embassies and among newsmen, inviting them into his "select" circle as soon as they arrived in Moscow. He competed not only with others acting as middlemen for the artists — Nina Stevens, the wife of correspondent Ed Stevens was one — but with artists who shunned his services and tried to reach newcomers themselves.

In this first meeting there was no hint of salesmanship. A quiet young man, whom Tyuman introduced as a rising artist but who spoke no English, was already at the apartment when we arrived. Tyuman's wife, one of the Soviet Union's most talented young cellists, whom we met later, was away on tour, and their little boy was staying with his grandmother. Tyuman's English is limited but adequate to exude hospitality and good fellowship. He served us bread and sausage with hot tea. Jerry and I shared one cup because he had only three, badly chipped. After the tea we drank red Georgian wine, a combination that made us all warm and heady. He told us about the various painters whose works we could look at after we ate, and promised to introduce us to them. After we had seen the new paintings he showed us his treasure — a realistic landscape with a lady in a long red dress. He claimed it was an early work of the pioneer abstractionist Kandinsky. We learned later that Tyuman's painting was a very questionable Kandinsky, but that night, in the glow of the single light bulb, we admired it wordlessly.

As the evening drew to a close Tyuman purported to feel a growing affection for both Jerry and me and as he helped me with my coat he gave me a friendly hug. Then he reached over to the wall above the bed and took down a small brass and enamel ikon, a triptich that he folded and dropped into the pocket of my coat. I protested that he was too generous but he insisted on presenting the gift to his newfound friends. A few weeks later a British diplomat's wife described in intimate detail a similar experience at Tyuman's home, shortly after they arrived in Moscow. We laughed heartily together and agreed that we were not insulted enough to give back the ikons. Nor were our feelings too hurt to accept his subsequent invitations to art showings or his offers of tickets to his wife's concerts. But when it came to buying paintings, we tried to deal directly with the artist. This had its pitfalls.

I once made the mistake of going alone to an artist's studio with the artist — a man named Misha, who had been introduced to us by Nina Stevens. When Misha came to our apartment for dinner, he was warm and affectionate, as Russians often are who trust and love you on first sight because their friends have told them you are worthy of it. Misha was tall and robust with a shaggy blond beard and watery blue eyes behind gold-rimmed glasses. He wore a plaid shirt with the sleeves rolled above his elbows. He invited me to meet him in a remote square of the city, from which we would go to an apartment where his paintings were stored. I never stopped to consider the indiscretion of going with him alone, the possibility that I was being drawn into a planned provocation to embarrass my husband.

We met in a busy open-air market in the shadow of a decaying Romanesque church. Bright sun lent a deceptive cheer to the streaked ocher walls of the church and the gray weatherbeaten boxes on which the street vendors set their wares. He greeted me with smiles and we spoke English on the walk to the apartment house. The studio was in a new five-story block with metal-rimmed windows and tan bricks to offset the grimness of the precast concrete walls. The gray wooden floors of the studio were unpolished; the only furniture was an old desk and chair, an armless cloth couch, and an easel. Against the walls, along the walls of the partition, everywhere on the floor and window-sills were paintings and drawings.

He showed me his work: an abstract landscape, old doors, studies of old iron locks. He had superimposed layers of paint one on another to give a sense of three dimensions, of decay and rust, of texture. I looked at all his paintings avidly, carefully, and silently. Before me lay the real problem, the true embarrassment in having come alone: what was I to say if I didn't like his work? If I had stood on a dais with lights shining on me and an audience waiting for my word, I could not have been more vulnerable than I was in those minutes with Misha eagerly waiting for my reaction. I sat down thoughtfully and we faced each other in anguish.

"Obviously," I began, "you are well trained and you can paint very well." There was no lack of technique in his work. What his Russian heritage could give him he had learned well. He leaned forward eagerly, waiting for the "but." I tried to make little value of my opinion — I had no degrees, I said, no professional training. I was only an occasional collector, a lover of art, I had no credentials, there was no reason for him to be concerned with my criticism. He insisted nevertheless on knowing what I liked and what I didn't like. What did I think of those drawings against the wall? They had been done by his friend, an older painter whose work he looked up to and who had achieved recognition abroad. Yes, I liked them, I answered, they were very well done. They were less behind the times than Misha's sad, simple paintings. But for the technique, his work might have come from one of those ladies in shorts and sun hat who take summer courses on Cape Cod.

Finally we spoke openly to each other. His subjects and his approach I said, had been popular and had then been discarded in the West fifteen or twenty years ago. How many current vogues had reached their peaks and been superseded since then! They had passed Misha and his colleagues by without their even knowing that they had existed.

Yes, he agreed sadly, the antimodernism of the Soviet regime, both present and recent, had cut them off from the world's artistic currents. Even to attempt to paint nonsocialist art they had to hide their work. This meant they could rely only on each other for stimulation and criticism. Also, they were touched somewhat by the demand to produce something indigenous. Misha pointed to his rusted locks. "I wanted to paint something Russian." In the same way the painter

Oskar Rabin often weaves a herring, a samovar and a church into desolate still lifes of the Soviet spirit. Others reinterpreted old ikon styles. There is nothing fresh or daring.

As we talked, Misha shrank back into his seat. By this time we both felt very tired and wanted to be away from one another. He walked me out to get a taxi, and held my arm brusquely when I spoke, warning me not to speak in the presence of a couple just vacating the taxi. The sun and his light mood had gone. He was suddenly afraid to be seen with a foreigner.

But our Russian friends also provided us with lighter moments. Our bachelor friend Volya had long complained to us of the difficulties he met in seducing girls in a communal apartment. First you had to get the young lady through the common foyer. This meant that everyone knew whom you had brought home and whether it was the same girl as the night before. Since his apartment mates didn't particularly like his lifestyle, they could make nasty cracks for the girl to overhear as he and she came through the hallway. Then, once in his own room things were better, but the walls were so thin it was hard to get the girl to relax. One time we drove him home but he didn't invite us in — the house, which was on the edge of the city, looked like the bleak wooden barracks of some obsolete army camp. Here reception for the Voice of America was not as jammed as in the central city, but his apartment mates looked askance on his early morning habits of listening to the Voice of America "Breakfast Show" (rock music) and the seven o'clock BBC news broadcasts.

And so it was with great glee that he announced to us that the bureaucracy had made a mistake in his favor. He was about to be given an apartment of his own, a large room plus kitchen and bath in one of the new cement prefab apartment buildings in the maze of new construction south of us. Certainly if they knew what they were doing they would give precedence to a family, but he was not about to call up and tell them they had made a mistake. Even though we had spent many delightful evenings together, and had shared his searing humor at the expense of the Kremlin leadership, this "mistake" was one more ambiguous clue to Volya's identity and his relationship with us. The USSR is a classless society except for those privileged people who are rewarded with special favors like foreign clothes and new apartments in return for special services to the state.

The next weeks were filled with vaudeville-like renditions of his adventures with his new apartment. For example, there was the day he bought a small new refrigerator and then had the problem of getting it home. Usually people hire a pickup-truck taxi but since there were none to be gotten, he talked a regular taxi driver into carrying it for him. Either it wouldn't fit into the trunk, or the taxi driver was afraid he would be stopped by a policeman, so they put it into the back seat of the car and Volya rode with his arm lovingly around it.

He invited us to dinner at his new home. He also invited his brother, a tall athletic teenager, and Evelind, Stevo, and two of his girlfriends. When we arrived we were struck by the universality of young bachelors' quarters. There was the bare light bulb covered by a paper bag decorated with a colorful drawing of St. Basil's. There was the room itself, spare, containing only his bed, a worn wooden desk, and an old-fashioned bookcase with glass doors; behind them were some dark-bound classics his father had given him. On the wall was a photograph of Volya, grinning mischievously, with a Josef Stalin mustache superimposed on his face.

He poured us drinks, using the desk as a bar, and assured us that dinner would be ready soon — the girlfriends were in the kitchen cooking. We leaned into the kitchen to say hello. They were rushed but friendly, obviously excited by the chance to play house. Then came the elaborate preparation of the table. The desk and the kitchen table were put together, with the backboard of the desk in the center, to make room for everyone to sit down. He had enough chairs. He also had enough plates, though most were chipped and had been gathered from a hundred years of broken sets, but no one apologizes for their tableware in the USSR because it is so seldom available in the stores. The girls had prepared a tasty dinner of fried liver and onions with potatoes and a salad of cucumbers and tomatoes, the first of the spring. We all ate avidly in the dimness of the paper-covered single light bulb.

Volya kept us laughing through dinner with his adventures as a city slicker drafted for a weekend of hoeing potatoes on a collective farm. When he protested that his expensive new raincoat had been stolen, he was told that it was his fault for bringing such a raincoat to the farm. He was serious for a few minutes while he recounted the social chaos and the hardship he saw there. He said that the only men left on the farm were alcoholics of no determinate age, the young healthy men having all left for city jobs or military service — anything that would get them away. With a lifted eyebrow and leering smile he added, "The only children born there are sired by men just passing through." He described the dormitory where the workers lived. It was crowded and smelly with body and cooking odors. Dressing and undressing, cooking and copulating all went on in these barnlike sleeping halls. Once a year the men from neighboring farms lined up with poles and chains for a violent confrontation that released the repressed tensions for a while.

Volya told us that during another draft of city men for manual labor he was assigned to work at a central receiving warehouse for agricultural products. Fruits and vegetables were shipped from this center to state-owned food markets all over the city of Moscow. He said that the workers who lifted and stacked the heavy crates were all women, who had taken these jobs to get off the farm. They found the living conditions the same and the work harder. Some of the women signed a petition asking for better working conditions; the response was to send them back to the farm.

After dinner we removed the kitchen table so we could dance to Volya's beloved collection of American records. Everybody danced; we exchanged partners and danced cheek to cheek and laughed a lot. But after a little while one of the girls became pensive and shrugged off Volya's attempts to get her to dance with him. She was a slim and pretty girl, who wore her dark hair pulled back in a severe topknot, which was more stylish than the hairdos of most Moscow girls. Her eyes were sharp and clear, but her pouting, unformed lips revealed the unsureness of the late teens. There was something distinctly urban about her; she had none of the little hints that betray how few years the family had been off the land. The pale thinness of her cheeks, her thin-armed, erotic slouch showed that she had never carried a bucket of water. She did not look particularly intelligent, but she did have a look of knowing her way around. She knew that she didn't belong in this dimly lit apartment playing forbidden music with children of the enemy. She was not so much in danger from the neighbors and other watchdogs of the lower Party machine — she had pull at a higher level than they could touch — the threat, she suddenly realized, came from her father. There would be a devastating scene if he found that his daughter, fed and housed and clothed with his earnings, his privileges as an officer of the secret police, had allowed herself to be reported in so indiscreet a situation. She was too frightened to make a scene, to demand that Volya take her home. She wasn't noisy about it. She just hugged her knees to her chest in a corner of the room and watched us with sick, unhappy eyes that silently upbraided Volya for getting her into this. Volya was half-sympathetic but his good humor was undaunted — he laughed and whispered to us that she was not sick to her stomach, it was just that her father worked for the KGB.

We danced and laughed and drank some more Georgian wine and as the day turned we thought it was time to go home. Volya and his brother were enjoying themselves too much; they wanted to dance all night and then go to our house for breakfast. Did Volya like us so much? Or was he getting pleasure out of tormenting the KGB colonel's daughter? At last we reached a compromise. We would go home since we were too old and our children were too young to stay up all night, but the others could go on dancing and then come to our house for breakfast. With hushed laughter and cheerful smiles, the four of them saw us off from the parking lot behind the apartment house. They showed us the easiest way out through the mud and onto the new macadam toward Leninsky Prospekt. From there we would know our way home.

It seemed as if we were riding forever through an aesthetic wasteland of white prepoured boxes, five, six, seven stories high, the recently churned ground all mud between them. Brand-new reassuring streetlights along the new roads seemed to lead only to more new roads. At last we recognized Lumumba University and the red airplane warnings on the roof of our own apartment house, and with a great sigh of relief turned onto the main highway that would take us home. It was by now past two in the morning and we fell into bed confident that we wouldn't be hearing from them that day. We slept until eight-thirty and were just putting on coffee when the doorbell rang. We hugged Volya and his brother and were politely introduced to a young girl we had never seen before. She was much taller and more muscular than the girls of the night before, with a kind of heavy-handed brashness that took in every detail of this foreign sanctuary with a hungry curiosity. She smoked and ate with a clumsiness and a lack of false modesty that was familiar in Moscow, the hard-to-erase traits of farmers' daughters a half generation away from the collective farm. We talked quietly in Russian over breakfast and then Jerry asked Volya in English what had happened to the two girls. He shook his head and repressed his laughter. "They just couldn't make it for breakfast."

8

Covering Moscow

BEFORE I WAS ASSIGNED to the Soviet Union, I became aware that Moscow, unlike Tokyo, Paris and London, does not have a *Time-Life* building. Nor are there office buildings of any kind for foreign correspondents or foreign businessmen. The Soviet Union is still catching up with its World War II housing shortage. The seventeen American companies authorized to do business in the Soviet Union utilize hotel suites and apartments scattered around the city. West European and foreign Communist correspondents use a room in their cramped apartments for offices, but are unable to muffle the staccato tattoo of the TASS news wire and the Telexes that link them to their home offices. American newspapers and wire services have converted separate apartments to news bureaus.

Time-Life's Moscow bureau is at 14 Kutuzovsky Prospekt, in two ground-floor apartments that are part of a block-long apartment house inhabited by foreign diplomats, journalists and East Europeans. My next-door neighbors were *Newsweek* and Kyodo, the Japanese news agency. By Moscow standards *Time* has choice offices, centrally located with good mail service and easy access to buses and taxis. There are public telephone booths on the street handy for unbugged calls to Russian friends. The Ukraine Hotel is within walking distance for long lunches. Needless to say, the usual militsioner is on guard duty, and Soviet citizens who enter are required to show their identification cards and are subject to harassment for coming to see a foreigner.

Broken floor tiles, tricycles, baby carriages and the smell of cabbage soup in the entryway soon became familiar. As I arrived at the office each day it gradually stopped being incongruous to greet neighbors carrying string bags full of bread and vegetables or covered enamel pails filled with fresh cottage cheese or sour cream from the nearby farmers' market. We would chat as they waited for the rickety elevator next to my bright-red office door with its dignified brass *Time* and *Life* plaques that I had brought from Japan.

With a wall of bookshelves, teak paneling from Copenhagen and new green carpeting from the Moscow dollar store my office was a spacious oasis. Old *Life* pictures of the poets Yevgeny Yevtushenko and Boris Pasternak enlivened the walls. The cover portrait of Nikita Khrushchev holding an ear of corn on his visit to the United States in 1959 made mine the only office in Moscow where Khrushchev's portrait was still hanging.

In the West the standard practice of foreign correspondents is to rent offices in the headquarters of major newspapers so they can be close to the action and have ready access to wire service tickers. In Moscow it is unheard of for *Pravda, Izvestia,* or TASS to rent space to foreign correspondents in their tightly controlled central offices. The official, decreed nature of news in the Soviet Union separates foreign correspondents from their Soviet counterparts. The dominant daily feeling for us is one of isolation, of being kept away from life and the news.

In Moscow, news is an extension of Communist Party policy, a means to explain and control ideas. The only acceptable constant companions for foreign correspondents are the leased TASS wire in English and Russian, *Pravda, Izvestia, Trud* (the trade union paper), and the Soviet weekly press. From reading and culling the press one can weave only a bland mosaic of Soviet life. The normal human foibles of personality, power, sin, crime, fire and accidents are not considered worthy of newsprint. Statistics on crime or the prevalence of alcoholism are never released in absolute figures but only in percentages, so there is no base for useful comparison.

One day a team of policemen came to our apartment house with

German shepherd dogs to investigate a robbery in the Sudanese con-
sulate on the third floor. Leona casually asked one of the police officers
what they were doing with the police dogs. "We have come for a fire
prevention inspection," the blue-uniformed officer told her with a
straight face. Another day the children came home from school flushed
with the news that the school garden had been swarming with police
because a young woman was found murdered there. The neighbors
told us that it was a crime of passion; a young man killed his girlfriend
because she spurned him. The crime was never reported in the Moscow
papers. We only learned that there was an increase of crime in Moscow when the local newspaper, *Vechernaya Moskva,* reported that
home burglar-alarm systems linked to the central police station would
be available for rental. Even a five-alarm fire in the middle of Moscow, across the street from the Lenin Museum, was not considered
news. Only recently has the government officially acknowledged air
crashes at the Leningrad airport and at Sheremyetevo Airport, outside
Moscow. Details are always minimal and the cause of accidents is
never officially reported. News of the crashes is occasionally given out,
however, when foreigners are involved.

The subordination of reality, or as the Russians prefer to say,
"life itself," to a utopian picture of "building Communism" takes
strange forms. Access to sources is curbed physically and psychically.
There are specific formal limits on foreign correspondents restricting
which Soviet citizens they may see and under what circumstances. Private warnings are given on what is considered "unfriendly" or "not
conducive to improving relations between the United States and the
Soviet Union."

In one of my first briefings at the Press Department of the Ministry
of Foreign Affairs I was politely but firmly told that the department
would arrange all interviews and contacts with Soviet citizens for me.
If I wanted an interview I had to ask the Press Department. According
to a 1947 law all contacts with Soviet institutions or their employees
by "representatives of foreign institutions" must be arranged by the
Foreign Ministry. The definition of foreign institutions includes journalists, diplomats and businessmen. The law thoughtfully does not
require that the notification and permission procedure be followed
before one buys a newspaper, goes to the post office, a restaurant or
the cinema, or calls a doctor, the police or the fire department.

Because of this regulation, developing sources is the biggest single problem in covering Moscow. One cannot pick up the telephone and call a ministry or an official to obtain figures and information. When I called the Press Department to ask for the Soviet Union's position on talks between the late President Nasser and Brezhnev, I was told: "Read it in *Pravda* and *Izvestia*. All the information is in our press." Soviet citizens who provide information or opinions to correspondents without official permission are subject to indictment for defaming the Soviet Union, a crime which can draw three years in prison or five years in exile. Although the law is difficult to enforce, it is used as a club to restrict correspondents from visiting Russians. In January 1968 foreign correspondents were warned of the law and threatened with "severe measures" if they went to the home of the mother of Aleksandr Ginzburg while he was being tried for supporting Sinyavsky and Daniel. Four American correspondents who tried to defy the ban were barred by plainclothes security agents. The same practice is sometimes used when correspondents try to visit Jewish protestors at their homes. Correspondents who attribute stories to Communist sources are reprimanded and reminded of the regulation when their stories displease the Press Department.

Only within this web of restrictions are social contacts with Russians permitted. The normal camaraderie of shared intellectual or cultural interests is poisoned. During our first winter Leona came back from skiing on the hillside outside our apartment house and told me she had met a red-bearded Russian who was a China scholar. The children had struck up a conversation with him and told him we had lived in Hong Kong and Japan. She chatted with him and he told her he had been to China to study several times, but not since 1966. "Perhaps we should get together. I think you'd enjoy meeting my husband. He's a journalist who has been covering China for years," Leona suggested. The Russian laughed and skied off.

To obtain official permission to travel on short notice takes one day at the minimum and is granted only in cases of illness or other special humanitarian necessity for leaving the Soviet Union. For internal travel at least three days is needed. Even a simple trip to Leningrad on the overnight train requires that one's internal passport be visaed and stamped. Correspondents are provided internal Soviet passports for travel outside the twenty-five-mile limit.

Traveling on one's own is theoretically possible but difficult. The Press Department was reluctant to grant permission unless I made my arrangements in advance through Intourist or Novosti.

The only alternative was seeing the Soviet Union on the official trips arranged by the Ministry of Foreign Affairs (MID). MID gave access to such out-of-the-way places as Murmansk and Central Asia. The tours always had a standard format: visit World War II battle sites and war memorials, tour textile factory, lunch with state or collective farmers, attend local theater group or folk opera in the evening.

For non-Communist Western correspondents there was no contact with Communist Party officials in their capacity as members of Regional or factory Party organizations. The Communist Party is off limits to non-Communists and even members of the Communist bloc are treated with caution. I met Party members who were directors of factories and state farms but never, despite repeated requests, was any of our group of foreign correspondents introduced to or allowed to interview the secretary of the local or Regional Party organization. The Communist Party is the power center and the control mechanism and it operates with relentless but secret omniscience. For the foreign correspondent the Party secretary, from General Secretary Leonid Brezhnev on down to the local Party secretary, is a figure of mystery whose influence and actions are never subject to the outside checks and balances that restrain a Western leader. The strict discipline imposed within the Party and the fear of being deposed are the restraints on a Soviet leader. Efforts to question the daily habits or political style of Party leaders are discouraged. The Politburo members who determine Party policy rarely meet with the press or give press conferences.

Lenin's idea was to preserve the Revolution through the Communist Party. As Stalin put it, "Not a single important political organizational question is decided by our Soviet and other mass organizations without guiding directions from the Party." The Party, a separate hierarchy that parallels the government bureaucracy on every level, controls the government and the ministries. It operates as the mechanism to execute commands while at the same time uprooting and destroying any challenge to its authority. Trying to change the Party is, as Aleksandr Solzhenitsyn has said, "like throwing peas against a stone wall."

For American journalists in Moscow the Party and its inner activities are off limits and any effort to probe them or speculate on them leads to warnings, isolation, harassment and expulsion. How policy is made is never publicly discussed, but the results of secret Party deliberations are revealed in the press after the Central Committee meetings and Party Congresses.

By traveling as much as possible outside of Moscow I hoped to break this ring of isolation and find in small villages or outlying Central Asian Republics the human elements of Party power, which remained hidden in Moscow. I went on all of the trips to which I was invited. The best part of the travels was often the long train rides. I would talk with young sailors on leave or share a compartment to Leningrad with a colonel in the artillery who remembered crossing the Elbe at the end of World War II to meet the Americans in Berlin.

One evening in Kazan, in the Tatar Autonomous Republic, Jim Clarity of the New York *Times,* whose specialty is human interest stories, excitedly knocked on my hotel-room door to report that a strange girl with a soft voice had called his room and asked for Igor. " 'This is Jim, not Igor,' I told her in my best Russian," Jim vowed. After more small talk mixed with his Irish charm, Clarity arranged to meet Nadya and her friend on the street corner one block from our hotel at 9 P.M. Clarity asked me to join him to make sure he was not being set up by the KGB. It was our free evening in Kazan on a Foreign Ministry tour and we were both delighted with the prospect of going on a blind date instead of typing our notes. Nadya and Margarita greeted us shyly and with reserve. They admitted they were in the habit of telephoning the hotel for blind dates but usually they met young Russians on *komandirovka,* official business trips. Had we come upon two semiprofessional young liberated ladies, we wondered, as they agreed we should have a drink. Where do you have a drink in Kazan on a weekday night after nine o'clock? The restaurants were closed and neither we nor the girls wanted to return to our hotel. The girls suggested the buffet of the main railway station.

Railway stations in the Soviet Union are overflowing with open activity. Fresh-faced soldiers, sailors, poor peasants with sacks on their shoulders, officials with leather suitcases and wizened old women suggest the complexity of Soviet life behind the bland phrases of official propaganda.

Our suspicions that the KGB was setting us up with the girls soon lightened. As we talked around the table in the cavernous, brightly lit buffet we were convinced that we had met two girls who were looking for a change in the dull routine of their daily lives. Like others at the crowded tables, we drank sweet Russian champagne and munched on thick pieces of white bread, cheese and sausage. Nadya was attractive, with long blond hair and a soft complexion. She worked as a salesgirl in the Kazan department store. For Margarita, a university student, this was a new experience. Dark-haired and pensive, she had been asked along by Nadya and had to be home by midnight. We got through the first bottle of champagne discussing their daily routine. Then Clarity asked the girls if they had read Solzhenitsyn. "Yes, I've heard of his book, *Ivan Denisovich,* but we are not interested in that kind of writing," said Nadya. They preferred novels in a lighter vein; they did not want to be reminded of labor camps. They wanted to marry and have only one child and were amazed when I told them I had five children and Clarity had four. Our escapade turned into an interview.

By midnight, when we took the girls home by taxi and shook hands, they were bewildered, fascinated and disturbed by our conversation. We had briefly entered their world, but not their lives.

Most trips did not allow for such spontaneity. The normal high point was a state-farm banquet with toasts to peace and friendship among the peoples of all countries, toasts to the people of the United States and the Soviet Union, and toasts to peace and friendship — *mir i druzhba.*

On one trip to Smolensk we were joined by the North Vietnamese correspondent Pham Que Lam. He was a dignified, quiet fellow who had been in Moscow for four years. His colleague from the South Vietnamese National Liberation Front, Chuong Quan Than, was also in the party; I was the only American. The toasts that day were a strain. The Russians departed from the usual toast formulas to attack aggression and the American bombing of Hanoi and to praise the Democratic Republic of Vietnam. In my reply I stressed the need for negotiations, an end to the bombing and the war. I got polite mild applause. The two Vietnamese were loudly cheered.

One of the favorite "games" on trips was for the Soviet hosts to pick out a correspondent and test his drinking endurance. John Dornberg of *Newsweek* found the practice so objectionable that he refused to drink at all on our visit to Kazakhstan.

We spent the day visiting a cotton textile factory and touring the state farm where the most remarkable thing was the contrast between the homes of the Kazakhs and the Volga Germans who had been forcibly resettled in Kazakhstan by Stalin during World War II. The Germans had built their own wooden homes with neat kitchen gardens and livestock pens — German farms in the middle of Kazakhstan. There was even a brewery on the state farm. The Kazakhs, who only recently had lived a nomadic life in tents, now had two-room apartments with concrete floors and ceilings, a family of five in two rooms. The Germans had re-created their lifestyle but the Kazakhs had still to find a new one.

The banquet at the state farm outside Alma Ata was elaborate, with a whole roast sheep, heaping salads and numerous bottles of vodka and cognac on the table. I was the target for the day and I decided to try and play the game. It was a mistake. I handled the vodka well enough. When the sheep's head arrived the steamed brains were removed and mixed with chopped green onion, then passed around as a delicacy for all to taste. Then there were more toasts to peace and friendship, to our wives and children, to peace in the world, to a big crop in Kazakhstan and to the joys of meeting new friends.

I excused myself and went to the men's room, an outhouse one hundred yards from the dining room, where I relieved myself of the vodka Roman style. I returned to the banquet refreshed to find the game had only just begun. The attack team switched to brandy, a cheap no-star local brand that had a heavy aftertaste of sulfur. In a relay of three against me the toasts multiplied. It was too late to turn back and I soon felt heavy and hazy. I managed to get back to the bus on my own power but quietly passed out on the ride home.

The next morning I awoke in my bed at the hotel with all my clothes on feeling as if I had been flattened by a roller. All my bones ached. My colleagues laughed when I wobbled weakly into the dining room just as they were finishing breakfast. I learned that a German TV cameraman had carried me to my room and Bruce Winter of the Baltimore *Sun* had watched over me to see that I was sound asleep and the lights turned off. That way he was sure there would be no uninvited callers of the night or embarrassing photographs. Winter and I agreed that the way our hosts had double-teamed me was intended to stimulate more than peace and friendship, but their true purpose remained unclear. Maybe that's just the way they drink in Kazakhstan.

Old Moscow hands insist that the job of a foreign correspondent is easier now than in the 1950's. The old-timers recall their battles with the censor; they remember living in a hotel room during the entire period of their assignment as proof that it's easier now. True, the physical amenities may have improved, but the psychic pressures are as intense as ever, and in some ways worse.

Censorship was lifted in 1961 by Nikita Khrushchev, ending a system that had existed since tsarist days. The Soviets never officially recognized it as censorship. The Italian journalist Vero Roberti of *Corriere della Sera* recalls that Leonid Ilychev, head of the Press Department of the Ministry of Foreign Affairs in 1960, used to tell correspondents that *glavlit*, the censorship office, performed only a "literary function." According to Ilychev, his job was not to censor articles but to improve and perfect literary style, a declaration which he repeated often and with great seriousness. Roberti described Ilychev, now the chief Soviet negotiator with the Chinese on border disputes, as "a man whose head was as hard as [former Foreign Minister] Molotov's backside."

In those days, the censor sat behind a glass door covered by an ugly green curtain at the international section of the Central Telegraph Office on Gorky Street. Nobody ever saw or talked with the censor and it became a matter of pride for the correspondents to try and discover who he was, but that was one battle lost. Roberti tried to tempt the censor from his lair by offering him a prized series of fourteen tickets to an Italian film festival in Moscow. Roberti watched in vain for an entire week for the seats to be filled but they remained empty.

Beating the censor was the Moscow game. Robert ("Bud") Korengold, then a UPI correspondent, recalls that even Nikita Khrushchev was censored in his off-the-cuff remarks if they did not fit the Kremlin's official political line. Stories were sent with Khrushchev's quotes excised. Tom Lambert, then of the New York *Herald Tribune,* explained how much a certain Soviet official was disliked by saying he was "as popular as Sherman in Georgia." The censor's knowledge of American history did not include General Sherman's scorched-earth policy during the Civil War and the phrase got through.

In the early days of the Sino-Soviet dispute the Russians would not allow correspondents to identify "the dogmatists" being attacked in lengthy editorials, although everybody knew they were the Chinese Communists. One day at the end of a long article against the "dogmatists" Roberti had an inspiration and wrote as the final sentence in his story: "Marco Polo went on a journey." When the censor allowed it to pass he rushed and told his colleagues that he had found a way to tell his editors that the "dogmatists" were the Chinese. The others — Lambert, Max Frankel of the New York *Times,* and Preston Grover of the Associated Press — tried the same formula and it worked; it got past the censor. Unfortunately, the editors back home, like the censor, missed the point of the reference to Marco Polo.

Beating the censor enforced camaraderie and esprit de corps as the correspondents met in the Central Telegraph Office to get their copy approved. Censorship ended when the Russians realized it was self-defeating. News from Moscow leaked to other capitals a day or two later and there was little that the Soviet authorities could do to stop it.

The Press Department lifted formal censorship but replaced it with an informal but equally insidious system which has become known as self-censorship. What amounts to a proscribed list of subjects is pointed out to correspondents, illustrated with examples of official actions taken against colleagues who write on them. An Italian correspondent who wrote about prostitution was not granted a visa to return to Moscow. Henry Kamm, a correspondent for the New York *Times,* had his travel in the Soviet Union curtailed because of too-detailed and consistent coverage of the activities of dissidents and of the human rights and democratic movements. Henry Bradsher, then with the Associated Press, had a bomb placed under the hood of his car on a Moscow street in 1968. Fortunately, he was not in the car when the bomb exploded, destroying the car and breaking windows in nearby apartment houses.

The most sensitive subjects are the Soviet leaders themselves, past and present, their private lives and personal peccadilloes. If Leonid Brezhnev does not like the portrait that *Time* chose for its cover a correspondent's visa may not be renewed (Stanley Cloud, for instance, was the victim of such an administrative expulsion by the Press Department in 1970).

Speculation about leadership changes is considered provocative and can form grounds for expulsion. The series of articles by Anatole Shub of the Washington *Post* in the spring of 1969, which forecast the removal from power of General Secretary Brezhnev, led to Shub's ouster.

Stories about public disturbances or discrimination against minority nationalities like the Uzbeks or Tatars are frowned upon and discouraged by the Press Department. Soviet officials would have the world live with the fiction that the Soviet Union with its fifteen Republics and more than one hundred nationalities lives in a state of harmony and bliss. Riots at soccer games in Baku and Tashkent between Muslims and Russians, which occurred in 1969 and 1970, were never directly reported in the press but only alluded to in commentaries. An effort to solicit confirmation and details from a Russian official in Moscow brought only the reply: "What can you expect from those people?" In everyday life the Russians mock the slowness of Tadjik or Uzbek waiters and slur their Oriental background. Discussing such contradictions to the image of the egalitarian socialist state is not considered within the purview of "serious" Western journalists.

The correspondent who writes on forbidden subjects or who is considered "unfriendly" in his treatment of Soviet life is subject to a wide range of intimidations. To show its dissatisfaction with stories on dissidents, the Press Department will refuse to telephone a correspondent to notify him of a press conference or a trip outside Moscow that the Foreign Ministry is sponsoring. The diplomatic service bureau may refuse to honor a request for apartment repairs. Further articles may lead to phone calls at 3 A.M. from an "irate Soviet citizen" insulting the correspondent in his native language. Newsmen who try to visit dissidents are sometimes roughed up by "angry Soviet citizens," actually plainclothes KGB agents. In extreme cases, as during the anti-Jewish campaign in the fall and winter of 1970, the windshield was smashed on one correspondent's car and Holger Jensen of the Associated Press had the tires of his car slashed. Windshield wipers, side-view mirrors and aerials are periodically found missing from foreign correspondents' cars. Nobody is ever certain if this is harassment or petty thievery. The shortage of spare parts makes for a lively secondhand market in Moscow and correspondents follow the standard Russian practice of removing the windshield wipers when they park in an open area.

Soviet journalists insist that the harassment of Western correspondents by the KGB is no worse than the harassment they receive from the FBI in the United States. During a long lunch with a *Pravda* correspondent shortly after I arrived in Moscow, I raised the whole subject of harassment. We drank vodka toasts to friendship and then he said: "Your FBI is no better than our KGB. When I was nearing the end of my six years in the United States the FBI tried to recruit me as a spy. When I refused I was certain that somebody tried to kill me by tampering with the brakes of my car. You know that every time I go to the United States now the FBI goes through my luggage. It's an unwritten rule that we Soviet journalists must leave our suitcases unlocked when we leave our American hotel rooms. On my last visit I spent all my spare dollars on two negligées for my wife at Bergdorf Goodman. I thought of placing the gifts in the safe deposit box of the hotel when I got to Washington, but decided that was silly. Instead, I locked my suitcase. When I returned that night the negligées were still there but the locks had been neatly cut out of the suitcase." We both laughed.

Then my friend gave me some unsolicited advice. "We have heard you are a serious journalist. I concerned myself with policy matters and foreign affairs when I was in Washington. You'll find your stay here more valuable if you do the same. We look to serious journalists, not those who engage in personal sensationalism about our leaders."

Under the unwritten, but carefully enforced rules of self-censorship foreign correspondents can write what they want, but there are penalties. The highest is expulsion. Every correspondent has his own way of interpreting the rules and has to choose quickly how he is going to run the gauntlet.

The dissidents and the democratic movement, the attacks on Solzhenitsyn, and the spreading drive to prevent Jewish emigration all became a major part of the Moscow story. I had to balance these subjects carefully against the ongoing diplomatic story, the positioning inside the Politburo, the intricacies of Soviet economics and new trends in lifestyles and consumer demands.

In my first weeks I wrote letters to the Press Department requesting interviews with the head of the State Planning Commission and the top man on the American desk of the Foreign Ministry. As with my request for an interview with Solzhenitsyn, there was no reply. I soon realized that official sources could complicate my life but would do little to facilitate my work.

I began to understand how the Soviet system of control and influence worked the first week I arrived in Moscow. I paid a courtesy call on Henry Shapiro, the UPI bureau chief. The doyen of the wire services, Shapiro had covered Moscow for forty years before he retired in 1973. His wife, Ludmilla, is Russian-born. Shapiro's office was decorated with pictures of himself with W. Averell Harriman and Nikita Khrushchev. Shapiro was a young man, thinner and balding in the pictures. Sitting before his plain, cluttered desk I could see how the Russians had dealt with him over the years. The Soviet effort to exert control over journalists had worked its way into his own system through a kind of osmosis.

The press corps, explained Shapiro, was divided into "camps." UPI and Agence France Presse were joined together against the Associated Press and Reuters. The obstacles to reporting laid down by the Soviet police and the Soviet bureaucracy demanded this kind of system, he said. His camp had the benefit of his own vast experience and contacts. In addition, he would provide free access to his office and use of the UPI news wire twenty-four hours a day. His staff would call to alert me on major news breaks. In return I would be expected to be completely loyal to him and his camp. I was not to share my information, samizdat material, or scoops from Russian sources with anybody else.

I politely but firmly told Shapiro that I would not join any camp but preferred to feel my way. He agreed to a trial period of informal cooperation with no binding rules, but warned that I would have to make a decision to join the camp or be excluded when the trial period ended. It never did. I got along well with him and with my colleagues at Reuters, AFP and AP. But Shapiro's system made it difficult.

Sharing a story is a violation of all the canons of American journalism. Being first and right is the rule to follow. Unfortunately, it is hard to follow in Moscow because being first and right too often about dissent is a sure way to expose your sources to the KGB and win the prize of expulsion for yourself. Although expulsion is a personal badge

of honor it causes competitive problems for major newspapers, magazines and wire services: it breaks the continuity in their coverage in
Moscow and leaves them without a man on the spot. An editor will
defend his man, but doesn't like to have him expelled.

It became necessary to set up an informal network of cooperation
and sharing of material received from the dissidents and members of
the democratic movement. The system was in effect when we covered
the activities of Pyotr Grigorenko, the fearless former major general
who defended the Crimean Tatars and their efforts to regain their
homeland; when we reported on the writings of historian Andrei
Amalrik, who questioned the premises on which the Soviet government operated; and when we reported the ouster of Solzhenitsyn from
the Writers' Union in November 1969.

The sharing of material, first of all, was a good way to check au-
thenticity and make sure that false statements were not picked up and
published. A ruse of the KGB is to try to plant a statement critical of
the Soviet government and have it published. Then the journalist who
publishes the false statement and the dissident movement, which supposedly issued it, can be discredited. Our sources asked us to share the
information they gave us because it was too difficult for them to reach
a number of correspondents without being discovered or apprehended
by the KGB. They naturally were more interested in having the widest
possible audience than in giving one correspondent a scoop. In October 1969 I received a detailed report on the arrest in Tallin of three
Soviet naval officers. The officers were part of a group of intellectuals
there who were preparing a program for the democratic movement
in the USSR. The group criticized the invasion of Czechoslovakia and
advocated sweeping changes in Soviet domestic and foreign policy.
My source handed me three copies of the materials and asked me to
deliver the two extras to the New York *Times* and the Washington
Post respectively. To have published the story alone would have
singled me and my sources out to the Soviet authorities. A continued
pattern would have led to expulsion. By sharing the dissident material
it was easier to divide responsibility. Thus, our stories carried the line:
"According to a statement widely circulated in Moscow." Even with
this rudimentary defense there was a constant battle to avoid directly
involving our Soviet sources and pointing to those who had given us
the material.

Under normal competitive conditions the wire services would race to file a dissident story, but in Moscow the consequences often weighed against breaking a controversial story first. UPI, and at times Reuters, held back on stories involving abuses in Soviet prison camps and the harassment of Solzhenitsyn, insisting it was a matter of "news judgment." Shapiro wanted to know what was "circulating" around town, but he sometimes declined to put a story on the wire. Instead, he would get the details of a protest and keep it in his top drawer. After AP or Reuters had sent the story UPI would get a call back from London asking why UPI did not have the story. Then Shapiro would file the story. By such a low posture Shapiro maintained favor with the Press Department. He was rewarded with advance information about Soviet space shots or given the right to call the head of the Press Department for official answers to such questions as whether Prime Minister Kosygin was sick or whether a foreign head of state was really in Moscow when his arrival had been reported by rumor alone.

The press alliances also had a natural geographic base since the camps were located on opposite sides of the city. Reuters, the New York *Times* and most of the British correspondents are housed in the same apartment house on Sadovo-Samotechnaya Street. The UPI, the Washington *Post, Time* and *Newsweek* are in the Kutuzovsky complex of apartment houses. The Scandinavian correspondents also lived on Kutuzovsky Prospekt. They and the West Germans often visited Shapiro to trade information and rumors.

One of Shapiro's closest confidants was Hermann Porzgen of the *Frankfurter Allgemeine Zeitung* who had been in Moscow before the war. Shapiro had traded information with Porzgen since 1941. In 1941, two days before the Germans invaded the Soviet Union, Shapiro arrived at Porzgen's apartment with a cable from UPI in Stockholm which read: "German troops will cross Russian border stop please watch." Porzgen recalled that Shapiro asked with resignation, "How can I watch?" When the German press attaché awoke Porzgen in the early hours of Sunday, June 22, to take him to the German Embassy for safety, Porzgen managed to get word to Shapiro: "Please watch." With that signal Shapiro had a potential historic scoop; but censorship prevented him from filing before the official announcement of the invasion was made by Foreign Minister Molotov at noon.

Shapiro had an unsurpassed depth of background and a finely tuned sensitivity to changes in Soviet policy. When a general died he could recall his military career in minute detail and remember whom his daughters had married, facts that were not on file in the Soviet Union or in encyclopedias. He could sense policy shifts by small word changes in *Pravda* and he knew at a glance how to assess a communiqué. His range of contacts and sources was massive and if he decided to go after a story he had no peers.

Yet the camp system led to friction within the foreign press corps and Shapiro administered his alliances firmly and often bitterly. He was judge and jury and he barred from his office offenders who shared news with the opposition. Given the problems of dealing with the Press Department the divisiveness of the camp system seemed to me to be self-defeating. Shapiro, subjected to the Soviet methods of control for as many years as I had lived, understood their ways. The camp system gave him his own sense of power.

In contrast to Shapiro stood a relative newcomer, the wry but persistent Italian correspondent Pietro Sormani of *Corriere della Sera,* who also lived and worked on Kutuzovsky Prospekt. I went to have morning coffee with him soon after I arrived. From him I learned about the unofficial art world in Moscow and the rules for survival as a journalist. Sormani became my link to Solzhenitsyn, but one of the rules I learned to accept was that he could not reveal his sources to me. Often we exchanged information, but nothing was used on face value; I always checked information three ways before I put it into a file to New York. Sormani agreed that I should not join the UPI camp and he gave me wise advice: "You can write almost anything as long as it is not couched in openly anti-Soviet terms. Be sure of the facts on which you base your judgments. These are the two most important requisites if you want to keep on reasonably good terms with the authorities. Of course they will object to your stories as they do to mine, but if you are sure of the facts and use moderate language they will not take strong measures against you."

For my first six months in Moscow there was no Telex machine in the *Time-Life* office. That meant filing through the Central Telegraph Office with duplicate copies every evening. Each page had to be addressed separately and numbered. From Moscow to New York took five to eight hours on long stories. The cost was eight cents a word at the ordinary press rate, and thirty cents a word for urgent cables, which I soon learned didn't move any faster.

The Central Telegraph Office, like the railway stations, suggests the diversity of people and lifestyles in the Soviet Union. There is always a line of people waiting to use the long distance telephones — Georgians, Armenians, Uzbeks, people from the Baltic states. Even at midnight the telegraph office, with its big doors and wide steps opening to the broad counters and booths, is alive. There is the feeling of stepping into a theater in the middle of a pantomime played by a constantly shifting cast. Meeting colleagues at the international telegraph counter was always a good way to check the latest rumor or newsbreak. When the Telex came to the office I looked back on the visits to the Central Telegraph Office with mixed nostalgia. The convenience of being able to dial Paris or New York directly from the office replaced the nightly drive past the Kremlin and Red Square to file. The extra copy I made for the telegraph office was no longer necessary. All outgoing Telex messages are centrally monitored. I knew, as did my colleagues, that nothing was personal or confidential to my editors although it might be so marked. Sometimes I wrote cables I hoped would be read by the authorities who monitored the Telex. By explaining to my editors that self-censorship was in effect they would know that there was more to the story but that it could not be filed and would be coming via a "pigeon," a friendly traveler or fellow journalist leaving Moscow who would post a letter or deliver a cable.

In an atmosphere where I was constantly being watched and monitored I tried not to use the telephone for detailed conversation. The phone was for making appointments. With Russian friends I would use a pay phone. Even then, we arranged a meeting place in advance, and I would only say: "See you at eight at the usual place." The system added drudgery to the day. Normal telephone interviews required an advance appointment by phone, then a trip back and forth across town; minutes of work became hours.

Visiting East European colleagues was most pleasant. The Yugoslavs and Romanians invariably offered a cup of thick coffee and a light native brandy to stimulate our exchange of news and views. The Communist world had its own hierarchy that matched roughly the level of each country's state and Communist Party relations with the

Soviet Union. The Poles and East Germans were on the top since they conformed best both in foreign policy and internal matters. Then came the Bulgarians, the truck gardeners of the bloc, the source of Soviet fresh fruits and canned vegetables. Their journalists, like the Hungarians, were well informed but lacked the scope and influence of the Yugoslavs and Romanians. The Yugoslavs and Romanians were at the bottom of the Communist hierarchy because of their independent leadership. Nevertheless they were the most sophisticated of the Communist correspondents and the least dogmatic. They were loyal socialists but understood the nuances of national self-interest that were sweeping through the bloc. Thus, they were the least trusted by the Soviet authorities. The Czechs, imaginative and daring during the days of the invasion, had turned docile. Their correspondents were shifted and the Czech press brutally disciplined for "the events of August 1968," as the Russians preferred to call their invasion.

The only way to get a line on what happened at Warsaw Pact meetings or on talks between the East Germans and the Russians was through Communist colleagues. What they told me then had to be triangulated with other sources. The Communist correspondents had more access to the Ministry of Foreign Affairs than Westerners and they were briefed by the Central Committee of the Communist Party. Their ambassadors had ready access to Soviet officials and through their own bloc network had developed a sharp sense of Soviet policy toward Europe and the United States. But when it came to Communist China, Soviet policy remained a blur, even for members of the bloc. As tensions increased between the Soviet Union and China during the border fighting in 1969, the East Europeans became more accessible and more talkative. Ideological control and conformity loosened markedly among the East European Communist allies despite the outward show of unity. The new threat from the East changed our lives in Moscow.

Clinging wet snow and a sharp, chilling wind whipped across the wide boulevard separating the Embassy of the People's Republic of China from Moscow University. The still of the enveloping whiteness was broken by the throb of diesel engines. Buses poured on to Friendship Street and disgorged hundreds of workers who waved crudely lettered slogans painted onto bed sheets and cardboard placards: "Shame on Mao," "Hands Off Damansky Island," "Mao

Tse-Tung Is an Imperialist." A straw-stuffed effigy of Mao with a rope around its neck was borne on the shoulders of the crowd as it swirled past the locked front entrance of the embassy. Hundreds of policemen in blue greatcoats with red epaulets and white billy clubs lined the street, arm in arm, to maintain order.

The demonstrators emerged from the buses at one end of the street, marched past the embassy shouting epithets, then climbed back aboard the buses, which had followed the marchers' route and were now waiting at the other end of the street. Other traffic was backed up for blocks, settling helplessly into the snowfall.

TASS reported that the demonstrations in front of the Chinese Embassy were "a spontaneous outpouring of public wrath," but the eye could see that they had been carefully organized. The Chinese had harassed Soviet diplomats in Peking and barricaded the Russian Embassy there following the outbreak of fighting over Damansky Island in the Ussuri River on Sunday, March 2, 1969. Now the Soviets were retaliating. After the vicious initial skirmishing along the Sino-Soviet border, propaganda and "rent-a-crowd" demonstrations were carried on to fight the ideological battle.

I joined the stream of marchers past the Chinese Embassy. Fathers carried small children on their shoulders and mothers held youngsters by the hand as they marched. Per Egil Hegge of *Aftenposten* in Oslo reminded me that it was International Woman's Day, a public holiday in Moscow. While many of the marchers clenched their fists and shouted in anger as they reached the front of the embassy, they seemed to enjoy the holiday diversion in the snowfall.

The initial demonstration had taken place the previous day, when "angry citizens" hurled bottles of colored ink against the yellow exterior of the embassy living quarters. They threw stones at windows and broke street lamps.

On the second day, since mothers and children were present, orders had been given for a nonviolent demonstration. Four sound trucks with loudspeakers shouted the cues for slogans: "Soviet borders are inviolable," "Shame on Chinese provocators," and "The Maoists are in collusion with American imperialists."

Covering the border war in the frozen East five thousand miles from Moscow was impossible. I submitted a letter to the Press Department as soon as the fighting was announced on March 5, asking to go to the area separating the Soviet Union's maritime territory from Manchuria. I never got a response. Nor would the Press Department permit foreign correspondents to fly to Khabarovsk, the closest city open to foreigners, forty-five hundred miles away. The only way to learn what was happening was to read Soviet press reports and to meet with Soviet correspondents and photographers covering the fighting. Yevgeny Yevtushenko joined the battle with a poem titled "On the Red Ussuri Snow." Wrote Yevtushenko: "A heavy hand creeps across our border, the Chinese god Khan." TASS distributed pictures of armed Chinese soldiers on the Ussuri River ice and on Damansky Island. One picture contained only the blood-stained identification card of a soldier. The Russians said he had taken the pictures just before he was killed by the Chinese.

On March 15 the fighting broke out again as the Russians mounted a counteroffensive to remove the Chinese from the small island and demonstrate their firepower. Although the Soviet press reported clashes between infantry and light artillery, Soviet newsmen who covered the fighting had a different version. Over vodka and smoked salmon at the Ukraine Hotel I met with a Novosti cameraman fresh from the front. He reported that in the twelve days since the initial Chinese attack, which had killed thirty-one Soviet border guards and wounded forty-one, the Soviet military had massed firepower in the area. The aim, he explained, "was to teach the Chinese a lesson. The ice was black with shell bursts as we massed Katusha rockets and bombed and strafed the Chinese with helicopters and jets. Tanks and armored cars headed the assault," the photographer told me. To the world the fighting was supposed to be an infantry battle in which the Soviet troops had defeated the Chinese on equal terms. But for the Chinese the Russians massed the best of their conventional firepower, demonstrating their superiority on the ground with armored personnel carriers and tanks, and in the air with jets and helicopters for close-in support.

The border war with China changed the atmosphere and working conditions in Moscow. The tension and aloofness that followed the invasion of Czechoslovakia broke. There was a perceptible official softening toward American correspondents. Russian sources were willing to talk about the border war and were anxious to learn American views about China. There was a new threat to "the motherland" that dwarfed the fear of loss of Soviet control in Eastern Europe. The Russians have a racial memory of Mongol and Tatar invasions from the East, of being overwhelmed by a "yellow peril." At Vladimir, the capital of the Kiev state in 1400, the Tatars swept into bloody control, and the museum walls in the old capital are still hung with lurid scenes of the conquest. The population pressure of China — 870 million versus 250 million in the Soviet Union — remains a constant threat. There were bitter jokes that spring about how the Russians could win a war against China only if the Chinese practiced birth control. The Russians mocked the Chinese as being quarrelsome, irrational and warlike. The cultural smugness and self-sufficiency of the Chinese rankled.

Beneath the stilted language of the formal attacks on Mao, racism was rising and spreading like a poison gas. In April, at the time of the Ninth Chinese People's Congress in Peking, *Izvestia* denounced the "Maoist clique," and attacked the Congress as "a new organization which has nothing in common with the Communist Party of China and with international Communism." In private conversations the Russians were more pointed. It was not the first time that I had heard the Russians privately warn against the danger from the Chinese. In Laos in the early 1960's when Khrushchev and Kennedy were trying to prevent an open conflict between the United States and the USSR, Russian journalists, after a few drinks, would warn that "we white men must prevent the Chinese from taking control in Asia."

In 1969 the fear spread along the four-thousand-mile border between Russia and China. On both sides of the border there are minority nationalities — Uighurs, Kazakhs, Buryats and Uzbeks. Through propaganda broadcasts, minority programs and infiltration teams, each side was trying to strengthen its own frontiers and sow dissension in the enemy camp. In winning the allegiance of the minority peoples the Russians have a distinctive disadvantage — their skin color. The Russians feared that if the Chinese created enough turmoil, the Uzbeks, Uighurs and Buryat peoples might be encouraged to form separatist movements.

Nationalism is the political virus the Soviet leaders fear most. Separation of one minority could lead to the breakup of the Union of Soviet Socialist Republics. The Ukraine, the Baltic States, and the Central Asian minorities might all follow if any one of them broke away. Only the Chinese have the real potential to create a separatist movement along the border.

The Russians cannot fathom Mao Tse-tung as a revolutionary. He has always been an enigma. He won China over Stalin's early opposition and without his support during World War II. Mao succeeded by following his own policy: fostering peasant nationalism and winning the Chinese Revolution in the countryside. Stalin and Marxist doctrine would have had him win in the city with workers. When Stalin returned Port Arthur and Manchuria to China in 1950, he signed a twenty-five-year treaty of friendship with Mao, but not before he kept Mao waiting for six weeks in Moscow, treating him like a dubious young upstart. Now the Chinese were reminding the world that Lenin had promised to return lands the tsars had taken from China. The days of China's recognition of the Soviet Union as the leader of the Communist world were over. The Chinese attacked the Soviet leaders, calling them Russian imperialists following in the footsteps of the tsars. National interest predominated over Communist ideology.

By April there were reports that a Soviet military buildup along the border was in progress and that troops were being shifted from European Russia to the Chinese border. The Russian troops were to increase there from 250,000 to more than 500,000. Over morning coffee in his office in the American Embassy I asked the American army attaché if he could provide hard details on the buildup. Turning up the recorded background music to foil any attempts at bugging, the colonel said he had heard reports from fellow attachés of the movement of both troops and equipment.

The colonel told me that he had paid a courtesy call on the army chief of staff, Marshal M. V. Zakharov, who had been the Soviet commander in Germany when the colonel was serving on the headquarters staff during the Allied occupation. Zakharov welcomed the American with whom he had often drunk toasts at long banquets. After recalling their postwar days, he talked about the new border war and told the colonel: "Mao is a madman capable of starting a nuclear war." There was, however, no criticism of Premier Chou En-lai. Chou was the man the Soviet leaders felt they could negotiate with. I heard a similar line from my Russian contacts. Chou was a rational statesman, they told me, while Mao and his Cultural Revolution had nothing to do with Marxism-Leninism. At *Pravda* the word was that Mao had started the border war as a diversion to win support and tide him through the closing days of the Cultural Revolution as he sought to control the power of the army.

On a trip to Kazan, capital of the Tatar Autonomous Republic, five hundred miles east of Moscow, I asked to meet with university students. We broke up into small groups and enjoyed the usual talk about the differences between American and Soviet student life. Then, I asked if the students had any questions for me. A thin, bright young man in an open-necked white shirt asked: "What would the United States do if there was a nuclear war between China and the Soviet Union?" I explained as best I could that the United States would try to avert nuclear war between China and Russia, but that we would not take advantage of the dispute or openly side with either party. Certainly, there should be peaceful coexistence practiced between Communist states, I offered. "The Chinese are not Communists; they are barbarians," replied the student.

The Russians were fascinated and threatened by the Cultural Revolution. They saw in its pattern of revolutionary excesses a grim warning, a preview of what could happen if their own youth were infected with too much revolutionary zeal. They believed that the Cultural Revolution masked a deep Chinese leadership struggle. Not only was Mao trying to instill revolutionary ardor in a generation which had not known war or revolution; he was also struggling for supremacy in the Chinese leadership.

Chinese motivations became a favorite dinner-party subject. At the Canadian Embassy, Teresa Ford, Ambassador Robert Ford's charming wife, told us how she had offered her unique interpretation of affairs to a senior official in the Ministry of Foreign Affairs. What was really happening, she explained with a straight face, was that Madame Mao and Defense Minister Lin Piao were having an affair. That accounted for the military support for and the influence of the Cultural Revolution group, of which Madame Mao was vice chairman. A week later the suggestion of personal affinity between Madame Mao and Lin Piao appeared in a Soviet journal, Mrs. Ford recalled. "The next time I saw the minister I told him that if he wanted me to run his propaganda organization, he would have to pay me," she said and her guests laughed.

My years in Hong Kong and Tokyo had initiated me as a China watcher, and I now enjoyed the company of Burt White, the Canadian Communist, who was in Moscow after ten years in Peking. He was jovial, open and never dogmatic. Burt had joined the Canadian Communist Party through the labor movement, and now wrote a weekly column for the *Canadian Tribune*. He and his wife also worked

as translators. Puffing on a Cuban cigar he would recall his own organizing days in the mines of Canada. To Burt, Communism meant
organizing the labor movement, and he retained a strong belief in the
importance of individual rights and liberties despite his Party affilia-
tion. He was an anachronism, a holdover from the early idealism of
the Communist Party in North America; he retained his charm and
earthy, nonideological approach to life. He found bureaucracy difficult
to stomach in any society.

The Whites invited Leona and me to a party he was giving for
his old friends. Out of the Moscow woodwork, the obscure institutes,
and the Party offices came the China watchers whom White had known
over the years in Peking. It was a strange gathering. Adam Kellet-Long,
the Reuters bureau chief, his wife and we were the only non-
Communists there. The rest of the guests were Russian journalists
who had served in Peking and now analyzed Chinese developments in
Moscow, and some American Communists who had come to Moscow
in the 1930's and lingered on. There was a young Russian engineer
with a Canadian wife. The group was outside both the diplomatic list
and official lines. The scotch flowed freely and so did the talk. There
were old-boy tales about how difficult it was to work in Peking. Yet
even in the atmosphere of professional intimacy there was no comprehension of the Cultural Revolution in China. No one seemed to understand what Mao was trying to do with an entire generation of young
people who had experienced neither the Long March, nor the war
against Chiang Kai-shek and Japan, nor the Korean War. The Russians I met during that long evening aspired to be privileged people
in a classless society. They wanted cars, blue jeans, scotch and wigs
(which were then the most popular new ladies' style). For them revolution was a process which brought summer dachas, fancy appliances
and phonograph records. The Chinese were a race apart. Mao would
lead the world into war for the sake of his revolution, and they had
had enough war. Late into the night in the smoke-filled shabby Moscow apartment the appeal was repeated: let the white men of the world
protect themselves against the yellow hordes from the Ussuri River,
from the deserts of Sinkiang and the Pamir Mountains of Central Asia.
As long as Mao lived, reconciliation would be difficult, they told me,
indicating that the propaganda attacks on Mao would increase.

Throughout the summer of 1969, the Russians continued to warn the Chinese of the danger of going to war. The respected poet, novelist and playwright Konstantin Simonov, who had been a war correspondent in World War II, went to Damansky Island and wrote an angry series of articles for *Pravda*. "War cannot always be stopped — history has taught us that. It is our duty to remember it," he warned. Then in August, only a week before the first anniversary of the Soviet invasion of Czechoslovakia, small-scale fighting broke out again at a frontier post. There was talk of a "preventive" Soviet nuclear strike against the Chinese atomic bomb facility in Lop Nor in the Sinkiang Desert. *Pravda* accused the Chinese of playing with nuclear fire on August 28, 1969, in an editorial titled "The Chinese Adventurist Course": "In view of the existing techniques, lethal weapons and modern means for their delivery, a war, should it flare up in the conditions of our times, would not leave a single continent unaffected." In Communist jargon this was a blunt threat of nuclear war against China.

I met Dmitri the first week I was in Moscow. He came to the office and Felix introduced him to me as a "friend of the office." Dmitri had begun his career translating for one of the first *Life* photographers in the bureau. His English and French were excellent. Now he worked for Novosti as a special correspondent.

Of medium height, with a ready smile and tight eyes, he had an air of complete control. He told me we would meet periodically, and he would help me to travel inside the Soviet Union and introduce me to Russians. Felix later explained that we provided him copies of *Time* and *Life* every week and obtained the latest English language books on Russia for him. "Is he really only a correspondent for Novosti?" I asked Felix naïvely. Felix smiled and shrugged.

Dmitri was helpful the first week after the invasion of Czechoslovakia. He told me there would be a new Czech government named within days and gave me possible names for the new cabinet. When the puppet government did not materialize I realized that Soviet plans for a quick takeover had gone awry.

Cautiously, I felt out my colleagues to see if they had similar relationships. Dick Reston of the Los Angeles *Times* mentioned one day, "My plant told me the space shot was coming." Other correspondents indicated they had a Russian source who backgrounded them on sensitive subjects. One of my colleagues referred to his unofficial source as his *mamka,* literally little mamma or babysitter. The term has come to mean a combination of ideological handholder and stool pigeon, depending on the context in which it is used. Mamkas usually work for the Committee for State Security (KGB). Every Soviet delegation abroad has a mamka to report back on the behavior and ideological deport- ment of the members and to prevent defections. Among foreign cor- respondents the term *mamka* or "my plant" was used to define the so-called Soviet journalist who "mothered" us. The mamka might offer tidbits of news and details not available in the Soviet press. Or he would try to spread disinformation about the private lives of dissidents or writers like Solzhenitsyn who were in disfavor. The job of the mamka is to report on and assess the work of the correspondent, to ascertain his sources and provide the material for his dossier that is kept by the MID. A sophisticated operator like Dmitri tried to discover trends in American attitudes, spot new policies and glean information that could be of value to his superiors. I soon found that only corres- pondents from newspapers and magazines of large circulation — the only ones considered "serious" (the Soviets never acknowledge that the Western press is influential) — rated a mamka.

Some correspondents resented the system and limited or cut off their relations with their mamkas. Others, myself included, accepted them as part of the Moscow lifestyle and tried to use our mamkas more than they used us. A good mamka provides glimpses into the Party and state security apparatus, and thus can dispense details and nuances far more valuable than anything that comes officially or even unofficially from the Press Department. Distinguishing between this information and actuality is the hardest part of the job in Moscow. In a closed system the worst enemy is isolation. Thus, even the plant and the line he is promoting is officially motivated. However, only a hard bit of news like a space-shot schedule can be taken at face value from a plant.

Shortly after I arrived Dmitri called to say that there would be a space shot in six hours. It was early in the week; the shot would be public knowledge long before my deadline came. I decided to build some credits with my colleagues who worked on daily and wire service deadlines and called around town announcing the space-shot news. The shot came off that evening as Dmitri predicted and I was pleased.

The next time Dmitri came to the office for his magazine I asked him to tell me about a scheduled meeting between the Russians and the Egyptians. He smiled and said, "How can I tell you anything when it spreads all over town?" I changed the subject but his remark confirmed a fact I had suspected. I knew that the rule of not talking about anything important on the office phone was not a figment of unwarranted paranoia. Dmitri had obviously been testing me, but I had also tested him. Now I was certain my phone was tapped.

I wondered what he had in mind next. Felix had told me that Dmitri was interested in American attitudes toward the Soviet Union but that covered a lot of ground. Soon Dmitri invited me to lunch. We met at the House of Journalists on Suvorovsky Boulevard in the Arbat section just off Kalinin Prospekt, Moscow's "golden mile" of new shops and office buildings. A former nobleman's house converted into a club, the House of Journalists was closed to Western correspondents except on Thursday nights. Dmitri had reserved a table and seemed to know the redheaded waitress well. She hovered over us making recommendations. Dmitri carefully ordered three hundred grams of vodka, a bottle of red wine, mineral water, caviar, sturgeon with horseradish, and an assortment of finely chopped herring, liver and eggplant in pastry shells, then fresh tomatoes and cucumbers (out of season) in a sour cream dressing.

After a toast to our wives we settled down to conversation on my problems in Moscow. There was no telephone in my apartment, I complained. Dmitri promised to help. Part of his charm was that he promised to do almost everything I asked, yet I rarely knew if he made good on any of his promises. Still, having him there to talk to was helpful: a live, interested Russian was fielding my requests and possibly doing something about them. When it came to my story ideas, requests for interviews and trips, he was full of enthusiasm.

For the main course Dmitri ordered giant fillets of beef with fried onions and potatoes. Dessert was a Moscow sundae: ice cream with strawberry jam and a ladyfinger. Turkish coffee and three hundred grams of brandy followed. Dmitri told me that his wife was completing a thesis on radical political movements among American blacks. As we downed our second brandy and ordered more coffee Dmitri asked me what I thought of Svetlana Alliluyeva's second book, *Only One Year*. Her first book, *Letters to a Friend*, published after her escape to the West, was an instant bestseller that had subjected the Soviet system to widespread publicity and criticism. I had read *Only One Year* and followed the reviews closely. Aside from its descriptions of life among the privileged Politburo set, the book lacked both a sense of history or any real insight into how the decision-making process occurs in the Soviet Union. It was a series of remembrances: poignant, brutal, yet sometimes quaint. Svetlana's life as an isolated Politburo princess came through clearly. When Dmitri asked me, "What do you think the best way to treat the book would be?" I was somewhat surprised.

"The best response would be no response," I replied. "There are critics in the West who have made telling points about Svetlana's personality." I mentioned the review in *Commentary* by Richard Poirier in which he said that the only way to read her book "is not as history but as a romantic novel." I argued that any official Soviet attack would raise the importance of her book and would heighten tensions caused by her taking refuge in the United States. "She is hardly a political force and should be left alone to live her life."

Dmitri listened carefully. "Thank you, that's a very interesting analysis."

Then I referred to what Svetlana had said about life inside the closed upper circle and asked Dmitri if the pattern of privilege still existed. I mentioned Brezhnev's penchant for foreign cars and asked Dmitri if it were true that Brezhnev drove a Rolls-Royce, a Jaguar and a Mercedes. Dmitri avoided a direct reply on the cars, but went on to tell me that Brezhnev, Podgorny and Kosygin had spent the weekend together at a Politburo dacha outside Moscow where all three had gone cross-country skiing. Kosygin, who was ill, had not been seen in public for weeks. His liver ailment, however, was improving, and Brezhnev and Podgorny, according to Dmitri, had come to visit him. Dmitri assured me there was no split in the collective leadership. I made a mental note of the date and circumstances he described, planning to check with other sources.

Lunches with Dmitri were never casual. He would try to find out who my sources were for dissident stories, or how correspondents had received a certain statement from the physicist Andrei Sakharov. I smiled and told him that I could not reveal my sources. Then, in a roundabout way he talked of the need for balanced coverage. It was important, he said, not to emphasize the activities of a few people who did not represent the broad mass of Soviet opinion. He never openly warned me not to send material on conditions in prison camps and on the persecution of political prisoners in psychiatric wards. Still, a warning was hardly necessary. His more indirect approach told me I was endangering the status of the new bureau by not providing "balanced" coverage.

Most of the time Dmitri and I discussed the Vietnam war or the goals of the socialist state and whether or not they were being fulfilled. I always tried not to be critical in blunt ideological or cold war terms; rather I pointed out how Soviet actions would be interpreted in the West and argued from the logic of mutual self-interest. We didn't discuss arms control, military matters or budgets. These were off limits and could easily be misinterpreted as areas for espionage. Dmitri was particularly forceful in discussing the abuses of the Chinese; he stressed the way in which they were pushing the Soviet Union into confrontation along the border.

There were long lapses in our contacts. I took these as a sign either that relations between the United States and the Soviet Union were strained or that internal problems were forcing the leadership into other concerns. When we met again after each lapse Dmitri acted as if the interruption had never occurred. He tantalized us with promises: the family would go skiing, or fishing and camping in the summer; he would give us a taste of Russian country life. None of these grand plans ever materialized. His friendship was carefully controlled so that except for an evening he and his wife spent with Leona when I was out of Moscow, we saw him at home only once. On that occasion, he came without his wife and traded stamps with the children.

Although he often spread vicious rumors about the private lives of dissidents, Dmitri was also a source of information that was both credible and valuable. While most of the space shots he forecast came off on schedule, one did not. Thus we had a key clue that there had been an accident on the launching pad in Central Asia.

In Moscow, finding out the official line is often itself news. On January 22, 1969, there was an assassination attempt in the Kremlin. The Press Department would admit only that shots had been fired near the Kremlin gate.

The shooting occurred during a celebration for the cosmonauts who had successfully docked Soyuz 4 and 5 in space. They proceeded from Vnukovo II, the official airport, down the Leninsky Prospekt VIP route to the Borovitsky Gate of the Kremlin. Although a number of correspondents were standing at the bottom of the gateway to the

Kremlin they neither saw nor heard anything. The shooting took place after the motorcade had passed the gate post and had turned out of sight onto the cobblestones inside the Kremlin next to the Armory. I went to Vnukovo II to watch the arrival of the cosmonauts and then returned to the office to watch the ceremonies on television. There was a brief blank on the screen as the cars turned into the Kremlin, then the scene shifted to the stage of the Palace of Congresses. For ten minutes the camera focused on the empty stage until the cosmonauts came out and the ceremony began.

That evening the word began to circulate that there had been a shooting at the Kremlin. The story was all over Moscow; cab drivers, maids, diplomats and correspondents began to sort out the details. By Thursday morning the Press Department was besieged with calls demanding confirmation and details. In one case, a rival wire service was told by a Press Department official, "Call Agence France Presse, they have the account." An enterprising British colleague walked up to the Borovitsky Gate and asked a policeman to describe the shooting. "You'll read about it in TASS," replied the guard, turning away from the journalist.

As I sat in my office phoning around town I began to develop a picture, but two big *W*s, who and why, were still unknown. A Mongolian journalist who had been inside the Kremlin wall had seen the actual shooting. He described the assailant as a man dressed in a policeman's uniform who helped control the crowd inside the Kremlin. Then, as the cars began to enter, the "policeman" turned, knelt and fired six shots from his revolver at the second car in the motorcade.

Midmorning on Thursday Dmitri called. He volunteered sketchy details. He said the gunman was twenty years old and "mentally disturbed." The crowd jumped on him after he fired the shots and he was quickly taken into custody by the policemen inside the Kremlin. The gunman resented the cosmonauts and was disturbed by the long week of praise they were enjoying. Dmitri said, "His name and identity are still not available." From what Dmitri told me I knew the motive had been officially established and the Soviet authorities had decided how they would deal with the assassination attempt. The Soviet press held the view that assassinations in the United States are not the work of individual madmen but are part of broader conspiracies.

If the assailant was aiming for the cosmonauts why had he not fired at the first open car, where a group of them were riding? Instead

he fired at the closed second car, which contained Cosmonaut Beregovoi who looks very much like Leonid Brezhnev. Beregovoi was wearing the same sort of tall gray Persian lamb *shapka* (hat) that Brezhnev
wore in winter. Their broad flat faces, both with wide noses and heavy
eyebrows, their gray fur hats, and their bulky, stocky physiques made
them markedly similar.

I found it odd that Dmitri could tell me the man's age and that
he was mentally disturbed, but could not tell me his name or other
details of his background. By emphasizing the gunman's hatred of the
cosmonauts, the government line clearly aimed at discouraging speculation that the attempt had been directed against Brezhnev, Nikolai
Podgorny or Dmitri Polyansky, who were all in the motorcade.

The Press Department had not even confirmed the details of the
shooting when at 6:30 P.M. on Thursday, twenty-eight hours after the
shooting, the first sketchy TASS story with the headline "provocation"
appeared on the wire. According to TASS, "a provocation took place
on Wednesday when the pilot cosmonauts were welcomed to Moscow.
Several shots were fired at the car in which the cosmonauts Beregovoi,
Nikolayeva-Tereshkova, Nikolayev and Leonov were driven. The driver
of the car and a motorcycle driver who accompanied the motorcade
were wounded. Not one (repeat) not one of the cosmonauts was in-
jured. The person who fired the shots was detained on the spot. The
investigation is being conducted. Item ends."

Try as I might to get him to give me more details, Dmitri gave
me nothing more. He indicated he had been briefed before he called
me and what he presented was an authorized background account. I
attributed it to Soviet sources in my file.

Soviet citizens were at first incredulous on hearing the news, and
then wondered if the shooting was a prelude to a purge as part of a
wider plot. The Kremlin shooting brought back lurid images of the
assassinations of Sergei Kirov, the Leningrad Party leader, on December 1, 1934, which triggered Stalin's great terror, the purges of the
1930's.

How did the assassin get into the Kremlin in a policeman's uniform? Where did he get two revolvers? Guns are carefully controlled
in the Soviet Union.

I exchanged my early information from Dmitri with Ed Stevens
of the *Sunday Times* of London and we sat trying to piece together

what we knew about the shooting. Stevens's wide range of Russian contacts came in handy. By Saturday morning he had learned a few things from a theater manager who knew the policemen at their headquarters near the Kremlin. The gunman was an army lieutenant from Leningrad who had come to Moscow and had taken his brother-in-law's uniform and gun. He already had one gun of his own as an army officer. One version said he was a topographer, but we still could not get his name. The details thus far fitted with the account from Communist journalists who had been inside the Kremlin gate when the shooting occurred. They added a further fact: the gunman, after firing five shots from two pistols, was beaten by the crowd before he could swallow two cyanide tablets he had pinned to his blue greatcoat.

The first report — that the man firing the shots was dressed as a policeman — came from Ed Stevens. He sent it to the *Sunday Times,* but a copyeditor in London changed Stevens's story to read that the gunman was dressed as a Kremlin guard, a key difference. Speculation rose anew of a plot against Brezhnev. A press conference with the cosmonauts on Friday elicited nothing more than a repetition of the TASS account by Cosmonaut Leonov, who avoided any new details and instead shifted to a description of weightlessness. Leonov said he preferred to talk about how he felt in space, not how he felt at the time of the shooting.

Tony Shub of the Washington *Post* found out that the gunman was named Ilyin, but he was wrong in reporting that Ilyin had swallowed the cyanide capsules and had died. Dmitri called a week after the shooting to confirm the name and insist that "the gunman was an amateur." By amateur he meant that he was working alone. The provocation, he explained patiently, was not a conspiracy. Dmitri confirmed that there was an alarm out for an army lieutenant missing from his unit in Leningrad.

My colleagues began to write about the shooting in the context of tensions within the leadership. Premier Aleksei Kosygin had not been seen in public since the end of December and questions were being raised more and more openly about his presence and status. The Press Department suddenly decided to leak to a favorite that Kosygin was on vacation. The week after the shooting they announced that Kosygin would return to work in a week.

The shooting coincided with reports of a rift in the Kremlin. By

March there were rumors of a letter from Politburo members criticizing Brezhnev and Kosygin. The letter's existence was officially denied by a government spokesman, but the rumors persisted.

We waited and watched for the investigation report. Although we made periodic inquiries, nothing more was said publicly about the shooting. In the spring of 1970 the head of the Kremlin guards was changed. On March 20, 1970, under a headline, "In the Supreme Court of the U.S.S.R.," *Izvestia* carried a brief story that said: "As has been reported in the press, on January 22, 1969, during a ceremony honoring the cosmonauts in Moscow, an unknown citizen in the crowd fired several shots at the car in which cosmonauts — comrades Beregovoi, Nikolayeva-Tereshkova, Nikolayev and Leonov — were riding. As a result of the shots, the driver of the car was fatally wounded and a motorcyclist who accompanied the motorcade was slightly wounded. The man who did the shooting was detained. He appeared to be Ilyin, born in 1947 in Leningrad. During the course of the investigation a forensic medical examination was conducted by full member of the Academy of Medical Sciences A. V. Snechnevsky, corresponding members of the Academy of Medical Sciences V. M. Morozov and G. V. Morozov and other scientist-psychiatrists. The examination established that Ilyin suffers from chronic mental disease in the form of schizophrenia. After it considered the report of the investigation, heard the findings of the experts and interrogated witnesses, the court found that Ilyin committed the socially dangerous actions in an unresponsible mental state.

"Taking into consideration that Ilyin is a socially dangerous person, the court decided to isolate him from society and sent him to a special psychiatric hospital for compulsory treatment."

The announcement that Ilyin was declared insane appeared to be timed to end speculation that there was an assassination plot against Brezhnev. The government decided not to hold an open trial involving his family and implicating others. The word was spread that the assassination attempt was directed against the cosmonauts. Our children heard at school that the assassin was aiming at the cosmonauts. For the correspondents, as well as for some Soviet citizens, the probability lingered that the gunman aimed at the cosmonaut who looked like Leonid Brezhnev. The story making the rounds in Moscow was that the gunman fired at the second car because Brezhnev usually trav-

els in the second car in a motorcade. On the day of the shooting Brezhnev switched cars under a bridge near the Kremlin and entered through
another gate, missing his usual place in the motorcade and the assassin's bullets.

Leona. When Dmitri came to dinner it was obvious that he spoke
English well and yearned to speak it better. He reveled in English as
a connoisseur luxuriates in his collections. Each new idiom or bit of
slang was an acquisition to be prized and savored. He expressed his
feelings best in his admiration for Nabokov. "Every Russian I know
who really knows English is jealous of Nabokov. Whether or not you
like his writing, look at what he, a Russian like us, has done with
English."

English is necessary to his job, which among ourselves we tagged
"messenger of disinformation." Ostensibly he worked for Novosti, and
was assigned to befriend a few foreign journalists. At the same time
he held, covertly, a major's rank in the Committee for State Security
(KGB), we learned later from an American diplomat.

His friendship with Jerry was an obvious game, which we named
"Who can use whom more?" The informal rules called for us to bring
him ski gear from Paris or parts for his motorboat from Helsinki.
Dmitri promised trips to Siberia and to cities where foreign journalists
rarely trod. Soon after he and Jerry met, Dmitri held out the promise
of a meeting with his beautiful wife, over whose charm he waxed eloquent after a little vodka. Galya, he explained, was brilliant. Her doc-
toral thesis on American blacks would break new ground in the Soviet
Union. Her forefathers, he confided proudly, were aristocrats, one of
the princely families leveled by the Great October Revolution. Dmitri
and Jerry planned an evening at the ballet for the four of us, and I
looked forward to meeting them.

It happened that on the day of the ballet Jerry was out of the
country, so I went ahead alone to meet Dmitri and Galya. We had
never seen each other, but they knew I would be waiting in front of
the theater, wearing a red fox coat which would easily distinguish me
from the crowd.

I arrived a few minutes early and leisurely watched the theatergoers entering the row of glass doors. They in turn eyed me with
curiosity; they could tell at a glance I was not one of them. A few had

changed into festive clothes for an evening at the theater. One wore a deep-necked brown velvet dress, reaching just below the knees, with modest but fine gems on the tips of her pierced ears, reminiscent of a prewar era. Had her mother worn the same dress back in the twenties, perhaps to a performance directed by the great Meyerhold? Or had she found it in a commission shop, where occasional elegance showed up in the racks of old clothes on sale by consignment?

Most of the ladies who had dressed for the occasion wore the square-cut Italian knit jacket sweaters with matching skirts available in the hard-currency stores. How they had laid hands on the dollars or the coupons held almost as much mystery as the origin of the brown velvet dress. What favors were spent on these fashions not available to the average Russian? Had they earned their knits as file clerks in the offices of the secret police? Or by active attendance at the cell meetings of the Communist Party in their apartment houses?

Most of the theatergoers had come straight from their offices in the same homemade synthetics or brightly colored handknit sweaters they had worn all day. Communist Party members or government officials like Dmitri can obtain tickets on short notice, but these shopladies and office workers had waited in long lines months before to buy tickets for this night's performance. It would take too long to travel home from work and back again to the theater, so a come-as-you-are informality is the look of most of Moscow's theater crowds, even at the Bolshoi.

I waited patiently, then impatiently as the stream of ticket-holders faded away. The hopeful ones looking to buy last-minute extra tickets gave up, and I was left alone. At last Dmitri and Galya arrived, just in time for the curtain, explaining with apologies that they had been to lunch at a friend's house. The eating and drinking were still going on and they had barely managed to pull themselves away, at almost eight in the evening.

Dmitri greeted me with an uneasy boyish smile. He was of little less than medium height, trim but not thin, pleasant-looking but not handsome. Only his dark, intelligent eyes were bold and sparkling, and he managed to hide them behind dark-rimmed glasses. He introduced himself and Galya to me breathlessly as we rushed to check our coats and find our seats before the lights went down. She wore an undistinguished gray sweater with a darker skirt over a fullness of figure that is not considered overweight among Soviet women. Her face, skin and hair, borne high by her straight carriage, justified the obvious pride Dmitri felt in being with her. She was a classic Russian beauty, blue-eyed with clear pale-pink skin, the color just a trifle higher over her fine cheekbones. Her gossamer hair was not the yellow of her Scandinavian forebears but a soft pale blond. Galya's lips were clear of line and with strong natural color, for which paint would have been superfluous. She wore small diamonds on thin gold wires that went through the tips of her ears.

We found our places with no time to spare. Onstage a young Canadian company performed with freshness, color and humor, a welcome change from the technically proficient but repetitious Bolshoi. The Soviet ballet buffs cheered and showed their pleasure, stood up and begged for more.

I wondered that Dmitri and Galya could stay awake after all they had had to eat and drink, but they seemed genuinely enthusiastic about the dancers. Afterwards Dmitri insisted on driving me home. They agreed to come up to our apartment since Dmitri felt a strong need for some coffee.

We had moved into Yugozapad about a month before and the apartment was beginning to take form, but it was still unsettled. Kitchen utensils lay on makeshift shelves, paintings and prints stood propped against the walls, the light bulbs in the living room still hung bare. While I prepared the coffee Dmitri strode back and forth the length of the now-combined living and dining rooms, the ruby red of the Central Asian rugs in stark contrast to the new white parquet underfoot.

"Amazing," he muttered over and over. "I haven't seen a room like this in all of Moscow." He was particularly interested in every detail of the decorating because they were in the last stages of refurbishing the apartment they had lived in for years. I described my bargaining session with the floor polishers, in which I had to pay overtime and find the wax myself if I wanted to avoid the lacquer these men were accustomed to brushing on new floors. I implied that I was the victim of the bargaining, having to give in on every step because I was a foreigner.

Dmitri's laugh was a snort. "I am a Soviet citizen so I have to bribe double. They know that I know there is such a shortage of workers who do anything right that I must give them favors to keep them. At least you have UpDK to keep them on the job — I have to compete in a bigger market. When I buy vodka to bribe them I have to pay in rubles at a much higher price than you pay in dollars. If I don't look at what they're doing they leave me a sloppy job; if I go to have a look they catch me for some more vodka or overtime." Then he added, "UpDK has the best-quality paint, but it's not available in Soviet stores, so either I must have a friend at UpDK or I must have a friend who will bring me paint from Helsinki." The same was true for doorknobs, drapery, curtain rods, nails, wall hooks, wallpaper — all of the niceties of life that Dmitri had developed a taste for on his trips abroad.

We three sat around the dining room table under the dim light of the rice-paper Japanese lantern we used as a chandelier. I poured coffee into heavy beer mugs and said I was sorry I couldn't offer coffee cups; all of ours had disappeared in moving. Dmitri and Galya, in one voice, admonished me gently: "You are new here, you will learn that in the Soviet Union it is bad form to apologize for what you don't have." We sipped the hot black coffee and there was a mood of tired truth about us all. It was too late at night for wariness and poses.

"You have such a rich country, why can't you have all these things that are ordinary in the West?" It was a rhetorical question, best answered with a shrug.

Dmitri answered with the self-satisfied smile of the Soviet bureaucrat: "If you could only appreciate what a leap we have made since the Revolution, if you could have seen where we started from. My grandfather was a cobbler, so poor he couldn't imagine what it could be like not to be so poor. I remember his bent shoulders. My deepest wish is that my grandfather could have lived to see how his grandchildren live now."

I said I could appreciate his feelings, but why did Soviets always use past wars as an excuse for what they lacked now? After all, Tokyo was burned to the ground and look where the Japanese are. All I ever heard from Russians was, "We have always been at war. The Germans were only the last of many. Before them it was the French and the Swedes and before that the Tatars." I described the Intourist guide who first took us around Moscow. I innocently asked the young man what contributions the Tatars had made to Russian culture. He gritted his teeth with fresh anger and said, "Contributions? Yes, they managed to ruin our cheekbones," brushing his cheeks with his fingertips.

Dmitri and Galya laughed. "Yes, it's true that Russians feel that way, even educated ones."

"But that was five hundred years ago!" I protested.

Galya leaned her chin on her wrist and her laughter turned to introspection. "Our memories are all of sadness. We have a national psyche of suffering and melancholy. It is for all the wars, the pogroms, treatment of the serfs, for the workers. We are motivated by sadness in our racial memory."

"But if you look into yourselves that way why isn't there more skepticism, more criticism of your own system?" I asked.

"Yes, we criticize, too," Dmitri assured me and Galya assented. "Among ourselves we exchange bitter, searing jokes against everything in our way of life."

We talked about the absence of any aesthetic quality in everyday life. I pointed to the practical ugliness of the bathroom in this new, advanced building, and contrasted it with Japanese efforts to create a sense of beauty and pleasure, a oneness with nature, in the baths of even the poorest people. Dmitri thought it was marvelous that almost all Russians now have bathtubs in their homes. For the present, one could not ask for more material comfort than had been gained in what seemed to him only a few short years. Galya, still in her historical mood, disagreed. "We need a sense of beauty and pleasure in our lifestyle to civilize the masses, to lift them from the brutalized state they lived in before the Revolution. The government should teach the people some of this aesthetic spirit in their home life."

On the one hand they had an ingrained belief in the all-healing, all-educative power of socialism, a faith in their system and a pride in Russianness; on the other hand a cosmopolitan outlook, a yearning for material things, a certain cleverness in manipulating the system to get the things they yearned for. This dualism left Dmitri and Galya in a vulnerable position toward the next generation. They mouthed, and indeed meant, their belief in the Revolution, in carrying it on, in revitalizing its goals of community and self-sacrifice in the upbringing of their children, but the disparity between their words and their example was evident.

Months later, at a cocktail party, Dmitri and I found ourselves standing next to each other, and cut off from the conversations going on around us. In response to my simple "How are you?" he confided his troubles with his stepson, Galya's son, who couldn't seem to apply himself to study or work.

"He is nineteen, handsome and strong. He is not a bad boy, but you know how easily he could become one if he does nothing all day but lazy around with other boys who are doing nothing."

"I know," I said with a sardonic laugh. "Even in that we are ahead of you in the West."

"If he doesn't work he can be arrested for parasitism. There has been so much trouble with young hooligans, the police are cracking down."

"What kind of work can he do?" I asked.

"With great difficulty, I assure you," Dmitri said, raising his eyebrows meaningfully, "I have managed to get him a job as a truckdriver. I only hope he will stick to it."

9

Rites of Spring: Mud, Cleaning, Dissent

THE SPRING CRACKING of the ice in the Moscow River is accompanied by the great Russian mud. It was my father's salient memory of his boyhood. The melting snow sits deep on the flat plain so that knee-high rubber boots aren't protection enough to cross an open field. Around our apartment building the uneven two-by-fours set up to span sidewalks not yet built, shook and dipped into bottomless puddles. Our children had seamless rubber boots from Helsinki, but the Russians searched their own stores in vain and had to rely on leather snowboots that leaked, or thick felt *valenky* with shallow rubber overshoes that are designed for dry Siberian snow.

The Russians have never quite come to terms with the mud, even though it has defeated invaders. Lyuba would throw up her hands as the children arrived home from school, scream at them not to cross the saddle of the front door, and hand them a broom and bucket to clean up the mess they'd made in the corridor. Couldn't they find a piece of wood to scrape off the wet mud before they came into the building? was her daily chorus. She got somewhere with the older ones, but Barney and his friends gloried in the ooze. They appeared at the door proud of how much they had been able to make stick to them.

Barney. One night Robert and I went outside to walk in the mud where they were to build a parking lot later on. We walked out into a sea of mud and the only shore was the cement around it. When we got out into the middle of it all we headed back but after not going far we discovered that we couldn't lift our feet—we were stuck in the mud. We pulled and pulled. Robert's foot came out of his boot. I got so disgusted I pulled off my boots and ran in my socks to the cement. Doveen and some other kids who were watching thought it looked like fun so they went in too. Soon everyone was going in and it became a big game.

Summer was moving in, the weather got warmer and each day just a bit sunnier than the one before. The gooseberry patches at the nearby buildings were getting ready but the gooseberries were still green. My Afghan friend Halette and I and sometimes other kids sneaked over to the buildings and got lots of gooseberries until one of the wrinkled-up old ladies stuck her head out of the window with her rotten teeth and dull scarf covering her head, and scolded us. We ran as fast as we could to our building to share the berries with some of the kids. They were sour but good.

In the spring at detsky sad on the playground we dug and found beetles and played with them and let them go. One time I caught a queen bettle and one kid liked it so much he took it and said it was his and convinced everyone that what he said was true so I couldn't argue. Besides, I didn't really know how to say in Russian what I needed to say to argue with him.

We played war with shovels as guns and we used small harnesses and put them on each other so one person would be the horse. We took partners and took turns being the horse. Everyone wants to be a Russian soldier and not German so everyone called, "I want to be Russian." One time I was a Russian horse and the boy who held the harness said to me, "I don't want you as a horse, you keep running me into Germans."

There were only one or two Russian families who lived in our building. The Russian kids who lived in the building did so because their fathers worked there. All the children in the building formed a gang.

At the bottom of our building there were glass storefronts which were empty. The Russian workmen were always working on them but they never got finished. They had big sheets of glass that they broke trying to put them in. When they laid cement stray cats from around the building came and walked on it. So did the children. A Peruvian boy would go in there and bend small metal bars in front of his friends to show his strength. The workmen needed the bars to reinforce the concrete.

The radiators in the stores worked. Sometimes when it rained, our gang of kids sat on the radiators to warm our butts. We played telephone in Russian, the only language everybody knew. One person thinks of a word and whispers it to the next and so on down the line. The last person says the word out loud. It usually comes out funny because someone somewhere along the line doesn't hear correctly. One word we used was Mary Poppins. The other kids didn't understand the English words and got them mixed up. Mary Poppins would be whispered down the line and the person at the end, rather puzzled, would say, "Poppa Lenin?"

At the end of winter the frozen lake was melting. There were flat pieces of ice floating around the lake. Boys from a building nearby came with me and we stood on the ice and steered with long sticks using the ice as boats. Stevo came along and saw me and took me back to the apartment, where I got into trouble. I had been told before not to go out on the ice.

In Russia there were no playgrounds near our building so we made our own. The other boys and I played in a construction site sometimes when there were no workmen around. We ran up and along scaffolding, in and out of unfinished rooms, and played war. But we kept an eye out for workmen. One time on a nice spring day we were looking in rooms and suddenly we saw a workman so we quietly ran over to the unfinished stairway and used it as a hideout until he was gone.

One time Halette and I were walking down the stairway and we saw some worker's clothes so we put on the baggy pants and shirts and ran outside laughing our heads off. We took off the clothes and put them on the trash pile.

One day there were some Russian boys outside our building who wanted to exchange handmade wooden guns for chewing gum. The guns were wood with wire triggers which shot small pieces of wire bent into a U shape. My friend Robert and I decided we wanted them so I got enough gum for each of us to get one. There was one boy who pretended he could speak English to impress his friends and he called chewing gum "ching gow." The Russian word for it is *zhivatchka*, which means cud like a cow chews. That night the same boys came by and asked Robert and me if we wanted to play army with the guns. We said yes and we divided up into teams putting me on a different team from Robert. We used the area around the buildings as a battlefield and had great fun. The next day my friend Halette and I were riding in the elevator and we found a lever we hadn't noticed before. Halette pulled it and the elevator stopped between two floors and the doors opened. I reached out and turned a wheel that was in the elevator shaft and the outer doors opened. Now if we slipped we would fall down the shaft. Laughing we jumped out onto the floor about four feet below. As the elevator closed and went to the first floor a woman came out of her apartment yelling at us. We gave a scream of surprise and disappeared down the stairs. We did the same thing many times again.

Leona. The first of May the steam heat is turned off, no matter what the temperature outdoors. Sometimes it is a blessing; one year the first week of May was in the eighties. Sometimes May comes in with a week of cold rain. But even if May starts hot it's sure to turn cold again, and that's just about time for the annual cleaning of boilers and hot water pipes. It is a kind of Russian irony, that in the sub-zero months of winter one can keep warm in furs and central heating, but in May there's not even a hot bath to relieve the bone-chilling damp of cold apartments. The Soviet people don't complain; when the hot water comes on again, running faster and cleaner than they can remember since the same time the year before, they look upon it with the pride of a housewife who has just finished her spring cleaning. They never dream that plumbing exists anywhere in the world that doesn't have to be shut off two weeks a year.

Evelind. Spring brings the people of Moscow into the streets.

In school every student is expected to work during his double-period shop class, or if the trees have to be pruned, during biology class. All students in a grade section work collectively at washing the windows and walls of their homeroom. To clean the rest of the school each homeroom is assigned a section. Outside, the students shovel the dirty mounds of unmelted snow into the sun, pick up the trash and pieces of broken windows that have accumulated over the winter. (If we planned it right, we could sneak off and buy ice cream before the next class.)

By comparison, pruning the trees and picking insects off them is light work. After the shrubbery bloomed in the spring we picked off the unopened buds and clusters of black inchworms, dropped them into buckets, and emptied them into an open fire prepared by the boys. Once, the boys hit something hard as they were digging the pit for the fire. Expecting to find buried treasure, they hurriedly uncovered it. It turned out to be a city sewer pipe, and with the nervous approval of the teacher, they quickly buried it.

At home, everyone in the apartment building contributes time to work on the land around the building, planting vegetables and flowers. The old grandmothers can marvel over the growth of the neighbors' kid and ask him if he's being a good Pioneer. The community is out together again, one big family, bickering, loving, watching, listening, chiding the children maternally, it does not matter whose they are.

Besides all the volunteers, the paid construction and maintenance crews get to work. New apartment buildings are finished every day because the roads are cleared to bring in the prefabricated parts. Long trucks, carrying concrete walls with tiny inset windows or enormous plates of unprotected glass, are a common sight. The larger pieces of glass are dropped, broken and replaced at least once before the workmen get them in right.

To repair the roads, crews go out and fill in the potholes that are the result of a long, harsh winter. They fill in the holes, but do little to make them level with the existing roadway, so the roads stay bumpy.

The main cleanup events of the spring, however, are the *subotniks,* Saturdays on which everyone in the country gets outside to do something for the appearance of the community. These workdays commemorate the Saturday in 1919 when the railway workers gave an extra Saturday without pay to help make the Revolution a success. Schoolchildren are expected to stay at school all day and work. I managed to slip away after a little while and wasn't hassled because I was not a Pioneer.

Stevo. Marya Illyinichna was first in command for our end-of-the-year cleanup at the school. She was a prim red-haired lady, and she took to the job well. Marya Illyinichna knew a lot about plants, discipline, yelling, and perfectionism. She was very concise and upright, at her best commanding battalions of schoolchildren.

I thought for some reason that I would be able to get away without working. I soon realized, however, that the only way to get my daybook with grades was to report to Marya Illyinichna.

I was the last person for whom she had to find work, but she managed to dig out some skeletons that needed help. There were two rodents in little glass cases that were collapsing.

I reported for four hours of work at eight o'clock on the Monday after school had let out. I listened carefully as she gave me tape and glue, and vaguely demonstrated my task. I sat down and started to fiddle around with it. My head began to spin. What the hell was I doing this for! I was finally finished with school, and I had to come back to get my dumb daybook. Damn it, I could have gotten someone to steal it for me. When I finally went at it in earnest, I broke out in sweat. The job required me to apply the glue onto some old tape, and somehow coax the plate of glass, which was still attached on the bottom, over to the tape; without upsetting the skeleton. By the time I was sensitized to the balances of the case, my hands were shaking, and I was red in the face.

The first skeleton was in fairly good shape, but the second one had a loose skull. I thought I could fix the glass sides, and be done with it, but the head wobbled at the last second. Marya Illyinichna gave me a little ball of clay, and I stuck it onto the metal frame. I had to nudge my fingers past the other twenty minute white pieces, and adjust them perfectly so that he stared blindly ahead.

I worked on the skeletons for four hours that day, but Marya Illyinichna noticed how white I was when I left. She found some grass for me to plant on the remaining days. I worked hard and happily in the dirt. She gave me fives for all aspects of my work.

Leona. The first week in May the bare city takes on a cheering greenness, for Moscow is a city of trees. Along the banks of the Moscow River, in the back reaches of Gorky Park, in the hundreds of courtyards around which apartment houses are built, in the narrow island parks that run between double avenues, in the poets' squares — the small parks that each surround a statue of one of Russia's revered writers — where young dissenters meet for politics or love and wrinkled babushkas gossip loudly, the fulsome trees hide the drabness of the gray stone city sitting squat on its giant plain.

When the mud dries it is time for picnics in the woods.

Katie. I liked Kaarina best of all my friends because she wasn't as demanding as the others and we could play together without even thinking about the fact that I was a foreigner. Her father had a job that took him out of the country sometimes, so she didn't always ask me for chewing gum and other foreign things the way the other kids did.

Next to our apartment building was a man-made lake and a forest. It was there that Kaarina and I had our picnics in the summer, got muddy sliding around in the creeks in the spring, played soccer in the fall, and went skiing, skating and sledding in the winter. Sometimes we went swimming in the lake, but it was very polluted. We played beside the lake and in the forest almost every day.

One day as Kaarina and I walked down the aisles of evergreen trees in the forest I noticed that a man was following us. I recognized him because ever since we had been living in our apartment building he had often followed me down to the lake. He was tall, with a kind baby face, and he looked as though he were in his early thirties. Once, when my mother and I were taking a walk, he came up to her and said, "That's a very nice daughter you have." Afterwards my mother told me he was just a little bit crazy. But he never talked to me or bothered me, so I began to get used to him and did not pay any attention to him.

That day Kaarina and I had brought our lunch and we found a nice spot on a little hill and spread out our blanket. Then we emptied the basket, which contained two oranges, a can of chicken, some radishes and a loaf of black bread. We played catch with the oranges but got tired of that because every time one of us missed, it would roll down the hill into the stream which had formed from the melted snow.

We sat down to eat but found that neither of us could open the can of chicken. I heard someone walking behind the trees so I got up to see if the person could help us, but as I got closer I saw that it was the man who was always following me. I was about to turn back, but then I decided to get the chicken open first. He opened the can without any trouble. I thanked him and started to turn away but he caught me and took me behind a tree. I was frightened but by this time there was nothing I could do. He put his arm around me and bent his head down until his lips were close to my ear.

"Bring me some chewing gum tomorrow at the left end of the lake," he whispered.

"Yes," I said, and I broke away from him and ran.

When I got back to Kaarina I told her what had happened while we ate the chicken that he had opened.

I never brought him any chewing gum. I don't know why they don't have gum in Russia, but they really should because everyone is hungry for it.

Evelind. One by one, clutching their belongings and eager to be off, everyone arrived at the front parking lot. The late ones, having just come back from the May Day parade in Red Square, called out from their windows for us to wait an extra minute.

The kids that gathered in front of our apartment building were from the Eastern European bloc of Communist countries; their parents were either diplomats or journalists. Although we are Americans, we were accepted into the group with no credential other than that we spoke the common language, Russian.

We helped the younger children, tripping over their canteens and toys, down the hill past the artificial lake choked with thick green and brown algae, and into the regular rows of the planted pine forest. The clearings would be filled with people because of the May Day holiday and the warm weather. We scattered among the pines, and within a couple of minutes we followed excited shouts to a sunny opening in the trees.

We dumped our lunch baskets, blankets, books, toys and a sack of potatoes in a pile. The little ones pulled everyone into the center to play a winking game that the Polish girls had taught us. After a few rounds the youngest were giggling and happy, but wanted to play something else. We decided on "sardines," my American contribution to the games, which is an opposite version of hide-and-seek. One person hides and as others find him they hide with him; the last bewildered person is the loser.

For lunch everyone brought sausages, cheese, black bread and some treat from his or her home country. Among the delicacies were jelly candies, pressed fruit rolls, meat pies and my peanut butter and jelly sandwiches.

After lunch everyone stretched out in the sun and fell asleep or talked. We compared schools, the merits of teachers and the everyday problems of living in a foreign country, especially in Russia. We never discussed politics because we knew it might cause arguments and bad feelings. We relaxed until one of the fathers came to make us a fire.

Everyone raced around, picking up firewood. Soon the fire was hot and we tucked the potatoes under the ashes. We roasted our "high tea" of leftover sausage, cheese and apples. We played riotous games of tag. As twilight came we stopped running around and huddled in a circle, telling jokes and singing songs.

When the potatoes were done, there was a race for the salt, but the potatoes were too hot to eat. With a lot of blowing and laughing we gobbled them down, sooty skins and all. They were fabulous! Our hands and faces became black and when the last mouthful was gone we sat around, exhausted. No one was willing to move until a scout came back with the news that our parents were wondering where we were.

We parted grudgingly and I invited everyone to come up later and listen to our new records. They smiled, but refused. I smiled back, a little sad, but not hurt. It was all right to go on picnics together but they couldn't come up to the Americans' apartment. It might cause their parents difficulty at work.

Leona. The Soviet picnickers in the birch and pine copses behind our apartment building came to enjoy the warm weather, pick wild-flowers, and talk to each other without listening walls. We too felt the urge to get out of the house and out of the city.

One midweek morning Evelyn Bausman, wife of the Associated Press bureau chief, called to suggest that she pick me up in her car. We would go to Peredelkino to see the beautiful old church in Solzhenitsyn's Easter story. From our apartment on the edge of the city it was only a short ride to the ring road; only a few minutes later there was a sign that would take us onto the overpass that was the main road to Minsk. This was the direct road to Peredelkino. There are back roads and side roads to Peredelkino, often used to visit Soviet writer friends who didn't

Evelind (standing second from left), Barney (reading, seated below her left arm) and Doveen (to his left) pose with their East European friends from our apartment building at a picnic in the woods. (Photo by Jerrold Schecter)

want us to bother getting special permission, but it was a bright and warm morning, unfit for deviousness. Why should we not be allowed to visit freely this suburban enclave for Party intelligentsia? We came off the ring road and crossed the bridge-overpass. But after another hundred yards we were stopped by an elderly, kind-faced policeman.

"You have correspondent's license plates. Do you have a letter from MID?" he asked.

Ask the Ministry of Foreign Affairs for a letter to visit the church in Peredelkino? Do they have a special form to cover spontaneous sunny mornings? "We want to go see the church in Peredelkino," Evelyn explained. It was no use. He made a sweeping motion with his arm instructing us to turn around, smiled warmly, and shrugged his shoulders to show he had no choice but to send us back.

About a week later we made all the necessary preparations to visit the old cathedral town of Zagorsk, forty-five miles from Moscow — full tank of gas, picnic lunch and a letter of permission from the MID. We met our Soviet friends at a Metro station near their house and set off.

The white walls and blue roofs of the churches seemed almost Mediterranean in the hot sunlight, but indoors the chanting of priests, the brooding colors of the icons and the waft of incense were dark and northern. Heavy-legged peasant women and frail old men stood looking upward in wonder at the cathedral paintings. Outside, a long line of pilgrims waited to be sprinkled with holy water from a well supposed to have magic powers. The children wanted to wait with the pilgrims but most of the adults, who were sleepy in the languid heat, wanted to find a shady spot of grass for the picnic. The cathedral area was filled with people and beyond the parking lot the town began. We drove around the town without finding a likely place. So we took a side street and headed out of town toward woods and open fields.

We had barely reached the edge of town when a figure in the familiar blue-gray uniform of a policeman signaled us to stop. Foreigners could not proceed past this point. All we could see was foliage. "We are only looking for a place to have a picnic," Jerry said. Like the policeman on the Minsk road he was affable but helpless to change the rules. He told us we were about to ride into a military installation, and directed us back into town. We gave up our plan to see more of the cathedral complex after lunch, and had our picnic on the way back toward Moscow.

The two major galleries of art, the Pushkin and the Tretyakov, are heated all winter, but some of the small museums in Moscow are housed in old stone buildings that cannot keep out the chill, so we had to wait until spring to visit them.

The Ostankino Palace or Serf's Palace, is twenty minutes from the center of the city, but few tourists ever see it, even though Intourist guides take their clients to the Exhibition of Economic Achievement nearby. The palace is a graceful neoclassical building covered with salmon-colored smooth stucco and built for the beautiful serf whom the nobleman Sheremyetevo took as his mistress when she was only thirteen. In tune with the intellectual currents of the late eighteenth century, this enlightened despot, who owned six hundred villages, hired tutors to train his beloved in the arts of the stage. He created a company of musicians and stage artists, all former serfs, to complement her talents, and he had the palace constructed with a stage on rope pulleys that could be lowered onto part of the ballroom floor to change the room into a theater. Then he invited all the Russian nobility to see her perform, in the hope that when they saw how beautiful and accomplished she was, they would accept her into his social class, and he could proceed to marry her without scandal. The privileged of Moscow came to eat, drink and be entertained, but they would never countenance the beautiful, educated serf's being admitted to their own ranks. He married her secretly when she was thirty, but she died of cancer a year later.

In his sorrow he formally gave the whole staff of the palace their freedom. However, the Soviet historical plaque tells us that in the preindustrial world of eighteenth-century Russia there was no place for men without defined status, and most of them starved for lack of employment.

The interior of the palace, garishly decorated in French Empire style with velvet-covered walls and sphinx-armed chairs, and hung with paintings by long-forgotten artists, is kept at a controlled chill that maintains the original quality of the artifacts. In the ballroom is a table model of the stage and its system of pulleys.

The warm weather made it possible to satisfy some of the curiosity we had restrained all winter, when it was too cold to wait in outdoor lines or take adventurous bus rides or casual walks.

Evelind. In Red Square, about twenty feet from the Kremlin wall, stands what appears to be a huge block of cold gray-black marble. On closer inspection, but not too close or you bump into the grim guards at the doorway, you see that it has steps carved on the sides, leading up to a platform on the roof. Over a normal-sized front door, in gold lettering, is inscribed LENIN. Three long steps lead up to the door, and two immense wreaths and two ominous guards on either side of the door face onto the square. The dark, oppressive structure is the Lenin Mausoleum.

On important holidays, such as May Day, the Soviet leaders climb the steps to the platform on the roof and give speeches to the people who have assembled to watch the parade of weapons and decorated floats that pass by.

One chilly Sunday morning in April, I set off to see Lenin entombed within this edifice. As a foreigner I was given preferential treatment, and the Intourist guide put me about half an hour from the front of the line. Behind me, the line stretched along one wall of the Kremlin for more than three and a half blocks — the Soviets who had come to pay tribute to their near-Godlike hero. They were huddled in twos and threes along the line, wrapped in warm cloth coats and hats, a sign that spring had finally come and the winter's fur could be put away. Many had brought something to eat — the wait would probably be more than two hours. I smelled the garlicky salami and pungent cheese as I walked by.

Eventually I came to the long steps that led up to the door. The guards on duty did not even blink, although I knew they were real because I had seen the terse changing of the guard earlier. The wreaths were enormous, larger than a man, and made of fresh flowers. This fact was amazing because flowers are exorbitantly expensive on the Soviet market and very hard to find, except during the middle of the summer.

Once inside the door, it was darker and cooler. An officer barked at the people in line to keep their hands out of their pockets and walk double file — something I found annoying because it was harder to see everything that way.

I followed the line down a steep flight of steps — marble like the rest of the structure — into the lower chamber. The only light came from electric lamps set in the black marble and the air smelled like you might expect a tomb to smell — dank, musty, damp and raw. Every ten feet there was a guard, for in the center of the room lay Lenin, enclosed in a glass case. No one said a word. This was the man that had made the Soviet Union, whom everyone had spoken of since they had learned to speak. He looked like all his pictures and his clenched fists seemed to symbolize the strength he had stood for.

We were forced to move at such a fast pace, however, that I only had a quick glimpse. He looked a bit too good to be true. Perhaps the Soviets had made some secret agreement with Madame Tussaud . . .

A guard motioned to me to take my hands out of my pockets. He didn't speak but rapidly demonstrated pulling his hands out of his pockets a few times. I wondered why. Was the rule to prevent photographing Lenin with a hidden camera?

Outside again, the meager sunlight was a shock. Before being urged onto the street I passed the tombs of famous heroes, some set in the Kremlin wall itself, including John Reed, the American journalist who covered the Revolution and died from typhus, and Stalin, who lay under a gravestone. Stalin was an exception, though, because he was the only one who had been given to the worms after first being embalmed and set next to Lenin, before Soviet history was rewritten.

I was back on the street. I had seen Lenin and would never again be curious about the contents of that block of mysterious marble, unless the Soviets tried rewriting history again.

Leona. One sunny morning in April I set off, shopping bags in hand, with Barney and Doveen, and Robert, Barney's Dutch friend from the twelfth floor, for the rynok (farmers' market) nearest us. I wasn't exactly sure how to get there, but my Russian teacher, Tamara, suggested I try the Number 42 bus which we usually took to get from the Metro station to our apartment house. "You know," she said, "if you just stay on that bus past your house, it will take you to the Cheryomushinsky Rynok, which is a very good market."

To do as she suggested meant venturing into uncharted territory; the bus went away from the main avenues that we used every day to and from the office, back and forth to school, to shop for food and home again. If I happened to be at the office at the end of the day, Jerry and I came home via Komsomolsky Prospekt for the pleasure of watching the painters refurbish St. Nicholas in Khamovniky, the weavers' church, in its original bright green and orange trim against fresh whitewash and restore the gold leaf to its cluster of small onion domes. We liked to stop in at three stores right near each other across from the church: a small cigar shop that carried Cuban cigars; the Gift of Nature store, which offered frozen bear meat, honey and dried fruits; and a *komissionnyi magazin* for antiques, where we often added to our lode of old *vareniye* pans, broad-rimmed shallow copper pans for the long slow boiling of preserves and jam. I was curious to see the rest of our neighborhood. I always had my eye out for restaurants we hadn't tried or a komissionnyi no one had told me about.

The three children and I watched a Number 42 come into view across Leninsky Prospekt to our stop, just a few hundred feet from the wide double avenue. The bus was not very old, but like all Moscow buses it had become doddering, dusty and ancient. We four climbed aboard and placed our 5-kopeck coins in the ticket machine, pressed the lever, and collected our paper chits that entitled us to ride the bus as far as it would go.

The lever of the machine was worn smooth, as were the indentations in the rubber carpeting that showed the main internal traffic lines. At this time of the morning, after the rush hour, there were only a few women riding with us, sturdy peasants in flowered dresses with babushkas on their heads, red-cheeked and blond, the true Russian type. Only one older woman had a city appearance: the knitted dress, the fine earrings through pierced ears, an office rather than a farm look.

When we got on, I asked the driver, "To Cheryomushinsky Rynok?" He nodded absently. We began to ride straight out of the city, whereas I expected him to turn toward the center within a few blocks. I asked one of the women and when she heard me say Cheryomushinsky she took on a worried frown. Then she shrugged and said yes, it would go there, but it would cut a wide circle first. It was a long way but it would turn eventually.

Soon we were out into open countryside, except that there were curbs and long iron fences. The road seemed to have been cut through fields, and across them construction was never out of sight. We passed factories isolated on the flat plain, with whole towns of new apartments going up near them. New roads, streetlights, neat traffic islands were already in place for these suburbs in the process of creation. From afar they seemed still uninhabited. The bus pulled up to its appointed stops, with their freshly painted sheds and benches for waiting passengers, and

I wondered where the passengers came from. Then the bus turned back toward the city, and in the embankments between the angles of the roads old cabins came into view, huddling onto hillsides for dear life against the onslaught of the coming city. In the ravines downhill, each of the izbas had a wooden picket fence to delineate a neat vegetable garden, its churned black soil a raw contrast to the dry grass of the hillsides. We rode a little further and came upon a town, a copy of a Moscow shopping center, complete with a dry cleaner, food store, restaurant, and a branch of Children's World.

We rode on. The skyline of the city we had left could be seen in the distance, but Cheryomushinsky Rynok was only a vague hope. The children were restless, got up from their seats, and were busy examining the effect of air coming through a small hole in the floor as the bus moved. One of the passengers tossed her head in the direction of the children and said to another woman across the aisle, "Look at her," referring to me in a loud voice. "If I had three children out of their seats I'd be nervous and screaming. She sits there totally unconcerned. I can't understand how she can stand to have three children and not be nervous."

Did she think I didn't understand Russian? Was she trying to start a conversation? Was she complimenting my calm demeanor or suggesting that I was well conditioned to motherhood? If she thought I was not doing my duty in protecting my children from danger, she would not have hesitated to discipline the children herself, seemingly the right of every Soviet citizen toward all the children of the collective society. So it was not criticism in a specific sense.

I decided to answer her in the same loud tone. "Two of these are mine and I have three more at home. Why should I be nervous?" Both women turned to me and shook their heads in wonder and pity.

"How do you manage? Do you have some household help? Do you go to work, too?"

I told them that I didn't go to work, that I had a maid to help me, that I managed very well, that four or five children in a family were not so unusual in America, but that of course we had more living space. Then they nodded their heads in a way I was to see and hear often. "Rich mother," they said, not in the sense of economic wealth as another American might say to me, but rich in motherhood, as only a Russian woman can feel who is torn between her "liberation" and the desire to have more children, to stay home and raise them.

Their change in tone embarrassed me, so I tried to change the trend of the conversation. I pointed to the new apartments as we passed them and asked if the people living there worked nearby or in the city. I asked if it wasn't a lot of traveling, implying some vague criticism of socialist planning, which professes to place workers' houses near their work. This brought forth a paean to the marvelous new apartments they lived in, the shrubbery (it was newly planted and hardly voluptuous), and the clean air they enjoyed in the new suburbs. They raved on, one inspiring the other, telling me with pride how much construction was going up, how much living space and modernity they enjoyed, how fast the country was moving ahead. Each family had one large room plus a good-sized kitchen and bath. "We have tables in the kitchen covered with a wonderful new plastic from Finland. You can take a pan straight from the oven and put it on the table without burning the table," one woman said, representing the others, who nodded in agreement.

I was sharing their awe and their appreciation of the wonder of Formica when the bus came to a stop at a large terminal and everyone got up. "Cheryomushinsky Rynok?" I asked apprehensively. My women acquaintances told me to get a transfer from the driver and showed me where to wait for another bus. "How much further?" I asked in desperation. We had already ridden an hour and fifteen minutes. Not far, they assured me. After five minutes of waiting a bus approached and I looked questioningly at my friends. No, they shook their heads, not this one, wait for two more. Finally the right bus came and we mounted the stair. We sat down, expecting another long ride. Within a few minutes, I began to recognize familiar streets and suddenly there was the market. We clambered out of the bus excitedly.

We were greeted with a splendid display: little piles of baby carrots, barrels of pickles and of sauerkraut, tubs of homemade sour cream and cottage cheese, buckets of fresh carnations and gladioli. The rynok is as big as an old-fashioned airplane hangar, with skylight windows, and has the same shape. There are four entrances and over each massive series of doors is a painting of a harvest cornucopia in bright reds, greens and blues. Enormous beefy round women, advertisements for their own wares, offered me a taste of their creamy cheese, butter and sour cream. Some of the peasant women selling their home products had come from only as far as the izbas we had seen a half hour away. The flower sellers, swarthy Armenians and Georgians with black mustaches, flirted as I walked by. Seeds and potted geraniums, cacti and jasmine were on sale, carefully tended by old ladies who brought them from their heated apartments.

Barney. We got to the market and the smell of coleslaw and sauerkraut filled the air. There was water running through the tile gutters of the market. Old *babas* were all around biting into radishes and snitching cherries.

The old ladies behind the big barrels of coleslaw and sauerkraut took their wooden tongs and stuffed the sauerkraut into bottles with half of it hanging out and watery. They worked their stands while they gossiped with all their friends. I stood at the stands looking and the old ladies pinched my cheeks and pulled my nose and gave me a flower and said how cute I was and that I was their darling.

Leona. They came from the south, from city windowsills and from surrounding farms, these agricultural products that were higher in price and better in quality than any that were available in the regular state-run stores. The rynok is a free market, a socialist compromise with individual initiative. Farmers bring produce from their private plots, middlemen haul flowers and vegetables by airplane from the south, to sell for profit. Outside the rynok such activity is dubbed "speculation" and is against the law. Prices are inflated: In winter cucumbers were ten rubles a kilo ($11.10 for 2.2 pounds) and tomatoes 13 rubles a kilo ($14.43 for 2.2 pounds). Even in spring new potatoes brought 2 rubles a kilo, but the official distribution system was so inefficient that citizens willingly paid the price for something fresh to eat now and then. People muttered about the prices but they paid them, because the real problem was to find something to buy with their money. In the Soviet Union food is the foremost luxury, except for vodka and cognac, and the free market, a continuation of the traditional village market, is the place where Russians can spend their extra rubles on luxuries. The only vegetables available in state stores all winter long were root vegetables that could be stored for long periods — carrots, beets, cabbage, potatoes, onions — the makings, with a bit of meat, of the cabbage borscht that most Russians cook once a week. The average family, with the mother working, ladles out a bowl of borscht from the same reheated pot until the next weekend, supplementing it with good crusty white bread or pumpernickel, various sausages and preserved herrings.

By the end of winter, before the new crop comes in, even the root cellar is empty. While I was at the rynok, a farmer and his friend attempted to unload a truckful of onions that they had obviously withheld, hoping for high profit when there would be scarcity, but they had held their prize too long. The stench of soft, rotting onions swept the market, and with it a whisper almost like a chant: *"Speku-lant!" "Spekulant!"* The two farmers, with shamefaced smiles, started to unload, but the irate citizens who sold fresh goods in the other stalls got together and forced the two onion farmers to depart with their load of soured hopes.

The three children and I walked up and down the aisles of stalls and I bought fresh flat-leafed parsley, carrots, and a potted jasmine plant. Then we started out again to find our way home.

Wizened old women from the countryside stood at open stalls outside the market to hawk their mushrooms for soups, stews and that great Russian specialty, pickled mushrooms. They gathered the mushrooms themselves in the damp birch forests and their presence at the market was a tradition that predated the Revolution.

On the sidewalk out in front, I decided to walk in the opposite direction from the way we had come by bus. It was then that I suddenly realized where we were. We were only one block from Leninsky Prospekt, the wide avenue that runs in front of our apartment building, and only ten blocks down the Prospekt from home. The bus had taken us in a two-hour circle. We could have walked home if we had had the energy left. But with our arms full we decided to get into a taxi and ride home.

Evelind. One afternoon in Moscow I was to meet Sasha at a Metro station farther down the line than I had ever ventured. Sasha was a young man with wire-rimmed glasses, thick blond hair and a short full beard. He was an English teacher whom my father had met on the street while covering the trial of Pavel Litvinov. They had started talking and Sasha was invited to our home after that. I suppose he felt that he had little to lose talking to a foreign journalist, since his presence outside the trial was already sufficient declaration that he held views clearly frowned upon by the Soviet regime. As our friendship with him developed, Sasha showed us monasteries and other out-of-the-way places in Moscow and we in turn invited him over to dinner to taste new dishes and listen to American music. When we discussed politics with him we turned the volume on the record player up high to confuse the "bugs."

On this afternoon, Sasha was going to show me an old section of town and we would also practice Russian and English as we strolled around. It was spring; the weather was warm and the cottonwoods were shedding "spring snow" into every nook and cranny. When I arrived at the station a few minutes early, there was no sign of Sasha. I killed time by looking at the theater notices and saw that a few very old, obscure American movies were playing in my neighborhood. One of them was an old Mario Lanza musical dubbed in Russian.

After reading all the propaganda slogans and posters on the news-stands and on the walls, I began to wonder whether Sasha was ever going to rescue me from "Glory to the Communist Party" and "Lenin Lived, Lenin Lives, Lenin Will Always Live." Maybe all the "Workers of the World" would unite and carry me off before he got there. A minute later he arrived, wearing a dark plaid flannel shirt and the gray baggy trousers that all Russian men wore. He apologized for his tardiness and explained that he had been working.

We set off through a long park lined with leafy shade trees and benches where people sat reading newspapers or watching the pas-sersby and an occasional quiet drunk. Everything was calm. Birds twittered; every now and then a soft breeze nudged the trees lazily, brushing aside the still warmth of the day.

From the park we passed along a street lined with shops just opening after the daily lunch-hour break. We examined the shop displays and walked through a "buffet" cafeteria to see what it was serving. Sasha offered me a fruit drink, but the line was too long, a frequent problem, and I wanted to move on.

We walked through another smaller park with little children playing in the tiny playground and into the old quarter. Here there were low apartment buildings with peeling paint and even a few dilapidated houses that surprisingly had not been torn down to make way for some of the ugly new high-rise apartments that were so preva-lent in Moscow. We came to a church with golden onion domes and clean red brick, set in among the aging buildings like a jewel. Sasha pointed out the plaque that showed which years the church had been in use, because it was now locked, open only a couple of days a week for exhibition. It had recently been restored, along with numerous other churches that were no longer "working" churches, for preservation as a museum. We shook all the doors and tried to peek through the windows, hoping to see some of the old paintings and ikons. But the doors were chained and the windows too high. So we climbed over a wire fence and slid down a small embankment on the cotton fluff.

We found ourselves in a junkyard in back of a house. Actually, the house was a long, three-story building that served as an apartment building for quite a few families. There was always a housing shortage in the city. Coming around the side, we went through a stone archway between two buildings and into a rectangular courtyard. Here too, the tranquillity of the spring afternoon had seeped in. Grandmothers sat crocheting and gossiping quietly while children drew chalk pictures on the pavement. Some drew flowers or trucks or stick figures, while two little girls worked intensely on the elaborate floor plan of a house that no doubt had never existed and probably never would, except in their childhood fantasies.

We walked around the courtyard trying, without seeming too obvious, to see into the darkened rooms, looking for some clue to the people who lived in this somber, silent house on such a dreamlike day. When the grandmothers started to watch us suspiciously, we slid quietly through another archway and out into the dazzling heat and light of the open street.

We had known better than to tangle with the old babushkas who played such a large part in Soviet life, bringing up their grandchildren while the parents were working. These women were of an older order, the revolutionaries of the 1920's, not like their descendants who had never known the fervor of the Revolution. They felt a strong sense of community, one in which loyalty and mutual help were all-important and privacy was a petty bourgeois luxury. Everyone worked together for the good of the Party. The babushkas were also meddlers and gossips. They undoubtedly were curious about what we were doing in their courtyard and were probably on the point of scolding us for intruding, snooping on their little community. They might have enjoyed knowing that I was a foreigner, speaking their language and interested in their country, but surely they would have frowned on Sasha for fraternizing with an "American imperialist."

We walked on, passing crumbling buildings, some that had been recently renovated, and new government offices; down twisting streets and cobblestone alleyways until at last we returned to the little park to sit for a while under the shade trees.

By now the sun was relaxing in the sky. People were coming home from work and the quiet laziness had left the air. The line in the "buffet" was twice as long and all the shops were crowded. I said good-bye to Sasha and descended into the subway, carried along by the jostling, rush-hour commuters. The regular rhythmic clattering of the train soothed me, evoking the peace of the hypnotic afternoon in that fantastic part of the city. I was going back now to the present, to the miles and miles of cement high-rises that held no beauty but only the dismal, functional grayness of Soviet Russia. That spring afternoon had been for me a brief respite, a glimpse into what the past — good or bad — might have been.

Leona. Jerry and I had a glimpse into the Russian past, both spiritually and physically, when we arranged to join our dissident friends at an appointed meeting place on a warm spring night.

Yury and his wife Nadya waited for us at the Metro entrance for Dynamo Stadium, the massive soccer field and sports complex off Leningradsky Prospekt. We had gone to some trouble to set the meeting place without using the telephone. Jerry and I came in our Volvo and parked it on a side street nearby. Still, we wondered if the presence of a foreign car with distinguishing white K-04 license plates would not cause problems for our friends. We often felt that their fearlessness might be foolhardy. They worried about telephone calls being tapped but they weren't concerned with the obvious: having their neighbors see them with foreigners. In spring it was more difficult to blend into the Russian population. Although we were racially the same our clothes, shoes and hair styles stood out. In winter, with Russian fur hats, boots and old coats, it is harder to tell foreigners from Russians.

The prospect of being followed, of causing trouble to our friends by being there, of being singled out by observant strangers in this quarter of the city where foreigners seldom ventured — all this lay heavily on us that night because of the words a friend had spoken only a half hour before. Our first stop that evening had been a cocktail party in the apartment of the chargé d'affaires of the American Embassy. I stood talking with the wife of an American Embassy officer when a foreign journalist whose Russian wife was away stopped for a moment to ask if Jerry and I would join him for dinner afterward. I laughed and said, "Thanks, but it's one of those nights when we're meeting Russian friends in the subway," putting a note of mystery in my voice. He answered with an understanding smile, and continued on his way. The American woman reached over and whispered heatedly in my ear: "You shouldn't say things like that. You haven't been here long, but you'll learn. None of us are sure what his contacts are." She had no reason to suspect the man of double dealing; he spoke Russian and had a Russian wife, but these were attributes that fitted a number of our colleagues. She had spread the virus of distrust, and for the rest of the evening I wondered why the journalist had given us a ride back to the *Time* office so we could pick up our car, and whom he called when he left us. I scanned the vicinity for signs that we were being followed.

With Yury and Nadya, we walked quietly through the darkening streets to meet Pyotr and Natasha, who waited for us in their dacha-in-town, an izba, set with others like it in an overgrown field. It was a lost piece of a village from another era, forgotten somehow by Moscow's bulldozers as the city grew. Nearby were new concrete pre-fabricated apartment houses laid out in neat rectangular patterns.

Natasha and Pyotr rented their one-room hut for the summer as a respite from their parents, with whom they shared a two-room apartment. The hut had the great virtue of privacy, but little else. There was no gas or electricity, only an old, tile-covered, wood-burning central stove that had served the Revolution and evoked the harshness as well as the simplicity of nineteenth-century life. To us it seemed like a playhouse. The happy playmates called themselves husband and wife but they were not legally married. They couldn't make up their minds to take the step because of Pyotr's precarious existence as an English translator. He was arrested once for his religious activities and after a year in labor camp found it difficult to get regular work. He managed to keep going on the largesse of friends and through free-lance translations that paid a set fee. But this work was unpredictable and a visit to Pyotr's might be either feast or famine.

He worried about marrying Natasha for another reason. If he were arrested again on charges of parasitism or anti-Soviet activity

Natasha would suffer from guilt by association and her career as a musician would be aborted. She had a fine voice and worked with a choral group.

The inner walls of the izba were whitewashed and across one end of the room Pyotr had painted a colorful dragon. Furnishings consisted of a table, a bed and two chairs. Nails in the wall held a few cooking pots. Pyotr and Natasha were delighted that we had come and proudly laid out white bread, slices of sausage, cheese and a pot of strong tea. Heavy-set Natasha, who loved sweets, had bought a large chocolate cake with butter cream for dessert. There weren't enough cups to go around but we took turns.

Apart from the bright dragon, the izba's only other wall decoration was a photograph of Alexsandr Solzhenitsyn. It was the first but not the last time we were to see a photo of Solzhenitsyn on a friend's wall. Pyotr told us that Solzhenitsyn was working at the dacha of the cellist Rostropovich. Pyotr asked Jerry not to write anything about it yet because it would cause problems for Rostropovich and for Solzhenitsyn. "It is one thing for us to know and another for it to be published in the West," explained Pyotr, who regarded Solzhenitsyn as a moral exemplar and spiritual leader. Jerry said Solzhenitsyn's picture reminded him of the pictures of Ho Chi Minh that were tacked to peasant huts in South Vietnam. Neither Yury nor Pyotr had met Solzhenitsyn. They knew him from his writings and from his statement against censorship. They admired the way he refused to compromise with the authorities. His career and the publication of his works abroad had become a barometer of the times; an official campaign against Solzhenitsyn meant that the Politburo and the Writers' Union were mounting an offensive for conformity among intellectuals. Efforts to harass him were reported by word of mouth and his safety and freedom became a quiet cause. His writings spoke for many silent voices in Moscow.

We had seen the two couples we were with through the winter and we asked what dangers they faced in seeing us. We all felt certain that the walls of the izba were not bugged. Pyotr explained, "Under collective leadership there seems to be a new set of rules. As long as we pass samizdat materials amongst ourselves there does not seem to be a problem. It's when news from the camps in the 'Chronicle of Current Events' [the samizdat publication] reaches the West that the problems begin. Then the KGB goes wild and tries to find the source. We hear that they are even trying to use a computer to find the authors of the 'Chronicle.'

"Here, look at these," said Pyotr, as he took out five pictures of poor quality which had been smuggled out of Magdagen in the north of Siberia. A pair of German shepherd dogs, the bare, harsh outlines of a barbed-wire fence in what was obviously a prison camp — this was how they kept the prisoners in line. Pyotr also showed us pictures of Yuly Daniel in prison and of Anatoly Marchenko, a worker who later recorded his harrowing experiences in the book *My Testimony*. "There are also hundreds of prisoners in the camps for their religious beliefs."

"But what do you feel about the Revolution?" Jerry asked. He wondered what it was that they really wanted to see changed in Soviet law and life.

Yury and his wife said they believed in the great experiment of building socialism. "But," said Yury, "It is obvious that the authorities break the laws they are supposed to uphold. The Soviet constitution, even Stalin's constitution, provides for freedom but it is the way they interpret the law that is so discouraging. This leadership was raised under Stalin, under him they learned that the choice was to survive either by going along and signing death warrants or by committing suicide. Those who are left escaped by getting blood on their hands. Now they are faced with a world of technology and economic development. Kosygin is the only one who has the skill of a manager, but he lacks the drive and strength to really do more than follow the pack. They are tired old men who fear that innovation will remove them from power. Yet they are too scarred by the excesses of Stalin to go as far as he did. They know they cannot get away with mass terror so they practice selective repression and hope it will carry the day for them.

"Look at Czechoslovakia," Yury continued. "How long can they impose conformity and expect this country to survive in the twentieth century?"

But Pyotr with his sad, sensitive blue eyes and Christlike beard decried even the Revolution. For the first time we heard him speak from the depths of his spirit. He appealed for the return of the Christian values of the Russian Orthodox Church. "We were better off when we could appeal to human values, the values of the church. Our lives were richer and we had the excitement and mystery of holy days. We had a sense of man. Now all we have are empty slogans and corruption. The Revolution destroyed Christianity in Russia and it also destroyed the Russian spirit."

Pyotr had not seemed like a religious mystic. I was startled and asked: "But what of the brutality of life, the excesses of the Church and the feudal pattern of life that went with it? Didn't the Revolution sweep all that away too?"

"It was better than this dullness and torpor that we live with today," insisted Pyotr. Later we would realize this was a view that he shared with Solzhenitsyn, who also seeks to return to the values of the Russian Orthodox Church.

"What would you offer to the Jews with your return to the Church?" I asked.

"All the Jews I know want to convert to Christianity anyway," said Pyotr.

His naïveté shocked me into passive silence. The extremity of his position awakened in me a sensitivity to the wide differences among various groups in Russia. All of them opposed the regime, but often for reasons that conflicted harshly with one another. "Dissidents" or "democratic movement" was no longer for me a single-minded, unified category of Soviets who wanted to democratize the Soviet system and bring freedom to all. I began to read more cautiously the public statements of Solzhenitsyn. I began to differentiate Solzhenitsyn's yearning backward in time to the authoritarian orderliness of Russian life dominated by the Russian Orthodox Church, from the futuristic "convergence" of the physicist Sakharov, which would blend the best qualities of Western democracy and technology with a humanitarian concern for the security of the ordinary worker under socialism.

"Is anti-Semitism growing?" Jerry asked.

Yury explained that "since the Six-Day War in 1967 the Jews have found a new interest in Israel. At the same time the government policy has been strongly anti-Israel, pro-Arab. The government is forcing Jews to choose between the Soviet Union and Israel. By forcing Jews to sign statements against Zionism and Israeli aggression they are accentuating the issue of Jewishness in factories and offices. Right after the Six-Day War there was a strong feeling that the Arabs had let us down and there was admiration for the way in which the Jews had won. But now Israel's moral authority has been eroded and Soviet Jews feel threatened, as if they have to choose whether they want to be Zionists or not."

Pyotr and Yury were disillusioned with the venality and insincerity of Soviet politicians; they wanted to know whether we Americans felt the same about our own politicians. Subjected to *Pravda* and *Izvestia* every day and the tired clichés of Soviet political jargon, they wondered whether political rhetoric was capable of substance. They had been fascinated by the oratory of John Kennedy; they listened to the words of American politicians as if they had something to communicate. They were curious about Nixon, remembering him as a cold warrior and questioning whether he would be any different as president.

Yury had read George Orwell's essay on politics and the English language and was fond of quoting Orwell: " 'If thought corrupts language, language can also corrupt thought.' Not only has the bureaucracy of the Communist Party destroyed the lifestyle and the enthusiasm of the Russian people, but it is ruining the language. Only Solzhenitsyn seems able to retain Russian. Our young writers have all slipped into political jargon, or else they write with foreign expressions. There is no purity of language any more. Perhaps it is the nature of modern technological societies, capitalist or Communist," Yury mused. He was reflecting the same complaints Solzhenitsyn had made.

As we talked there was a rustling noise outside. We all stopped to listen. Then Pyotr smiled and said, "Don't worry, it's only the neighbor's dog." Speaking freely without inhibition we had all flinched at a strange noise, as if some intruder had come to spy on our thoughts and feelings.

On the way home I was angry with Pyotr and his obsolete religious ideas. Jerry reminded me that Christians, mystics and old believers were still serving in labor camps for their beliefs; Pyotr's romantic yearning for a Christian revival was a humanist counter to the dullness of Soviet life. But I argued that his hunger for a pre-Revolutionary past, like all romanticism applied to political solutions, provides a dangerous alternative to present woes.

The wet spring turned to dry summer and brought the close of school. I went to see the directress to make sure that she did more than promote each of the children to the next grade. By the end of the first school year the children and I agreed that they would have been better off with Russian children their own age, even if it meant starting at a harder level of Russian schoolwork. Doveen, who was repeating first grade, found the work more advanced than she had in American first grade, and she was with other seven-year-olds, so she had no difficulty. But Katie, Stevo and Evelind were with children a year or two younger than themselves. This eased the burden of doing work in Russian because they were in effect repeating a level of learning they had accomplished already, although in another language. But the disparity of personal interests and the differences in maturity between them and their classmates made them feel more odd and set apart than they would have felt if they had had to contend with the cultural and language differences alone.

Nadezhda Aleksandrovna accompanied me. She and I sat next to each other facing the directress, as on the first day with the children. We sat silent, waiting for her to finish reading the paper in her hand. Then she lifted her head with a scowl, and without waiting for Nadezhda Aleksandrovna to translate, lit into me. She shouted that she was fed up with my children for not doing any work and for upsetting the order of the school. I would have been frightened if it hadn't been so humorous, because all four children were famous with their teachers for earnest endeavor and for behavior that was perhaps a little unnaturally restrained. They hadn't relaxed enough yet to cause trouble, even the normal teasing and fights that well-behaved children occasionally get into.

Nadezhda Aleksandrovna and I burst out laughing and she stopped the directress to correct her. We both knew she was referring to another family, Canadians who were there for only one year and had two good-natured, high-spirited teenaged boys who could not be convinced that learning Russian would ever be useful to them again. The two boys thrived in Moscow weather, which was similar to the weather they knew back home; they helped Stevo change from a wobbly-ankled beginner into a self-assured whip on the ice hockey rink. They learned enough Russian for their sports needs and to engage the susceptible members of their classes at school in practical jokes and disruption.

"Ah, Schecter?" the directress said, straightening her memory of me and indicating a different attitude. She did not go so far as to smile at her mistake. Without waiting for my request she told me she had decided to jump Stevo and Katie over one class. I tried to persuade her to jump Evelind two classes, and failed. I argued that Evelind's work was successful and that it was most important for her at fifteen to have friends her own age. She agreed, but at the end of the eighth grade, where I wanted her to be, Evelind would have to take a set of examinations to be promoted to the equivalent of high school. The directress didn't think that in one year Evelind could learn enough to pass the exams. To have her try and fail was too great a risk. She didn't want to take the responsibility. There would be some students in seventh grade who were a year younger but others would be almost Evelind's own age. I couldn't make a dent. However, Barney could enter the first grade in the fall even though he wasn't old enough by Russian standards. She gave me the name of the government education office that would have to approve his starting school at six instead of seven. We knew he might have some difficulty in being with students older than he was, but if he returned to the United States at seven, never having attended first grade, he might be permanently set back a year in school.

When school was out the children enjoyed the freedom for a few days, but then time hung heavy on them. In Lenin Hills I had often passed the Pioneer Palace, a low, colorful building of modern design that housed children's craft studios, small theaters and sports facilities. Perhaps it would offer some constructive activities. I took a taxi and found the building open, but I couldn't find anyone in charge. I wandered through well-lit, pleasant studios until I found a teacher to ask how I could enroll the children. He showed me an impressive schedule but explained that I could not bring the children. Only organized groups from schools and youth organizations could use the Pioneer Palace. Sports facilities were usually used by school teams who came for training. Once a student chose an activity he had to devote a serious amount of time to it. As in other aspects of Soviet life, there was little room for individualistic experimentation.

After a few days of luxurious inactivity and a few more of boredom, Doveen decided she would try "city camp."

Doveen. When school ended for the year, I had nothing to do so I decided to go to city day camp. The camp was held at the school that I went to. They took the desks out of two classrooms and replaced them with cots for naptime. A room was set up for the girls and a separate one for the boys. We had to bring our own linen. I had to be there at nine every morning and went home at five.

For breakfast we were usually given hard-boiled eggs, mashed potatoes with a raw egg broken in the middle, or *maneya,* which was a cold lump of Cream of Wheat, and a piece of good wholesome Russian bread with a huge chunk of butter on it. The kids weren't given knives with their silverware (which was a tinnish metal) so they spread their butter with the back of their spoons. But the cook, a fat lady with her hair falling out of her bun, came and spread mine with her big heavy butcher knife. We had coffeemilk, tea, or *kompot,* which is a warm, cooked fruit drink.

When we got there we would go upstairs and have relay races and play with the toy blocks, cars and dolls in the playroom. On the walls of the playroom were painted enormous pictures of Russian storybook characters. During our playtime, the cook would come up to pick out her helpers for the day. We were excited because everyone wanted to be her helper. On the day I was chosen with my friend Maxim we got to set the tables for lunch, help the cook serve from the big steaming pots on her rolling table, and clear the table.

Everyone else got ready for our day's trip. Once we went to see Robert Louis Stevenson's *Kidnapped* in Russian. Another time we went to a big park in front of our school, behind some apartment buildings. The park had woods and grassy clearings. There were other groups of children, some in white aprons on outings with their day-camp teachers. We picked strawberries, wild berries and wildflowers. On the far end of the park was a tiny factory that made toys and school supplies. We were allowed to look in the window and see plastic toy dining room furniture being packed into cardboard boxes. The man demonstrated quickly for us how one of the small cardboard boxes was folded. Through the window he gave us each a plastic centimeter ruler.

Next to the factory was a small graveyard. On each gravestone there was a photograph of the person in the grave, in a decorative frame. The graveyard didn't seem sad to us because it was a beautiful day and we were having a good time.

Another day we went to the Moscow zoo. We went on the regular bus. The teacher brought bags of old bread and we all fed the ducks in the zoo pond. That day we wore our white aprons.

Leona. At the end of her first school year in Moscow, Doveen, just turned eight, wrote a geographical summary of her new home to a friend in Tokyo.

Doveen. Russia is a Communist country. Moscow is the capital of Russia. Russia is one of the Republics of the USSR. I have lived here a year. I went to Russian school. The dolls in Russia have white faces. Whenever some imported toys come to Dom Igrushki, the biggest toy store in Moscow, they are gone in one day. No one lives in a house. Everybody must live in an apartment building. I live in an apartment building that is only for foreigners. In Russia there is no gum so everyone at school begs you for gum. They don't have any Coke. In front of the university for African and Indian people there is a sign that says, "Russians will always have peace with people from other parts of the world." But if you ever see someone colored walking near to you and you are a Russian you will go over and shove him or her.

List of what they have in Russia:

Yes	*No*
kvass	Band-Aids
chocolate	gum
prune soda pop	felt-tipped pens
long lines	comics
Kremlin	Hawaiian Punch
smelly bathrooms at school	Coke
good steak	root beer
good black bread	Log Cabin Syrup
stuck elevators	cornflakes
white-faced dolls	
fat ladies sunning in their underwear	

10

Summer Love and Other Affairs

A FRIEND OF JERRY'S AND MINE from Tokyo who now lived in Calcutta cabled to say she would be stopping over in Moscow. She arrived late in the afternoon, checked in at the Metropol Hotel, and decided to have dinner and then rest. In the hotel restaurant, it took a long time, as is usual in Moscow, to be served. While she was waiting, a good-looking young Russian asked in English if he could join her. He began a long conversation, and was delighted to find she was a concert pianist. He, too, was well versed in music. Remarkably, he had heard of her teacher and of the conservatory where she had studied. A small world! He had studied Japanese for years. Could he show her around Moscow?

Charlotte is a chic woman in her late forties, whose face, though attractive, does nothing to hide her years. "First of all," she said, when she told me about it the next day, "I was too tired. Second of all, I'm old enough to know better than to start anything with a twenty-five-year-old." What intrigued her was the double coincidence of his knowing both the music world and Japanese. She asked if I thought he was planted to meet her, and if so, why? Who would have sent her name ahead to give the Soviets time to set this fellow in place for a provocation?

I asked if she knew any Russians in Calcutta. "Not really," she said. "When we first arrived some Russians came to see us who said they were friends of the Ovchinikovs, a couple who were friends of ours in Tokyo." Her mention of the Ovchinikovs took me by surprise — we also knew them. I asked Charlotte how they had come to know the Ovchinikovs. "No special reason, just friends. They love music and I often played at their house after dinner. They were very friendly to us in Tokyo."

Vsevolod Ovchinikov was the *Pravda* correspondent and the leading Russian journalist in Tokyo. He was in China and Tibet during the days of Soviet-Chinese friendship in the 1950's. During his stay in Tokyo, which lasted six years, he and Jerry met occasionally for lunch at the Foreign Correspondents' Club in Marunouchi, where they talked about the Vietnam war or their countries' foreign policies. But his interests ranged wider than politics. He was the author of one book on Chinese porcelains and another on Japanese pearl culture. When *Time* applied to reopen the bureau in Moscow, Jerry asked Ovchinikov to find out what the chances were for a favorable reply.

Ovchinikov was optimistic that the bureau would be reopened and we assumed his judgment would play some part in the Russians' decision whether or not to accredit Jerry. Months went by without an answer from the Soviets and we decided to go to Rome instead. Ovchinikov encouraged us to wait a little longer before making a final decision. He and his family were about to return to Moscow after many years abroad. They described to us the wonderful food and wines we would enjoy together, how easily we would find whatever we needed for our house, the comradely spirit that would prevail. Mrs. Ovchinikov, who was a housing engineer, told me that the only thing I couldn't get in Moscow was cocktail dresses. My mother asked Ovchinikov if Jews were allowed to live in Kiev without paying a special tax as they had to before the Revolution. "There's no more anti-Semitism in the Soviet Union," he assured her, and explained that large numbers of Jews now chose to live in Kiev.

The Ovchinikovs invited us to their home in Tokyo for a Russian dinner, after which we sat late into the night discussing the differences in philosophical heritage between our two countries, and the things we had in common. As if he were hearing it for the first time he listened to us explain the Puritan ethic that influenced not only America's history and character, but the crisis the country was facing in the late

1960's. We were like Russians, he said approvingly, prone to introspection and analysis of our own society.

A few days later we invited his daughter to join our children in a visit to the American trade exhibit, where live baby chicks were being given away. At first he accepted, but then he called back to say she had to go out of town.

We hardly saw the Ovchinikovs in Moscow. They found it difficult to see us except when we gave a large cocktail party and a contingent from *Pravda* swept along with them. It was just over a year since we had last seen each other, from April 1968 to May 1969. Mrs. Ovchinikov and I greeted each other as old friends and drew off to one side to talk. She complained that she did not enjoy her normal strength in Moscow, probably because she couldn't have the fresh vegetables and fruits that were available all winter in Tokyo. She was often ill, and it had been a hard year. Her husband was writing a book on Japan and they were shut away in a dacha while he worked on it. Ovchinikov broke into our conversation. I sensed that he wanted to cut short her disadvantageous comparison of Moscow to Tokyo.

"It's a miracle," he said in English, smiling broadly. "Only a year ago you couldn't speak a word of Russian and now you two can have a heart-to-heart talk in Russian. It's amazing!" In one blow he had restrained his wife and complimented me. His years as diplomat and journalist had not been wasted.

The book for which his wife suffered, *A Branch of Sakura*, appeared in *Novy Mir* (*New World*), the highly esteemed literary magazine, early in 1970, in two parts. It was a phenomenal success and Russian friends encouraged me to read it. They said they could not put it down once they had begun. I read some of it and found it sensitive and perceptive, but in its appreciation of Japan similar to a number of books by Americans who lived there. In the West it would have been just another well-written book about Japan, but in the Soviet Union it was a revelation. Coming at a time of hysterical fear, when Russians imagined Chinese hordes rampaging across the border into the Soviet Union, it was soothing for Russians to read about Asians who were gentle, perhaps comprehensible, people with whom Russians might get along.

I listened to Charlotte's tale and wondered if Ovchinikov, a gentleman of such cultivated sensibilities and literary talent, could have been the conduit for setting up Charlotte in a possible indiscretion.

Jerry was away when Charlotte visited, and when he returned I told him about her "coincidental" meeting with the well-briefed young man at the Metropol. Was it planned, and why Charlotte? He burst out laughing. "Don't be shocked," he said. "It's industrial spying [Charlotte's husband was an expert in advanced computers]. Just think what they could do with some photographs of Charlotte in bed with the young provocateur. They could present the pictures to Paul and threaten to show them around if Paul refused to give them the computer secrets they need so badly. They're far behind us in computers — Charlotte could have been a shortcut to catching up."

Another friend from Tokyo, Rita Peach, called one June day to say she was in Moscow. In fact, she said, she had been there two weeks.

"What?" I exclaimed. "Why haven't you called us until now?"

She was suffering, she explained, from the end of a beautiful but brief encounter. As was her habit, she clothed this disclosure in such cheery bravado that it was hard to tell how deeply she had been wounded. "We'll talk tomorrow," she promised with a meaningful low in her voice. We agreed to meet at 10 A.M. in front of her hotel and visit the Tretyakov Gallery.

When I met Rita as planned I found her shaken and upset. "I was standing out there waiting for you and a huge black chauffeur-driven limousine pulled up. A middle-aged man in the back seat shouted at me in Russian. He opened the door and was waving wildly at me to get in beside him. He finally gave up and drove on. You should have seen him wagging his head in disgust."

"Why didn't you go?" I joked. "From the description of the car he was at least Central Committee, maybe even Politburo. You're doing well."

"You say that with a straight face. You've been here too long."

I couldn't understand why she was so unnerved by the approach, crude as it was. She wore a bold black-and-white printed summer dress that clearly marked her a foreigner. She has the high round cheeks of a beautiful aging cherub; in her smile is the eternal friendly innocence of the American Midwest. Rita is tall and overweight, with golden blond hair swept up in a stylish twist. In other cultures her exaggerated curves might have been a drawback, but in Moscow they were appreciated.

At the Tretyakov we looked at ikons and Soviet works of art glorifying workers and partisans in the war against the Germans. Rita paid close attention to each statue and painting, as if she were trying to forget what had happened in front of the hotel. By the time we had seen everything in the gallery, she could feel nothing but thirst and aching feet.

We sat down to cold apple juice and stale pastry in the buffet attached to the museum. Under the long eaves only a few pencils of late-afternoon sunlight came through the windows. It was cool and quiet; only one other of the half-dozen tables was occupied — by two young men. The unpolished wooden floor was gritty underfoot and the plastic tops were permanently stained with the resigned grubbiness that permeates Moscow.

Then Rita told me what was bothering her. "I arrived in Moscow a week before Intourist expected me and they didn't know what to do about it. They made it clear that I would do what they told me to — they're tyrants. 'No, no,' I pleaded, 'don't make me join a group of African students on a short tour into Central Asia. I have friends here. They used to live in Tokyo. He is an American journalist. He works for *Time* magazine.' The guide explained that there is a separate telephone listing of foreigners, in English — all foreign newsmen, diplomats and business firms. The poor guide, she had the patience of a tired machine. Only she didn't have the book of foreigners and she didn't know how to get one. We tried calling the American Embassy but the numbers she had only got us a toy store and the circulation department of *Pravda*."

I was sympathetic but couldn't help laughing. "Finally, I gave in." Rita waxed dramatic as she related her ordeal with Intourist. "I realized that for the week until my reservation began I would be a nonperson. I was a Martian who had landed on a side street and couldn't read the signs that led to the main thoroughfare. When my week in limbo was over I would exist again and eat real Russian food, I would have the right to look at the churches I wanted to see, go to the museums and stores I'd heard about for years from all those White Russians I knew in the Far East. Obviously I had a White Russian list. But in the meantime I would stick to the Red list: get in and out of trains and buses as directed, eat the food offered on the coupons I clutched obediently, sleep in the hotels I was put into, and show visible appreciation for the scientific and cultural achievements of the heart of Asia, where only twenty years before there was nothing but wind, sand and nomads."

Rita finished this episode with a sweep of her arm, in a voice of sardonic exhaustion. Then her eyes sparkled again and there was deviltry in the corners of her smile. "But I won, after all." She laughed triumphantly. "The best part of the trip wasn't in my itinerary — Vladimir." What can even mighty Intourist do about love? "I met him in the dollar bar of one of their own hotels."

A dollar bar? The dollar bar of the Natsional Hotel in Moscow, just a short walk from Red Square, is a small room off the brightly lit main corridor that leads to the restaurant. It is one flight up the grand circular staircase. In the dollar bar the lights are low. One can just make out the bottles and the gleam of the chrome coffee machine. For nominal prices in hard currency it is possible to order Black Label scotch, well-aged French brandy, and dry Armenian champagne. The customers are foreign businessmen and young Russian girls in flowing black dresses and bouffant hairdos. I have often seen the girls freshening up in the ladies' room next door, barking vile-tempered orders to the attendant to get them cotton balls and clean towels. From the woman's angry stare and sulky obedience, I assumed she had no choice but to do as she was told: the young whores were in the pay of the state. An American foreign service officer told me that the American Embassy had a file of complaints and confessions by American businessmen who had the courage to report that they had been presented with photographs showing them in bed with these girls. They were later approached back home in America by Russian Embassy officials who demanded seemingly irrelevant information in return for discretion about the photographs.

It was in such a dollar bar that Rita met Vladimir. In a small spa town in Central Asia she had stopped for a nightcap in the dimly lit lounge of the hotel. Vladimir sat nursing his drink, apparently waiting for Rita to walk into his life. Like Rita, he had recently come out of an unhappy marriage. They found each other sensitive, intelligent, mutually receptive. He was an automobile engineer at Togliattigrad, where a new plant was under construction to assemble Fiats for Soviet use. His good command of English made him useful in foreign technical negotiations. It helped the two of them communicate even though they might have reached each other even without the convenience of words.

"He is tall and broad, fair-haired with light skin," Rita said.

"Pure Russian," I nodded.

"He has marvelous blue eyes. They searched into my soul." She imitated his accent but mocked herself. Then more seriously, she assured me, "Russian men are such great lovers." I stared at her in wonder. "Never," she said, "have I met such tenderness."

I found it hard to believe that Rita had found a Russian attractive and tender; with few exceptions the Soviet men I knew were masculine but heavy-handed, socially coarse, and seemed formless in their box-cut suits and layers of sweaters. Their sensuality was suffused with garlic and unwashed clothes. But more than the fascination that I felt in her attraction was the doubt in Vladimir's intentions. Try as I might I could imagine no reason why the Soviets might want to snare Rita into an embarrassing attachment with Vladimir as the bait. Rita and the Kremlin had no interest in spying on each other. Then what was Vladimir doing in the dollar bar, spending his foreign currency (perhaps earned in his negotiations with the Italians) on drink? Was it worth it for a little foreign scotch, or did he have hopes of meeting foreign women there? Did he have a particular desire for foreign women, or was his desire to meet any woman who would marry him and get him out of the Soviet Union? Whereupon he could leave her and go his own way? I wanted to warn Rita of my doubts, but she was as moody as an infatuated teenager, and perhaps as volatile. I decided to keep them to myself and listen to her story.

After Vladimir met Rita, he cut short his Central Asian holiday and set off for the capital. When Rita returned to Moscow, Vladimir was waiting for her, as he had promised, at the Minsk Hotel, which was not on the A or B lists (the best hotels, as officially designated by Intourist), but convenient to the center of the city. During an idyllic week they talked about marriage to each other. He knew of no way for him to secure an exit visa, but he was willing to try walking across the border, even though others had been shot in such an attempt. The obvious alternative was for Rita to settle down with him in Togliattigrad.

Would romance survive between a pleasure-loving woman who had lived in both the East and the West and an engineer in a small industrial city on the Volga? Past forty, with grown children away at school in America, she was not about to start a new family to keep her busy during the short days and long nights when Vladimir was at the factory. Perhaps she could survive on short trips into the outside world; she would still be an American citizen with foreign currency to spend. But how long would her bank account last when her alimony was cut off? Remarriage would automatically dry up the dollar supply that had given her the freedom to travel, to curb her loneliness in brief but heady affairs.

A new love after forty is sweet, but Rita had not become so intoxicated that she lost sight of the pitfalls. In a small city she would be totally dependent on the goodwill of his family and friends — how would they receive her and her foreign ways? Whom would she talk to in introspective moments when she needed a friend, someone who spoke her language in its native nuances? Would she be forced to become a Soviet citizen? And if the marriage didn't work after that, what would she do? Soberly, sadly, but realistically they agreed to part. The day after Vladimir left Moscow Rita got in touch with us.

Just as Rita finished her story, the two young men at the other table came toward us, smiling. One of them feigned curiosity about the heavy silver Laotian bracelet I was wearing, which provided just enough conversation to sort out who could manage in Russian and who would try to talk in English. They were both Armenians from Yerevan, the capital of the Armenian Republic, on a week's holiday. The shorter one, less handsome but shrewd-looking, knew a little English and practiced it earnestly on Rita. The lazy eyes of his dark handsome friend, my partner in conversation, betrayed his vain stupidity; he fitted my Russian friends' view that all Armenian men think they are sexual supermen and irresistible to women. He was delighted to meet me because he wanted desperately to go to America.

"I know for a fact," he said, "that Armenians in California are making $125 a week working in factories."

I agreed that this was possible, but warned him that it is expensive to live in America, and to make that much in a factory he would have to be skilled at some job. He would have to have a specialty.

"Every Armenian has four or five specialties," he assured me with a sneer. He said that Armenians are smart and ambitious, and that many are rich. That I believed; I had heard many stories about their shrewd profiteering. The familiar pattern was for an Armenian or Georgian "middleman" to fill a huge market basket with tomatoes, cucumbers, greens and cut flowers in the sunny south, buy an extra seat for it on an airplane going to Moscow or Leningrad, calm the stewardess with a lavish tip, and sell off the load in a rynok at the rate, say, of $6.50 a pound for tomatoes in January.

"It's easy to make money in this country," the young Armenian explained, "but there's nothing to spend it on. And without freedom to come and go, what good is money? The only way to be ambitious in a socialist country is to want to get out."

He looked over his shoulder to judge whether or not the counter-girl was listening and adjusted his voice to a seditious low. "I have a friend with good connections," he said, and paused ominously, "who told me that if I paid a thousand rubles and had a foreign wife, he could get me an exit visa." I perked up, for Rita and Vladimir's sake. He said, resuming his normal voice, that he would like to see me again. I felt threatened with complications, and at once abandoned the cause of Rita and Vladimir.

"Certainly I would like to see you again," I replied, "and I'm sure my husband would like to meet you too. Please meet me tomorrow morning at his office," and I reached for paper and pencil to write down the address. His spirits fell, but he wasn't giving up. Apparently noticing Rita for the first time, he asked if she were also married. I answered that she was divorced. He took a closer look at her, and motioned with his hand that I should keep writing the office address.

"Yes," he said with the beginning of a smile, "I would love to meet you tomorrow morning in your husband's office. Before we meet again, will you do me one favor?" His face now lighted up with bravado and joy.

"Of course," I answered.

"Please tell your friend I want to marry her."

On an early summer morning I was shopping at the Gastronom when I came upon Helene Levine, an old friend visiting Moscow with her husband, an economics professor. They were buying a few things to eat, but mainly it was a chance for her to do some sight-seeing. So I went to some pains to explain the absurd and complicated system of prices and the procedure for paying. I had already been in line and given my order to the clerks.

I explained to Mrs. Levine the two sets of prices: one applied to certificates issued to Russians at prices comparable to the Soviet market, which were about three times the dollar price. The other applied to hard-currency coupons at prices closer to world norms. This system was obviously designed to earn foreign exchange currency and to entice the members of the diplomatic corps and other foreigners like us not to use our privilege of importing food and liquor from Helsinki or Copenhagen.

I showed Mrs. Levine what I had paid that day for butter, clabbered milk, farmer cheese, sausages — all at approximately one third the ruble price. Then we came to the listing for caviar; for 250 grams (a half pound) I had paid 21.80 rubles ($24.19), while the Russian market price was only 9.80 rubles ($10.88). I told Mrs. Levine it was probably an error, and went to get it changed before I picked up my groceries. First the cashier and then the countergirls told me the bill was right — the dollar price for caviar was more than double the Soviet market price. I still protested that it couldn't be so. We called a junior manager, who verified that the bill was correct. I called Jerry; we agreed to skip the caviar and I went back to report that I didn't need the caviar after all. I would like my money back and would they please cancel the listing for caviar before I picked up my order.

The cashier and the counter clerk stood aside biting their cheeks to see what would happen. The junior manager said it was impossible to give me back my money if I had already paid. I protested loudly that I had paid but not yet laid a hand on the caviar. I demanded to see the senior manager. He came out of the accounting office and explained that once the money was rung up and the item recorded as sold on their stock list there was nothing he could do to refund my money. I argued as patiently as I could that if they made some mistake in an order sent to me at home or if they had charged me for something in error, there would be no problem crossing out the overcharged item. What was there to prevent them from crossing out the caviar on the invoice, their copy and mine, and giving me back the money?

The cashier mumbled to the junior manager, "Of course she doesn't want it, it's cheaper in a ruble store." The counter clerk explained with an embarrassed shrug that the price was unfair, but it was virtually impossible to find caviar in a ruble store. The manager didn't give an inch — it was against the system to give back money.

Finally, exasperated, but still in a tone of reasonableness, I pointed out that all over the world, if you bought something and returned it unopened and unharmed within a fair period of time, whether it was in London, Tokyo, Hong Kong, New York or Rio de Janeiro, you could get your money back. Here I hadn't even received the goods and they wouldn't refund my money. Their eyebrows lifted; they looked at me with large, questioning eyes: "All over? Is that how it's done all over?"

"Yes," I said, tired but still somehow patient, "that's how it's done in the rest of the world."

"Well then," the manager said, turning to the junior manager for agreement and at her nod turning to the cashier. "Give this lady her money back and take the caviar off her order." He checked to see that the clerk put the caviar back in the cold case and crossed it off the invoice. I thanked them and took my money and everybody managed not to laugh.

Summer, naturally, is the time when visitors come to Moscow with their children.

Stevo. One good place to take American teenage visitors in Moscow is Dom Plakata, the House of the Poster on Dzerzhinsky Square. When you come up out of the Metro, you see the big black imposing statue of Felix Dzerzhinsky, founder of the Soviet secret police, in the middle of the square. The massive building behind Dzerzhinsky is called the Lubyanka. It is the central headquarters of the KGB. I rarely saw anyone go through its thick high doors. To the left of the Lubyanka is Detsky Mir (Children's World), the big department store which is always full of people. Moving right, across the street from the KGB, is Dom Plakata, where books and stamps are also sold.

There is a story that Kosygin was walking through Dzerzhinsky Square, once very late at night. He suddenly heard a voice from the upright statue saying, "Lyokha! [the familiar form of Aleksei] Lyokha! Bring me a horse! I've been standing here all these years, and I need something to sit on." Kosygin was very perplexed. The next day, he decided to confide in Brezhnev. Brezhnev thought Kosygin was ready for a dacha by the Black Sea after he heard the story, but agreed to go with him that night. At two in the morning they walked into the empty square. Dzerzhinsky's voice rang out, addressing Kosygin: "Lyokha! Lyokha! I asked you to bring me a horse and you brought me an ass!"

I usually found the poster section in the House of the Poster doing less business than the other stamp, book, and postcard outlets. The few browsing teachers or business people gave the poster saleslady no work compared to us astounding foreigners who bought up thirty posters at a time. All the posters cost ten kopecks (ten cents) except for the occasional oversize ones. In 1970, they put out an eight-foot-high poster of Lenin, smiling, with *Pravda* sticking out of his breast pocket. On the bottom, it read: "1870–1970." One of my favorites is about Maxim Gorky. With a Soviet flag draped in back of him, Maxim looks grimly to the left at a jumble of skyscrapers with big surreal black fountain pens floating in between them. The pens are spattering ink from their points and they each have a word printed on their barrels: "Falsehood," "Racism," "Cosmopolitanism," "Provocation," "Militarism." The big print between Gorky and the scenario reads: "The Bourgeoisie Is Poisonous to Culture." The caption below says: "There it is, the 'spirit' of contemporary bourgeois 'culture,' a disgusting and shameful spirit." These are all quotations from Maxim Gorky.

Another poster shows two big white hands clasped in front of a clump of dark high-rise "capitalist" buildings. The central, highest building has a mean little face capped with a Nazi type of helmet that has a big dollar sign on it. The buildings have "BANK" and "TRUST" in English all over them. Perched on the buildings to the right is a big black bomb with an "A" on it. The caption below the hands reads: "We won't let them in."

The posters I have described are among the few imaginative gems that one finds occasionally. Most Soviet posters repeat the endless pattern of Lenin, Party, Homeland, Capitalist and Communist in a drab and boring manner. There is a whole series of black, gray, and brown Lenins, on a white background. For each different pose there is a caption: "Lenin — teacher," "Lenin — leader," "Lenin — friend."

One Saturday morning when I came into town to the House of the Poster, I saw a big crowd milling around out in front of the store. The fifty people standing there were mostly men, ranging in age from twelve to forty. They were all selling and buying stamps from each other. The venders had little stamp booklets with cellophane strips on each page to hold their stamps in place. The dealer held the book open for the group gathered around him to see. Everyone talked about the stamps, asked prices, and bargained. Some proposed a stamp of their own in exchange. People joked about the Lubyanka across the street. They pointed across the street and laughed nervously. The stamps were

"Aid American-style"

Poster honoring the fiftieth anniversary of the Great October Revolution.
The slogan under the statue of Lenin reads: "Forward to Communism!"

mostly foreign, although there were some old Russian ones too. Stamps from the West were the most expensive. I bought a terrific old Chinese stamp for about thirty kopecks. It shows Stalin on the left side with the Kremlin in the background, shaking hands with Mao, who is also standing bigger than life in front of Tien An Men Gate (from 1950). It was a lively business, and people were enjoying themselves.

I went back a couple of weeks later but the place was deserted. "Speculation" is not allowed in the Soviet Union, especially under the windows of the KGB.

Leona. Traveling with children is always a risk; they may be bored, become difficult, or get sick.

The first afternoon that Marshall Loeb, one of the senior editors of *Time,* his wife Peggy and their two children spent in Moscow they came to our apartment for lunch. Peggy said that thirteen-year-old Adam's restlessness was unusual, but I thought it normal for a boy that age to dislike sitting while his parents and their friends talked over old times.

The morning after they left us Marshall called from the Natsional Hotel to say that a Soviet ambulance was on its way to take Adam to Botkin Hospital. "Adam had a bad night," Marshall said. When they realized he had more than a stomach ache, the hotel helped them call a Soviet doctor, who ordered an immediate appendectomy.

Both the *Time* and *Life* interpreters rushed to Botkin to help the Loebs through the ordeal. Peggy, who is a trained nurse, and Marshall were very self-possessed and said they didn't need me to spend the day with them. We kept in touch by telephone and late in the afternoon Marshall said Adam would be out of the recovery room soon. If I came over I could visit Adam and have dinner with Marshall and Peggy. The interpreters had just left; they had been very helpful, Marshall said.

Jerry was out of Moscow on a story, so Evelind came along for company. Since children aren't allowed visiting privileges in hospitals, she waited with Peggy near the emergency room door while I went into the hospital with Marshall.

As often as he had been through the labyrinth of gray halls that led to the recovery room, he still thought he would get lost, so we were shown the way by a wizened old man with a whimsical smile whose

job it was to help carry stretchers from the ambulances. The old man
told me, "I can't count how many times I walked these halls today
showing your friend the way back and forth." It had been a heavy day
and he hung his bent shoulders a little lower to demonstrate how tired
he was. I thanked him for what he had done, and when he told me
again how strenuous his services had been I thanked him more
profusely.

An attendant tied Marshall into a white coat and mask so he could
go into the recovery room, but I had to wait with the old stretcher
carrier because I was not of Adam's immediate family. Marshall said
he wouldn't be long; he only wanted to tell Adam that we were going
to dinner.

After a minute Marshall came back to us, his face as white as his
coat. "Adam's not in the recovery room. I asked where he is and they
kept jabbering something about 'Korpus Pyat.' What is 'Korpus'?" he
demanded, fear rising in his eyes.

"Don't worry." I laughed, took his arm, and walked into the recovery area with him. "It means Building Number 5." The two doctors
on duty couldn't understand why the American father was so disturbed. They had done exactly what he had requested, which was to
move Adam to the diplomatic pavilion, Building Number 5. He was
on his way. In fact, the ambulance hadn't left yet and Marshall could
ride along with him. I told Marshall I would pick up Peggy and Evelind and we would meet him there.

The prune-skinned old man was waiting to lead me back to the
ambulance entrance and as we walked he told me again how much he
had done for Marshall. Again I replied in heartfelt tones, *"Bolshoye
spasibo"* (thank you very much), and went on: "How frightening it is
to have your child become ill in a foreign country, where you can't
speak the language; how wonderful that you were so considerate to
him when he needed help."

As we approached the emergency room he stopped and looked at
me. "I don't know how much Russian you speak but can you understand *'Bolshoye spasibo ne pashit shuby'*?"

I shook my head, assuming it was a proverb that was beyond my
comprehension. Resigned to not being understood, he walked off and
began to tidy the room. I stood where I was, repeating his words to
myself, and suddenly I understood. I burst out laughing and began to

dig in my purse for money, for of course, "a big thank-you doesn't sew a fur coat." There is a bit of Soviet hypocrisy that says that accepting tips is not permitted. So I waited until he was alone and pressed a three-ruble note, folded small, into his hand. He thanked me with his toothless smile.

Korpus Pyat had a rather frugal air for a diplomatic pavilion, but it was clean and well run. Adam's room was long and narrow, with two antique iron beds facing each other head to foot, and quaint veneer bedside stands.

He was very uncomfortable as he was transferred from the ambulance to the bed near the window, but he said it was nothing compared to the pain he felt during the operation. Hadn't he had anesthesia? Only a local, which hadn't lasted, and by the time it wore off it was too late to give him another local. He simply had to bear the pain, and more than that, his fear.

We asked one of the doctors why Adam hadn't had anesthesia and he looked at us contemptuously. "We never give more than a local for appendicitis," he said. He explained that because Moscow is on a large flat plain there is heavy static in the air, which makes it dangerous to use ether: it can easily burst into flame.

Other doctors gave us other reasons, but the real reason, apparently, was the shortage of trained anesthetists and safety monitoring equipment. Months later, Tolya, the office driver, also was given a local anesthesia for the removal of a long narrow growth at his waistline. As they opened his skin to cut it away they found that what showed was only the tip of a mountain; probing and cutting to remove the entire growth took hours, all on the same local injection. He was a bull of a man, able to lift heavy weights and work long hours, a man who normally made little of pain, but he said later that the pain was unbearable.

After Adam was settled we left him and walked to the Hippodrome, the racetrack a few blocks away, to have dinner. The ticket windows and the racecourse were dark and silent, but upstairs in the restaurant where winning bettors, sports writers and track officials ate in comfort on race days, diners were being served.

With the racecourse idle, the busy betting lobby echoed our footsteps. The streets around the Hippodrome, lit only by widely spaced streetlamps, were filled with the solemn dignity of the hospital and noiseless apartment buildings. The restaurant was nearly empty and the headwaiter seemed glad to have us to fill the void. The few quiet diners seemed lost in the high-ceilinged dining hall, trimmed ornately with red velvet and gold.

We sat down at a table set with damask and wine glasses. The food was the best of Moscow standard first-quality, approximately the same as at the Metropol or the Natsional Hotel. We started with black caviar and smoked sturgeon, dark bread and good fresh butter; then we all ordered fried chicken breasts stuffed with a vegetable dressing, a variation on Kiev cutlets. The food was well prepared and well served. We were just beginning to think about dessert when we realized that among us we didn't have enough rubles to pay for what we had already eaten. Both the Loebs and I had dollars with us and I had coupons representing dollars, but the restaurant was not authorized to accept anything but rubles. If we couldn't pay at least part in dollars, we were sunk.

Marshall called the young waiter and showed him our dollars. The waiter's pale-blue eyes lit up and he quickly looked around to see if anyone else had noticed. He told Marshall it would be all right but to hurry and get the dollars out of sight. The waiter's helper perceived what was happening and came to have a look, but the waiter motioned the younger boy to go away, stay nonchalant, and keep watch, all in one look. Implied in it too was a promise — if only they could carry it off without being seen by anyone else.

Satisfied that we wouldn't have to help in the kitchen, we each ordered a Moscow sundae: vanilla ice cream with fruit preserves spooned over the top and a cookie on the side. All of us were smiling benignly at one another and at the hovering waiter. When it came time to pay he took the rubles we had, but when Marshall tried to hand him the dollars he thought he saw the headwaiter coming and scampered away. His busboy kept looking to see if the deed had been done. The waiter, who was nervous enough, railed at him silently to keep his back turned to us, made two more sallies to take our dollars, and each time lost his nerve and withdrew. We sat with catlike grins just waiting. He stood a few feet behind Marshall, nervously pulling his waiter's towel through the palm of his hand like a watchful animal, ready to pounce or to fend off an attacker.

Then Peggy wrapped the dollars in the damask napkin in her lap and called out in a loud and imperious voice, "Will someone please take this dirty napkin away." She lifted it into the air like the shroud of a dead rat. The young waiter came running and grabbed it from her hand, relieved and grateful. We thanked him with pretentious aloofness, and feeling like partners to a not-very-serious crime, stole away.

At the end of August, leaving Adam Loeb at Botkin Hospital well on his way to recovery, the children and I set off for a shopping trip to Helsinki, the Hong Kong of the North, to outfit ourselves for the coming frost.

The Volvo, now a year old, needed repairs, which couldn't be accomplished in Moscow. Our pots and pans still stood on makeshift shelves because the promised Polish cabinets had never arrived.

My first plan was to drive the Volvo all the way to Helsinki, leave it there for repairs, and take the train back. Jerry, who was working on a story in Poland, would fly to Helsinki from Warsaw and drive the car back. We changed some of the plan because everyone in the office assured me it was too long a drive, especially with five children. Instead, Tolya would drive the car to Leningrad in time to meet us at the train station when the Red Arrow pulled in from its midnight to 8 A.M. run from Moscow. He would then drive us all to the border and hand the car over to me for the remainder of the trip to Helsinki.

Tolya arranged the train tickets and I made lists of everything we needed for the coming winter, for the apartment, and for Soviet friends who had lists of desires tucked away in drawers awaiting just such an opportunity. One friend yearned for a wig; another dreamed of velvet drapes and a coordinated bedspread. It seemed a heavy responsibility to choose for others colors and patterns they would have to live with for years to come, but they assured me they would like whatever I chose, and if they didn't it was never hard to dispose of luxury goods to their neighbors.

After a long wait in line, Tolya returned from the train station with six places on the midnight sleeper, and with an inordinate number of slips for each ticket. "What are all these parts of the tickets?" I asked as we drove to the Gastronom. He waved the back of his hand in the direction of the tickets and began to recount what they were for.

"One is the ticket to get on the train, another is for a place in a sleeper compartment." That accounted for twelve of the tickets; what about the other six?

"And another is for laundry."

"Laundry?" I asked, bewildered.

"Yes, for clean sheets," Tolya answered, seriously. What, he wanted to know, was so funny?

"Clean sheets?" I was now roaring and he began to laugh too. A separate ticket for sheets on the sleepers — all his life he had taken it for granted — suddenly struck him with its bureaucratic ridiculousness. He and I both had tears running down our cheeks, and he was so convulsed that he had to pull the car over to the side of the avenue until he could stop laughing.

We slept well on the midnight express. In the morning the children, who all, except Doveen, had become drinkers of strong Georgian tea, loved having it served by the conductor from his big samovar. We had brought our own breakfast, so that by 8 A.M., when we were met by smiling Tolya and the Volvo, we were ready to start for Vyborg.

We were soon out of the Italianate streets of historic old Leningrad, past the new parts of the city and onto the Baltic seacoast road. The salt air and scent of pines were a refreshing contrast to the static continental climate of Moscow. Tolya sang songs as he drove. He admitted he was glad it was the last stage of the trip for him, because the drive from Moscow to Leningrad was less than enjoyable. The road was wet and traffic was heavy all night. He had seen three accidents in which the cars were overturned on the slick macadam. He was tired and would be happy to get on the train in Vyborg; he wanted to sleep the whole way back.

The approach to Vyborg was a shock to us. We seemed to be entering the nineteenth century, perhaps Manchester in the first steam of the Industrial Revolution. The air was filled with a yellow fog of chemical waste. A frail and poorly dressed child spun a wheel frame down the littered street like an apparition out of the past. Decrepit, hundred-year-old tenements bulged with vertical rows of toilets built onto them.

Past the industrial slum the air cleared; there was a small well-kept park in front of the railroad station. We had lunch in the station buffet, where the borscht and fried cutlets might have been sent from a central kitchen in Moscow, so alike are the menus for this level of

Soviet restaurant. However, it was good and served hot, and in a shorter time than usual. We appreciated that because Tolya had to make a one o'clock train and we still had four to five hours' drive before we would arrive in Helsinki.

(What sad days had come upon this once-attractive resort center! Before 1941, when it was part of Finland, it was famous for its night life. Then the Russians claimed that the point of land on which Vyborg sits was necessary to its own security in the war against the Germans. The Finns at first defended themselves ferociously, slaughtering Soviet troops with their white-clad crack ski infantry. Stalin was surprised by the Finns and sobered by photographs of his own armored troops stuck in the deep snows. He finally sent in massive air support and the Finns ceded Vyborg in the peace settlement.)

Tolya remarked that I was nervous as he settled me at the wheel of the Volvo and pointed the way out of Vyborg to Helsinki. It was true that I had driven the car very little in the last year in Moscow, but a greater cause for concern was the road he showed me. It was a cobble-stone street and seemed more a byway than a thoroughfare for international travel. "Are you sure?" I asked him. He had checked, he was sure. We waved goodbye and drove off, but I stopped once more out of his sight and asked a bystander if this ancient street was the way to Helsinki. It was, and after a few minutes' driving I relaxed.

We still had about an hour's drive before we were out of the Soviet Union, and we still had to pass three border checkpoints. Of course we had proper exit visas, and the border guards had been notified that we would be coming through. The customs official at the main border station gave us only a cursory check and waved us on courteously. At the two military-guard points young soldiers stood at barriers much like the red and white warning gates at a railroad crossing. I thought they would count the passports and wave us through also, but instead they were grinning and curious to have a good look at the five children of one family. They carefully compared the photo of each child to its live counterpart. The children giggled at the scrutiny they were getting. I was suddenly reminded that they had received the same unusual treatment from the passport official at Sheremyetevo Airport when we had gone abroad; it was unlike the cursory glance that passport officials give children in most international airports. Then I understood the reason: within a group of five, might there not be a

Soviet child whose parents were anxious to smuggle him abroad? For example, an American we knew was married to a Soviet woman who had a young child by a former marriage. With some difficulty he might be able to get his wife out of the Soviet Union, but it was nearly impossible to get an exit visa for her child. The American would have to wait until his stepson was grown before his wife could begin to think of emigrating. Wouldn't we, with five children, be the logical object of a request to take their son out as one of ours? Therefore, in a country of closed borders, the counting of children was meticulous.

Once assured that all the children matched their passports, the gates to the outside were opened for us and we drove on. We passed small villages of wooden houses with elaborately carved window frames, some of the carving new and waiting for the first coat of paint. This surprised me because I thought the traditional peasant gingerbread decorations were only a remnant of the past and no longer a living craft. The village wells were next to the road, and from the sight of women carrying water we knew that indoor plumbing hadn't come here yet. These farms, like others we had seen further into the Soviet Union, were orderly but poor; now, in the last week in August, there were no visible signs of abundance or the imminence of a bounteous harvest.

The two-lane road dipped in steep and winding hills through some forestland, and then we were suddenly on the Finnish side of the border. The change was dramatic. It appeared that we had moved from a harsh and barren countryside to a starkly different latitude with a climate more conducive to human habitation. The grass was actually greener. Fields of deep-green, moist vegetation and grass carried my eye along the gently rolling terrain. Modest farmhouses were neatly painted white, often with green shutters; they had a cared-for look absent from the Soviet log cabins we had seen. There were more children at play, and even in their simple country clothes the fresh Scandinavian styling set them off from their drab Soviet counterparts only a few kilometers away. We drove through small towns where the colors, the abundance of cars, the atmosphere of prosperity and the sight of advertising proclaimed to us that we were out of the Communist world.

The sight of the Helsinki skyline was exhilarating, but approaching this bustling commercial metropolis at the rush hour was unnerving, after a day of having the road practically to ourselves and being used to the sparse traffic conditions of Moscow. We entered the city on a forked bridge in the midst of a stream of fast-moving cars reminiscent of London or New York. No one had warned us that we would have to make a choice of which fork to take, because no one in the office had ever driven to Helsinki. It was no longer important which fork was right, only to be decisive.

"Should we try left?" I asked Stevo, who sat up front acting as navigator. "Sure, left, " Stevo answered, sharing the blind decision. We drove left as if we knew where we were going, and continued until we found a quiet side street. Then we pulled off the busy avenue and stopped to check the map. We knew our hotel was across the street from the central railroad station. We were only a few blocks away. We plunged back into the heavy traffic, and found ourselves on a route that circled the station. We could see our hotel, but not how to get out of the circle. After going around twice we asked a policeman in sign language how to get to the hotel just a few feet away. He spoke English and broke into a broad grin. No turns were allowed out of the circle, but he stopped the car behind us and told us to back up, make a U turn, and drive into the hotel entrance. We thanked him and were about to back up, but I couldn't get the gear shift into reverse. My shirt seemed to be sticking to my back as all of the Helsinki rush hour waited for me to move. The policeman continued to smile good-naturedly and the other drivers took his lead. Finally the gear gripped, I pulled back a few feet, and we drove forward. I handed the keys to the parking attendant, who gave them to the Volvo mechanic the next morning.

Once in Helsinki I was taken in hand by Mrs. Keyworth, the wife of the resident *Time* stringer (part-time correspondent). She organized my shopping and accompanied me through the many floors of Stockmann's department store. Stockmann's would be just another big department store in any American city, but for Soviets and for foreigners who have been in Moscow for a while, it is the symbol for "yes" to the luxuries and the ordinary comforts to which Moscow is a symbol of "no." Helsinki is neither as far away nor as overpriced as Paris; Stockmann's is reachable by phone or Telex and their export department will put your order on the train to reach Moscow in eighteen hours. This excellent service, however, is of hardly any help to the Soviet who has no foreign currency and must get his order past Soviet customs. We could bring in anything duty-free for one year; after that the import tax was exorbitant. Diplomats didn't pay these taxes, and some of them even had large hothouse cucumbers, individually sheathed in cellophane, sent from Helsinki when the Soviet hard-currency store had none to offer in midwinter.

We shopped for three solid days and it was hard work. Life in Moscow, where there isn't much to buy, at least had the advantage of simplicity. You get along with what you have. In Helsinki we were confronted with a profusion of jewelry, cutlery, tableware, furniture, fabrics — all manufactured with an eye to the competitive marketplace. Even a plastic kitchen bowl was a joy for its color and design. In Moscow the only criterion was utility, and even by that measure the products were often clumsy. Now, faced with goods which had all been created with strenuous attention to attractiveness as well as to constantly improved utility, we found the choices and decisions exhausting.

The children bought woolen tights and ordinary stretch-knit ones for underneath. They found pajamas, and Evelind, now fourteen, chose a new dress and a jumpsuit. Stevo bought a hockey stick and skates; the girls found white figure skates and cross-country skis. Skates, skis, warm underwear, seamless rain boots for the muddy season, all part of the core of life in Moscow, had to be brought from Helsinki because they were so rarely available in the USSR.

The Keyworths saw us off on the train at noon on Saturday. We would arrive in Moscow at eight on Sunday morning. We were prepared with dark bread and sausage, seedless grapes (which the Russians don't grow), fresh raspberries, huge cucumbers. Stockmann's had delivered to our sleeping compartment all our purchases, with the exception of the steel kitchen sink and cabinets that would come later. We had bought a whole case of dry breakfast cereals. We had bought turnable handles to be installed in all the doors of our apartment, to replace the drawer-pulls that came with the original construction. We had replenished our stock of toilet paper and paper napkins. The adage in Moscow was "the harder a country's currency, the softer its toilet paper."

When the train pulled out of Helsinki we began eating up our treats and repacking our purchases into the empty suitcases we had brought. I thought we would attract less attention from the border customs that way. The conductor understood, and kindly got rid of the packing cartons as we emptied them. At the Soviet border two young soldiers with rifles slung over their shoulders inspected our cabins. They were not interested in the monetary value of what we had bought but instead opened and closed drawers and looked under the mattresses. "Do you have any pornography?" one of them asked in a routine tone. I laughed and said that I didn't. *"Ne pakhozhe na vas"* (It's not like you), he said respectfully, and departed.

As we pulled into Moscow we were pleased to return home, but I was forced to smile when I remembered a little joke I had heard from some Soviet friends: "Khrushchev said we will catch up and bury the Americans. First we have to catch up with the Finns."

11

Parents and Hooligans

WE CAME HOME from Helsinki on Sunday morning, the day before school began for the year. On Monday, September 1, all the students at Special School 47, dressed in clean uniforms, gathered a half hour early for an outdoor ceremony to mark the opening of school. Each class formed a separate line. At the head of each line a student held a bouquet of flowers to present to the directress after she gave her welcoming speech.

It was a busy morning finding the right lines for Evelind, Stevo and Katie, who had been promoted to more advanced classes, and for Barney, who was in the entering class of first-graders. Even Doveen, who was in the same grade as last year, had a time finding her old class. Barney got in line with his new classmates, but he wasn't sure he wanted to join them. He kept pulling away to return to my side. I was back to the situation of a year before, half cajoling, half ordering him to get over his fears and go to school. I persuaded him to march in with his class, and then I lost sight of him in the shuffle. The usually stone-faced directress, standing a step higher than the marching students, turned to me. "Your little one is crying," she said and motioned me into the school to find and comfort him.

Meanwhile, we tried to extend the benefits of our year's experience to our new Peruvian neighbors, who were entering their five children for the first time that day. They had arrived during the summer and their children had quickly made friends with Russian teenagers. Sixteen-year-old Raul, handsome and bright-eyed, had picked up a rudimentary knowledge of Russian from his hooligan pals, and one of their pretty daughters already had a blond, curly-haired Russian boyfriend who daily visited the Gutiérrez apartment on the far end of our building, always with three or four friends in his entourage. The Russian maid who worked for them complained at first about the abundance of visitors and tried to get rid of them. She warned the militsioner that Russian boys were visiting foreigners. But it was she who was exchanged for another maid; the boys stayed. Mrs. Gutiérrez and I concluded that the boys were officially encouraged. Russian and East European friends found it difficult to visit our apartment, but the Russians had recently normalized diplomatic relations with Peru and were anxious to promote "people-to-people" friendships. Mrs. Gutiérrez generously allowed Evelind and Stevo to come to these teenage gatherings every night after dinner, which provided not only a social life but language practice and insights into a Russian world they would not otherwise have seen.

Stevo. Raul was Peruvian, and his father was number-two man in the new embassy. The Gutiérrezes had five kids. Laura, the eldest, was seventeen; Raul, next, was a year younger, and Pilar was fifteen. Cucha, the youngest of the girls, was eleven, and Tito was four. The three teenagers had been befriended by a few of the physically strongest and politically most powerful hooligans of our quarter. I always wondered how Raul had managed to meet all these people. One reason was that two brothers, Lyokha and Slava, were very attracted to Laura and Pilar. Laura and Lyokha became quite close. Raul was one of them from the beginning. He had had an ulcer at sixteen from weekend drinking parties on Taiwan. I told him about being robbed in the woods, and he told me that if this guy, whom he knew as Shibayev, ever bothered me again, he and Lyokha would be sure to take care of him.

A few months after I met Raul we were walking up to the clump of stores near our building, when Shibayev wobbled over to us with a friend of his. He hailed Raul like an old friend and asked him for some whiskey. Raul thought he was a slob and tried to shrug him off. My insides turned cold when he came over to me and put his arm around my shoulder, asking if I had any good foreign booze up in my apartment. I answered no again. He left a little irritated. It's possible that he remembered who I was.

The third and last time I saw Shibayev was a little more than a year after he robbed me in the woods. It was December 5, Constitution Day, and we had no school. The blanket of winter cold had dropped down on the city during the night, and the rain that had fallen the day before was frozen on our sidewalks in a nice, slightly bumpy surface, almost perfect for skating. So I was out there running around on my skates with Raul, his sisters, and mine too. We had been skating for about half an hour when Shibayev and his friends came around stone drunk, barfing in the gutters, intimidating little kids, and asking everyone for money. Recognizing Raul, the foreigner, Shibayev asked him for cigarettes and whiskey. Raul didn't even bother to be nice, and told him right off that Lyokha was up in his apartment, and he'd call him any minute. Shibayev interrupted Raul, and looking at me said, "Hey, don't I know you?"

"No," I muttered, "go to hell!"

"What was that?" Shibayev grumbled.

"Listen, Shibayev, you'd better get the fuck out of here," Raul said.

"All right, all right," said Shibayev with his eyes half-closed. "Eh, guys, let's go." He moved off, falling every few feet. He ran into Volodya, a Polish guy who lived in our building. "Got a cigarette?" Shibayev called. Volodya pretended not to notice. "Hey, you son of a bitch! I said do you have a cigarette?"

Volodya turned around nervously. "Here you go." His hand shook as he handed Shibayev one.

"Light? Nice lighter you got there. Can I have it?" Grabbing it, Shibayev walked off into the dreary snow that was beginning to fall, to terrorize the kids in some other building.

The last I heard, they had shipped him off to jail for stealing a case of vodka.

The city of Moscow is divided into four main regions, and is further subdivided into numbered quarters or *kvartals*. Most teenagers in these quarters were called hooligans by the police for their rowdy and unruly behavior. They met in the afternoon and at night in the parks and courtyards of the city to talk, play music, smoke cigarettes, kiss girls, and get drunk. Most of the students in our special school were not hooligans because they were committed to their schoolwork and the future that their knowledge of the English language would bring them. A lot of the hooligans I knew in our quarter went to another school, where they did hardly any work and often skipped classes. They told me how they smoked cigarettes and drank wine in the bathrooms and improved their grades by changing their marks in the teacher's log. The hooligans grouped themselves into gangs by quarter, and they ruled over their respective territories. The gangs usually terrorized the recreational area in their neighborhood. Small or weak kids, and even solitary eighteen-year-olds who went to an amusement park, a playing field, a park, or woods that were not home ground were liable to have their money taken. Some neighboring quarters were quite friendly but little arguments between them started off full-scale fights with poles and chains. A friend at school told me that hooligans who hung around a park where we played soccer had killed a policeman the year before. My older hooligan friends were known as the biggest and strongest in our quarter, and they would talk quietly and in hints about rumbles they had been in. The police were after hooligans for these rumbles, so it was not anything to boast openly about. In my friendships with them, I was never involved in any violence — I was simply too young to have been included — but everything we did tended toward it. Drink put us into a mood where our insecurities were less easily defended, and we were carried into group rowdiness. This rowdiness could easily have turned into true violence.

I once asked Lyokha where he and Slava were from. "A small city in the south," he said. He smiled and remarked, "There we all knew each other."

"Everyone?" I said incredulously.

"No, you fool," he smirked, and he lowered his voice. "All of us hooligans."

Sasha was the most soft-spoken of the hooligans. He was a swimming champion and was always loaded with money. We went through the woods one day, with a couple of other guys, drinking Polish cognac. It was soft and steaming, turning me and the world into those qualities.

The thick covering of leaves on the ground turned spongy like a bed of moss, floating and drifting us through the trees that were losing their leaves. Sasha talked about poetry, and started to read his own love poems. He was looking out of the window over his sleeping girl's head, contemplating the night, or lamenting in philosophical boy-girl equations. My concentration on Sasha became total. The rest of the world was a void that carried me along slowly and gently. My only frustration was the language. I couldn't understand some of his more complex poetic words.

Soon we were out of the woods, and I had to stretch my eyes open to accommodate the wide sky. We came to the Lumumba soccer field and watched the African students play. The goalie at our end of the field was more concerned with looking valiant than with blocking the ball. He tried to save a ball on one side of the goal by flopping full-length in the dust on the opposite side. I laughed until my cheeks hurt.

Late in the afternoon, during the height of the winter, the hooligan elite of our quarter used to gather over at Raul's. We all sat around the Gutiérrezes' living room playing cards, watching television, and listening to music. The music was Western rock 'n' roll. The Beatles predominated. The card game was almost always Russian: *bura* (boar), which is an extended form of blackjack. The stakes were card slaps on the ear. At the end of the game, the losers drew two cards. The first one determined how many times you would be slapped, and the second one was the number of cards to be used. A thick wad of cards moved swiftly across the flexible area of the ear is much more painful than one. It was a great show of *macho* to quietly withstand the thwaps that turned your ear into a very red and stinging piece of flesh. Vavo, who was one of the most sensitive and kind people among the hooligans, taught me how to play. He was a medical student, and he did a lot of things with me that the others didn't have the patience for. When we met out on the lake where people were playing hockey, he would come over and pass the puck around with me, having a good time. The others considered themselves in another league, and played separately. When we were skiing on the slopes, Lyokha was always proving himself by doing tricks on one ski and jumping. Vavo did the same things, but with a looseness and fun that made it a comedy act.

One evening I got into an argument with Lyokha and Slava about Soviet leaders. They said that Khrushchev was a bumbling fool, while

I argued that he had brought about important reforms. They said the purges were all the work of Beria, and that Stalin had been unaware of these crimes. I, of course, argued that the purges were all Stalin's doing. They told me I was a chump, and I should go back and read my history books.

Later in the evening at Raul's someone would arrive with a bottle of wine or somebody would go to the store and buy one. We went out to the stairs of the apartment building by the incinerator chute and stood around in a circle, chugging it down. It was sweet and warm as it went around. Although I was only twelve, my friends liked to see me drink with them. It brought us together onto the same plane of rowdyism and enjoyment. After a couple of bottles had been drained, it was usually time for the hockey game on TV. Russian hockey games are excellent to watch. They're very fast-moving with a lot of skilled players. One problem was that they were often slowed down on account of broken sticks. The Russians still make their hockey sticks from one or two lumps of wood which are not very strong, besides being quite heavy. The Europeans and Canadians glue thin strips together to make an extra-strong and light stick. I had one of these which I had bought in Finland and it was highly admired. I gave it to Vavo when we left.

Although we used to drink a lot, I don't remember ever getting totally smashed. When the others would take four or five gulps, I would take one sip. I enjoyed it much more that way. The others, however, often drank themselves into irresponsible insanity. I remember one night when Sanya did it to himself.

It was late Saturday afternoon and Dusko, the Yugoslav, had a bottle of good American whiskey. Vavo, Sanya, Sasha, and a few East Europeans were with us when we headed over to the woods.

We had planned to sit on the bench that was tucked right into the edge of the forest. It had a nice view of the lake, but some people were already sitting on it. My friends whispered a few things to each other, and started to make a little fire on the pine-needle floor. They kept moving the clump of smoking debris to the left, then a little to the right, finally a little forward. We put a lot of leaves on it, and the smoke belched through the trees, straight on course to the bench we wanted to sit on. The people there started to choke, cough, and gag. They looked back, but could see only a thick smoke screen. We had a nice blaze going. A few of the people tried to stick it out, but they didn't last long. A few minutes later, they were all gone, and we were swigging whiskey in sedentary comfort. Here we built a flaming wood fire. By the time we had some good coals, we were starting in on the cognac and people began to come by. Hooligans, out on a Saturday night. Some came staggering up, supporting each other, trying to talk coherently. They seemed to have been drinking all day. They always asked for a drink, but we always hid the bottle well in advance. When others came to play their guitars and talk, the bottle went around freely. They talked about mutual friends, what was happening, fights, women. At one point, some solitary girls were walking past us down by the lake, and Vavo cooed loudly to them, *"Heeeey, dyevushkiii!* [Hey, girls!] Come on over here." When they didn't respond, he yelled, "Oh, come on over, or do I have to come down and get you?" They looked pretty alarmed at that, but Vavo just laughed and took another swig. I never saw many pretty girls with hooligans, though.

As it got later, Sanya turned out to be very drunk. He was a guy who lived in our building because he was the son of the maintenance man. Sanya was an expert at electronics, and with all machines, especially tape recorders. He was studying English. Lyokha and Slava, the two tough brothers, didn't like Sanya very much. He was a little too soft-spoken for them, I guess. Vavo and Sasha got along well with him, though, and they assumed the task of taking him home when he started babbling in English to one of the Yugoslav girls, "I love you, love you I? *Chort vozmi, kak tam idyot?"* (Goddamit, how does that go?). He put up some resistance at first, but he was in no shape to fight, so Vavo and Sasha caught him under each arm and started up the hill to the building. I took up the rear. We were constantly stopping because Sanya would turn to Vavo and say, "Hey listen Sasha, will you go away, I want to talk to Vavo." He got angry when Vavo tried to explain and turned to Sasha. "Well, Vavo, will you go away so that I can talk to Sasha. Come on." He babbled in English and Russian all the way up to his apartment. His little sister was the only one home, and we suggested that she put him in the bathtub. She seemed a little scared, and I think that we all felt sorry for her, but there was nothing else to do.

I heard that Sanya woke up in the empty bathtub the next day with an enormous headache.

Leona. Stevo and Evelind went to the Gutiérrez apartment night after night, and I wondered how they passed so much time without getting tired of sharing repetitive evenings with the same friends. What did they talk about with the Russian boys? Stevo only hinted at his own drinking, but told me how much Raul drank. Stevo sometimes got into political arguments with the Russian boys; they followed a narrow, well-learned line without embellishments or imagination. With predictable points of view they attacked the Vietnam war, capitalism and racist imperialism. Although they called themselves hooligans, and flouted the authority of police and parents, many of them continued to work toward serious goals — careers in medicine or electronics. They continued to believe in the socialist principles on which they had been brought up. One of the reasons they had banded together was that they needed a group defense against violent gangs from neighboring *kvartals.*

The lifestyle of hooligans involved thievery, serious alcoholism and violent enforcement of hegemony over parks and recreational areas. Parents, teachers and government officials were concerned with the rapid breakdown of the communal discipline and motivation that had marked previous generations.

Until recently the Soviet government would not admit publicly that the new generation of teenagers had gotten out of control. The problem did not appear in print or in literature because a principle of socialist realism in art is the happy ending. Even the conclusion of the ballet *Swan Lake* was changed to depict the lovers, very much alive, facing the dawn after the black prince of evil has been vanquished. This made all the more remarkable a film called *Accused of Murder,* which appeared in early 1970. *Accused of Murder* is a courtroom drama with flashbacks, in which a group of boys of seventeen or eighteen, out at night drinking in a pack, come upon a boy their own age talking quietly with a girl in the shadowy street outside a school dance. Laughing and teasing they begin to beat him, and in their drunken frenzy deal him a fatal blow to the head with an empty wine bottle.

Dramatic tension builds at their trial as the girl puts off testifying against the gang because she is afraid of reprisals. The film criticizes not only the behavior of the young hooligans, but also other antisocial behavior: the silence of witnesses who see the fight from their apartment windows and the lack of direction and discipline from the boys' parents, including a young divorced woman whose disorderly life has led to neglect of her son. Lyokha and Sanya, Stevo's friends, appeared as extras in the film and they were the first to encourage us to see it. *Accused of Murder* was well done and created a sensation by its open acknowledgment of social ills in a socialist state. Russians flocked to see it and discussed its frightening implications.

One, not often mentioned, was that it documents the beginning of affluence in the Soviet Union. Youthful energy is no longer channeled into building the nation. After the Revolution and during the post–World War II years, restless young men were organized into youth brigades who tilled the Virgin Lands or helped build dams and factories. There was little time left over for dissolute street-corner idleness. Now the Russians face the same problem as the rest of the industrialized world: what to do with its underskilled young who are unsuited to the technological jobs that require more training and offer delayed rewards.

The physical destruction of World War II and the shortages that followed remained vivid memories for those who survived it. These memories could be appealed to with effect until the late 1960's. Combined with the need to overcome the nation's postwar impoverishment they bound the people together in a common effort. By 1970 the old appeals had worn thin. Patriotism based on World War II unity had not been replaced by new ideals; for twenty-five years no war had touched the homeland and the galvanizing effect of war psychology had faded.

Nevertheless, billboards and slogans still depicted the hardships of the war, still evoked fear of the Germans. At the Moscow circus the show began with a pair of Russian soldiers trampling a German Nazi flag. At school, incidents of personal sacrifice and bravery in the war against the Germans were still the models held up for the children to emulate.

Katie. Zoya was only fourteen when the war began. She was strong and healthy, so of course, she volunteered to help. Zoya was put into a group that was to spy on a German camp that was near the front in a dense forest.

They slept for many nights in the cold and wet forest, watching and learning what was going on in the enemy's camp. One night the leader of the group sent Zoya and one of the boys on a mission. They were to free the horses from the German stables. Zoya and the boy decided that she would sneak into the stable and let the horses loose while he knocked out the stableboys. That night they crept down to the camp. The boy slowly opened the stable door and quickly knocked out the German guard on watch. Zoya slipped in from behind and turned the horses out. Smacking them on their backsides, she sent them galloping out into the snow. As fast as they could Zoya and the boy ran back to their camp. They had accomplished their mission successfully.

A few weeks later, when things had settled down at the German camp and everything was pretty much back to normal, Zoya was assigned another mission. She was to burn down the stables, alone. That night Zoya once again crept down to the German stables. This time the Germans were ready and she was caught.

Zoya was put into a cold room with a wooden table in it. For many nights she slept on the cold wooden table and every day they tortured her, trying to find out where her group was hidden in the forest. Zoya resisted even the worst tortures and so they had to hang her. Today Zoya is remembered for her bravery, like many other young people during the war. She is a fine example to all of us. That was the story of Zoya Kosmodemyanskaya we were told in the fourth-grade class before we went on our field trip to her memorial.

We all piled into the bus that had been obtained especially for our field trip. Everyone was very excited because this was the first class trip we were going on and it was to be for the whole day. The ride outside of Moscow took about an hour and a half, but the time passed quickly with all the jokes and chatter in the bus. Soon we left the apartment houses of Moscow behind and passed lines of white birch trees along the road. Finally, we stopped on the side of the road and we all jumped out to look around.

There was a field, and in the distance a metal gate, but I couldn't see what was inside it. The teacher led the class into a house that had been made into a museum in memory of Zoya. In front of the house was a life-size statue of her and around her neck there was an old battered-up Pioneer scarf that supposedly was hers. Zoya looked about fifteen years old. She had short dark hair and pretty features. She looked like many of my older schoolmates.

We walked into the house and took off our coats. Then we were allowed to look around. There was an old newspaper clipping from

НИКТО НЕ ЗАБЫТ. И НИЧТО НЕ ЗАБЫТО

*Poster reminding Russians of World War II: "No one is forgotten.
And nothing is forgotten"*

the war with a picture of Zoya being hanged and she was half-naked. She was surrounded by snow and German soldiers. When I heard the story of Zoya in school I thought her death had been exaggerated, but when I saw the picture I realized how terrible her death had been and that it was all really true.

Then we all went outside and walked across a large field. Soon we came to a square garden surrounded by a black metal gate. We went in and looked around. On every tree branch and gatepost was a red Pioneer scarf signed and dedicated to Zoya from each of the classes that had come to visit. There were hundreds of scarves. Some were so old they were practically white, while others were brand new and bright red. One of my classmates wrote a dedication on our class scarf and we tied it to a branch.

As we left all the red scarves looked beautiful fluttering in the wind and it never occurred to us to be depressed. I thought that Zoya was lucky to be remembered with such respect. It was spring and as we walked back to the bus we jumped over little creeks and had races, laughing because for us there was no reason to be sad.

The memories of World War II still lingered in Moscow. There were posters of the war and we were always told about it in school, even though Moscow did not show signs of being broken down from the war.

One day a Hero of the Soviet Union came to give a talk at our school. I had seen a television show at Kaarina's house about him. His plane had been blown up while he was flying it and he landed in a dense forest. When he became conscious he realized that both his legs were blown off. He dragged himself over to his wreck and found a pack of cookies, all the food that remained in the demolished plane. For many days he dragged himself over snow-covered ground through the forest, trying to find out where he was and where he could find his fellow Russians. One time he came very close to a German camp, but instead of giving himself up he hid until night. He stayed in the forest two weeks. It was hard to find food because it was the middle of winter but somehow he survived. At the end of the second week he dragged himself into a Russian camp where he was immediately taken care of. He was awarded many medals for his courage and loyalty.

He got wooden legs and practiced very hard to walk again. He had to wear big shoes but he never needed a cane. As soon as he could walk with ease on his new legs he decided to go back to the army. Of course he couldn't get back his old job but he was given something he could do. For his act of loyalty he was made one of the most honored heroes of World War II.

Leona. During the war the Russian people looked up to Stalin as father and protector. After his death they endured the trauma of having his crimes revealed and his embalmed body removed from its honored resting-place next to Lenin in the Red Square mausoleum. For ten years Khrushchev led the nation in foreign adventures and attempts to modernize production at home. His ambitious plans for agriculture as well as his "cult-of-personality" antics are remembered with scorn; most Russians feel that he shamed them with his attention-getting outbursts. When he was deposed from power in 1964 the collective leadership that replaced him searched for a new unifying symbol. The fading of the postwar spirit and the loss of the beneficent image of Stalin left the nation emotionally starved for an idol. In the middle 1960's, therefore, Lenin rose from his more modestly venerated place in history to become the sacred figure in the folklore of the Soviet people. He has taken the place of Christ in their iconography; his bigger than life-size portrait appears in classrooms, in all public places, in lights projected above the city of Moscow on his birthday. Although his deification is recent it is omnipresent, so that for schoolchildren he has been the central figure of attention in their environment since they began their education.

Stevo. I was thirteen, in the Russian equivalent of eighth grade, and had lived in the Soviet Union for a year. The teachers started to call on me regularly to "retell" the lesson assigned the day before.

Like everyone else, I was taking physics that year, and it was probably my least favorite course. We had a new young teacher who was trying to prove herself. She was very impatient and was always screaming. The few moments when the teacher chose whom to question made everyone's heart beat very fast. There would be a complete silence as she ran down the list of names, and a very audible exhalation by all the students would follow, as the victim walked to the front of the room.

I climbed up to the science floor, put my bag and an extra book on the wooden floor, and proceeded to murmur formulas to myself, checking them in the physics book. One of my acquaintances, Kolya, came over and said, "Pick that book up off the floor."

"What? Which book are you talking about?"

Kolya could be very nice, but he was a little full of himself. He would tell all of the boys about body-building, using himself to demonstrate his lecture.

"That book is about our great leader, Lenin," he said almost shrilly. I looked at him, at the book, and back at him.

"Pick it up yourself, if you want it done," I chuckled. I didn't believe his seriousness.

I went back to my physics book, but his hand shot out and knocked it onto the floor. I picked it up, and looked at him. "You idiot," I yelled. "How can you take something like that so seriously. You're just programmed like everyone else into thinking that Lenin and Communism are the most important things in the world. Why don't you wake up?" My voice was getting desperate, and Kolya was getting very mad. I remember the open-mouthed stare of his twin brother as he listened to me shouting my guts out. Kolya's fists were clenched, and a few people had gathered to stop him.

I hurried away up the stairs to the attic storage space. I sat there on the steps exploding and subsiding. I regretted not fighting with him very much, but it was too much of a contradiction for my psyche to handle. I was the nice American kid who helped all the English teachers and was such a *molodets* (good boy) when called to answer before the class. The yelling threats of the teachers terrified me the first day I came, and I had tried to completely avoid their irrational anger from then on. I got used to their methods of dealing with disobedient children, but I did not want to be dealt with like that myself. This had such an effect on me that I couldn't even open my full aggression on a student. I could express my incredulity and frustration, but I couldn't strike out against it. I had to wipe my eyes and clear my throat for another round in physics class.

Leona. After a year in Soviet school Stevo had learned to fit in and conform, but the demands of conformity were on varied levels, often conflicting. Could he be a good boy at school and a hooligan after dinner? Could he sing patriotic Russian songs with his classmates, show a proper respect for Lenin, and at the same time retain his American

Stevo on the school steps. The plaque reads: "Polytechnical School Number 47." (Photo by Jerrold Schecter)

reluctance to make Lenin into a godhead? Stevo's image of Lenin was akin to what Russians earlier thought of Stalin. It was how Americans who grew up in the thirties looked upon FDR — as a beneficent figure with the courage of his convictions even when the odds were against him, and with a tremendous intellectual arrogance, which made people follow him. In the late 1960's we, like other American parents and children, were discussing the value of revolution as a means of correcting social injustice. After a little more than a year in Moscow, I argued that no violent revolution could accomplish democratic aims because by its very nature it breeds the violence of a police state to maintain its victories. Stevo answered thoughtfully that if Lenin had lived a few years longer the Revolution would not have deteriorated into brutality. "But it was Lenin who initiated violence. It was by his order that thousands of the bourgeoisie were executed. Once that begins it doesn't stop," I argued. When he returned to the United States Stevo searched out pamphlets in Russian by Lenin that related to our argument. He wrote a paper for school on Lenin's advocacy of the elimination of class enemies as a means of social change. The last appeal — "what might have been if Lenin had lived" — was thus destroyed, and Stevo achieved a clear-minded rejection of Communist methods as a step in his intellectual growth.

After starting first grade, Barney became an Oktyabryata and wore a pin with Lenin's picture on his lapel every day. In most ways he conformed outwardly, but inwardly he thought his own thoughts. At home we assured the children that we would not judge their performance at school as we would in an English-speaking school; Barney took this to mean that it wasn't very important whether he did well in Russian school or not. He didn't voice his interpretation openly, he simply decided to do only what work pleased him. When his teacher shouted at him in frustration, he managed to look as if he cared. Stevo had had the same teacher the year before, and he described her as constantly shouting, harsh and demanding. The combination of Barney's attitude and her lack of sympathy were an unproductive combination, for he was not only a foreigner, he was left-handed as well.

She made fun of his left-handedness, proclaiming that she had never seen this phenomenon. She ridiculed his smudged writing with a fountain pen, even though it was his first try and the other children had been primed in penmanship by their babushkas at home for years.

Barney watched jealously when the rest of the class modeled little animals out of clay; we couldn't find any to buy anywhere in Moscow, but the teacher never encouraged the other children to lend some to Barney. She blamed him when he defended himself but looked the other way when he was picked on.

"If some boy in my class couldn't write very well I'd go up to him in the playground and tell him not to worry, that it would get better, but here not one boy has done that for me. They're all bullies and glad to have someone to laugh at." In Tokyo kindergarten he had been a jaunty little leader. Now he was "nobody, just a foreigner, less than nobody," Barney said angrily.

Barney. When the trolley came we squeezed on and in and under people's feet smelling their breath, which smelled like garlic and sausages. Finally we found a place on the floor and sat down on someone's feet. The people at the bus stop who decided to wait for the next bus would see coattails between the door. Old ladies cursed the driver because he closed the door on them. Then we rode down Leninsky Prospekt feeling every bump on the road because we were on the floor.

When I got to my room it was 8:30, which is when school started. Everyone sat down. When the teacher walked in everyone stood up and said "Good morning, teacher," in Russian. Then the teacher said to sit down.

In Russia they graded us with numbers — five was the best and two was the worst. The bathrooms were horrid and there were no seats on the toilets. We went home at noon, but we also went to school on Saturday, and sometimes on Sunday.

The first subject was handwriting. We used a fountain pen and wrote in a thin notebook called a tetrad. All the Russian kids had perfect handwriting because it was a big thing in Russia. Their grandmothers had helped them at home since they were about three years old. Since my handwriting wasn't so good, the teacher would hold up my papers in front of the class and make fun of me. Also she made fun of me because I was left-handed and it is not common to find a left-handed person in Russia. When she came to me she lifted my tetrad up to the class and said, "Look at this paper," and taking the paper from the boy in front of me turned to me and said, "Why can't you do it like this?"

I knew that we were going to leave next year so I thought to myself, "Oh, I'll be out of here next year so why should I do my homework?" So I didn't do my homework and sat there with a solemn face as the teacher lectured me and once more I got away with it.

One time the teacher told everyone to get new clean tetrads. Coming to me she found I didn't have mine. She said to me loudly so everyone could hear, "We will be going ahead in these nice new clean tetrads while you're writing in these old ones." It seemed stupid to me that you should buy new ones before you use the old ones.

Another time I was writing and the girl in front of me turned around, looked at my paper, and said, "Strange."

Next we had reading. We were each given a small story booklet. The teacher would call on us to read in front of the directress and if we made one slight mistake we had to stay after school to read. The directress hadn't come yet but we started reading anyway. It seemed that almost everyone was making mistakes. Suddenly it came my turn to read and naturally I made a mistake and the teacher cut me short and said, "Okay, you stay after school. Next." Then the directress came in. Then, when someone made a mistake the teacher corrected them and said, "Very good," although everyone knew she wouldn't say that if the directress wasn't there. That day I got a three in reading and a new boy to the class got a two. Later he walked up to me with some other boys and he said, "You got a three because you're a foreigner." Then he picked up the book we read out of and said, "You couldn't read this in a month." I knew he was right. The teachers have to be easier on foreigners, but I didn't like her to give me an easy grade.

One day children were called up to the teacher's desk to read aloud. One girl read a very long time and she started to get weak. The teacher, who had been staring out the window, said, "Oh, I forgot. You may go to your seat." On the way back to her seat the girl fainted and fell on the floor. Then the teacher screamed, "What is everybody sitting there for?" Everybody including me ran down the hall to the doctor's office but before we got far the teacher said, "Where's everybody going?" So everybody ran right back into the classroom. Then she sent one child to get the doctor. The doctor came with smelling salts and put it under the girl's nose. She woke up instantly and started crying.

In Russia when you are bad they take you to the corner by the ear.

Next we had music. We all walked up one floor and went into the music room and sat down. The teacher's name was Yury Petrovich. He was loco. He made us laugh so he could say we were bad. If we wanted to use the school's music books to write our notes before we got our own we would have to pay twenty kopecks. It sounded like he was just trying to get some money. When he called the attendance there was a Polish boy named Peasal but the teacher made fun of him and called him Puzel. We would sing songs and sometimes see movies of Russian bravery. After music when everyone was walking out, the teacher held me back and said in a serious tone, "Next time bring me some gum or comics or some felt-tipped pens."

Art was taught by the homeroom teacher. She would pick up something in the room and everybody drew it. In art everybody had to do the same thing. Everyone brought their own materials. This time it was a pad, paper and paints. Everyone stared at my American paints because they weren't like the Russian watercolors, little squares of paint loose from the package, but instead were locked in place by the box. We had to draw a watering can — first outline it, then paint it in. The teacher said mine was too small and gave me a three; other times we worked with clay which was nonhardening soft clay, the only kind they had for artwork.

The next and last class was gym. The gym was in the basement of the school, just above the tenth-graders' coatroom. It was a fairly big room with a high ceiling. There were ropes hanging from the ceiling and ladders built into the wall and mats spread out on the floor. Everyone wore gym shorts and if you forgot them it would lower your mark. First we ran around the room over the mats. Peasal tripped over one of the mats and I tripped in the same place, so the teacher said if I tripped once more it would lower my mark.

He gave us all sticks and we marched around the room holding them as guns. All the boys had crew cuts, like soldiers. He said we had to do this because we should always be prepared to defend our country and if we didn't know how to march we couldn't get into the army. We should always be prepared to defend the Soviet Motherland.

Leona. We decided to attend a parents' night at the children's school. We felt that our Russian was good enough to be able to listen better than the first few times we had gone, and perhaps we could help Barney. I complained about the teacher to Lyuba and Tamara, and they helped me prepare a little speech of protest. But once there, faced with a room full of Russian parents, I wasn't so sure I had the courage.

Jerry and I entered the classroom and squeezed into two children's desks at the rear of the room. Almost without exception, the Russian parents were overweight with a doughy formlessness. They were carefully dressed and combed, the women all in similar flowered or navy-blue knitted dresses. No farmers were in the room; there was an urban look to them all. Even in their discomfort and tension, they bore an unexceptional sameness. The teacher, a trim, good-looking young woman with short-cropped black hair but not a trace of softness in her expression, read down the list of first-graders. She stopped after each name and established who the parents were. Then, while the other parents listened and waited their turn, she described the performance of each child. The parents whose children were criticized adversely showed no embarrassment; instead, there seemed to be a solidarity of oppressed parents. They listened with hushed resignation.

Jerry nudged my elbow with his and whispered, "This is no different from the Chinese. It's public self-criticism."

When the teacher finished she asked if she had skipped anyone. One of the men raised his hand. So did we.

"Yes, Schecter," she acknowledged us. She told us across the room of parents that our son was a lazy dreamer who often did not complete his notebooks and sometimes didn't bother to hand them in. He didn't have his supplies in time. He worked in a careless and messy manner, but there was some hope for he had improved a little recently. Any questions?

My heart was beating hard. I leaned against Jerry and he whispered, "If you want to answer her go ahead." I had promised Barney to speak up for him.

I stood up and spoke in halting, incorrect Russian. The parents craned their necks to have a look at me and listened in absolute silence, much in the way an American PTA would strain to understand a foreign mother struggling in English.

"Why is the boy always frightened? More than once he has come home and related that his teacher told the class that if they received too many *dvoikies* (twos, like D's) their mothers would become nervous and die and they would have to go off to an orphan asylum." The verb forms were wrong but they understood me perfectly well. A gasp of repressed, shocked laughter went up from the assembled parents and they looked straight at the teacher for a denial or explanation. One could sense joy in their reaction. For once someone had talked back to the teacher. They could not. There is still a strong feeling of gratitude to the state for educating the children, and especially to this school, which is considered to be on a higher intellectual level than others. If you questioned the teacher, therefore, you had to be careful how you phrased your displeasure; it was important not to draw attention to yourself as a troublemaker. This young teacher in particular thrived on her authority; she put unbending, puritanical demands on the children and the parents, but this unexpected thrust from an outsider had thrown her off guard.

"He didn't quite get the idea. He misunderstood the meaning of what I said," she explained hurriedly. She bent in conciliation toward the parents who watched her with stony gazes. She didn't deny our accusations. She simply tried to explain that she only wanted to get the children to work harder.

Jerry and I got up and left in the middle of all this. As we left we heard her telling the parents in warm tones that we had five children in the school, a goal to emulate in Moscow with its depressingly low birthrate, and therefore we had to go on to other classrooms.

In Doveen's class the teacher berated the parents for their children's poor performance in reading aloud. She boasted, upon seeing us, that the Indian child, Mandit, and Doveen outshone the Russian children in reading Russian aloud. She didn't know how much of it they understood, of course, and her extravagant praise didn't endear us to the other parents.

In Katie's class we settled down to a longer session. A heavy-set old woman, crippled, with a chest full of medals, to whom everyone deferred as a Heroine of the Soviet Union, read a long article from a newspaper decrying the lack of discipline among children. The teacher was not impressed, but she tried to lead a discussion on the article as impartially as she could. Backing the old woman, a man in his sixties stood up and blamed the lack of discipline on the young mothers. The teacher looked pained and tried to rally the parents. She told them in detail what their children were learning. She reminded them all that this was to prepare the children for the much harder year to follow, the fifth grade, which in Russia is a big jump from the fourth. The younger mothers were smoldering at the attacks and they looked at each other, trying to decide whether or not to fight back in the presence of foreigners. One muttered a defense in angry undertones, her head bent, looking into her lap. The teacher asked her to speak up. With the obvious agreement of the others the young mother said, "Let us stay home, and then we can be responsible for the behavior of our children. How can we go to work and be home raising our children at the same time?"

Among Soviet women in their late forties and fifties, there was an assumption that going to work was natural. For a woman, staying at home was a fetter on her personal freedom. But among this generation of women in their twenties and thirties, the trend was away from the post–World War II spirit, toward a desire for domesticity once they became mothers. Many young women expressed dissatisfaction with public child care, and longed to be liberated from the necessity of bringing home a paycheck.

The regime is of two conflicting minds: the Kremlin leadership would like to see the urban birthrate go up, but cannot provide adequate living space for larger families and cannot spare the work hours the women contribute. Even young professional families cannot get by on one salary; women are forced to work. Until recently, Soviet families had faith in the ability of public institutions to raise their children for most of the day. Raised communally, the children would grow up with a uniform ideology and escape the individualism they would learn at home. The Soviets have learned, however, the same lesson that Americans have slowly come to realize: only parents can build character in their children, only parents can supply the motivation needed for achievement. Problems of "hooliganism" and "dropoutism" are rising concerns of the Soviet state and are forcing a reappraisal of the role of women.

After we left Katie's class I went to the woman who had first helped us settle into our new life, Nadezhda Aleksandrovna, the head of the English department. I explained Barney's problem to her. At first she was skeptical. Then she recalled how years before she had refused to believe that her son was unhappy when he was away at summer Pioneer camp, only to learn later that he had been mistreated. As she told the story tears came to her eyes and she got up from the desk. With the exception of Barney's teacher, who taught Stevo the first year and about whom Stevo confirmed Barney's reports, the teachers, aside from their excessive yelling, were like Nadezhda Aleksandrovna, concerned and affectionate toward the children. She said she would do some discreet observing for herself.

I met Barney's teacher in the corridor later and she looked at me coldly through narrowed eyes. I looked back at her the same way. Within a week Barney reported that she had changed her attitude toward him and as a result the children were following her lead. He now had some friends in the class.

While I consulted with Nadezhda Aleksandrovna, Jerry went to Stevo's class and then to Evelind's. In these classes of older children, thirteen and fourteen, the parents were questioning their children's marks. They listened attentively and asked how the marks could be raised. They wanted to know what record and recommendations were necessary for their children to be assured of passage from Young Pioneers to Komsomol. (Komsomol is the youth organization for Soviet citizens aged fourteen to twenty-eight who aspire to Communist Party membership later.)

Special School 47, which specialized in the teaching of English, might be compared to American private schools. One teacher went on at length about the higher caliber of work expected from these children. While their performances would be considered good or even exceptional in a "mass" school, these children, from whom future Party leadership would come, had to work much harder. I was taken aback to hear the teacher refer to *massevoi* students in contrast to the children of the elite. It was a startling contradiction to the democratic "comradeship of all the people" that we heard constantly promoted as the unique progressive quality of the USSR.

It was evident that these elitest parents rode herd on their children to produce good academic work. Many of them worked for the Academy of Sciences and therefore expected a lot from their children, knowing that academic achievement had got them good apartments, dachas, coupons for foreign currency stores, and entrance for their children into a superior school. The children hadn't had to struggle; they hadn't experienced the scarcities of the war and the years after it; they didn't feel the need to achieve — it would all come to them.

Biting at their heels were the children of truck drivers and grocery-store clerks, still living in communal apartments, who had been sent to this school because they worked hard and were Party loyalists. These children didn't have to be pushed. Their whole attitude toward life and life's goods was different. One of them, Evelind's friend Olya, came over after school to study and play. She said they would soon get an apartment of their own, but she wasn't sure if it would be better. I sympathized with the difficulties of living in a communal apartment but she sternly corrected me. When her parents were away at work, she said, and the parents of the other children were away, the little boy of the other family was a loving little brother to her. She would miss living with him. For the young children of a society with one- or two-child families, companionship had a higher value than privacy.

At the parents' meeting Jerry and I felt we had come closer than ever before to the driving motivations of Soviet life; in fact, what we saw was the serious preoccupation of the privileged classes, whose children were our children's classmates. Quite different they were from the students of the *massoviye shkoly* (mass schools). How petty were the infringements of discipline in this elite milieu. A grandmother sitting next to me at a school music program remarked as the children responded to the bell with a chaotic rush out of the room: "You may think this group is undisciplined. You should see what goes on in ordinary schools." An American professor of Russian history doing research in Moscow for a year sent his teenage sons to a neighborhood high school (not one of the special schools, such as our children attended); he described it as a "blackboard jungle," in which the students were unresponsive to the teachers but quick to violence.

The separation of the elite in education had its counterpart in medical care. A special diplomatic clinic and reserved wards of hospitals served the needs of foreigners; certain clinics and specialists were at the disposal of high-ranking Party members. Nevertheless, the special care afforded some Russians didn't interfere with good medical services for all Russians. Jerry surveyed Soviet medicine for three weeks before writing a story on it for *Time,* and found this the area of greatest achievement in the government's attempt to meet its socialist goals. Medical care in the Soviet Union is free and makes a sincere attempt to reach every citizen. The warmth and personal concern for patients, by doctors who are mostly women, were inspiring. He found differences in style and methods of practice from the West, but the general level of competence and dedication was high.

Dental services were universally backward. At school a visiting dentist pulled baby teeth without ever asking parents' permission. Tolya told me that his wife, a dentist in a factory clinic that served thousands of workers, "dreamed of the day she would have a modern speed drill." The only one I knew of in Moscow had been brought in by a Finnish dentist, the wife of the Finnish military attaché, who practiced in her apartment under a special dispensation from the Soviet government. She could only take foreigners as patients.

There was no preferential treatment, however, when you called a city ambulance.

On a September afternoon I tried to cut the last slices from the end of a loaf of dark bread and instead sliced deep into two fingers of my left hand. The cuts bled profusely, and as the bleeding continued I became panicky. Lyuba tried to calm me, but Jerry had been away in Poland for two weeks and I was feeling sorry for myself. The blood began to congeal, but the gashes looked ugly, and I thought they might need stitching. I decided to call a doctor. Lyuba dialed the central Moscow emergency number, 03, and they sent an ambulance within twenty minutes.

The ambulance had a complement of three: a young male doctor, a driver who also helped carry stretchers, and a boy, apparently still in his teens, who was a *feldsher,* a paramedic. The young doctor was bored with the two cuts. He told me not to worry because I had not touched the nerve areas. Then he told the feldsher to clean and bandage them. I wondered if this were the boy's first day out of the institute; he was hesitant and clumsy, and showed no sign of the self-confidence I would expect after three years of training. He cleaned my wounds with trembling hands and wrapped sterile gauze loosely around them. The uncertain bandage meandered up and down my hand. The doctor stopped his distracted pacing back and forth and gave out a noise of disgust. From his fierce look I thought he would rip it off and do it again himself. Instead he took a deep breath and ordered the boy to take the gauze off and do it again. This time the doctor stood over his charge and directed his movements. The feldsher tied a reasonably neat bandage and they bid me goodbye. The doctor had about him the defeated air of one who feels that what he is being forced to do is hardly a job for a man.

At the end of September Doveen came down with the flu.

Doveen. When I first got sick, the usual white car with "Medical Help" written on it in red lettering came with a lady doctor and a man driver. She prescribed tetracycline and said I had to stay in bed. I was just getting over the flu when I had a strange feeling in my body. I had a tingling in my hands and couldn't feel anything with them. My mom got worried and thought it was a reaction to the antibiotic the doctor was giving me for my flu. This time Mom called the clinic in such a panic that the doctor on duty, who knew us, decided to send an ambulance.

Just then, Lyuba came to work. When Mom told her that an ambulance was on the way, she opened the back and front doors of the apartment and started yelling down the shaft to keep the elevators clear. At least twice a day the elevators got stuck and she didn't want it to happen then. Lyuba's idea was to keep me moving, in case it was an allergic reaction. She made me make the bed and unmake it and make it again. Then she and Mom and I played three-way catch with a pillow. Lyuba and Mom were half crying while they played catch with me.

The ambulance driver was a man and the doctor and her helper who came were women. They were not from our regular clinic but from the city ambulance service, so we didn't know them. The doctor said I was not having an allergic reaction. She said it was something you get after the flu. Since they did not have the equipment with them to be sure, I would have to go to the hospital for observation. My mother couldn't understand everything they were saying so she took a Russian dictionary and called the translator from the office to meet us at the hospital.

Lyuba had a cardboard carton stuck between the doors of the elevator to keep it from moving. She bundled me into my coat and put my socks and shoes on for me. I was dizzy and my mother was upset at the idea of going to the hospital, but Lyuba had calmed down and was telling Mom over and over that the Soviet hospital was very good and it was the best thing to do.

I was scared and leaned against Mom going down in the elevator. Outside the kids from the building stared and asked each other what was the matter. Once in the ambulance I relaxed. The doctor sat next to me as I lay on a bed covered with warm blankets, and Mom was riding with us near my head. The ambulance ride was short, about ten minutes, because Morozovsky Children's Hospital is on the same side of the Moscow River as we lived. We rode through tall gates into a compound of gray buildings with tree-lined streets between them.

They took me to a small room with two benches, a desk, a cabinet and some chairs. On each wall in this room there was a large window that either looked out into a nursery or a laboratory. It was like a Marx Brothers movie because there was a doctor for every part of my body. For example, one doctor came into the room and examined my ears, said something to the nurse, who wrote it down, and then the doctor sat down on a bench. Then another doctor came in, looked at my eyes with a special light, gave his report to the nurse and sat down next to the first doctor on the bench. Finally, there was a whole collection of specialists on the bench. When they were finished they said I had pneumonia and that I would have to stay in the hospital. I ended up staying for eight days.

When we got to the hospital room a young doctor who wasn't sure the committee of specialists was right kept on examining me because he thought I had appendicitis. He worked over me until he and I were both exhausted and then he gave up, because the blood-test results could mean pneumonia as well as appendicitis. A year later I had to have my appendix out; maybe he was right.

The room they gave me was fairly large with three great big windows that looked out into the hall and two other rooms on either side of me. The fourth wall had two smaller windows that faced into a courtyard. In the room there was a toilet in the corner with torn sheets of *Pravda* for toilet paper, a large crib in which I slept, a bed for the parent, a sink and a bathtub. The toilet, the sink and the bathtub were not in a bathroom but out in the open so that you had no privacy from the people on the other side of the half-glass walls. When I started to get better and could have a bath, I asked the nurse to cover the glass walls so she tacked up some sheets but she said I was a pain in the neck.

The first night Mom stayed in the big bed but the second night she went home. After she left I couldn't sleep at all so I went out into the hall looking for someone to talk to. The young nurse on duty hurried me back into bed and drew pictures with me until she had to go. When I tried the same thing another night, the big fat nurse on duty yelled at me, "Go back to bed," which sounded convincing. I would often watch her through the glass, testing the hypodermics up toward the ceiling before the other nurses came around with them.

I was in the foreign section. There was a Swiss boy on one side of me who seemed to be about thirteen years old and was rarely visited. He was always working on complicated train models. On the other side was an Ethiopian lady. She had to take care of her two babies, who both had dysentery. She was only able to go out once a week because she had no one to help her. She spoke only Italian so she couldn't even talk to my mother or the nurses. When I was strong enough to get out of bed I danced around the room swinging my arms and singing "Oh, What a Beautiful Mornin'" and "Do Re Mi" and "My Favorite Things." The Ethiopian lady couldn't understand the songs but she laughed and seemed to enjoy my performance.

One day I was to have X rays and I had to walk to another building where there was an X-ray machine. It was fall and fairly cold out so I put on some ski-pajama pants under my nightgown and my coat over it. We passed some Russian kids sitting on a bench and they all laughed at the elastic ankles on my pajamas.

As I walked I saw all the Russian children hanging out of their windows and yelling down to their mothers and throwing paper airplanes with messages written on them. The ground was full of paper airplanes being dashed about by the wind. It was then I realized no Russian patients were allowed visitors. The Soviets were giving special treatment to the foreigners.

When I first came to the hospital the nurse gave me a knife, a fork and a spoon made of a tinny metal that was so soft it bent in your hands. I was always trying to straighten them because they bent so easily. She told me I had to wash them after I ate and keep them in my room, not let them be taken away with the dirty plates.

I didn't like the food very much. The milk had a layer of fat on it and the noodles looked as if someone had purposely poured water on them when they didn't need it. For breakfast I got mashed potatoes and herring. They clucked their tongues and shook their heads, wondering why I didn't eat much. The food came on thick white plates, handed out from a rolling cart, without a tray, but there was a little table at the head of the bed to put it on.

Since I didn't exactly love the food, my mother brought me American cornflakes and homogenized milk from Helsinki, which we had just started getting once a week through the American Embassy. The nurse said my mother was spoiling me.

There was no TV in the rooms and no magazines to look at. My mother brought me paper, colored pencils and some felt-tipped pens to draw with. When the nurse came to give me my medicine she saw the felt-tipped pens and said, "Could I try some of your eye makeup?" She kept saying over and over that she had never seen so many colors in eye makeup. Then she came out with the question that she seemed to keep in so long. "Could I have one of the pens?"

My mother was very nice and explained what they were. She told the nurse that these were in a set that she didn't want to break, but she would bring another pen from home the next day that she visited me, and she did.

Every day I would get three penicillin shots, one in the morning, one at noon and one in the evening. I woke up every morning with a needle in my rear end, and on the other end of the needle would be the hand of the nurse. She always smiled and said how brave I was when it just so happened that I was crying my head off.*

Sometimes the nurse would put mustard plasters on my chest and on my back. There was one nurse who put them on and forgot and my mother was the only one around to rescue me. Some days I was taken to a room where they put an electrical vest on me. It was padded and had heating wires going through it. It was supposed to clear my chest.

The penicillin, the mustard plasters and the electrical vest all seemed to work, and after a week and a day I was well enough to go home. I had to rest at home for a month, and then I was checked by the pediatrician in the clinic we always went to. We called before we went so the receptionist could tell us whether or not there was a long wait, otherwise we would have to sit in the waiting room for hours. When we got there, only an Indian family and their Russian interpreter, plus a Mongolian family who spoke perfect Russian, were ahead of us. My grandmother from New York was visiting and she came along for the checkup. She couldn't get over the fact that all the

---

* *Leona's note:* Doveen's tears were justified. Each morning when I arrived I found her wilted from crying after the first of the day's three penicillin injections. The needles were thick, of a gray metal, and though properly sterilized each time, they had become blunt through repeated use. Her buttocks resembled black and blue pincushions.

doctors were women and that they were so friendly and called me by name. The doctor looked me over and said I could go back to school at the end of October.

Jerry. Doveen was not the only one with medical problems in September. According to the rumor mill, Lin Piao had coughing fits and Chairman Mao lay near death after a stroke, but their illnesses turned out to be more political than physical.

On the morning of September 11, 1969, my "personal contact" at Novosti, Dmitri, called to tell me in a matter-of-fact manner that Soviet Premier Aleksei Kosygin had stopped over at the Peking airport for "open discussions" with Chinese Premier Chou En-lai. Kosygin was on his way back from Ho Chi Minh's funeral in Hanoi and had detoured in southern Russia to fly to Peking. I was excited by the news. It signaled an important new attempt to end the bitter recriminations between China and the Soviet Union, and an attempt to rebuild state and Party relations. China and the Soviet Union had been engaged in border fighting and skirmishing since early 1969 and the incidents had continued throughout the summer. The Peking meeting was a major news and diplomatic break.

Dmitri's giving me the story early did me no good because it was Tuesday and my deadline was not until Friday. I went around to the office of two colleagues who were not competitors and told them the news, so they could break it if they wanted to. Then I cabled New York and waited for the announcement from Peking.

Propaganda activities are carried out on many levels. Communist Party study meetings are held to expound a new line; then party officials carry the word to local neighborhood cells. Within the government and the Party apparatus the degree of sophistication and detail of a briefing depends on one's status. At the neighborhood level, a Party expert from Agitprop — the Bureau of Agitation (the spoken word) and Propaganda (the written word) — is called in to give a talk and answer questions. There the public has a chance to go beyond newspaper headlines and formulas. The briefings often contain detailed statistics on crime or alcoholism that would be embarrassing if printed officially. In the case of China, Agitprop meetings spread the rumors of internal bickering within the Chinese leadership, but there were no hard details.

In September, after Premier Kosygin met Chou En-lai at the Peking airport, rumors began to circulate in the press corps and at diplomatic cocktail parties that Chairman Mao was seriously ill. According to one version, Mao had died and a double was taking his place at official functions. In the Soviet Union this news was not as outlandish as it seemed on first hearing. In the last years of Stalin's life the tale persisted that whenever Stalin left the Kremlin, there were five Stalins, each going to a different place to foil any assassination attempt. Another tale had doctors examining five men, all of whom looked like Stalin, to diagnose Stalin's disease. Thus nobody could tell if the real Stalin was ill. Although apocryphal, the tales were indicative of the mood of the time. The story that Mao had a double was taken as an indication that the Russians believed the Chinese leader was nearing his final days.

There was no way to pin down a direct Soviet report of Mao's illness. There was no way even to link the rumor to official Russian sources. From Moscow the Russians were still, officially and scrupulously, trying to avoid interfering directly in Chinese internal affairs. The Soviet journalist Victor Louis had filed a story to the London *Evening News* that the Soviet Union was considering a preemptive nuclear strike against Chinese nuclear facilities. Since Louis has policy-level government connections, the story was widely held to be officially inspired as a warning to the Chinese. Still, there had been no official Soviet public speculation about the Chinese leadership.

I wrote a memo to New York about both rumors, Mao's illness and his alleged double. The memo questioned whether this was a piece of "disinformation" to influence the leadership struggles in Peking, or whether Mao had really been taken ill.

On a Friday night at a party with Russian friends I heard how the story of Mao's illness had been circulated and the details surrounding these rumors. Middle-level Communist Party officials serving in government ministries were being told at classified Party briefings that Mao had suffered a stroke on September 2, 1969, and was critically ill. The Party officials were also told that Mao was alternating between periods of coma and consciousness, and was in no condition to take part in leadership decisions. The top decision-making in Peking was being shared by three men: Defense Minister Lin Piao, who was then Mao's designated heir, Premier Chou En-lai, and Chen Po-ta, who played a key role in the Cultural Revolution and was then a vice chairman of the Cultural Revolution group. Both Lin Piao and Chen Po-ta were said to have taken part in the meeting with Chou En-lai and Prime Minister Kosygin at the Peking airport on September 11. Chou En-lai had not seen Kosygin in Hanoi at Ho Chi Minh's funeral because Chou had to fly back to Peking on September 4 to assess Mao's condition and consult with Lin Piao on whether to meet Kosygin. This, according to the Soviets, was why the meeting had not occurred in Hanoi and why Chou left early.

The briefing, as recounted by Russian friends, contained hard details. Lin Piao, who sat in on the airport meeting, had been forced to leave the room three times because of sustained fits of coughing. The Russians were playing up Lin Piao's known weakness — he had consumption — and indicating that they thought he was too ill to succeed Mao. The Communist Party officials were told that Chou was infinitely preferable to Lin Piao as a successor to Mao.

The story broadened the meaning of the Kosygin-Chou meeting in Peking.

I had a major story. Even if I could not further confirm the report on Mao's stroke, I had a detailed rundown on Moscow Communist Party thinking on the top Chinese leadership. If the Russians were telling ranking officials that Mao was ill, it indicated one of two things: either they had new evidence on Mao's health or they were mounting a campaign to discredit him on a new level. How to be sure? I had gotten the story late in the evening and it was late in the week, nearing my deadline in New York. This was not the kind of story to share with colleagues. I had to protect my source, but I also had to indicate that the material had come from a Communist official. And I had to do it without pinpointing him. Often reports on China came from East European Communists in Moscow and were attributed to "Communist diplomatic sources" in Moscow. But that kind of sourcing, besides being inaccurate, would miss the point of the story. To say it had come from "Soviet sources" would make it appear that the news had been leaked to me; this was the usual way of indicating an official but unnamed lead from the Press Department. I decided to attribute the story to "Communist sources." This, I felt, would indicate it came from within the system but yet was indirect enough not to reveal the source or imply official sponsorship. I made a point in the file to New York of saying that this was what the Russians were telling their people.

There were stories at least once a year saying that Mao had disappeared from sight, that he was ill, that a double was appearing for him, or that he was dying from a disease of old age. I realized that the October 1 anniversary was only two weeks away, and that if Mao were alive, there was a good chance he would appear on the reviewing stand in Tien An Men Square in Peking.

To send the story I might be playing into the hands of the Russians trying to use me as a transmission belt for their propaganda. But I knew that my source was not involved in the disinformation business; what I had picked up was an authentic replay of what the Communist Party was telling its own trusted officials. Such insights are rare in Moscow and I decided to go ahead with the story and urge the editors in New York to print it. Still, I sought to find some way to triangulate and double-check the story. Going to fellow newsmen would be useless in this case.

At midnight I woke Sherrod McCall, a trusted friend in the American Embassy, who knew China, and told him my tale, without naming the source. He too had heard the rumors of Mao's illness but the story had stopped there. There was no way to check further. If it was a direct Soviet provocation against the Chinese and a part of the propaganda war, then certain things would not fit: the details of the Peking airport meeting, the explanation of why Kosygin had not met with Chou En-lai in Hanoi. Over black coffee we tried to piece together the evidence that Mao was really ill. This was the most difficult part to verify.

The story broke with a ringing of bells on Telex machines around the world and callbacks to the wire services in Moscow. It was picked up and played with big, black headlines, emphasizing Mao's illness. For Kremlinologists and China watchers it was an important link in assessing the Soviet stance toward China.

Two weeks later Mao appeared in Peking for the October anniversary of the Chinese Revolution. He did not speak, but he was certainly alive.

That week I had a meeting scheduled at the Press Department to discuss the arrival of a second man for the *Time* Bureau and to outline plans for a trip to Central Asia. At the end of the conversation, my China story was raised. "I have been directed to reprimand you. Would you like the reprimand today or when you return from your trip?" Deputy F. M. Simonov asked pleasantly. "I guess I better have it now," I replied, trying to conceal my surprise at his tone. Then, in his most serious manner, Simonov switched from English to Russian, the standard manner of indicating an official conversation. "Printing rumors is not conducive to improving relations between the Soviet Union and other countries," he said, and he reminded me that by citing "Communist sources" I had violated the regulations applying to foreign correspondents. I had claimed to have talked with sources without naming them or getting prior approval for my interview with the Press Department. "You should be more careful in the future," he admonished gently. At no point were the details of the story or its substance raised. I left feeling that the story, insofar as it quoted what the Russians had been telling their own people, was accurate.

Whether Mao had really been seriously ill at the time of Ho Chi Minh's funeral or whether the tale was an elaborate cover to explain Kosygin's trip to Peking still remains a mystery. There was no doubt that the Soviet leadership hoped Mao would quickly pass from the scene and be replaced by Chou En-lai and a moderate leadership.

12

Lost on the Metro, at Ease in the Baths

ABOUT A YEAR AFTER WE MOVED into Yugozapad we found ourselves suddenly inundated with cockroaches. They moved into every apartment in the building, in search of water. We found dead cockroaches wherever we left pans or dishes to dry and a few drops of water had accumulated. The electrician and maintenance workers blamed the roaches on the Asians in the building: our efforts to exterminate the insects, they said, would come to nothing unless everyone participated, and the Asians, presumably Buddhists, refused to kill any sentient beings. The children joked that the cockroaches, with their long antennae, were really electronic listening devices — bugs — set upon us by the Russians.

Lyuba was horrified. She was afraid she would accidentally carry some home and infest her own apartment. While we were away at New Year's she put poison into the sink with a little water, so that when we came back the kitchen was strewn with dead cockroaches. But when we were home I frankly preferred the bugs to having poison in the house, especially since the insects did not bite or spread disease. After mentioning the problem to a few Russian friends, we learned that all Russian buildings with central hot water systems were infested because the roaches climb the pipes; buildings like Lyuba's, where the source of hot water is a gas geyser in each individual kitchen, have no roaches.

The cockroaches were a small inconvenience in our lives. By the time they came, at the beginning of our second winter in Moscow, we had adjusted to the continental climate and had learned to share with the Russians the pleasures of the cold season. Only Doveen's stomach problems and my broken ankle marred the second winter.

About the middle of December Doveen began to complain that her stomach itched. I brushed it off as winter dryness and applied baby oil, but when it continued and pain developed, Lyuba said it sounded like the symptoms she had suffered years before when she had liver trouble. Her warning sounded far-fetched, but the pain persisted through our two-week vacation in France. It was hardly a holiday because the weather turned bad while we were skiing in the mountains and I broke my ankle and whiplashed my neck in a bad fall. A French doctor, the son of a Russian émigré, set my leg in a cast while his father translated my complaints from Russian into French for his son. When I returned to Moscow I put my broken ankle under the care of a Soviet orthopedic specialist at the clinic.

I stood in the hallway of the clinic waiting my turn to see the doctor, when a familiar face, the pediatrician who had checked Doveen, came toward me. "What happened?" she asked sympathetically, eyeing the white gypsum that covered three quarters of my right leg. I was touched by her more-than-routine concern, but assured her that the ankle was on the mend. My real worry, I told her, was the pain in Doveen's stomach. She listened patiently to Doveen's symptoms and nodded. When I finished she said decisively, "She must have a stomach probe," using the same word for probe as the name of the recent Soviet spaceship, *zond*. She explained that a stomach specialist would put a plastic tube down Doveen's throat and draw up gastric juices that would be analyzed for a clear diagnosis. "I'll be right back," she said, and rushed off. In a moment she was back with the appointment book from the gastroenterologist's office, and wrote Doveen's name down for an early morning date the following week.

The zond was as uncomfortable as it sounded, but Jerry held Doveen's hand and told her newly made-up fairy tales during the ordeal. After an hour the technician administering the probe said she had got as much as she could, but she had not got near enough to the liver to be able to tell whether or not it was functioning properly. The analysis showed an inflammation of the gall bladder. It seemed incredible in a child of eight, but with a careful diet and daily doses of a molasses-like syrup, the pain disappeared and she became her usual cheerful and energetic self. Months later the American Embassy doctor asked me what the outcome of her problem had been. I described the treatment the clinic doctor had given Doveen and told the American doctor that she had responded well. He scoffed, refusing to believe that her gall bladder was inflamed or that the glucose and liver extract was helpful. "Nature made her well," he said, "not the Russians." I never knew which helped Doveen, nature or the Russians.

What relief I felt when the Soviet orthopedic doctor allowed the big cast to be taken off my leg and a small walking cast put on. She was a shapely and handsome woman of about forty-five, who had a good-humored relationship with the fair-haired, beautiful young doctor who assisted her. They both kept me laughing with their cynical jokes, and the younger doctor demonstrated with flair the Russian dances she would teach me as soon as my leg got better. I said one day that Doveen wanted to be a doctor, and as one voice they both said, "Tell her not to!" While I was in her office the older doctor was at the telephone every free minute checking on her own child who was sick at home. Had Grandmother arrived as promised to take care of the child? Had her fever gone down? The younger woman had a small child who came home full of energy from the crèche where she stayed all day. "I come home tired but she has had a nap all afternoon and wants to play till midnight." They both felt the pull of two professions, motherhood and medicine, and were constantly exhausted by the conflict.

When the walking cast came off, the doctor prescribed both therapy and massage for my ankle. I was back three times a week with the therapist, prudent Maria Gregorovna, and after she finished I would cross the hall to the masseuse, an enormous but gentle young woman who was as full of stories and liveliness as Maria Gregorovna was taciturn. Each woman made faces at the other behind her back; they barely managed a civil tone. Neither approved of the other's style, and both were constantly looking for something to criticize in the other.

The one time that Maria Gregorovna showed her softer nature was when three American astronauts were on their way back to earth

from the moon and the world waited in suspense to see if their mal-
functioning electric system would get them back safely. An announcement of official compassion and concern was broadcast on Radio Moscow, which set a pattern for citizen behavior. Both Tamara at our
Russian lesson and Lyuba when she came to work had expressed, almost in the same words, their human concern for the endangered
Americans. When I arrived for the therapy session that day, Maria
Gregorovna made a similar speech: fear for the astronauts, she said,
cut across all boundaries. There was no quality of parroting Radio
Moscow in her voice when she added, "I know how their families must
feel. My brother was lost in a submarine accident in the war."

Getting my ankle massaged was only an incidental part of my visits
with Masha. The massage was often interrupted by personal telephone
calls and she would go off to answer. She always apologized for leaving
me, but I didn't mind because she told me all the details of the call
when she came back. The first time it was a friend who wanted to
arrange a blind date for her — they would go out in a foursome. She
refused, but she was still considering it. She liked the girlfriend but
her mother didn't approve of her. "My mother is right. She has a terrible reputation. Only twenty-one years old and already she has had
five abortions — just like a cat." Another time the call was from a
friend who had been on a trip to Paris and had brought back a number of fake fur coats. She was asking 500 rubles each for them. I knew
that they cost about $100 in the West. At the official exchange rate 100
rubles was $111, but it was possible to buy rubles abroad at a rate of
between five to eight rubles to the dollar. (Some African and Arab
diplomats were bringing in cheap rubles, and although Soviet officials
knew it, they didn't want to offend these Third World governments
by clamping down. As a result these diplomats were paying inflated
salaries to their servants and driving up the price for the rest of us,
who refused to or didn't dare fool with unofficial currencies.) Therefore, Masha's friend was asking a modest black-market rate. The average Soviet citizen didn't mind the price when a chance for a luxury
came. Even the official price of cabbage went up to $1.50 a pound in
midwinter, so to pay five times the dollar value of a foreign coat didn't
seem exorbitant to Masha. Her mother was pushing her to buy the
coat. What did I think? she asked. I told her that the artificial furs
are not warm enough for Moscow winters.

I sometimes found her in a mood of despair, which she attributed to her love life. Some years before, she had been in love with a young engineer, who asked her to marry him and go with him to the Pacific island of Sakhalin. He knew it was a hardship post but they would be together and could save some money. Later they could ask for a more favorable location. Anton Chekhov went to Sakhalin in his first post as a young doctor. Masha was willing to go, but her mother discouraged her by pointing out that she, a girl who had never lived outside Moscow, would be unhappy in such primitive living conditions. How would she manage without toilets and running water in the house? Masha and the engineer agreed that he would go first, see what it was like, and then send for her. For a while he wrote her glowing letters; then the mail stopped. It was months before she heard from him again; he had been in an accident and had lost an arm. In the hospital he took to brooding: he was sure she wouldn't want to marry him now, a belief reinforced by the nurse who cared for him. Subsequently he wrote to tell her he had married the nurse.

She had no shortage of lovers, but they were shallow and insincere. She was in the midst of an affair with a married man, who told her that he had married his wife only because she became pregnant and refused to have an abortion. He kept promising Masha that he would get a divorce and marry her, but he was still living with his wife. One night she and some friends were drinking wine; feeling heady they went off together to the apartment of her lover. They pretended to be a group of his friends, but Masha was sure his wife suspected that Masha, desperate to have a look at her, had led them on the wild jaunt. Now, the morning after, as she worked over my ankle she was remorseful. She worried that the errant husband wouldn't see her again.

Occasionally we were not alone at the massage sessions. A girlfriend of Masha's who worked as a nurse in the clinic sometimes came down to the basement for a break. The nurse told me she made 65 rubles ($72) a month after studying years for a nursing certificate. She was considering forgoing the prestige of a profession to become a housemaid for foreigners. What did she need to know, and what was the usual salary? My emphasis on the difficulties of the job could not dispel the fact that I was paying Lyuba 160 rubles ($177) a month.

The last time I went to see Masha I asked her if massage was useful in getting rid of fat. "Yes," she said, laughing. "What do you think all those Arab women come in here for? They don't all have broken legs!"

After more than a year in the Soviet Union, all of us had our lives in place — friends, winter sports, favorite pursuits. We had stopped being painfully new in town.

Stevo. "Hey, Pilar, watch out," I shouted, slashing by on my new Finnish ice skates. The three Peruvian sisters stood in the middle of the frozen lake below our apartment building in their fancy foreign leather boots. The hundred Russians there were all wearing skates. Laura, the oldest sister, was talking to a Russian boy she had met, while Cucha and Pilar stood by watching and envying the skaters. There were a couple of other guys who also found the two worth harassing, and as they sprayed foamy ice on the girls with their sliding, daring stops, they said, with a laugh, "Exkyuss mee," in a foreign accent. One of them called me over and after finding that I spoke Russian, asked, "Shall we steal their sled?"

"OK," I replied.

"I've got an idea," he said. "Since you're a foreigner, go over and talk to them. Be sure to keep them occupied, and we'll grab it from the back."

"Are you buying a trolleybus or a bus pass next month?" I ventured to the girls, trying not to smile too much.

"What difference does it make?" Pilar asked.

"Not much. They're both full all the time. 'Bye now," I snickered as I raced to catch up with the Russians. We curved around the concrete-enclosed ice with the sled in tow, leaving their wails and Spanish curses behind. We exchanged names. His friends had left, so Grisha and I talked mostly about me, where I was from, and the usual first question about America was asked: "Is it really as bad as they tell us?"

"No, not quite," I answered. "There are people starving, and there is discrimination against blacks, the Vietnam war is terrible, but everything is so exaggerated here. Everything is about half as bad as they make it out to be." But by then we were back around to the girls, and we threw them their sled, blocking their attempts to catch us.

As we carved the icy perimeter of the lake with our skates for the last time that evening, he said, "Do you want to be friends?" Since we already were, I thought it a bit strange, but I said yes, and we shook on it. I presumed it was a ritual he enjoyed.

"See you here tomorrow."

"*Poka*" (see you later).

The next day we went ski-jumping. There was a shoulder-high jump on the steepest part of the hill, reinforced with a few boards, that served the purpose quite well. There was also a nice stiff wind blowing from behind us that added a great extra push. I bit the snow with my poles, freeing my skis from their stillness. I shoved the packed snow out of my way, tearing into it again and again, tossing chunks out of it. The clenched arrow of my body waited for the moment, the split moment to push, shove, and kick out, to fly. Up! A moment later, my tiger's ferocity switched to a sailing calmness flying straight on target to the goal, the aim, but, no, crunch; it was the ground: the virgin snow swallowing my skis in brave gulps. I turned and climbed up the hill to watch Andrei have his hit. I wrote this poem then, when I was thirteen:

> I stand at the top of the hill.
> The jump is a few yards below me.
> The wind thrashes behind me,
> And then, with a huge push, I'm off!
> There's the jump, I crouch like a tiger,
> And then I'm there, and I jump — up, up, up!
> I'm free! Free from everything:
> ABMs, the Middle East, Indochina, heroin, speed,
> Kent State, everything except gravity.
> I crouch again and slap! I land.
> The shock is so hard that
> My spine still hurts from the time
> When I used to land with a straight back.
> I stop, and climb back up the hill
> For another moment of freedom.

After another ten jumps, exhausted and exhilarated, we unsnapped and went to sit on the ground floor of my building. It was to be a store at some point in the very indefinite future, but meanwhile the bare and dirty concrete waited for a parquet covering, and the large windows on all sides were broken while others lay in jagged heaps outside, smashed by inefficient packing before they even reached the frames. We sat on the radiators, which carved designs on our asses, and talked about different types of skiing and skis, the advantages and disadvantages of cross-country style and downhill, different kinds of skates, different types of liquor. He told me about some very strong homemade liquor, *samogon,* he had drunk. During a lull in the conversation, he said quite suddenly, "You know, my father is a colonel in the KGB."

"Oh," was my only reply. I valued his friendship even more after that because he represented the extreme Soviet part of Russian society. Western historians and journalists write about the secret police and the rest of the government, but I was getting it from a unique point of view. I knew the son who told me that his father was sure to get him a job in the KGB, maybe even overseas.

In our quarter, a lot of the hooligans practically lived in the woods near our house where Grisha and I went cross-country skiing in the early bearable days of the winter. Between the two of us, we knew most of the hooligans in our quarter, and therefore we could still count on the forest to blanket us in quiet and protection from the wind. Swinging and swishing rhythmically through the trees, we were very comfortably alone. The best part of skiing in the forest, however, was a couple of snaky paths through the trees on a slight incline, so that you gathered a very nice speed schussing down in the quiet privacy of the big black branches against the sky. Leaning, sometimes slowing down, usually just missing the trees on the curves, you would burst out, in the end, onto the arterial road of the forest, suddenly in the open again, yelling for the people to get out of the way, and peering through the blur of windy tears to see if there was a nice girl to run into.

We also played hockey at the rink up by Lumumba University, where you could almost always find a game. The African students who ventured onto the ice with their wobbly ankles were invariably knocked over at least once during the afternoon, in the course of the weight-swinging hockey games. They were good, fast, passing games, but I wasn't much good at knocking people into the boards. We both got crunched ourselves at some points even though Grisha tried to warn me whom to keep away from before we started.

He was of medium height with flashing, often jeering, blue eyes; a hard but handsome face, and crew-cut black hair. One thing that made him uncomfortable to be with was his continuous, always alert striving to prove himself. He always insisted that his jumping was better than mine even though I landed farther from the jump. He was flashy in all sports even though he wasn't good enough to be. Our friendship often depended on a sort of trading of favors. He had the status of having a Western friend and was treated to a few of the "luxuries" of Western life at my house. It was a means of building his status as a young hooligan. I, in turn, had a Russian friend, and thus an opening into the real Soviet world.

When winter overshot itself, as it always does in Russia, and going outside was stepping into a world of numbness, Grisha came to my house a lot. In the beginning, we listened to records so that Grisha could acquire a taste in rock. He taped most of my Beatle records, which he liked the best. After I showed him my stamp albums and my coin collection, he started to bring Russian and Chinese stamps, some self-glorifying Stalin portraits, a few of Mao, and sometimes even tsarist issues. I also asked for North Vietnamese stamps, which are usually a propaganda scene: Ho Chi Minh–like peasants shooting down American jets, a young girl leading off a captured American pilot twice her size, or victorious soldiers standing on top of an American tank with piles of seized weapons in front of them, waving the flag of the Vietcong. There was heated bargaining between us as to how many pieces of gum, foreign coins, or stamps from colonies (in high demand) I would give for his stamps and coins. Grisha was fascinated with my younger brother's toy metal pistols because the Russians make only the real thing out of metal. While I looked over the stamps he had brought, he would have draws with my brother and shoot at every figure he could see, including the posters of Lenin on the wall. He had never had any American whiskey so he tried our scotch, gin, and bourbon, taking monstrous swigs from the bottle, trying not to let his eyes tear, and then complaining that "veesky" wasn't strong enough, and that he would stick to vodka. We played a few good Monopoly games at that dead part of the year. Of course Grisha condemned it at first for its capitalist orientation, but when he played he won like the shrewd Russian capitalists of tsarist times.

Grisha was always a little hesitant to come over because of the dangers involved. First of all, there was the militsioner, who might stop him and ask him his name and address, and what was he doing. He would be reported to his school or his parents. When I went out with him, there was no danger, though. Grisha said that his parents had told him not to go to foreigners' houses because they would plant foreign currency or some capitalist goods on him, and then take photographs as they pulled the goods out of his pocket. It was a complex paranoia. Grisha was willing to gamble it for the status and material he could accumulate through me.

I only went over to Grisha's apartment a couple of times, and it was always when nobody else was home. It had four rooms including the kitchen, and he, being the only child, had his own room, unlike most Soviet children who sleep on a couch in the family living room. The rooms had nice wooden parquet floors and atrocious wallpaper. A couple of beautiful rugs hung on the wall. There was a bedroom for his parents and a living room with a television and a tape recorder that was now blaring the Beatles. We were sitting in the kitchen over some hot Georgian tea, and we started a political argument. We were already true believing defenders of our respective ideologies, and we argued our points vehemently, as if we really knew what we were talking about. "There really is contradiction and injustice in your capitalist country with the privileged rich in their mansions and the proletariat starving," he remarked.

"That's not true, there are only a few starving, while most are on a middle level between rich and the poor. At least you can buy shoes that fit and food that's edible. And there's freedom also unlike the repression here. Take Czechoslovakia for example."

"We did the Czechs a favor saving them from capitalist infiltrators, you idiot." The dialogue was much more broken than that from our constantly interrupting each other, but in the end it boiled down to our news sources. Unknowingly, both of us were right when he said that the Voice of America was a capitalist propaganda station, and I said, in turn, that *Pravda* was full of gushy stories about the socialist paradise and workers overfulfilling their norms. Eventually, the telephone rang; he turned down the music and picked it up. I listened to him talking to his mother about meeting her at "Lyuba" (obviously a nickname for the Lubyanka prison where the KGB headquarters are located) and looked at a picture, probably taken in one of the buildings in the Kremlin, of a few rows of men and women lined up in military uniforms, medals bristling in the bright light. When he got off the phone, he pointed out both his father and his mother. He had to go downtown so I walked him to the bus stop. On the way we stopped by his school, and he asked me to wait outside. He emerged about ten minutes later with a big smile on his face. *"Vsyo v poryadke"* (everything's in order), he said. He explained that he had recently got some *dvoikies* (twos, the equivalent of Ds), and he had some friends cleaning up the class that day. They let him come in and change the marks in the teacher's book which always lay on the desk. With a class of forty, the teacher hardly ever noticed. It was an established practice among the hooligans.

Grisha didn't follow through, though, in one situation where hooligan ethics required him to help me. I had a ten-speed Sputnik bicycle, which I kept out in the hall on our floor. One afternoon, I stepped out of the elevator, and saw that my front wheel was missing. I asked around, and Grisha told me that his friend had been riding his bike near my building and had crashed. He needed a new front wheel, and happened to know about a bike up in one of the hallways. He replaced his wheel without much effort. It was mine. Grisha promised he would get the wheel back for me, and he did bring me one that had a flat tire. I should have kept it, but I told him that I wanted mine. The conversation dragged on for weeks. Soon school was out, and I never did get my wheel back. One of his friends stole a silver dollar when we were trading. I never got that back either. These incidents reminded me of the Polish girls' warning: "Those are bad boys. You shouldn't play with those boys, Steve."

Our friendship of favors is what finally broke us apart. He eventually demanded more than he could give. It was a constant badgering for a few more cigarettes and just one more piece of gum. I liked his rough style, but Grisha was sickeningly uncool when he pleaded for Marlboros. I became better friends with the older hooligans because they took what they got, and knew it was the best way to get more. We got high together on their liquor. Grisha only boasted. He brought me deeper into hooligan society, but Grisha was still proving himself and establishing his position in the hooligan ranks. I didn't have to deal with these problems because I was a foreigner.

Almost all the kids at our school were pretty smart and studied a lot, but Andrei was our class clown. He never learned the poetry that we all had to memorize, and he would stumble along, making funny mistakes when his turn came. He got into vicious fights with the geography teacher. She would call him something nasty when he had not learned the lesson, and as we all gasped, he would return something worse. Marya Andreyevna got so mad once that she pulled his hair.

Andrei was medium-sized for a twelve-year-old. He had thin hair that was usually scattered about, and too long for the school's liking. His face was rough and simple with a prominent nose. His eyes were daring and defiant, full of humor, but with an unsettling turn of sadness and depression. I saw him cry once, and his defiance was broken. It was sad because he seemed so vulnerable.

He smoked cigarettes with the avidity of all true hooligans. I surprised him once when I joined him for a smoke. After we'd taken a couple of drags, Andrei asked me if I always smoked. I said no, and he asked me why I was smoking. I was thinking of an answer when he plucked the cigarette out of my hand and threw it away. "It's no good for you," he said.

"How about you?" I asked.

"I need it," he replied. A schoolmate who was with us was glad that Andrei had thrown my cigarette away. "You shouldn't do it if you don't have to," he said.

Andrei thrived on the respect he earned through his hooliganish mystique, and his notoriety around school. Why and how he managed to channel his creativity into achieving this stature were his own sad secrets.

One Friday afternoon at the beginning of the winter, six of us, led by Andrei, took the Metro to the Lenin Hills. We all had our skates and hockey sticks. There was a stadium nearby that had a wide manicured ring of ice around it, where we set up some goals. Teams were chosen, and we started to play. There weren't any boards along the side to crush people against, so it was a better game. Speed on the ice, and quick accurate passes were needed. A water truck had just glossed over the surface, so the ice was rock hard and almost glowing. The game was getting good, and I had made a few goals, when a policeman on skates came by, and told us we couldn't play. He told us that the ice was only for free skating. Andrei took the lead here, and acted as if we were going to leave. We picked up our stuff and set up in a different place.

We were too tired just to outrace each other to the goals now, and our passing offensive strategies began to take shape. Andrei and I made some very smooth goals together. Another policeman came by and we agreed with him to stop playing. After the cop left, a couple of guys were seriously talking about quitting, saying that it wasn't worth it, but Andrei insisted that we continue.

Our third round of hockey did not last more than ten minutes. Two policemen together, hardly saying a word, grabbed all our sticks, and told us to get our stuff. We yelled and held onto our sticks, but Andrei was very cool and didn't even protest. Soon we were all skating down the ice after the policemen.

It was just getting dark as we skated along, muttering between ourselves at first, but then carving our way in silence. Andrei was quiet the whole time, he had a half-smile on his face, and looked quite confident. Most of us were pretty scared, though, especially me. But when I looked at Andrei I realized that there was nothing to worry about and that this was just going to be a formality. When our formation of eight reached the open part of the stadium where the coffee shop and the police station were, it was quite dark. We passed under the bright lights and through the people. Hooligans were in groups, some boys showing off in front of their women.

We walked into the stadium on the hard plastic floor with our skates on. As we went through the anteroom of the headquarters, I saw a framed piece of paper with a list on it. The word "hooliganism" blared out from it at me. I started to get nervous again, but the policemen were being almost friendly now. One of them prepared to write down our names while the other looked through our sticks. He picked mine out and exclaimed, "Hey, is this real?"

It was a Finnish Kono stick, and far superior to any that the Russians make. The stick itself was laminated, and the bottom was coated with a hard protective plastic layer. It was very light and strong. Russian sticks are lumpy pieces of wood, that break quite easily, but many kids write foreign brand names on them, to show their obsession.

All of my friends tried to answer his question at once.

"Yeah, it's real."

"It belongs to this guy."

Katie in Red Square on May Day, 1969. The slogan under the group portrait of Lenin, Marx, and Engels says, "Forward to the Victory of Communism!" (Photo by Jerrold Schecter)

"He's a foreigner."

"He got it in Finland."

"He's an American who goes to our school."

The officer had been swinging the Kono, and when he heard this he told me to come over. He asked me if it was my stick, and then told me to come with him. I looked back at everybody, but they were waving. Andrei was giving his name and address.

"This is a really nice stick," the policeman said. "Here, take it. Your friends will be out in a few minutes." I thanked him, and went to sit on a bench outside. They all came out smiling and joking ten minutes later, and we walked back to the Metro station.

Andrei was kicked out of our school at the end of the year.

Katie. Every Tuesday and Friday I went to ballet lessons in an old palace that had been built before the Revolution.

As I stepped up the huge winding staircase with beautiful dark wood banisters I could hear the faint sound of music on the top floor. I got excited, thinking my class had started and began to run. But even though I hurried I imagined myself as a princess climbing a never-ending tower.

When I reached the top I found out the music I had heard was for the younger girls' class and I still had time. I also found out that my Peruvian friend, whom I was supposed to go home with, hadn't come and this caused a big problem. How was I to get home? But I didn't worry about it too much because I was busy getting into my leotard.

The dressing room was quite big and completely covered with mirrors. The classroom was like a ballroom except that it had ballet bars and one wall covered with a mirror. Everyone faced the mirror and in one corner a lady played a piano.

The lesson was typical of any ballet lesson with only two exceptions. One was that all instructions were given in Russian and French, and second, the teacher was much stricter than any other ballet teacher I had ever had. For example, if your leg was bent when it was supposed to be straight he would come around and slap it. He also had a little watering can and if anyone made too much noise he would sprinkle it on the floor around them. This made the floor slippery.

The ballet teacher was a chubby man who seemed in his early thirties, but although he was strict I enjoyed the class.

After class I got dressed and called home to see how to get there. I was told to take the Metro. I had been on the Metro alone coming to class many times and with my sister going home, but I had never been on the Metro going home alone. My sister gave me instructions and I said "Bye."

I walked down the steps and into the wind and cold. I walked out of the palace grounds through the gate of the fence surrounding it.

It was about two blocks to the trolleybus I had to catch. I walked past a grocery store with people pushing to get in and a man on the sidewalk selling shriveled-up apples.

I came to Tchaikovsky Street, where I caught the trolley. I got on in a big crowd and walked shakily back to the last car. I sat down by a window and gazed out. We passed about five portraits of Lenin and I thought about all the times my friend and I would pretend we didn't know who he was and ask each other why we were always seeing him. It all seemed so obvious to us then: Lenin was the father of Communism and we all should respect him. The more I thought about it the more I got sick of the whole idea and my best remedy was to dream about America. We passed the American Embassy and even though I had only lived in America about two years altogether in my whole life I still felt very American.

My stop was coming up soon so I got up. An old babushka was sitting next to me and as I got up I saw that the bus was much more crowded. We stopped and I started to push through so I would be ready to get off at the next stop. Then suddenly I heard a big clunk on the top of the trolley. The rail had fallen which attached the trolley to the wires that it runs on. This meant that we would have to wait a while for it to be fixed. I didn't worry because this had happened before going to and from school.

About fifteen minutes passed while the men climbed on top of the trolley and fastened the rail back to the wires. Then we started to move again.

I got off the trolley. It was dark at 7:30; I was already half an hour late. I walked into the warm Metro station with people bustling around. Outside people were selling ice cream, cake, and flowers, and there was a stand where they were selling meat.

I put my five-kopeck piece in the slot and pushed the bar. I walked to the escalator that was straight in front of me. The escalator was enormous, about three or four times as big as one in the States. I felt as if I were going down into the center of the earth. I stepped off the escalator and went over to the side where a train was coming in. All around me were big arches and in between the arches were murals painted on the walls. The murals portrayed workers, either working on farms or doing construction jobs.

The train came clattering in. You never had to wait too long because trains came every four minutes. The train came to a halt, the doors opened and people got off and on. It wasn't too crowded in my car. I sat down next to a young man in a gray suit. The train started with a jolt and I grabbed onto a bar. The train went very fast and everything was pitch-dark outside the windows. We passed a few stops and even though I didn't recognize the names I didn't worry. But when we came to the fourth stop and I still didn't recognize it I started getting upset. Besides, I couldn't remember the name of my stop. So I asked the man next to me when would we come to the university, the only stop I could remember on my line. He said I was going in the wrong direction. I had made a mistake and had walked to the wrong side of the platform when I got on, taking a train going to the north side of the city instead of the southwest where we lived. The man said I should go back on the train across the platform from this one, at the next stop. He said he would take me back and I didn't object because by this time I was pretty scared. Maybe it doesn't sound too frightening but at the time I was eleven years old, a foreigner, some place on the other side of Moscow, and I couldn't remember the name of my station.

I told the man the only name I could remember, which was the name of the bus line I took home from school. He said that would help a lot.

At the next stop we got off. This young man who offered to help me home didn't know what he was getting himself into. We spent two hours going up and down escalators, up and down steps, getting off and on trains, and pushing through crowds.

All that time a thousand things ran through my head. When he explained to me how to get back home it all seemed so easy, why were we going through all this trouble? God, it sure does stink, why don't the Russians have antiperspirants? God, it's hot, I wish I could take my coat off. I wonder what time it is. A quarter to nine. I could have been home by now. Many other things ran through my mind but they were all confusing.

At last we came out of the hot Metro station into the cold winter night. The air felt good as it blew down my neck and through my sleeves. The man who was guiding me showed me to a bus that would take me to my bus stop near school. He said I should transfer there to the bus that would take me home.

I thanked him and boarded the bus. As I sat looking out the window at the lights in the apartment buildings that seemed to blink on and off as we rode by I realized it was already a quarter to ten. This didn't shock me too much even though I usually got home at seven-thirty. With all I had just been through it wasn't very surprising!

The bus came to my stop in only a few minutes and it occurred to me that the man who had just helped me had taken me straight across the city. In the gutter a drunk lay all wet and cold while some people tried to help him. I got on the bus and laid my head against the window but it was too bumpy so I sat up. I got off at our stop and trudged across the street, climbed the bank of snow to get to the boards, stepped across each board, and soon I got to the path of hard-packed snow. Everything seemed like such a drag. I started running and slipped. I fell on my tailbone. All I wanted to do was get home, but I still had a way to go. I crossed the long field more tired than I could ever remember. I passed the building next to ours and climbed another small snowbank to get to our building. As I walked along to get to our entrance I kept looking behind me to make sure no one was following me. All around was complete silence except for the wind biting at my face and neck. There was no policeman on duty in the guardbox. I walked into the door, went up in the big metal elevator and opened the door.

Everyone was glad to see me and wanted to know what had happened. My mother and brothers and sisters were very worried. Daddy was working late in the office. I told them everything and someone laughed and said, "We thought you were kidnapped."

I told them, "You didn't have to worry 'cause there's no crime in Russia." We talked and laughed a bit more and then I went to bed. In bed I wondered why there wasn't any crime or at least very little in Russia and laughed at myself for looking back when I was walking home.

I never saw the man who helped me again and I never knew his name, yet he took me from one side of Moscow to the other.

Every Sunday there is an open-air bird market in Moscow.

Our whole family went there a couple of times. There were farmers and babushkas selling many different kinds of birds and small animals. One stand sold German shepherd puppies and right next to them a dozen geese waddled around waiting to be bought for someone's Sunday night supper. There were canaries, chickens, a few turkeys of a European breed and a variety of other birds for pets or for eating. There were European hedgehogs being sold for pets. They don't have long quills like American porcupines, only short stubs that don't hurt at all. We found out, however, that they are nocturnal animals and wouldn't be good as pets. Sometimes there were kittens, gerbils, mice and other harmless rodents. Well, I really shouldn't say that because Barney was bitten by a gerbil when he put his hand in the cage to pet one.

The animals all the kids liked best were the rabbits. I thought how terrible it was that most of the birds and rabbits would be killed by the next day. We found one vendor who was selling baby rabbits that could fit into your hand. My father agreed to get two because we didn't have any pets and these could survive easily outdoors in winter. My mother was doubtful about getting them but agreed as long as we got brown ones. She said that brown rabbits are always much smarter than white ones. My father bargained with the old man who was selling them. The man said he needed the money to buy vodka. In the end he settled for three rubles.

We took the bunnies home and made them a little house on our balcony. We got dried grass from the woods and made them some beds. We fed them all our peelings and leftover pieces of vegetables and fruit. Every day we would come home and play with them, holding them, petting them, putting them on places where they would have to jump down. They survived the winter and spring easily and grew bigger and furrier, but we could still hold them and play with them. It was easy to keep them on our balcony because whenever we had to clean it we just swept everything off and most of the mess got blown in all directions.

When summer came and we were going out of the country on vacation we needed someone to take care of them. The van Hijftes, our Dutch friends who lived a few floors below us, volunteered for the job. Mr. van Hijfte worked for KLM and every week he received a special shipment of Dutch vegetables flown in from Holland. The leftovers of the shipment could go to our rabbits.

When we came back from summer vacation we couldn't recognize them. They were huge. Each of their ears was about a foot long and they were so fat and strong you couldn't hold them for more than a second without their wriggling away.

We tried to keep them but it became impossible. They were so big they needed more space. So we gave them to the kindergarten across the street. Barney went over to visit them once in a while, and one day he came home and told us the rabbits were gone. Some couple had taken them. We never found out what became of them. Lyuba kidded us that they were probably eaten. Secretly, I hoped they were too strong and got away.

Doveen. Everyone got in line to go to the auditorium on the fifth floor for an assembly. There was a big picture of Lenin above the stage. On the other walls were exhibitions of the students' art.

After we sat down a girl from a higher grade did a dance from the ballet *Swan Lake*. She did it like a professional, I thought, partly because when her crown fell off she didn't stop to pick it up. After that some boys and girls did a play, but I didn't understand much of it.

Then came the big surprise that we had all been waiting for — Father Frost. He is just like Santa Claus who brings presents on Christmas Eve except that Father Frost brings presents on New Year's Eve because no one can be Christian in Russia. He took a big sack of toys over his shoulder and handed out toys to all the children. I got a plastic doll carriage. After that we sang a song about Father Frost and went back to our classroom.

Barney. I went to the coatroom and got my coat. By this time I knew how to ride the bus alone so I didn't wait for Evelind. I set out for the bread store. When I got there the lady behind the counter wearing a baker's coat gave me a big fork to feel the buns and see which one I wanted. I picked out a round white bun with powdered sugar on top, which was my favorite of all of them. When I got the bun it was still hot and soft and it warmed me up. I tried to stay in the store as long as possible without finishing my bun because it was cold outside. The old grandmothers in the store yelled at me for eating with my gloves on. Then I went out into the cold. I went to the bus stop and waited for the No. 42 bus which brought me the closest to our building. I got on the bus and didn't put any money in the machine because I didn't have any. I sat down and a lady behind me said, "I don't want to see you on the bus again. Why didn't you pay?" All through this I was mumbling that I had a pass. I mumbled because I knew I didn't have it with me. I'd left it at home. Katie told me how she did the same thing and how Doveen did it too so I didn't feel so bad. The lady kicked me off at the next stop so I had to walk farther than I expected. I walked up to the field that we crossed in the morning. The cold wind pinched my face and I started seeing red blotches. I was wearing a Russian fur hat with ear flaps, a sheepskin-lined coat and fur-lined boots, but it was still cold. I felt as if I were walking across the desert in a cold sandstorm.

I caught up with Stevo. I was running up to him and I slipped and fell flat on my nose on the icy path. I started seeing stars and black for a minute but then I got up and started crying. Then we walked on through the parking lot and into the building and up in the elevator to our warm apartment for lunch.

Jerry. At the top of the hill leading to the *bani* (baths) my friends and I each paid forty kopecks to a peddler who hawked switches of green birch leaves for the steam room and fresh linden shavings curled round and round so they formed a rough scrubbing brush called a *mochalka.* Then we entered the Sandunovskiye Baths where the dark wooden-beamed and fretwork ceiling shone with the gloss of age. At the bani dry heat purges the body of the poisons of vodka and the stale odors of the office. The baths restore health with primitive simplicity: heated stones to force sweat, green birch leaves to rouse the blood, pine shavings to wash away dirt, and cold water to balance the heat and soothe the self-induced fever.

Long lines of people stand patiently for admission tickets to the men's and women's sections, which are separate, each at the head of a grand, winding wooden staircase that seems to be leading to a ballroom, not a public bath. There are all kinds of Russians at the baths, young and old, each with a small paper-wrapped package under his arm containing a *vobla,* sun-dried and salted river fish with black and white scales that are related to American freshwater white perch. Together with vodka and beer, vobla are a necessary part of the regimen.

The main hall of the bathhouse is divided into cubicles separated by partitions of heavy dark wood. The attendant gives each bather a clean sheet as he enters. He took my money and watch to be checked, my shoes to be shined and my pants to be pressed.

Like a Finnish sauna, the heat is dry. I stood first at the entrance to adjust to the extreme blast of heat that engulfed me as I entered through the heavy door. Gradually, I walked up the steps, to a corner where I could feel the full force of the temperature. Gradually the heat penetrated and my body warmed. Simply waving the birch switches caused the air to circulate and increased the heat and its penetration. We took turns with the birches which gave off a fresh smell of resin and woodlands. Then we struck each other with the birches and pressed their hot wet leaves against our legs and arms and stomachs so that the heat burrowed beneath the skin and into the vitals. Sweat began to pour and soon the tips of my toes, the last to warm, felt the heat. One of our party brought a glass of beer into the hot room. He threw the beer against the stones and the hiss spread across the room carrying the smell of roasted hops, a full deep crunchy odor of warmth and pleasure. The heat and alcohol drove through our bare skin and my body began to vibrate. My sweat ran in sheets of water.

It was time to plunge into the swimming pool and do a few laps, then run to the shower for a scrubdown with the pine shavings. The pool was dark and the white Grecian columns were mildewed. The plaster on the walls was peeling, but the water was icy and bracing.

The washing room had white marble slabs to lie on, and an ancient but strong bath attendant with a rubber apron scrubbed me hard with the fresh white pine shavings. It felt as if he was rubbing my skin away; my arms were red and tender; the bucket of water he poured over me cooled and refreshed me.

Then once again we went into the inferno for another purging of the ill humors of Moscow's daily existence. The anger of calling the Press Department and getting no answers, the inability to meet Soviet officials, the cancellation of trips outside Moscow, the decisions of New York to hold over stories, the frustration of having the radio antenna and side mirror of the car stolen for the third time — all melted away with the heat. There was only my hot skin and a deep warming through my body. Although the heat made my blood flow faster it calmed me into a kind of heat-induced meditation. Then we went into the shower to cool again. The attendant handed us each a crisp white sheet to dry ourselves with.

We sat down in our cubicle: American correspondent Ed Stevens; Sasha, a thirty-five-year-old art restorer who worked on ikons for Ed's wife; Pavel, Ed's friend from Krasnodar, which is in the black-earth farming region of the North Caucasus; and Grisha, a young engineer. The vodka was icy cold, and we passed the bottle. Sasha ripped open a vobla, carefully removed the skin and licked the salt from his fingertips. I followed his technique. The fish and the roe were firm, dry and salty, chewy but tasty. After a few bites our body juices began to flow again. The salt from the fish restored the chemicals removed by the steam.

Sasha regaled us with the latest Moscow jokes. His favorites revolved around the civil war general Vasily Ivanovich Chapayev and his faithful aide Petka. Example: Vasily Ivanovich asked Petka for a virgin and he provided one. "She was lovely, Petka," said the general the next morning, "but she wasn't a virgin." Petka promised to do better and repeated the procedure. Again Ivan Ivanovich complained that Petka hadn't brought him a virgin. Finally Petka brought his general a beautiful girl and the following morning Ivan Ivanovich approached with a smile on his face. "She was lovely," he said, "but she wasn't a virgin."

"Oh, yes, she was," insisted Petka. "I tried her myself."

Sasha told political jokes about the invasion of Czechoslovakia. One was a play on the word *dub*, meaning oak trees: why did the Russians pick all the acorns in Czechoslovakia? Answer: so there wouldn't be any more Dubceks.

We talked about the shortage of meat and potatoes in the Moscow markets. We all praised the superiority of Czech beer we were drinking over Moscow beer.

Ed Stevens had organized the visit to the bani. It was part of the old Moscow he had known when he first came from the United States as a Columbia University graduate in the 1930's. Ed worked as a translator before becoming a correspondent for Reuters. Later he became

chief of the *Time* and *Look* magazine bureaus and now he was correspondent for the London *Sunday Times*. Ed was a genial and generous host, and he and his Russian-born wife, Nina, were the only ones
in the foreign press corps who had a private house.

Although Nina had become an American citizen during World
War II she was loath to leave Moscow permanently, preferring to
make long visits to her son in New York and her daughter in Rome.
Nina collected the works of young Russian painters, which she sold
by appointment to Moscow's foreign community. She converted the
basement of their house into a log-walled izba, leading out to an En-
glish-style garden, the only place where foreigners and official Russians
could gather. It had apparently been declared safe ground.

Over the years Ed and Nina collected writers, poets and artists.
Nina had spats with the artists over their share of the price of their
paintings but they always seemed to make up with her and come back.
They did not want to miss the new faces or the blinis and kilos of
caviar on the antique wooden tables inlaid with the crest of Peter the
Great. Nina had managed to salvage the tables from the secondhand
stores of Moscow and from private sellers.

Through Ed and Nina we saw a side of Moscow that was otherwise difficult for foreigners to reach: writers from the Writers' Union,
actors and directors and moviemakers, the sons of Politburo members,
poets and translators. From Ed's connections in the film business — he
was agent for Avco-Embassy Films in Moscow — there was a steady
flow of visitors from New York. The Stevenses also acquired friends on
their visits around the Soviet Union who would drop in when they
were in Moscow. That was how Pavel, an Armenian visiting Moscow,
came to be with us at the bani.

Pavel was a friend of a friend in Krasnodar. He arrived at the
Stevens house at 11 Releyev Street one evening with a basket full of
mountain trout from Armenia wrapped in ferns. Pavel was a *tolkach*
(expediter), which is Russian slang for an independent entrepreneur,
derived from the verb *tolkat,* to push. Characters like Pavel existed
for me only in cartoons in *Krokodil,* the Soviet humor magazine, as
objects of scorn. Pavel's wide smile was relaxed and self-assured, dis-
playing a gold tooth that gave him a worldly air. I judged him to be
in his late forties, a man of medium build with black wavy hair. His
springy step and active motions indicated the energy with which he
was used to functioning.

Pavel was a successful construction contractor, an illegal middle-man in a socialist state. His operations centered in the rich black-earth region of the Kuban in the North Caucasus where he was the go-between for the bureaucracy and the giant collective farms and state farms. Pavel's function was simple in concept but difficult in execution. Using his smooth charm and skill at organization he expedited the shipment of construction equipment and building supplies to farms. He built roads and drainage ditches, provided for electrification and sewage. He operated as a private building contractor in a society that officially forbade entrepreneurship, but he was never prosecuted because he was needed. His clients were big farms that needed to get approval for major improvements but found that the normal bureaucratic chain was too slow and inefficient. Coordination is a middleman's skill that was eliminated during the building of socialism in the USSR and Pavel's job was to grease and link the bureaucratic chain. His clients were rich in rubles but poor in organizational skills. They had no idea where scarce supplies were to be found and how to install them. Even if much-needed drainage pipe was allocated, where were they to get the heavy equipment to have it laid? Pavel responded to problems with a flexibility that the bureaucrats from the Ministry of Agriculture and Light Machinery could not match. The bureaucrats were hampered by the rigid norms imposed on them by central planners. The planners, in turn, failed to coordinate with each other or with the needs of the farmers working far from their ministries in Moscow.

Pavel's secret was that he assumed responsibility. Without him there was too often nobody to take charge. His resources were remarkable. He had no office except his pockets, no supply depot or motor pool. Instead, he had friends at tractor stations, cement factories, and construction equipment centers, and he knew the ministries like the palm of his hand. He could supply skilled labor from a pool of friends in Armenia, bulldozers, wiring and heavy pipe. When he promised a job it was done on time and executed well. He knew how to present his schemes with a genial ease and efficiency that pleased all concerned. His prices were high but money never seemed to be a problem; it was materials and equipment and making them work that counted.

Pavel was a master at making the system work for him. He knew whom to pay and how much to pay in the ministries so that permissions and supplies flowed smoothly. Sometimes state plans were altered to fit his projects but no one complained because the results served the acute need for roads and drainage systems. At other times he craftily arranged his projects to fit into the prescribed plan. Whichever approach he used, the results overfulfilled the norms required both of the farms and the ministries. His function and his fees never had to appear on their ledgers.

Pavel's fees kept his pockets filled with rubles and he entertained liberally. In the Soviet Union that meant he had a kilo of fresh black caviar with him in his hotel room for breakfast, together with a couple of bottles of twenty-year-old Armenian cognac, as well as fresh tomatoes and cucumbers, in the midst of winter. The day we went to the baths Pavel arrived with delicate, tangy goat's cheese and still warm flatbreads from the Armenian restaurant where the chef was on his payroll.

Pavel traveled often and he described for us the delights and complexities of his ventures. His luxuries were a car, a dacha, and plenty of cash. He enjoyed his work and the good fellowship he generated. He never admitted to having a capitalist instinct; rather, he insisted he was simply filling a need to get the work done. He invited us to visit him in Krasnodar and promised to show us the work he did. We accepted readily.

Krasnodar, in the Kuban region of the North Caucasus, is the richest black-earth wheat-growing region in the Soviet Union. From the air the Kuban River meanders gracefully through the dark black fields.

It was spring — mid-April. Ed Stevens and I, after tedious applications and postponements, finally received permission from the Press Department of the Ministry of Foreign Affairs to make the trip on our own without a guide from Intourist or from Novosti, the Soviet Press agency that usually arranged foreign correspondents' trips for a fee. We made our reservations through the diplomatic service bureau and were making the trip without an interpreter, who would be superfluous since Ed speaks fluent Russian. This was the only time I was able to make a trip in the Soviet Union without a mamka to keep watch over me. It seemed at first a heady freedom, but the officials who allowed it made sure it was difficult and frustrating.

Ed and I set off for Krasnodar aware that the usual facile contacts provided by Intourist and Novosti would not be waiting for us; we were on our own and it would be hard work. The chance to move around freely and talk to people without the inhibiting influence of an official interpreter would allow us, we hoped, to choose whom we wanted to speak to, see what we wanted to see, to assess for ourselves the prospects for the coming wheat crop without the interpretation of *Pravda*. But meeting with farmers in an atmosphere without government surveillance was to prove even more difficult than we imagined it would.

Flying over the black earth in an Ilyushin-18 we could see that there were only occasional strips of green winter-wheat shoots. The winter had been a stormy disaster and spring had come three weeks late. There should have been full fields of fresh thrusting winter wheat for July harvest, but the winds of hurricane force in January and February blew away the spare snow cover and uprooted the young shoots and the topsoil. Wheat was sprouting in woodlands and pastures and some had even taken root in the city of Krasnodar where, scattered by the winds, it was growing in the cracks of sidewalks. Everywhere except in the wheat fields.

Krasnodar is the capital of the *oblast* (region) and has a population of five hundred thousand. The Kuban River borders the city, which is laid out with the straight streets and clean lines of a farming market community. In the contemporary center are the required Revolutionary Square with an opera house, local and regional Communist Party headquarters, and the newly built concrete blockhouse, the Caucasus Hotel, an example of the shoddy finishing that is the trademark of Soviet building standards. On the balconies of the apartment houses lining the wide streets, strings of vobla, the river perch we had eaten at the baths, hang in the sunlight to dry — a humanizing touch.

Krasnodar is a city with few distinguishing characteristics. It has the raw look of being built to plan on a giant scale, the stamp of socialism under collective leadership. The postwar buildings have the oversized gigantism of Stalin; a rush of cheaply constructed housing marks the Khrushchev era. Krasnodar's monument to the recent past is a giant agricultural exhibition complex that was built under Khrushchev's orders and then abandoned. The gates and buildings stand, weather-worn and spotted, unused, a memorial to Khrushchev's aspirations for agriculture that never materialized.

Pavel and his friend Igor invited us for dinner at the new Caucasus Hotel. The main dining room was spread out like a soccer field and lined with crystal chandeliers. We arrived after 9 P.M. and the tables were full. Pavel, the supply agent, arranged for us to sit down only after talking to some of his waiter friends on the side of the dining room and paying them. A flow of wines, vodka and *zakusky* (hors d'oeuvres) emerged. There was an elaborate menu in English, Russian and French but the only choice available was shashlik. This was typical of Soviet restaurants; despite the menu only one or two dishes were available each day. It had become a bad joke between Ed and me that whenever I asked for the Kiev cutlet on the menu the waiter would say, *"Kievsky nyet."*

The band and the dance floor harked back to an image of America in the years just after the Second World War, the late forties, when America was feeling the flush of growth and power. The people on the dance floor were out for a good time. The women, fat by Western standards, were clad in shapeless flowered-print dresses of no particular style. The men, heavily built with beefy arms and necks, wore white shirts and narrow ties. A group of Georgians asked the band leader to play a well-known song of fast tempo and the men began to dance singly with a grace and animation that livened the entire dining room. Then the band began to play a quiet two-step. I watched three black Africans move toward some Russian girls seated at a table near the dance floor, with the obvious intention of asking the girls to dance. As the blacks approached, a group of young men rose from their table and stepped between the Africans, who appeared to be students, and the Russian girls. The Russians surrounded the blacks and firmly edged them off the dance floor, pushing them away from the girls. "They don't want those blacks dancing with Russian girls," said Sasha, who had joined us in Krasnodar. "We don't want those blacks marrying our girls. In Kiev last month a black student married a Russian girl and people threw stones at them after the wedding." He spoke with marked approval.

Then, to change the subject, Pavel proposed a toast to friendship between the Soviet People and the American People and between our families. At the dinner were Ed, Sasha, Pavel, Vadim, a foreman in a small factory who was a friend both of Pavel's and Ed's, and myself. Pavel's friends stopped by the table to shake hands and he introduced me. Each of his friends and I drank vodka together; bottoms up was the rule. The small glasses were filled and the first toasts were delightful. The liquid flowed through my body like a sudden burst of power from the afterburner of a jet fighter. Spirits rose, cares dispersed, and the world seemed relaxed and manageable, but keeping the fire burning and the mood in balance was difficult. The black bread and caviar, the smoked salmon and sturgeon were all rich and tasty and banked the heat of the vodka.

Pavel explained that it is perfectly all right to ask young women who are unaccompanied to dance and he suggested I approach an attractive girl in a brown knit dress. She was a university student home for spring vacation who was studying French. Her father was a Communist Party official in Krasnodar, she told me as we danced to a two-step that took me back to high school days. My tablemates nodded with approval.

The next morning, Saturday, we went to the collective farm market in Krasnodar to watch preparations for the Russian Easter. The market was alive with people: old peasant women with boots and babushkas, office workers with string bags, old bearded men, young boys and girls doing the family shopping. The fruit and meat counters were crowded; the green painted stalls seemed like a tableau from the past. This was a rynok where farmers sold vegetables, chickens, pigs, and beef grown on their own private plots. Fish caught by individual fishermen were for sale: big-mouthed river pike, three rubles each, lay shimmering on wet wooden stalls. Spring onions, parsley, chives and small leaf lettuce were the only vegetables ready in mid-April. The other counters offered last fall's crop — apples, dried fruits, nuts, mushrooms and seeds for private plots. Each mound of seeds had a primitive hand-painted picture on wood of the fruit or flower that would grow from the seeds. As I took pictures of a counter of green vegetables a woman in the crowd shouted "Speculators, speculators. Show their pictures on television with the prices they charge," she encouraged me. People turned to look at her and smiled in embarrassment.

"*Molodoi chelovyek, molodoi chelovyek*" (young man, young man), called an old woman as I passed a stall of pickles and sauerkraut whose briny smell quickened my taste buds. I smiled and approached as she offered me a sample of her wares. The pickles were full of garlic and spices. As I bit into one I remembered Mr. Sax's "appetizing" store in the Bronx where I often bought a pickle on the way home from school. The taste was exactly the same.

The local river fish were fresh and plentiful. We bought vobla to take back to Moscow. There was no sense of abundance, only a continuity of the seasons, another year on the faces of the wrinkled women and weather-browned farmers in rough clothes. People shouted and haggled over prices, laughing and counting their kopecks. It was more primitive than Moscow, closer in spirit to the black earth. The new concrete shell of the city was a façade that could not manage to hide the earthy flavors of the market. Nothing was packaged; the shoppers brought their own jars for pickles and expandable string bags in which to carry home fruits and potatoes. For the time being there were no supermarkets. The state stores, with centrally controlled prices and distribution, could not equal the freshness or the supply of fruit, vegetables, eggs, cheese, or sour cream that came from private plots. The timeless ritual of Saturday afternoon marketing at the collective farm market is a holdover from pre-socialist days. The holiday atmosphere in the market before Easter Sunday is part of the old pattern of life that remains.

That night we rode through the city. Krasnodar Cathedral was jammed with old men and women celebrating the traditional symbolic midnight resurrection of Christ that is an essential part of the Russian Orthodox Service. The faces were all those of people more than forty years old. Outside the cathedral curious bands of youths gathered and pressed against the heavy iron-railed fence. Some carried guitars and transistor radios. Many of them came from the Caucasus Hotel. After dining and dancing they had wandered off to the cathedral to gape at the ceremonies. They seemed curious to observe the ritual but they weren't encouraged by the police. Heavy security had been set up to avoid the jeering and riots that had marked the Easter service at some churches in past years. Inside the courtyard policemen and plain-clothes security police patrolled. Supported by lines of *druzhinniky* (volunteers), they stood firmly at the doors of the cathedral, arms locked in a chain to keep order, and to prevent the crowds from crushing the old men and women who hobbled forward into the high-domed church.

The priest sang the deep, somber liturgy and two blue neon lights shone the letters *X* and *B* over the altar, the Cyrillic letters abbreviating the phrase "Christ is risen." Celebrating Easter was not encouraged by the state, but neither was it forbidden. Benign neglect was the policy. Easter observances, like all religion, would dwindle and become vestiges of the past, a side current of Soviet life, quaint but not significant. This had already happened among the young people. Religion for them was a cultural relic. The older people inside the cathedral were stirred by the richness of the service; for them it fulfilled a spiritual need that praising Lenin and building socialism could never satisfy.

The next morning Ed and I called the Intourist office to rent a car. We were told we could pick it up in an hour. Hertz had recently signed a contract with the Soviet government to set up branch offices for its Rent A Car service. I wondered if I could use my Hertz credit card in Krasnodar. It was a ludicrous thought; I might sooner get to use it to rent a spacecraft on the moon.

When Ed Stevens and I arrived to pick up the car the stalling began. The car would not be ready until the afternoon because there was a problem with the motor. It would be fixed by 2 P.M. We knew that something was wrong but agreed to return. We learned later that the Intourist man called the Press Department in Moscow, told them that two American journalists wanted to rent a car, and asked for instructions. He was told not to rent us the car. We called the Press Department to complain and were told angrily that if we wanted an Intourist car and a guide we could have one but there were no cars available for self-drive rental. The message was that we could visit Krasnodar but we would receive no cooperation. No, a Hertz credit card will not help you in Krasnodar.

Our friends, however, were undaunted. Igor managed to get an old Volga to take us to our long-awaited fresh sturgeon roast on the banks of the Kuban River. We drove to the home of Pavel's assistant, who brought forth giant hunks of fresh contraband sturgeon, flatbread, cheese, tomatoes, cucumbers, vodka, and beer. Outside the city we drove past a willow-lined road to an open area along the Kuban, and followed a dirt embankment that paralleled the river. There, on dry flat gravel we started an open fire with twigs and driftwood. The day was bright and the spring light fell in soft shadows from the willow trees. We were alone in the open, ready to enjoy a sturgeon as it should be prepared, roasted over an open fire.

Pavel's assistant was loath to explain how he had obtained the fish. Ed Stevens smiled and explained that it was another of the mysteries of Pavel's operations. It was against the law to take sturgeon from the rivers. The valuable dollar trade in caviar made for a tight state monopoly on sturgeon. But Pavel had friends. He was proud to produce such a delicacy for our picnic. We placed the fish on skewers and held it above the fire, which had burned down and now gave off a strong constant heat with little flame. The sturgeon was plump and heavy, with thick white meat streaked with orange fat that simmered, and then spit and hissed as the fat dropped into the fire and forced a flame to rise. The sturgeon browned on the outside and basted in its own juices. Within minutes it was ready to eat. Pavel showed me how to make a sandwich with flatbread and tangy green parsley that heightened the flavor of the chunky white meat. The sturgeon was firm yet light to the taste, its flavor nutty and earthy yet delicate. It was full of a fragrant freshness. Vodka and beer went well with it. We talked of spring in America and I explained how we barbecued hot dogs, hamburgers and steaks, but never fresh sturgeon. We laughed together and Igor said, "Americans and Russians are really not very different."

Across the river we could see farms and wheat fields. Pavel pointed to a stand of Lombardy poplars in long graceful lines. These were a windbreak, he explained, part of the agricultural plan in Stalin's time. Khrushchev disliked the idea; he considered windbreaks a waste of valuable arable land. He urged farmers to plow deep and plant corn; by increasing the grain yield they would increase meat production. Unfortunately, the deep plowing and the unchecked wind eroded the soil. "But look around," said Pavel, "wherever there are windbreaks the wheat has been protected from the storms and the losses have been low. Now we'll go back to planting trees around the fields."

Pavel's business was booming. Despite the storms the morale of the farmers was high. "The black earth is so rich here that whatever you drop into it grows. If the weather is good we can recoup most of our losses with other crops," Pavel said.

"The real problem is coordination," he explained. Although thousands of tractors were mobilized for a drive to increase the summer crop, he said, and hundreds of volunteers were brought to the Kuban, the campaign was not working. "How can you have a round-the-clock effort without adequate lighting?" Pavel asked with a shrug. I mentioned reports of a crash program in *Pravda*. The government was trying, Pavel said. Fliers and planes were shifted to the Kuban, where 80 percent of the spring wheat crop had to be replanted. Their double wing yaks drifted over the fields dusting down clouds of fertilizer. But farms without cash reserves were forced to rely on government insurance claims to compensate for losses from the storms. They were experiencing the usual bureaucratic delays in replacement of equipment.

I asked if there were anybody in the regional Communist Party organization who was outstanding and might be a candidate for the Politburo. "No," said Vadim, the foreman, "we don't know them well. We don't see them; they have their own world. Polyansky was the last regional first secretary from here who went to Moscow. He had a reputation for being very tough and was not well liked here, but I guess that's what they like in Moscow."

Rarely did Russians speak of Politburo members or party matters with a foreigner. It was as if such conversation, and the criticism it implied were disloyal. Even as we spoke Igor motioned across the road to a sound in the bushes. Two men in suits, white shirts and ties were about seventy yards away. Their car was on the side of the road; they could have stopped to relieve themselves, but our friends were suspicious and reckoned that we were being followed.

We doused the fire and started back for Krasnodar. Two men in a Volga followed us and a glimpse at the license plate convinced our friends that we were being followed by the local Committee for State Security (KGB). Later we learned that Vadim was called in for questioning and warned not to entertain foreign correspondents.

From the riverside picnic we went to Pavel's apartment in a new concrete block on the edge of the city. Pavel proudly introduced us to his wife, who made us a delicious supper of *piroshki* (meat-filled pastries), and to his young son, who was learning English. In addition to the living room they had two bedrooms so that the boy had his own room, a luxury in the Soviet Union.

As we said goodbye, Vadim suggested that Stevo write to his son Misha, who was the same age, to trade stamps. Stevo wrote to Misha but he never received an answer.

13

The Theater Is Still Alive

MOSCOW IS A WONDERFUL THEATER TOWN. Jerry and I discovered that at least a dozen worthwhile plays were being shown at any one time during the winter season, most of them performed by repertory companies.

The Moscow Art Theater not only offers grand productions of Russian classics in its main theater, but also repertory plays by secondary companies in its chamber auditorium.

We saw a sensitive production of Gorky's *The Lower Depths* done by the Sovremennik ("The Contemporary") Theater group in a workers' theater on the edge of the city.

We particularly enjoyed the Revolutionary poet Mayakovsky's *Bedbug* at the Satire Theater because we had met the leading actor, Andrey Mironov, at a party. Mironov sat at my left involved in a conversation at his end of the table, while I spoke with friends to my right. One of my friends offered me vodka, but I did not have the right glass to accept it. Suddenly Mironov picked up the way I said "glass" in Russian and addressing the whole table, mimicked my pronunciation. There was a stunned silence. I could sense that my friends were ready to rebuke him if I took offense. I had to decide quickly. I laughed, perhaps a little too loudly, but it broke the tension so everyone else could laugh too. It was an old party trick of Mironov's. He then began to entertain us with imitations of British, Frenchmen and Germans speaking Russian, and invited Jerry and me to visit him at the theater. Mironov played the part of the crude Ivan Prisypkin to pithy perfection. *Bedbug* is a humorous fantasy about a worker who is accidentally preserved in ice and revived in the future; we were surprised that it was not shut down for its satirical jibes at the benefits of Communism. However, Jerry and I were the only ones in the audience to laugh at those jokes; the rest of the audience sat coldly through them. We wondered if they thought them not funny, if they were annoyed at them, or if they were simply afraid of being noticed laughing.

Few of the plays performed in Moscow were new. Most were part of established repertories, and the scripts were often available in translation, or printed in a magazine of current plays. We would get a copy and read it at our Russian lesson with Tamara before the performance; if we couldn't follow all of the dialogue we could at least pick out lines that we remembered and in that way follow the action. During *The Cherry Orchard* there was enough light to follow the play from a translation into English that my friend brought with her.

Our favorite theater and the one we attended most often was the Taganka. When our close friend from Tokyo years, Nanette Meech, visited Moscow we went to see *Pugachev* there. She found the stark production of Sergei Yesenin's ode to the unsuccessful eighteenth-century peasant rebel visually gripping and emotionally powerful without understanding a word of Russian. The theater's bold uncovered beams, the skill and harmony of the actors, the response of the audience — all communicated the excitement of the play even without language.

Jerry. Ticket in hand, I was pressed through the Taganka lobby by the surging crowd. The entrance was barred by a bearded soldier with a bayonet on the end of his rifle. He plucked the ticket from my hand and neatly pierced it with the point of his bayonet, adding it to the pile.

The play for the evening was *Ten Days That Shook the World,* a pageant based on John Reed's record of the Great October Revolution. A soldier dressed as a revolutionary guarding the theater entrance was the kind of unexpected touch that makes Yury Lyubimov's Taganka Theater the favorite of Moscow's intellectuals and young people.

They not only like Lyubimov's innovative techniques, they like his stimulating ideas and his willingness to experiment. Often he stretched the bounds of socialist realism to the breaking point, putting on the controversial works of the poets Andrei Voznesensky and Yevgeny Yevtushenko. The walls of Lyubimov's office backstage are decorated with autographs and inscriptions from celebrities who visited the Taganka. After Arthur Miller watched a Lyubimov production in 1967 he wrote on the wall: "Once Again the Theater Is Saved."

Lyubimov's theater is the only one in Moscow that combines modern dance and rhythmic choruses with lights, music and poetry to express ideas. Social satire abounds in Lyubimov's productions; a new play is both a social and intellectual event, for this is the one theater where the stale and shopworn are scorned, the imaginative and challenging courted.

We saw productions of Peter Weiss's *How Mr. Mockinpot Solved His Problems;* Bertold Brecht's *The Good Woman of Szechuan, Galileo,* and *Mother Courage;* Molière's *Tartuffe,* and Voznesensky's poem *Anti-Worlds,* which was performed in dance, chorus and theatrical revue form. Some works, such as Gorky's *Mother,* or Yesenin's *Pugachev,* convey a lesson in Communist ideology: there can be no successful revolution without the Party. Nevertheless Lyubimov was often in trouble with the watchdogs of cultural purity.

Officials from the Central Committee or the Ministry of Culture would attend a performance and complain that he was mocking the bureaucracy or that his interpretation of revolution was wrong. Lyubimov had his enemies in the theatrical and literary world, and when he agreed to stage Voznesensky's *Look Out for Your Faces* (*Beregite Vashi Litsa*) the battle lines were drawn.

Voznesensky, along with Yevtushenko, was the rage of the 1960's; his poetry recitals drew thousands of admiring Soviet youth, his foreign trips were sellouts. In a bid for approval Lyubimov planned two premieres before making the play part of the Taganka's standard repertory. The opening night was a gala occasion and the Moscow intellectual world turned out in force. Composers, ballerinas, poets, journalists, young film makers, and party watchdogs were all there. Voznesensky was attempting nothing less than a sweeping poetic review of the human condition as he saw it in March 1970. Amidst the flood of propaganda for the one hundredth anniversary of Lenin's birthday on April 22, 1970, his fanciful, free-wheeling imagery was fresh and even slightly unorthodox.

He made his bow to Lenin as the "spirit" of an age and then moved on to such contemporary issues as youth, the Soviet Writers' Union, the Vietnam war and the Chinese Cultural Revolution. Voznesensky's range was both cosmic and comic, dissecting contemporary Soviet and American life with his own Soviet-trained, but still highly poetic and individualistic, vision.

The evening was delightful. Around the rich frame of Voznesensky's poems, with songs by a popular balladeer, Vladimir Vysotsky, Director Lyubimov wove an elaborate theatrical tapestry of music, pantomime, dance, light show and shadow play. Nothing like it had been seen in Moscow since the dazzling Meyerhold productions of the 1930's. Lyubimov has a unity of style and imagination that reflects the spirit of his chosen exemplars, Bertold Brecht, Stanislavsky and Meyerhold, and the director Vakhtangov, under whom he studied. In a nation that lionizes poets, Voznesensky also represents a tradition. He is a disciple of Boris Pasternak, yet he has developed his own style of soaring imagery that rings clean, his own voice.

He speaks for a generation that was reared after World War II, that never experienced the Stalin terror. His lines do not have the staid ring of propaganda, his ideas are subtle and richly timbered. There are complex levels of meaning. In daring to deal with the problems of a superpower in poetic form Voznesensky courted controversy. Always he comes back to his main theme: the shame of man and the need for the poet to expose sham. The young rebel has become the maturing prophet who questions even as he tries to believe that

> *The truth is in the asking*
> *Poets are the questions.*

He decries violence and barbarism, deplores political assassination, the Vietnam war and the Chinese Cultural Revolution. There is a particularly sensitive moment when he compares the dying Robert Kennedy to the Soviet poet Sergei Yesenin:

> *Wild swans, wild swans, wild swans,*
> *northward, northward bound.*
> *Kennedy . . . Kennedy . . . the heart*

breaks at the sound.
Of foreign politics
not much may be understood;
but I do understand
a white cheek bathed with blood.

For the first time student dissenters were shown on the Soviet stage carrying posters that read "I Love Kennedy," "Make Love Not War," "Exploiters, Serve Yourselves." Voznesensky is careful to point out that the dissenters are "theirs, of course, not ours." Yet he also had a young student explain how difficult it is to portray contemporary youth because youth is always changing. The overriding theme of the evening was the need to preserve one's own individuality.

The high point of the evening came when Vladimir Vysotsky, with his gruff, virile voice, sang the "Wolf Hunting Song." Vysotsky described a pack of dogs hunting a brave, lone wolf. The symbolism was obvious: the assassins were hunting down Bobby Kennedy. The Taganka audience saw a broader meaning — contemporary society crushing the individual no matter what his social and political order.

After the two premieres Lyubimov and Voznesensky were told they would have to revise the play. Among the offending scenes was the one on how difficult it is to portray youth accurately. The "Wolf Hunting Song" by Vysotsky obviously hit too close to home.

Voznesensky's poem "And the Moon Disappears," a plaint that the moon has lost its mystery because man "had trod on her soul," was interpreted as an unwarranted reminder of the Soviet Union's failure to land a man on the moon before the United States did. The whole format of *Look Out for Your Faces,* with its multimedia, theatrical approach, including a dance sequence in which the dancers wore flesh-colored tights, proved too heady for the socialist realists of the Ministry of Culture. Voznesensky and Lyubimov could not have both their play and their faces. The show was canceled.

While we were saddened by the closing of *Watch Out for Your Faces,* Stevo inadvertently benefited.

Stevo. My father took me with him to visit the poet Andrei Voznesensky at his apartment. It was in an old building with many entrances. The apartment numbers had been painted through stencils onto the doors. It took us a little while to find the right entranceway.

Voznesensky's apartment was large by Soviet standards. It seemed cluttered. We all sat down and he talked about a new book that was being published and how they never printed enough copies. His books sold out very quickly in the Soviet Union. We were interrupted a few times during this conversation by the telephone. His publisher was trying to reach him but kept getting a bad connection, a common Moscow malady. Voznesensky showed us some of his latest word sculptures. They were ingenious arrangements of letters that add further dimensions to the words they spell. I'll never forget *alunakanula*, which means "the moon has vanished," printed in the shape of a crescent moon. It spells the exact same phrase backwards! Andrei said the authorities did not like that one. They thought it referred to the space race. Voznesensky is in good standing with the government compared to a few years ago. He showed us a poster promoting socialist realism that pictures a well-known Soviet sculpture of a proud and well-muscled couple striding forward, torch in hand. Just underneath these heroes of socialist labor is a little, ratty-looking beatnik grasping a triangle shape that says "Triangular Pear," a poem by Voznesensky. You have to look carefully to make out this vagabond who is meant to be Voznesensky.

Before we left he rummaged around in a cabinet, where I saw glossy colored pictures of each of the Beatles. He pulled out a pedometer and presented it to me. "It measures your steps, I hope you can use it," he said.

Leona. Ivy Litvinov, the British-born widow of Maxim Litvinov, knew of us and we knew of her long before we met. We had eagerly waited to meet Madame Litvinov, a writer whose short stories often appeared in *The New Yorker.* Jerry first heard her name at the trial where her grandson Pavel was sentenced to five years of exile for protesting the invasion of Czechoslovakia in Red Square. It remained for the late Mary Leatherbee, the ebullient *Life* writer, to introduce us.

Mary came to Moscow with a letter of introduction from a mutual friend and quickly convinced Ivy to drop her ban on meeting resident foreign correspondents. Mary assured her of Jerry's personal and professional discretion. Ivy said that she had heard Jerry's name from someone who waited with him for the verdict outside the courtroom at Pavel's trial. She would like to meet us, she said, but because of Pavel's conviction the family was in a delicate position vis-à-vis the police. Some of the family feared that by seeing foreign journalists they would bring reprisals upon themselves.

Their relation to the police and the regime was ambiguous because of their identity as a leading Revolutionary family. Pavel was not only a dissident but also the grandson of Maxim Litvinov, comrade-in-arms of Lenin and a former foreign minister.

After some thought, Ivy decided that she could not shut off all windows to the outside, that at least for herself she had nothing to lose. At eighty, she was hungry for friends who spoke her native tongue every day. A friend who had previously lived in her apartment building came with us to show the way.

Ivy received us with the same delight we felt in meeting her, the consummation of a pleasure long postponed. She stared so hard at Jerry that the next time she met him she asked him what had happened to his beard — she had transferred it to him from the young Russian who had brought us there. She terrorized us that first meeting with questions about what we had read, testing our friendship with characters out of the classics.

She lived in a high-ceilinged apartment that contained two large bed-sitting-rooms and a foyer, plus a light and cheerful kitchen big enough to hold a table and chairs. She shared these quarters with Pavel's parents: her son Misha and his wife Flora. Ivy had her books and papers in the foyer and she had one big room to herself; the couple occupied the other large room. Each spring Ivy spent months holed up writing in a little dacha outside Moscow; she spent the winter months in a rented room in Sochi, in the warmer south. While she was away the couple could spread out in the apartment, which was grand by Moscow standards.

We left with the young bearded Russian and two of Ivy's family who had been visiting. We were anxious not to draw the concierge's attention to a visit by foreigners, so we all rode down in the ancient, open French-style elevator in taut silence. The cage hit the bottom, the doors opened, and we emerged to face a screaming concierge, his arms flailing about in dismay. "Did you want to break the cables, you fools? Why did you all come down at once? I bet you've put it out of order again." The tension of keeping silent snapped and we all broke out in loud laughter, which of course did nothing to mollify the old man.

A few days later Jerry received an American visitor at the office who was in Moscow on an unusual mission. Mary Jones, a magazine editor from New York, was there to see her sister Em, who twenty years before had married a Russian when they were both students at Cornell University. She moved with him to Moscow and took Soviet citizenship. When the marriage failed, she no longer had the option of returning to the United States. Nor could she move to her own apartment: for years she and her estranged husband lived in the same room. It was just as easy to prepare dinner for both of them as for herself alone, but they never had a conjugal conversation again. She supported herself with a historical research job at the Academy of Sciences.

This was Mary Jones's first visit to her sister in all those twenty years, and Em was making sure her sister was well received socially. "You've no need to take care of my husband and me," Mary Jones told Jerry. (I was in the office at the time; I had been shopping and was waiting for Jerry so we could go home together.) "My sister is showing us all the sights and has introduced us to all her friends. Last night we had dinner at Kim Philby's apartment. It was very congenial. Maclean and his wife Melinda were there."

Jerry and I barely managed not to say "What?" Every newsman in Moscow cherished the goal of meeting and interviewing the two former spies.*

Mary Jones was in Jerry's office with a message from Ivy Litvinov, a close friend of her sister Em's: she would like Jerry to visit her again. Jerry thanked Mary Jones for the message and said he would like to meet her husband and her sister. We invited the three of them for the following evening and she accepted. I walked her out of the office and down Kutuzovsky Prospekt to show her a taxi stand. "This looks familiar," she said. "It was right around here that we had dinner last night. Philby lives in one of these buildings, I'm not sure which." We were looking at a cluster of buildings that form one of the foreign ghettos of Moscow. By eliminating all the buildings I knew to be reserved for foreign newsmen and diplomats, I could deduce that Philby

---

* Philby, the spy of his generation, penetrated the British Secret Intelligence Service (SIS) for the Russians and headed the Soviet section at the end of World War II. He became the link between British Intelligence and the CIA and betrayed important secrets of Western intelligence to the Russians before he fled to the Soviet Union in 1963. Donald Maclean was a senior British diplomat who passed atomic secrets to the Russians and was befriended by Philby before he escaped to the Soviet Union in 1951.

lived in one that looked like the others but was set off from the compound for foreigners by a tall chain fence.

Now alert to his presence in the neighborhood I kept my eye peeled for Philby. A short time later we were driving up Kutuzovsky Prospekt when I saw him standing at the curb waiting for the traffic light to change before he crossed the street. He was sensitive to eyes that picked him out of the crowd; he stared back at me, saw the K (for *korrespondent*) on our license plate and looked away. By the time Jerry and I could pull over he had crossed the street and merged with the crowd of shoppers in front of the Russky Souvenir store, behind which stood the building he lives in.

Mary Jones, her husband and her sister Em came to dinner the night after her visit to the office. Em's entrapment was in her eyes and in the pallor of her skin. She met me with a look that was half a smile and half the snarl of a cornered animal. In a sealed society, the few expatriates guard their friendships jealously. I could have no idea yet that she saw me as a wedge splitting her close relationship with Ivy. Seated at dinner, the two women courted Jerry's attention and to an embarrassing degree ignored Mary Jones's husband. I deliberately drew out the old gentleman so he would not feel excluded. I didn't hear the two women's conversation with Jerry until Em raised her voice and eyed me slyly across the table. Ivy had asked to see Jerry again, not both of us. "She wants to see the husband alone," she repeated, teasing the last word, "not with the wife." One would have thought she was taunting me with a thirty-year-old blond bombshell, not an eighty-year-old woman. I returned her look blandly; it was probably some sort of warning peculiar to the conditions of news reporting in Moscow. Why should I object?

The next afternoon, when the late February sun had just gone down, leaving patches of bare sidewalk between formless mounds of gray snow, our doorbell rang. It was Ivy. She couldn't waste time waiting for us to come to her. She only wanted to rummage through our library to see if she could find something to read, she said with child-like apology.

She had not, of course come to look at books. "What did you think of your dinner guests last night?" she asked bluntly but with coy laughter. The question was a blatant provocation; what kind of friend was I willing to be?

After a moment's hesitation, I plunged. I told her that I hadn't heard much of the sisters' conversation because I was busy talking to the husband, whom they shamefully ignored. Ivy said they had done the same when the three visited her. "It's because he's a Jew. They both think they're too good for him — they're intellectuals, he's a businessman; they're New Englanders, he's only a Philadelphia Jew." As she spoke she made a mock-snobbish face, then jutted out her lower lip, as she often does when she wants to make a point of some horror.

"That's why they paired me with him," I said laughing. "They probably thought Jerry isn't Jewish."

Ivy's eyes opened wide. "Are you Jewish?" she asked. I nodded. "And Jerry too?" I nodded again, wondering why the fact affected her so much. She hugged her arms and said, "It gives me the chills to hear it. I hardly think of myself as Jewish, but it's so important for the children."

In the Soviet Union, the children of Maxim Litvinov, a founding father of the nation, are not considered Russians; they are Jews. "There are Russians and there are Jews. There is no such thing as a Russian Jew," one of them explained to me later.

It takes only a moment to become friends. We talked about writing and Ivy said she would love to help me with mine. From that afternoon until we left Moscow Ivy and I got together every free day.

Robust and still buxom, this white-haired matriarch of an illustrious Soviet family often held court at tea around the kitchen table of her Moscow apartment. During Pavel's exile she rationed herself; she allowed only a counted number of visitors and scrupulously kept away from political discussions or political reminiscing with the few foreign contacts she had. She gave in once, laughing, when I asked if she had ever met Stalin in all the years she was wife of the nation's foreign minister. "Maxim and I were receiving the foreign minister of Sweden and his wife. We four were seated at a table and Stalin walked into the room. He thought I was the Swedish woman so he came and shook my hand. That was the only time I saw him face to face."

Against the rays of the late afternoon sun, tea at Ivy's was tea in the English sense, with multiple boilings and steamings of the teapot, but with Russian makings — Georgian *chai* (tea) with thick apricot preserves, Ivy's own homemade fresh curds, a pile of thinly sliced Russian cheese, apples peeled and sliced, and a plate of heavy-crusted white bread already buttered. Once when I was present she began with a few kind words about the talents of each person around the table and then proceeded to entertain with a story. "The Englishman walked to the edge of the cliff and looked down and there was a beach." She enjoyed great gulps of tea and bread as she talked. "And there on the beach below, glittering in the sun was a golden mermaid flecked with emeralds." She never ended the story for us; she only wanted to capture us. When the story appeared as "Bright Shores" in *The New Yorker* months later it was new and even better than I'd remembered it.

Since 1966 when her first story was published in *The New Yorker*, Ivy Litvinov has been a literary mystery. Some recall her name from the war years 1942–1945, when the Soviet ambassador to Washington and his British-born wife, known for their charm and poise, made frequent copy for ladies' magazines and the fashion sections of American newspapers. A few remember *Moscow Mystery*, which she published while she was in America. It has recently been reissued in England. But there is hardly a soul alive who remembers *Growing Pains*, her first novel, which was published in England in 1913 under her maiden name, Ivy Low, and soon followed by *The Questing Beast*. Both were banned from lending library lists for their too-overt discussions of sex, about which she will assure you she knew much less than her readers. During the diplomatic years as wife and mother of a "Kremlin family" she had little time to write. Later, after her husband's death, she began to write again and her stories in *The New Yorker* were gathered in a book, *She Knew She Was Right*. ("Do you think everyone will say I cribbed the title from Trollope?" she asked.)

Her stories reveal with a fierce sensitivity the elusive internal world of human relationships in the Soviet Union. They bring us inside dachas, holiday resorts, markets and communal apartments, making sense out of behavior as unpredictable to us as it was to the young English bride who learned to cope with it. Ivy was never interested in travel or seeing the great sights of the world. "I could pass the Taj Mahal and never turn my head," she said. "I have always lived inside myself," and in the world of the English novels she reads over and over again. She is a tyrannical name-dropper, not of the political personages she has known, but of her intimate friends, the characters in the novels of Jane Austen, James Joyce, Dickens and Trollope. She likes to read Norman Mailer, and loves to waste a little time on "sweet poison," the weekly news magazines. She usually reads a page or two of the latest bestsellers and casts them aside as stylistic pollution.

Ivy Litvinov was born in Bloomsbury in 1889 and grew up in its Fabian socialist atmosphere, which she describes as "suburban-cum-Bohemian." Her father, a Jew, came from a family of distinguished Hungarian political exiles; her uncle was Sir Sidney Low, editor of the conservative *St. James's Gazette* and author of *The Governance of England*. Her father died when she was six, however, and her mother severed relations with his family when she remarried. Ivy's stepfather was a classical scholar on the staff of the British Museum.

The atmosphere in her stories of her early years is frighteningly English, pre–World War I. She offers no roseate sentimentality to soften the hypocrisies, the hurts and constrictions on the life of a young woman in the last years of Victorianism. She re-creates the tawdriness of respectability without money.

From her father Ivy inherited a shelf of Russian classics translated into English, which she is convinced "prepared me for marrying a Russian." When she met and married Litvinov he was thirty-nine, a seriously engaged revolutionary who was procuring arms for the Bolsheviks and waiting only for the call to action; she was twenty-five, intent on living her own life away from her family in Hampstead but bewildered by the ideals that motivated him. The story of their courtship and marriage is told with light-handed charm in "Call It Love."

The Revolution came and Litvinov was appointed the first Soviet ambassador to the Court of St. James's. Ivy was invited with him to luncheon and dinner parties in Westminster, Mayfair and Downing Street, where she recalls sitting next to Ramsay MacDonald and opposite Bertrand Russell. "I asked Russell what he thought of Freud," she said. "He fixed his eagle eye on me for a moment but hardly troubled to answer my brash question."

In Paris a few years ago I asked a well-known British journalist sitting next to me at dinner whether he had ever known Ivy. "Is she still alive?" he asked incredulously. "I remember her at parties in London in the late twenties when she would lecture us for half the evening on the accomplishments of the Soviets and British decay. Then, gracious lady that she always was, the second half of the evening she would turn the conversation around to the strengths and sophistications in which no one can equal the British."

As the snow melted, Ivy's afternoon visits to our apartment became more frequent. Lyuba asked me once who she was, and I answered that she was a British lady who had lived in the Soviet Union for a long time. That was all I said, but when Ivy reappeared, a knowing smile on Lyuba's face indicated to me that she had made her own inquiries. It shouldn't have needed too many questions to learn the identity of an eighty-year-old British woman who spoke fluent Russian and was perfectly at ease getting around Moscow.

Ivy had her own transportation system, which it would take a foreigner some time to learn. She was too slow afoot now to ride the science-fiction escalators that take you in and out of the Metro. The Metro was built deep into the earth to double as a bomb shelter. The vista of a long, snail-like stair, grinding slowly down, down into the bowels of the city kept even some of my younger friends off the Metro. Instead Ivy picked up gypsy cabs, official government cars whose drivers were moonlighting between runs or after work. She and others, I found, knew how to spot their official license plates and would hail them, especially late in the day when it was difficult to find regular cabs. The accepted price was one ruble for a short or a long run, it made no difference. Ivy told me it was all right to give the man two rubles for taking me and three children from their ballet lesson in the center of town all the way out to Yugozapad. I was never sure how to interpret this common practice; was it a way to cheat the government, or did every citizen feel that the government and its official cars belonged to them, too?

Ivy had other means which either presumed upon her status as an aged woman or were a hangover from her Kremlin years. One day she arrived feeling rather outraged by the treatment she had received from the dispatchers of official cars at a government building. I wondered what she had been doing there, but listened sympathetically. She had passed the building a number of times but had never realized before that there was a pool of cars parked there. "I thought I'd just ask if they had a car coming this way."

I tried to imagine myself strolling into the parking lot of the Treasury Department and inquiring of the drivers sitting about waiting for orders if any were going in the direction of my friend's house in Chevy Chase. But of course in Washington there are no signs in the streets proclaiming "Our Aim — Communism" nor do we anticipate the withering away of the state, at which time we can help ourselves to whatever car is handy.

"They couldn't seem to understand where I wanted to go. Yugo-zapad is a new quarter of the city, and they had never been out here. To explain better where it was, I said I wanted to go to the new building for foreigners. Then that stupid old man and that foolish hag started lecturing me that I shouldn't visit foreigners. Can you imagine such presumption? Such an attitude?"

What made her action stranger still was that our friendship had begun on a note of tight security. Her telephone name was "Edith" and I was not to drop in on her without calling first, from a pay tele-phone, since we both assumed that our telephone was tapped.

The weeks that followed our initial caution showed, however, that the will to be oneself is more demanding than the will to hide. When I arrived at Ivy's one afternoon, I found her mulling over and over the events of the previous night.

In the early hours of that day, about 2 A.M., Misha had taken their pet Scotty down into the garden area between the buildings of the apartment complex on the Moscow River embankment. This was a much-beloved Fala, heralded for his expressive eyes, affectionate na-ture and loyalty. Once down onto ground level he reveled in his free-dom and was quickly out of sight. Misha took no notice but sauntered along enjoying the night air and the world asleep, confident that the dog, as always, would hark to his whistle when it was time to go home. Misha was alone when he was suddenly confronted by a man in a business suit and an overcoat who demanded to know what Misha was doing there at that hour. Misha answered affably that he was walking his dog. The man said he didn't see any dog. Misha whistled, but the Scotty was too absorbed in his own pleasures to come immediately. There goes that alibi, the stranger's look said. He then asked Misha to produce his identity card, which Soviet citizens are required to carry at all times. Misha's genial cooperation turned to consternation, and he refused. The man flashed a card indicating he was an off-duty policeman, but Misha stood his ground. He insisted that he was a man walking his dog and had not behaved in any manner requiring him to subject himself to interrogation. He turned his back on the plain-clothesman and stomped off in search of the dog.

I found Ivy worrying over Misha and his obstinacy. She was convinced that it was a provocation, and that it was a signal of more harassment to come. Misha insisted that it was his right as a Soviet citizen not to have to identify himself, even to a policeman in uniform, if his most suspicious act was to take a walk at 2 A.M. Ivy's point was that the stranger didn't need Misha's identity card to know who he was. Her fears turned out to be only the family's usual sensitivity over their name, and Misha continued to take his nocturnal walks without further interruption.

Ivy's caution and Misha's self-assertion were both warranted, but it was often hard for them to decide which attitude to cling to and when, which was precisely the atmosphere of uncertainty and conformity the state aimed to generate. Misha was always friendly but because of his work as a physicist and his position as the father of a man in punitive political exile, he never came to our apartment. When we met we talked about nothing more dangerous than skiing in the Caucasus. Ivy flaunted her disdain far more than did her son. She walked boldly past the wily Cerberus who guarded our apartment building in broad daylight.

A telephone call after Ivy returned home from visiting me one day made me shake my head in wonder. Amazing the power of human dignity in the face of whatever ambiguous oppression the police state could devise.

Ivy had tried that afternoon to educate me in the art of English tea making, to raise my sights higher than the tea bags I was wont to hang over the edge of a pot of water. Her own pottery teapot, she said, was beginning to crack and might not survive another steaming over her open kettle. Before she left I climbed up and pulled down from a storage shelf a Japanese teapot, buff with brown brushstroke bamboo leaves, which I had replaced in daily use with a larger one. It was old and stained but still worthy. She had to be sure I didn't need it before she would accept what I hardly termed a gift, and then she glowed with pleasure. Finding a new teapot or any crockery in Moscow meant a search of usually frustrating result.

She happily clutched the pot as I walked her out of the building and across our rutted access road to Leninsky Prospekt, where she quickly spotted and hailed an MK license plate. The driver stopped and welcomed her into the front seat beside him. "Is it all right?" I murmured, with the American's fear of hitchhiking with strangers, but she only laughed with the self-assurance most Muscovites feel for their safety, at least from each other. She rode off and I returned home, back across the muddy road, along the quivering boards that marked the path over brown puddles, past the militsioner and up the big service elevator, barely in time to answer her telephone call.

"I feel terrible," she wailed. "I left the teapot in that man's car. We got to talking and he was such an exceptionally kind young fellow, I told him what I rarely tell anyone I don't know, that Maxim was my husband. He was so respectful; he said that Maxim was our greatest orator and one of our most revered patriots. He refused to take any money from me. Do you think maybe he'll come back with the teapot? He'll remember where he left me off."

Faithless me, I couldn't reassure her that he would come back. Instead I made little of the value of the teapot and promised to find her another.

Before two hours had passed she called again. The young man had returned, learned her apartment number from the concierge, and delivered the teapot to her door.

In late winter and in early spring Ivy was in Moscow, using the Foreign Language Library, seeing friends and writing at her makeshift desk of boards propped against the wall of her bedroom. The walls were decorated with drawings by her great-grandson and stylized animals torn bit by bit from candy wrappers by Misha.

"From the Belly of a Whale" was the whimsical return address on her letters from Moscow. Even when she hadn't signed her name you knew who it was; she often read the story of Jonah aloud to friends as an example of the "perfect short story." She, who left English middle-class comforts to marry a penniless Russian political exile and follow him into the eye of the Revolution, well understands the faith that carried Jonah far from home. Ivy made no more attempt to explain the workings of the Soviet state than did Jonah to understand the divine pattern.

In Moscow, Ivy lived on the edge of a colony of British and American exiles — all of whom had fallen into the whale's mouth. There were women who had given up their native citizenship when they married Russians who later died or divorced them; there were those who jumped in to get out of the cold: the Philbys and Macleans.

They came on winter afternoons to borrow books or play quiet games of anagrams.

Ivy was at our apartment one day when I received a troubled telephone call from a Canadian girl I knew who was married to a Russian. He had been fired from two jobs, she said, because he had a foreign wife, and she was afraid the next reprisal would be worse. She was convinced someone would kill him. "Tell her not to give up her citizenship!" Ivy yelled across the room.

In Moscow, half forgotten by the world that was once hers, she wished that like Jonah she could be coughed up and out again.

Khrushchev let her go in 1960, and she spent a year in London enjoying herself but writing long letters to her daughter Tanya. Finally she went back to her Russian home. Then, in 1972 the magnet pulled her again. She moved to England to live her last years there.

Ivy was eighty-six in June 1975 and faces the future with characteristic wit and equanimity: "Next stop — crematorium." She is still writing but complains that she can only work in fits and starts. After a cup or so of tea she may reminisce about her life with M.M., as Maxim Maximovitch was known in the Moscow household. "Like all Russians he was devoted to Pushkin and there was always a volume of Pushkin on his night table to the very end. He liked it when I told him Pushkin was the best thing that ever happened to Russia." He read Trollope, her favorite, to understand the English "because they never change."

Jerry and I were leaving Ivy's after tea one afternoon in mid-May when Tanya telephoned. She wanted her daughter Vera, who had been visiting Ivy, to come straight home. Their friend, the poet Joseph Brodsky, was on his way to Tanya's apartment. Because Brodsky lived in Leningrad and was not often in Moscow, Tanya was gathering the family together so that no one would miss his visit. As soon as Vera hung up, Jerry unashamedly asked if we could come too. Vera immediately called back and Tanya welcomed us.

When we arrived, Tanya's older daughter, Masha, and Masha's husband, Grisha Freidin, were already there. Brodsky sat in a plain wooden chair and smiled brightly at his friends, but his eyes were sad. He said that he had just come from the Writers' Union, where he had intended to meet a friend. Brodsky did not belong to the Writers' Union even though he was the finest lyric poet in the Soviet Union. Another writer, with whom Brodsky had long been acquainted, came along and pretended he didn't know Brodsky from Adam. He even told Brodsky that nonmembers were not permitted to stand in the entrance to wait for anyone. Brodsky left immediately. The others all asked him how he could possibly care about the behavior of such a hack; they teased him and made jokes and soon pulled him out of his hurt mood.

Jerry and Brodsky talked in bits of English and shards of Russian. Brodsky, then twenty-nine years old, remarked how strange it is that Americans like to read Dostoevsky and Russians like to read Melville, though few of their own countrymen read either author; perhaps it is refreshing to deal with someone else's neuroses for a change. Brodsky wondered how much Russia and the United States have in common; there is something similar, he said, in the national experiences of countries with a great land mass and histories of deep violence. Brodsky said that even though he had once been arrested and sent to a labor camp as a "parasite" because his classically formed poems of love, beauty and the subconscious do not meet the demands of the Soviet state for socialist realism, he loved his country and wouldn't leave. Brodsky was unable to collect his royalties from abroad and could not get his poems published in the USSR. He said he loved Leningrad and could manage to live there on very little income. "Let the publishers in England enjoy the furniture and the refrigerators they can buy with the royalties from my poems."

But if he could have what he wanted from America, Jerry asked him, what would he ask for? He pondered the question for a moment. "Blue jeans and a little democracy," Brodsky answered, holding back his mirth in the way he does, as if it is dangerous to laugh too heartily.

Two years later the decision whether to leave or stay was made for Brodsky. In 1972 the police "invited" him to leave, posing the alternative of another sentence like the one he had served earlier: hard labor in an Arctic village. Since his exile he has been living and writing in the United States. At first he was poet in residence at the University of Michigan and a visiting lecturer at Queens College in New York; later he became professor of poetry at the Five College Program in Massachusetts.

Of the participants in the conversation at Tanya's apartment that May afternoon, only Tanya remains in the Soviet Union. Masha and Grisha were divorced and left the Soviet Union separately, of their own volition. Vera accompanied her husband, Valery Chalidze, the fiery Georgian legalist and dissident, on a speaking tour of the United States, and while they were in New York the Soviet Embassy revoked his passport, so that he could not return to the Soviet Union. They have remained in New York, where Vera gave birth to a daughter in 1973.

The first time I saw the writer Yury Nagibin was at Dom Kino (House of Film) at a showing of *Barbarella* for people from the movie industry. We were invited by Ed Stevens. Ed and Jerry waved hello to a bullnecked man in a white turtleneck sweater. Jerry told me in a brief aside that he was a famous writer and the second husband of the poetess Bela Akhmadulina, who was Yevtushenko's first wife. I nodded, but the names and shifting relationships left me confused; what excited me was to see a current American film, bad or good I didn't care. The image of Nagibin's turtleneck sweater — obviously imported from the West — fixed itself in my memory because it identified him as a member of the privileged intelligentsia, which had access to foreign clothing.

The audience, most of whom knew one another, exchanged greetings, found places among the rows of portable chairs, and quieted down; then Jane Fonda, tanned and bigger than life, stripped before us without a flicker of the screen. The public display of nudity, the open references to sex, which long ago had ceased to cause comment among even conservative Western moviegoers, hushed and embarrassed this supposedly sophisticated Russian audience. They laughed enthusiastically when the pushbuttons didn't go off in the Revolution scene and the actor said with a shrug, "Nothing works." When last I heard, *Barbarella* had not been released to the Soviet public.

I met Nagibin months later at an informal dinner Ed Stevens gave for Kitty Carlisle when she visited Moscow. We took to the party a close friend, Marc Leland, a classmate in Russian school in Monterey. Marc had come to Moscow to arrange a research program in Russian law for the Harvard Law School. His plan was to stay with us a day or two, and then move into a hotel. After he arrived and had tasted the Russian winter, we all decided he should sleep in the living room on our *futons,* which are folding Japanese mattresses. It was easier than having to go out into the cold after dinner every time he came to see us. He stayed with us for five weeks, making the first pot of coffee in the morning, sometimes walking Barney to school, playing but not finishing games of Scrabble in Russian with Stevo.

The evening started with fewer than ten at dinner. Later, noisy groups of men, all of them Ed's friends from the theater and the film industry, began to come and go. Nina Stevens had a fire burning in the small fireplace she had converted from an old Russian stove. The roving bands of friends warmed themselves by its heat, aided by many a cup of vodka. They laughed and embraced each other with great bear hugs and drank toasts to Ed's bit part as a racing driver in a film they had recently finished. Among them was the bullnecked writer Ed and Jerry had waved to at *Barbarella*. He sat next to me on the bench along the wall and Ed introduced Nagibin as a well-known and prolific writer who had collaborated with some of the boisterous guests on film scripts.

The troop of rowdy film makers left but Nagibin stayed. He was left alone next to me, and he became a quiet drunk anxious to impress me with his English. His steel gray hair was combed straight back, his lower lip heavy and mean in a face creased with fat — I hardly expected refinement or gentleness from him.

He told me he was very famous. He said he had written countless short stories, novels and movie scripts. "I am the Hemingway of Russia," he said. Like Hemingway, he confided, he had personal problems. The real reason Hemingway gave up on life, Nagibin said, was that he couldn't make love any more. If he, Nagibin, didn't succeed in making love by midnight tonight he was going to take the same path. He turned to look straight at me as he delivered his ultimatum. In his best English and throatiest voice he asked, "Will you halp me with facking?"

I repressed the urge to laugh and looked for help to Jerry and Marc, sitting just beyond reach, where Marc was earnestly trying to explain Kitty Carlisle's show, "To Tell the Truth," in Russian. "I would like to help you," I told Nagibin, "but I am very busy with five children, a husband and a house guest."

"Ah, you have a guest," he smiled benignly. "I understand."

Thus did Marc permanently acquire the title of "the guest."

After midnight we poured Nagibin's sleeping hulk into a taxi and sent him home. In the relaxed post mortem that is often the best part of an evening, when only a few close friends are left and have pulled off their shoes, Nina dismissed Nagibin with the back of her hand. "He has already been married six times. Each time he thinks the next one will cure his impotence." Another Russian friend once told me she knew of a few members of the official Writers' Union who suffered from impotence because of the double life they led: writing to please the state but fully aware they had sold their artistic integrity for security.

At our Russian class next morning I asked Tamara to find us a story by Nagibin so we could read it together. The story she brought was about a child who sells his big, crusty old turtle to have money to buy two small turtles that have caught his eye at the pet shop. After completing both transactions the boy wakes up in the middle of the night, remorseful and missing his old friend, and goes out into the dark to try and find the man to whom he had sold the turtle. The language and descriptions were startlingly sensitive, hard to match with the coarse image we had of the author. In this story, at least, Nagibin had accomplished both beauty of expression and the demands of socialist realism, for it was both a good story and a moral tale against mercenary attitudes. The next person I heard mention Nagibin's name was Yevgeny Yevtushenko, whom we met only a few months before we left Moscow. Stevo had met him long before Jerry and I did.

Stevo. The first poet I ever met was Yevgeny Yevtushenko. I was reading in my father's office when Rudy Chelminski, the *Life* correspondent, popped his head in and said, "Come meet Yevtushenko, he's in my office." I followed him back there and saw a man on the sofa sipping a scotch on the rocks. He could have been any Moscow drunk, but his light and alert eyes singled him out and confirmed his identity as a poet. He said to call him Zhenya and continued to talk excitedly about magic and supernatural powers. He swore some magician had levitated a chair before him. Then he was off on palm-reading and went around the room looking at everyone's hand. He thought mine was particularly interesting because two of my principal lines do not merge as most people's do. Zhenya said it was a rare hand. Rudy and Strobe Talbott, a *Time* colleague and family friend who was also listening, didn't seem to believe all that Zhenya was saying, but they talked of cases of supposedly supernatural happenings they had heard about. Soon it was time to go to lunch and as we stood up, Rudy asked if it was all right to bring me along. Zhenya laughed and said, "Sure, with a hand like that he can come any time."

We picked up Brien, Rudy's wife, and drove over to the Writers' Club. We walked back through the halls to the dining room. Different groups of people hailed Zhenya and he stopped every few feet to exchange greetings. He didn't try to introduce everyone. He looked from his Russian friends to us, smiling, and then kept walking. To me his look said, "Sorry I can't stop. I'm taking these foreigners to lunch." I got the feeling that the Writers' Club rarely entertained foreign guests, and Zhenya was being a little unconventional in bringing us there. It was an elegant old building. We sat down to eat in what had once been a ballroom. It had a little balcony with nice woodwork overhead that wasn't used any more. We didn't eat anything too special but we drank bottle after bottle of dry Russian champagne. Zhenya wanted to make sure I was all right when he refilled my glass over and over again. Rudy smiled and told him not to worry.

There was an almost paranoid tension that Zhenya kept creating and laughing off. Soon after we sat down he pointed out quite blatantly two men sitting a couple of tables away. They were, he said, "the KGB agents who take care of me." Later, when he was drunker, he turned around and asked them a little boisterously what they were doing there. They left soon after that, giving us dirty looks. During lunch he turned to Strobe, looked at his moustache, and said, "You know, you do look a lot like the young Stalin."

Strobe flinched and said, "I hope that's not a compliment."

"No, I suppose it isn't," Zhenya replied.

When he got drunk enough Zhenya started to recite his poetry at our request. He didn't stand up or speak loudly, but he was very impressive in the feeling he put into his words. I didn't understand much of the substance at that point in the afternoon, but I felt the romantic love and torture that these words brought together for him, soulfully expressed through his body.

As he was reciting, a young poetess came over and joined us. She had short dark-red hair and wore glasses. She said she would stick to her cognac, which she drank slowly but steadily. She recited some of her own poetry, but she didn't put as much of herself into it as Zhenya did into his.

Earlier during lunch, Zhenya asked Rudy for a light. Rudy pulled out his fancy French lighter and handed it to Zhenya. He examined it and used it to light his cigarette. Then he asked if he could have it. Rudy was a bit startled because it was quite expensive, but after a second's thought he said, "Sure, it's yours." During the poetry recitation the waitress had brought a huge can of caviar and Zhenya had quietly put it under his chair. Now he brought it out and presented it to Brien and Rudy: a kilo and four fifths of fine black caviar (four pounds) worth almost a hundred dollars. At first they wouldn't accept it, but Zhenya convinced them it was in return for the lighter and they took it. After some coffee to put us back on our feet, we walked out to the street. On the way Zhenya took me aside and gave me a little talk on life. He said one must always be a man. Whether as a pilot, a writer or an engineer, one should be strong, full and generous, living fully. His last words were, "Remember, always be a man."

Leona. Winter was over and early spring had come before Ed Stevens was able, after a number of tries, to find a night when both we and Yevtushenko could come to his house so that he could introduce us to each other.

Since the purpose of the evening was to bring Yevtushenko and us together, we expected there would be few if any other people at dinner. Instead, just as we arrived, Nina came home with a crowd she had attached to herself at an Italian Embassy party. It was an apparent act of spite aimed at both Yevtushenko, whom Nina does not like, and at her husband for inviting him, because at the center of the group was Bela Akhmadulina, Yevtushenko's first wife. Also in the entourage was Bela's husband, whom she had married after her divorce from Nagibin. Nina's manner was unusually loud and cavalier while she rearranged the tables and gave instructions to her kitchen staff to make more blini; obviously, she was enjoying the trick she had played on Yevtushenko and Ed.

Unfortunately, the other actors involved did not enjoy it. I stood in the garden just outside the door leading to the kitchen and the basement izba, where the Stevens always entertain their guests. I joined a conversation between a young British diplomat and Konstantin Simonov's son, who described the pleasure of collaborating on a script with his father. He explained that film making in the USSR is hampered by the high cost of celluloid, so that the director cannot shoot carelessly or too experimentally, but his labor costs are low. "In the West you shoot all the footage you like, film is cheap, but time is money because of the high wages paid to actors and crew." I tried to listen attentively, but right behind Simonov, in my full view, Bela sat on Yevtushenko's lap, her arms clasped around his neck, imploring him to listen to her. Bela was not drunk yet; she must have had a few cocktails at the Italian Embassy, but there was no burlesque in her performance, no irony. There was only pain in her face and voice as she begged him to love her. I was transfixed by the scene and didn't notice when Simonov and the British diplomat joined most of the guests on their way in to dinner. The sun had set and the first hint of night was falling over the city. Yevtushenko and Bela, a doctor and his wife who are close friends of the poetess, and Jerry and I were the last guests left outside.

Bela repeated over and over to Yevtushenko that she missed him, but her words didn't seem to reach him. He sat erect, his posture suggesting that he was trying to shake off the small passionate figure clinging to his neck. He looked not at her but at the rest of us, with an embarrassed smile, as if we could help him. "Let's run away together, Zhenya," she pleaded.

From inside the house someone called us to dinner. The doctor and his wife urged Bela to rejoin her husband waiting at the table. Bela allowed herself to be pulled away by her friends and the three of them left Jerry, Zhenya and me alone.

At that moment Yevtushenko and we had barely been introduced to each other, but he knew who we were. He turned to Jerry and began berating him for all the hurts and injustices he felt he had suffered from *Time* over the years. He said he didn't want anything to do with Jerry or anyone from *Time*, and stood up to leave us. Jerry laughed and reminded him of all the items *Time* could have printed about him yet had not. He was quick to remember and agree; perhaps he knew that Jerry had protected him at the time of the Czechoslovakian invasion, when Jerry learned how the text of Yevtushenko's telegram of protest to the Politburo had reached the West but buried the story. Yevtushenko's scowl changed to the beginnings of a smile, and Jerry helped it along. Jerry told him how I had laughed when I read his poem in *Pravda* about the Chinese coming across the border. Did he intend as a joke the line in which the yellow-skinned invaders would rip the onion domes off Russian churches and cook them in their Chinese soup? Of course, Yevtushenko said with a broad smile, of

course it was a joke. Then he took my arm to escort me into the house
for dinner. He told me he liked Stevo and hoped that Stevo would
always think of Yevtushenko as a child like himself, never classify him
as an adult.

The long dinner table was made up of two early eighteenth
century inlaid-wood dropleaf tables placed end to end.

For Yevtushenko, Ed had reserved the seat at one end with the
first places at his left and right for Jerry and me. Zhenya described to
Jerry in a mixture of Russian and English how when he was in
America he communicated with kindred souls without knowing
English. Both he and his American friends talked in their own tongues,
but from their hearts; after a while they began to pick up expressions
and words from each other's language. Soon they were discussing complex thoughts and understood each other perfectly.

Up and down the long table one could hear fragments of a dozen
conversations. Next to me were the Russian doctor and his wife, Bela's
friends, who had studied in Italy during the war and still had ties of
sentiment there, hence their attendance at the Italian National Day
party. At the other end of the table were Bela's husband with his
friends, many of them artists or writers. Across from me, next to Jerry
was the young British diplomat I had met in the garden before dinner.
He had the face of a peach in full bloom, pink and sensuous-lipped,
and he was delighted to be out of his embassy and on the town so that
he could use his Russian, which was very good. He was perhaps a little
too thrilled with the company in which he found himself. Next to him
sat a young and attractive Italian girl, the daughter of a former ambassador from Italy to the Soviet Union. She worked at the Italian
Embassy. Bela, now very drunk and with a deep sadness in her glittering eyes and wan cheeks, stood up and sat down intermittently, each
time giving a speech of a sentence or two, then giving up in defeat. She
puffed nervously at the cigarette between her long thin fingers; she was
a hummingbird with no place to perch.

The doctor and his wife watched Bela, reassured her with their
smiles, stayed on guard to see that she did not display too much of her
anguish. They did not want her to go too far, to cry or flail out, to
crush the fragile nest she had built as a temporary salvation with the
handsome husband next to her.

Yevtushenko talked with Jerry, then with Ed, then with the

British diplomat and with the young Italian girl, always watching Bela and trying not to. Then exaggerating, playacting, he told the others not to listen while he told me a secret. He whispered in my ear, "I don't like him," indicating the peach-faced boy attaché. "He smiles too much. What do you think, do you like him?"

I answered that I neither liked nor disliked him; I forgave his smiles because he was very young and had not learned to control how much he showed of his pleasure. "You must forgive me if I play the role of mother, but I understand why he behaves this way, therefore I cannot dislike him for it."

"Of course, I see what you mean, for I too am mother. I am mother of the world in pants," Yevtushenko said, laughing with glee. But his satisfaction didn't last long because Bela was on her feet performing for him, trying to reach him across the room.

He couldn't avoid the subject of Bela any longer. He turned serious and spoke to me in a confiding tone. "She is the best woman poet — no — the best living poet in the Soviet Union." He explained that they were married when they were very young, when she was only sixteen, and that they had constantly hurt each other. Then later she married the writer Nagibin, he informed me, as if the match were a sign of her importance. I nodded that I knew that. My mental image was of a delicate bird served up, still singing, on a silver platter to a greedy king of clubs. I asked Yevtushenko how he had survived the breakup — wasn't it terrible, to be in love and not to be able to make it work? Yes, he said, it was very painful for a while but the longer they were apart the less it hurt. Then his face took on a protective mask in the form of an introspective smile. "That is the worst part, the worst thing for a writer, when you stop feeling altogether."

14

Lenin Is Always with Us

"CAN YOU REALLY BUY MATZOHS in Moscow?" I asked my friend Margarita on a March evening. "We'll find some and you must come to us the first night of Passover," she said. I protested that with our five children we were too many, but she and her husband Kolya insisted and brushed aside all objections. Would we really get to see a Russian Seder, one like our grandfathers knew as children in the "old country"?

For most of the Soviet Union's three million Jews the Passover, or Season of Freedom, has lost its religious meaning and is vaguely connected with Easter and the coming of spring. In Moscow, the festival which celebrates the deliverance of the Jews from slavery in Egypt is marked by the limited sale of matzohs (unleavened bread) in state bakeries, a grudging acceptance of a religious past by the officially atheistic state. Even if they eat matzohs, few Soviet Jews can relate them to the story of Passover in which, according to the Old Testament, God punished the Egyptians with ten plagues for the pharaoh's refusal to free the Jews. After the tenth plague, when the Angel of Death visited the homes of the Egyptians, killing their firstborn sons but "passing over" the houses of the Israelites, the Egyptians frenziedly drove the Jews out of Egypt. The dough which the Jews had prepared for bread did not have time to leaven.

Margarita called a few days before the holiday to make sure we were coming, and told us happily that she had been able to get matzohs from her aunt who lived near the synagogue.

Naturally, I was delighted to be invited to a Soviet home, but as I put the telephone down after accepting Margarita's invitation a familiar unease came over me. I paused to wonder: Who is Margarita? Who is Kolya?

The first time I saw Margarita, standing pale and alone among the overweight, gossiping women jammed into the balcony of the Moscow synagogue on the Jewish New Year, I thought she was also a foreigner. Her limp brown hair hung straight to her shoulders in contrast to the frizzled curly coifs around her. She saw me watching her and responded with an amused, tolerant smile. She understood that I wanted to meet her and as we moved closer to talking I expected her to address me in English. Then, as I stood waiting for the next step, I saw that her foreign-looking shirt was mismatched with her skirt in a way no foreign woman with access to Western clothes would ever dress. Her chic was catch-as-catch-can. Then she spoke to me in such fast, colloquial Russian that I had to work hard to keep up with her. I wondered if perhaps it was not reticence that had delayed her but calculated timing designed to catch a foreign friend who would add a few gifts to her eclectic wardrobe.

She might be what the children called a "chewing-gum friend," one who cared nothing for you but only for what foreign goods she could wheedle you into giving her. But I was willing. I wanted to meet Russians. It doesn't take long years of residence in Moscow to change your standards: an American has to be ready to give a little both in material goods and moral acquiescence to make friends with Russians, who are taking much higher risks in having anything to do with you. Friendships in Moscow make allowance for all levels of human frailty.

My misgivings about my new friend soon disappeared. Margarita, an art historian, took me along on her afternoon "researches," and became my guide to the meaning of every hand gesture of the ikons, to the French Impressionist paintings, to the rotting but still beautiful yellow-ocher and green pastel plaster architecture of Moscow. She introduced me to the Rublyov Museum in the former Andronikov

Monastery, where Andrei Rublyov, the monk and ikon painter, worked. She also took me to the Boyars Romanov Museum, a small gem near the giant Rossiya Hotel. It is the restored house of a sixteenth-century lesser nobleman, with a workstand on which pearl-encrusted lace was made, and with ivory toys and samovars I had never seen elsewhere. (Later, I took the children to see it. They loved the hidden stairways and small proportions: people were shorter in the sixteenth century.) After a few of these meetings she suggested that we get together for a concert. It would be a good opportunity to meet each other's husbands and introduce them.

Kolya and Margarita became frequent visitors at our apartment, sometimes bringing along Kolya's brother Boris, a quiet athlete still in his teens. Or they brought a friend, usually a straight man for Kolya's exhibitionist humor. Kolya was always onstage, regaling us with the latest political jokes.

Kolya and his pals were a perpetually cheerful group whose bravado and love of vodka seemed to us always to mask a layer of passive sadness, underlain by an unpredictable restlessness. They had sought us out as friends, which made us suspicious, considering the burden on them if their political reliability ever came under question.

One evening Kolya read to us from the Komsomol (Young Communist) rule book, and with great hilarity translated some of the moral strictures put upon youth as budding members of the Communist Party, the ruling elite they could strive to join in their maturity. Kolya was an officer of his Komsomol group. His brother was in the Soviet astronaut training program; his sister was married to the son of a member of the Central Committee. Was it possible that simply for the sake of our company and an occasional gift of a rock record he would risk the scandal that might fall like an oil spill on his future Party membership, his sister's privileged married comfort, his brother's flight to the moon? Or was it more likely that as a Komsomol member with good English and the talent to make people laugh, he was given license to mock the hand that fed him and assigned to watch us and glean whatever information he could about our habits and activities? Were his friends also assigned to us, or was Kolya assigned to them, too?

Margarita, a vivacious, sparkling-eyed pixie, was neither solemnly intellectual nor as lighthearted as her husband presented himself. In her wisdom she knew that drastic domestication of Kolya would hurt their marriage, so she tolerated his friends even though she found most of their stories boring and their slightly off-Red lampoons of Soviet life offensive. She cared about her job, about the price of fresh vegetables from Georgia in the inflated free markets of Moscow, about getting a nursemaid, for not more than sixty rubles a month, who would be attentive to their baby and prepare a little dinner for her and Kolya. She could have left the baby in a government day-care center but she was afraid he wouldn't get the care due him as her one and only son.

Another subject that excited her was our mutual Jewishness. She wondered what I thought about the Soviet Jews who wanted to leave for Israel. She often thought how much better it was for Jews in Russia than before the Revolution. But in her delight that we shared her religion, she unconsciously betrayed the constant discomfort of being a Jew in the Soviet Union. To the extent that she would admit repression of Jews, she shrugged it off in the stoic manner of old men who accept some hard facts of life that are immutable. When she heard her husband discussing the works of Solzhenitsyn or admitting that he knew Jews, even young men, who wanted to leave for Israel, she shushed him and reminded him with a pantomime that even the walls listen. To her it was simply another hard fact of life like the price of cucumbers in winter.

In keeping with her Soviet upbringing, Margarita is not religious. It was only by the most offhand chance that I found her in the synagogue, she said. She was passing Arkipova Street, saw by the crowd on the steps of the synagogue that something was going on there, and wandered in. The only time her family went each year was for Simchas Torah, the harvest festival in October when all of young Jewish Moscow turned out to dance in the street in front of the synagogue.

Besides that, she knew she was Jewish in the one way she could never forget: Her identifying passport — all Soviet citizens must carry their passports with them at all times — bore the line "Nationality — Jewish" and was so clearly a part of her self-identity that she referred to her non-Jewish friends born in the Russian Federation as "Russians" but to Jews born in Moscow, capital of the Russian Federation, only as Jews.

Was I being naïve in assuming that my meeting with Margarita was purely casual? It is known that the synagogue is as well planted by the secret police as the lobby of the Metropol Hotel, that notorious meeting place for low-level agents, provocateurs and unsuspecting American tourists.

Such thoughts were never far from any friendship in the Soviet Union, even with people who had a long public record of dissent. It was whispered that Andrei Amalrik, author of the scathing critical essay "Will the USSR Survive Until 1984?" was a KGB spy because of the long delay between the publication of his book abroad and his arrest and sentencing to a labor camp. Only his arrest and jail sentence cleared his name from suspicion, for such is the distrust fostered by the KGB. This reserve with friends formed in every relationship an avoidance of personal secrets as if the friendship were enough of a secret.

But to refuse Margarita's invitation out of fear of a setup or provocation would have been to become paralyzed, frozen into a social life limited to our foreign ghetto; if we had been deterred by the experiences of other Americans who had arrived on invitation at their friends' door to be greeted by the flashbulbs of KGB photographers, we would have been boxed in the way the Soviet government wanted us to be: never hearing, seeing, feeling for ourselves the rhythm of Soviet life.

On the day of the first Seder I went to one of the Beriozka (White Birch) stores and bought a half dozen teacups as a gift for Margarita. We dug out our skullcaps for the boys and our collection of worn Haggadahs (readings for the Passover) and set off to Kolya and Margarita's apartment, anticipating an old world Seder.

But as we drove out of the Lenin Hills, the golden onion domes of Novodevichy Convent burning in the reflected fire of the sunset across the Moscow River, it occurred to Jerry that we might not discover the roots of our Jewish identity in the place we were going to that warm spring evening. He slowed the car and turned to me and the children. "Maybe it will be a Seder and maybe it won't. We'll play it by ear. If it's not don't say anything," he said. "Tomorrow on the second night we'll have our own Seder at home."

Barney asked, "Will we hide the matzohs? Will we open the door for Elijah? Will Elijah come to Moscow?"

Will Elijah come to Moscow? Under what guise, I mused silently, would come the long-awaited messenger of mankind's redemption from oppression, the prophet who went alive to heaven in a fiery chariot and will return to deliver pious Jews from modern pharaohs; in what form, as which guest or passing stranger will the guardian angel take his place at the Seder, the Feast of Freedom, and drink the cup of wine set out for him? "I don't know," replied Jerry. "We'll see."

Kolya and Margarita's apartment is in a high-rise apartment building set in a raw maze of similar structures on the edge of the city. Food stores and movie theaters with curved plate-glass domes served the new community, but the streets and approaches to the buildings were still unpaved and suffering from the recent thaw. The annual battle of the Russian mud is no longer the dread of Muscovites of the inner city, but in the urban new towns mud still suffuses the consciousness of spring. We bounced through the rutted lanes and arrived at the same time as Kolya's brother Boris and another friend.

Kolya had come down to the parking lot to scout for us, apprehensive that we might have gotten lost among the identical buildings with similar entries, all assembled from the same prefabricated parts. We were a rather boisterous party, ten in all, trooping up the four flights to Kolya's apartment, affectionately pushing, playing tag and stopping for breath. Most of the greetings to each other through the stairwell were shouted in English, but Kolya seemed to have no idea of concealing his foreign visitors from his neighbors, as other Soviet friends did. Was he unaware of the danger of having foreign visitors, putting the onus on us to protect him from his own naïveté, or was he "passed" and secure, making us wonder who was naïve.

Margarita was waiting for us wearing a plain skirt and rayon crepe blouse with a double collar, an elegance reminiscent of American styles of the late thirties. The baby had been boarded away for the week at the dacha of the babushka who normally cared for him while Margarita was at work. The apartment was scrubbed and ordered. Margarita had set the table with a white damask cloth and napkins, family treasures, and one large serving plate in the center, held onto from the days when Russia produced fine copies of French porcelains. Two brass candlesticks held white tapers ready for lighting, a surprise in Moscow where candles rarely appear in stores. Matzohs stood wrapped in damask on the table, and on the grand serving plate was a whole boiled fish. I looked in vain for other signs of a Seder.

The older children were so distracted with Kolya's newest jokes and his bubbling enthusiasm for the latest rock music he had taped from the Voice of America, and with the young future astronaut and his friend, who after all weren't light years older than our teenagers, that they quickly lost sight of what we'd come for. I looked on in wonder as Evelind, my little girl of a few moments ago, turned on her femininity to become (in my eyes) a Siren to the future space Ulysses, her easy flowing Russian nearly faultless after two years in a Soviet public school.

But the young ones weren't so easily put off. They darted quizzical looks my way: Was there going to be a Seder? So in as roundabout a way as I could I asked Margarita whether Kolya would conduct a Seder. "Oh, no," she said, "we won't bother, it's too complicated." Would you like Jerry to do it? "Never mind, it's too complicated."

While the younger children helped Margarita carry in a bowl of fruit and fresh salad, the offerings of spring in Moscow, I took advantage of this opportunity to have a good look at the comforts of a Soviet home.

In the room where the music blared was Kolya's small but impressive library of Russian classical authors and modern English and American works translated into Russian. The emphasis was on social realism: Dreiser and Jack London, plus Hemingway and Melville. The walls were filled with cut-out reproductions of Russian church monuments and classical Impressionist paintings. An armless couch, upholstered in dark tweed, opened at night to make a bed for two. There was a cluttered desk, and the makeshift cabinetwork for the phonograph and records was known to collapse if leaned upon. In the second room, besides the dining table, chairs and some padded leatherette-covered boards attached to the wall for seating space, was the heart of every Russian home, the buffet. In the government-run secondhand stores massive old cabinets with stained glass or leaded glass doors are urged upon foreigners for fifty rubles; the modern Soviet citizen wants them out of the way to make room for veneer and plate-glass models from Poland or East Germany.

But Margarita and Kolya have some feeling for continuity with the past. Through the glass panes of the upper cabinet were displayed the odds and ends that families treasure for their art or against all art: a dragon-encrusted cup and saucer from the Orient, chipped plates painted with Napoleonic scenes, an Art Nouveau vase, faded photographs, a carved bear. On the wall above the dining table hung a weathered plaque with old Church Slavonic lettering carved in it — a piece of a faded rural ikon. For Margarita and Kolya certainly there would be no religious significance in a church relic, but even their Christian friends collected ikons, they said, only as folk art.

The toilet and bath were in two separate cubicles, each without an inch of wasted space. The uneven composition-board walls were hung with airline calendars and a caricature of Mao Tse-tung; in the kitchen Kolya had pasted a collage of wine bottle labels to the wall. Margarita proudly showed me the new "plastic" countertop imported from Poland on which it was possible to place hot pans straight from the oven. For most Americans, the gas range on its curved iron legs, the rust-stained porcelain sink would have evoked a past era, but the kitchen was functional and did not have to be shared with another family — a recent luxury in the Soviet Union.

It was just getting dark outside when Margarita lit the candles and gathered us all around the dinner table. She sat the three youngest children on the padded bench against the wall, herself next to take care of them, the teenagers together, Jerry and me flanking Kolya. Kolya poured chilled vodka to drink with the fish. Sweet red wine from Georgia stood on the table, as well as Armenian cognac, which Russians drink throughout the meal. Jerry tasted the fish with the sweet and sour jelled sauce and remarked that it was just like the sauce his grandmother made. Barney wanted to know if we were going to dip hardboiled eggs in salt water, and Katie elbowed him to be quiet. I was a little embarrassed but Margarita was totally confused and asked what he wanted. My husband explained that "in America" at Seders we dip eggs into the salt of the sea that the Jews crossed when they came out of Egypt. Margarita and Kolya thought it was a quaint custom.

After the fish, Margarita served freshly puréed potatoes and piquant boiled sausages from Central Asia, not easy to find in Moscow. She had found them at a small collective farm market. The cucumbers and parsley, she said as she urged them upon the children, came from the same market. They ate the cucumbers gladly but were leary of biting into stalks of parsley. Then Doveen smiled brightly — these were the Seder's sweet and bitter herbs! What's that about, Margarita asked again, and again Jerry explained. Kolya laughed. "We Jews in the Soviet Union have a few bitter things to think about too," he said.

Later Jerry hid pieces of matzoh for the children to find, another "American" practice which our hostess and host looked upon as foreign and charming. After the excitement of the treasure hunt, Kolya, Boris and his friend each took a young child on his lap and proceeded to tell us Russian cowboy stories. (Cowboy went into a bar, drank a whiskey, asked for two pickles which he placed behind his ears and rode away. Second cowboy did same. Third cowboy asked for pickles but bartender had only tomatoes left. Cowboy put tomatoes behind his ears and was about to drive away. "Why do you put tomatoes behind your ears?" asked the bartender. "Because you have no pickles," he said and rode away.)

Then each child was allowed to tell a joke but Barney, astride Kolya's knee, had to be cut short because he was telling a joke Kolya had told us in the first place. Struggling to hold in his laughter, Kolya said, "Let him go on, maybe he'll improve on it." It was the comparison of history's three great heroes; Marshal Kutuzov, who let the French take Moscow, then waited for winter, and destroyed them; Stalin, who let the Germans approach the gates of Moscow, waited for winter, and slew his enemies; and Egypt's Nasser, who let the Jews into the Sinai and was still waiting for winter to come.

Staring into the flame of the candles as the laughter around the table quieted, I recalled Arthur Miller's story about the poor salesman who traveled from town to town in the southern Italian mountains, peddling his wares, but returned to his home every Friday night with a loaf of braided white bread as by a primeval command, without ever learning why he followed this weekly ritual. For Margarita and Kolya there was enough unconscious piety in their commitment to Judaism to overcome the bitterness of the identity the state had thrust upon them and to want to celebrate the Passover. But the blind manner in which they practiced their religion was graphic proof of the elders' lament, "What is happening to the Judaism of the young people?"

Margarita and Kolya represent the midstream of Soviet Jews: if they had been ten years younger they might have felt the way one beautiful twenty-year-old girl did who said to me later in the same week: "Tell me everything you do at a Seder. My parents are good Soviet citizens and call any religion superstition but my friends and I are hungry for all the silly ritual. If I'm to be cast aside as 'just a pretty little Yid' I want to begin a positive life as a Jew, rather than avoiding it until someone asks to see my passport." Perhaps if Margarita and Kolya had been ten years older their ambivalent position in Soviet life, in which they joined Komsomol, marched with Red banners on

May Day and found that for all their efforts less talented people were promoted above them, would have made them desperate to apply for an exit visa for resettlement in Israel.

Instead Kolya and Margarita went on from day to day with a quiet acceptance and hope that life would become a little easier; they looked back at how far they had come since the defeat of Germany, when their country was left in shambles and something to eat was enough to ask. They had never been outside to see what the rest of the world had done since 1945.

As we sat around Kolya and Margarita's dinner table that mild spring night, the glow of the candles highlighting our laughter, we ate fruit and traded forbidden humor. We Soviets and Americans laughed together as a family gathered on the eve of an ancient liberation, the Passover, which like Easter is the celebration of spring. Perhaps the revitalizing cycle of the seasons, perhaps the ability to laugh even with bitterness, perhaps Margarita's close attention to the everyday realities that spell survival under any conditions, are the ingredients that make it possible to build a relatively optimistic life even without political freedom. They took as normal their position as a marked and separate people within their society, and never missed most of the amenities of life we take for granted in the West.

It was getting late and sleepy children were beginning to squirm in the laps of their friends. Suddenly Doveen sat bolt upright and asked with near alarm if anyone had left the door open for Elijah. Jerry patted her hand quietly and smiled, "Don't worry, he's already come." I looked around the table and wondered: Who is Kolya? Who is Boris?

We planned a trip south for the children's spring vacation from school, which coincided with Easter. Because they attended Russian school, the children could fly at half fare on domestic Soviet airlines. Jerry, Stevo and a translator from the *Time* office left a day before the rest of us, to do a story in Tadzhikistan; the other four children and I met them in Baku, the capital of Azerbaidzhan.

We were met at the airport by a local correspondent of Novosti who presented me with a bouquet of sweet peas. At the moment that I accepted his kindness I thought it might be a routine welcome without individual motivation, but I changed my mind in the few days we spent with this thoughtful, sensitive young man. I concluded that it

was his way of telling us that even though our visit would be super-
vised in every respect, he was genuinely interested in knowing us. He
took unfeigned pleasure in taking the children to the best baklava
bakery in Baku, and promised us it would be worth the wait in line
to eat fresh sturgeon broiled over a charcoal fire in his favorite small
restaurant on the edge of the Caspian Sea. In his free time he wrote
mystery stories.

Doveen. When we went to Baku we stayed in an Intourist hotel.
After we had settled in our rooms, my mother, Katie, Barney and I
walked three blocks from the hotel, to a little park. There was a me-
chanical swing that twirls you around in the air. We asked the three
men who ran it if we could go on it and how much it cost. They saw
Barney and they said he was the holy child and they kept blessing him
and saying "God bless you." Then they would kiss their hands and tap
Barney on the head. They were very nice to us and let us go on free.
It made us all dizzy.

The people in Baku seemed more at ease and much more happy
with life than the people in Moscow.

Barney. In Baku, Katie, Doveen and I went with a guide to a stone
tower. The steps wound upward and it seemed as if they would never
end. There were landings on the way and on some of them there were
glass cases built into the wall. In them were small old daggers and
knives. When we got to the top it was windy and you could see almost
across the city. We saw the old stone walls that used to surround it. By
now the city had grown beyond them. Later we took a walk to the edge
of the old city. Katie, Doveen and I climbed on the crumbling walls.

Baku is known for its oil wells. We went to see the oil wells in the
Caspian Sea. We drove out on huge docks where there were lots of men
and machinery. It was very noisy. We stayed for a while and Dad talked
to some men.

On the way back to the hotel the guide told us a story. He said
that during World War II Hitler's generals gave him a birthday cake
with candy oil wells on it. They promised him Baku for his next birthday. The Russians shielded the city and the Nazis never conquered it.

Leona. A Russian we knew in Moscow told us not to miss the
Zoroastrian fire temple in Baku, but our official guides discouraged us
from going to see it. When we insisted they relented and arranged for

cars to take us on the short journey out of the city. We rode through poor but clean suburban enclaves where small cement houses had replaced village cottages; these were not the showplaces to which visitors were normally restricted.

The temple was a whitewashed structure of four posts with a roof over a perpetual fire that burned in a pit at the center. The natural gas escaping from the earth that kept the flame going was also fed through the hollow posts so that four smaller flames burned at the corners of the roof. We came there at dark and watched the dramatic spectacle of the sacred fires burning, hidden away in the midst of a rural town. For the first time I could conceive of the faith that sprang from the mystery of the continual flame.

Surrounding the temple courtyard was an old guardian wall which housed a small museum. In it a mounted map pinpointed Baku on the silk trade route that spanned the Asian continent from Constantinople to Peking in the first century B.C. I trembled with the sudden realization that we were standing at the crossroad where camel caravans passed each other carrying art, ideas, and technology from one end of the world to the other before the name of Christ had yet been spoken.

The next stop on our trip was Yerevan, the capital of Armenia. In the Intourist hotel there we met Japanese technicians who felt they had been exiled to the end of the world. Since Japanese trade replaced exaltation of the emperor as a national goal its heroes no longer wear kamikaze scarfs but they have not lost the spirit of sacrifice needed to remain in Armenia for two years.

The capital of the sunny republic looks like fondant candyland. Its pastel pink and green buildings, constructed with blocks of pale-colored tuff, a rock of compacted volcanic ash, look as if they might float away. It is a fitting image for the land of the flood — we rode out of the city and saw Mount Ararat, where Noah's ark is supposed to have settled as the waters receded.

We rode farther into the mountains and visited a monastery with chapels and stairways hewn from the stone of the hillside. In the courtyard a monk was roasting a lamb on an open fire in preparation for Easter. Christianity has been practiced in Armenia since the fourth century.

The next day we attended Easter services at Echmiadzin Cathedral, where the ornately garbed processional yielded nothing to the anticlerical state. The air was heavy with incense and the chanting of priests. There were no seats; the congregation and choir stood in the great marble hall beneath the altar, responding to the intonations of the priests. Large arched doors were open to the outside but no guards were needed to keep order. Here, far from Moscow and from urbanization, socialism had not replaced Christianity. Even a sprinkling of young people had come to celebrate the Resurrection.

On the way back into Yerevan the Novosti guide took us to see his friend, the curator of a museum next to the site of a church built in the fourth century and destroyed by Arab invaders in the tenth century. Until recently no one knew what the original church looked like, but a traveler found a bas relief of it in Paris. Since then new buildings in the center of Yerevan have followed the lines of the church's architecture. Bits of colored mosaic and broken stone pieces left after the Arabs filled the domed structure with explosives are sorted and waiting for the time when the church can be rebuilt.

On a wall in the Intourist hotel in Yerevan our Armenian guides pointed to a map showing Armenia's common border with Turkey. They wanted us to understand the bitterness they felt toward their neighbors who in 1915 slaughtered one and a half million Armenians who lived in Turkey, in a genocidal attack without provocation. The Armenians are nearly as bitter toward the memory of Lenin, who in 1920 arbitrarily gave the Turks a piece of Armenia which he said had been seized by an imperialist tsar. The Armenians have never appreciated his act of generosity at their expense.

In Yerevan the central market was abundant with fruits and vegetables. In a side bazaar of the market I bought cross-stitched linen napkins and a tablecloth. I also found two embroidered panels to make into a long dress. When Lyuba saw them she laughed. "They are a pair of curtains," she informed me. I made a dress out of them anyway.

The Georgians, like the Armenians and the Azerbaidzhanis we visited, live with ever-present historical memories of invasion by clashing empires meeting in confrontation on their soil. Artifacts of their prehistory are magnificently mounted and spotlighted in the Tbilisi Museum. The museum also houses a fine collection of lavishly bejeweled ikons and ritual utensils of the Orthodox Church. In the mountains overlooking Tbilisi, Evelind made a literary pilgrimage.

Evelind. The car wound up the road between the rolling green hills and through a light mist to get to the monastery that the poet

Mikhail Lermontov described in his work "The Novice," which we read in school. The monastery sits on the edge of a cliff overlooking the confluence of two rivers.

> *Not many years ago*
> *there where merging sound*
> *embracing each other like two sisters*
> *the streams Aragva and Kura*
> *was a monastery.*
> *No longer do monks say prayers for us*
> *nor does the blessed smoke rise under the church arches.*

The poem goes on to tell the tale of a young boy brought as a captive to the monastery, and his desire to know freedom outside the monastery walls.

Except for a modern chain fence that replaced the old one, the monastery was just as Lermontov must have seen it. Even the old gray-haired keeper who "brushes dust from the tombstone" was there, perhaps a descendant of the original keepers. The delicate mist softened the light to create an aura of timelessness, but did not obscure the awesome sight of the two rivers merging with a dull roar hundreds of feet below.

The essential structures — the altar, the chapel and the monks' cells — were all hewn out of rock and still stood. Only the ornaments, a few doors and the sacred smoke were needed to bring the small, intimate chapel to life. The tiny cells set in the mountainside seemed too small for human beings. No wonder the young captive of the poem yearned to stretch his limbs in freedom.

Translating literature was always a struggle because of the difficulty in pulling together all the parts of the complex Russian sentence. Finally the images burst out of the confusion of the foreign language and the sweet pleasure that comes with understanding is greater than if there had been no effort spent at all. I worked hard to translate Lermontov's romantic poem and loved it; now I enjoyed the reward of visualizing the poem and its story in its own setting.

Leona. As we bid Lyuba goodbye before we left on our holiday, she asked us to bring her some cognac from Armenia; there was little or none to be bought in Moscow. We visited a cognac factory, where we learned one reason why there was a shortage. The manager showed us thermostatically controlled "caves" where the fiery drink is distilled and aged in huge barrels. Then he took us to a guest hall where Jerry, his interpreter and I sampled brandies identified by how many decades they had matured. At the end of the tour we watched three-year-old cognac being bottled on an assembly line for which the designer had received the Order of Lenin. We could hardly believe our eyes; as the bottles moved along the wobbly conveyor belt young women capped them with plastic corks, then a machine came down on them with a seal. Every fifth or sixth bottle was broken by the sealing device and the cognac splashed onto the floor. The women had to stop the belt each time to take the jagged bottle off the line and throw it into a waiting barrel. The workers considered the losses ordinary and went about their work with no sign of dismay. Evelind whispered to me that in Hong Kong the Coca-Cola plant had glass walls so that people could watch the sterile, efficient bottling process that worked without mishap.

With spring came the one hundredth anniversary of Lenin's birth. When the mud had dried enough, we could walk around the pond below our hill, and our Russian neighbors could come out to stroll in the sun. It wasn't warm enough for ordinary mortals to swim yet, but three muscular young Soviet men came in their swimming trunks to try the water. They stood beside the pond, preening and testing the temperature with their toes, and showing off their bare chests to the ladies who happened by. They had something to show off: one had his upper chest tattooed with an unmistakable portrait of Lenin, the second had his chest indelibly printed with a head of Marx, and the third was tattooed with another bearded notable, whom I could guess but not for sure so I asked. Beaming with pride he pounded his chest and answered, "Engels!"

Jerry. As April 22, 1970, Lenin's birthday, drew near, the Press Department of the Ministry of Foreign Affairs invited a group of foreign correspondents to visit the Lenin Memorial Center in Ulyanovsk, his birthplace.

The strict, trim lines of the Lenin Memorial Center are of white marble from the Ural Mountains. The massive building, forming a square of 119 yards on each side, attempts the serious and yet spiritual quality of religious architecture. The mood is massive and awesomely pleasing. By Soviet standards the finishing is good and the complex conveys a sense of purpose, occasionally imagination. There is a hall and theater for fourteen hundred people, a museum with murals and mosaics of Lenin's life, and the Lenin Tower Room, the culmination of the cult of Lenin. A religious inner sanctum, the walls rise ninety feet in a mosaic of bright red, real gold leaf and smoked glass tiles. From the ceiling, spotlights focus on a white marble statue of Lenin, twenty feet high. After seeing the Tower Room a French Communist smiled and said: "I respect everybody's beliefs."

A high official in the Foreign Ministry told the correspondents to "Please remember, for us Lenin is an ikon." Like the Washington Monument or the Lincoln Memorial, the Lenin Memorial Center in Ulyanovsk is an architectural statement that attests to the society's ideals and the need to declare their permanence. Lenin as a man has been overshadowed by Lenin the ideal. Ulyanovsk has become a shrine. Lenin's family home and his childhood are portrayed in tales of sweetness and joy. Suffering came only when his brother, Alexsandr, was executed for an assassination attempt on Tsar Nicholas II.

Every detail of Lenin's early life is idealized to the point of exhaustion and dullness. Glimpses of the real boy remain only in the authors he read (Tolstoy, Cherneshevsky, Marx, Belinsky). Lenin's chess set, his report cards and his letter of recommendation to the university from Alexsandr Kerensky's father, who was director of the school young Vladimir Ilyich attended, record his brilliance and gentler days. Wherever Lenin lived, worked or studied there is a memorial.

The overkill of the anniversary preparations celebrating Lenin led the Russians to their favorite form of release: humor. So concentrated, repetitive and boring were the paeans of praise to Lenin that Soviet citizens could respond only by joking. Prizes would be given for the best jokes about the Lenin anniversary, it was said. The first three prizes would be fifteen years, ten years and five years respectively in Shushenskoye, the village in Siberia to which Lenin was exiled.

Factories competed to commemorate the anniversary and in Moscow the tale was told of the brassiere factory that sewed a new model called the Lenin Hills. In *Komsomolskaya Pravda* a critic branded as "illogical, absurd fervor" the production by a candy factory of special chocolate medals, emblazoned with a picture of a light bulb over the inscription "1870–1970 — the light of Ilyich."

V. Ulyanov (Lenin)

Another story finds a honeymoon couple checking into a new Soviet hotel on the night of their marriage. They are ceremoniously shown to the bridal suite and find not a double, but a triple bed. On the wall overhead is a sign which reads: "Lenin is always with us."

The jokes were not anti-Lenin or anti–Communist Party; they were a normal human reaction to the dull reiteration of Lenin's virtues in a society where Lenin's ideals have still to be realized. In the midst of the preparations a Russian friend, fed up with the extent to which Lenin was being idolized, told me that there had been a contest for the best statue of Pushkin. "Who won?" I asked, naïvely. "Well," beamed my friend, "the first prize went to a statue of Lenin reading Pushkin and the third prize was for a statue of Pushkin reading Lenin."

The backlash of humor was not lost on the Kremlin leadership. Articles in the Soviet press on the anniversary warned against using quotes from the "bible" — Lenin's works — to prove any convenient point. "Lots of people use quotes from Lenin as stones to hurl at one another," cautioned an article in *Yunost (Youth)* magazine.

Aleksei M. Rumyantsev, a former editor of *Pravda,* wrote in the literary journal *Novy Mir* that "one must always compare the scientific and political lessons of Lenin with one's own practical experience — not in order to find ready formulas, but in order to find a basis for independent thought and for one's own answer to questions which arise in a world that has changed greatly since Lenin died."

Summing up the reliance on Lenin was the story of the old Communist who was waiting for his new apartment. First he wrote to his local Party committee, then to the Central Committee. Finally, after receiving no answer, the old man trudged to the Central Committee headquarters and asked to see Lenin. "But comrade, Lenin died in 1924," he was told by the Party secretary. The old man sighed and replied: "How come when you need Lenin he is alive, but when I need him he is dead?"

For the Soviet leadership and Leonid Brezhnev, who was seeking to establish his paramount position in the Politburo, Lenin's legacy provided legitimacy. By emphasizing Lenin as the pure interpreter of Marx and the Soviet Union as the standard-bearer of the Leninist tradition, the leadership could make its case against Mao Tse-tung to the rest of the socialist world. The Lenin anniversary provided the

Soviet Union with a convenient rallying point and associated Brezhnev and the Politburo with Lenin.

When the great day of the hundredth anniversary finally came, Lenin's birth was celebrated with speeches and parties at the Kremlin. My Russian friends joined the observances. Then they told me about a schoolboy who was asked to describe Lenin on the anniversary of his birth. "Lenin was a great man. He was bald but had a red beard, wore a vest and a cap and was one meter sixty centimeters tall." His teacher was impressed and praised the youth. "But tell me," she asked, "How do you know how tall Lenin was?" The student passed the back of his hand across his chin and replied: "Well my father is two meters tall and he said he has had Lenin up to here."

Katie. Kaarina held her birthday party on Lenin's birthday the year I went to it. I'm not sure it was her real birthday.

I came alone but most of the other children came with their mothers. Only one of them, Katya, came from our school. We had little sandwiches and cakes and then went downstairs to play outside.

There were ten children so we decided to go in the big elevator. The mothers stayed in the apartment and had tea. Going down, some of the boys started jumping and soon we all started to jump. The elevator got stuck. We had all been laughing but as soon as the elevator got stuck we all became quiet and a bit frightened. We pushed all the buttons and jumped some more but nothing worked so we pushed the emergency bell. We knew it would take a long time for help so most of us sat down and started talking.

The elevator in our building often got stuck. We would stand near the shaft calling to our friends in the elevator not to be scared and assuring them that they would get out soon. I had gotten stuck many times before.

Some boys got the door open about a foot but it didn't help because we were in between two floors. The boys started telling us we didn't have enough air and tried to frighten us but we pretended not to be scared. We all just sat there and took turns pushing the bell for about an hour with no results.

In about an hour and a half we heard some old women yelling and scolding us. They were on the bottom floor so luckily we couldn't hear them very well. They got some men to work on the elevator, and after being in it for two and a half hours we came to the bottom and got out. As the door opened we could hear about half a dozen old women bawling us out for fooling around in the elevator.

As soon as we got out I realized how much time had gone by. I told Kaarina I had to go home because I didn't want to miss going to the Lenin Hills.

On Lenin's birthday they always had fireworks, and all the kids from our building planned to go together. There were at least fifteen of us, from five years old to sixteen and from at least five countries.

We took the bus to the Metro station and then got on a crowded train. We held hands trying to keep the little ones from getting lost in the mass of people.

When we got there, it was dark outside and the fireworks had already started. To get to the top of the hills we had to go up on an escalator that was enclosed in glass. The escalator was very long and crowded on both sides, going up and down. Outside the glass the firecrackers were bursting right in front of us and many looked as if they would have fallen right on top of us if there had been no glass.

We got to the top and watched for a while but the air was so smoky from the firecrackers that everyone agreed the best place to watch them was from the escalator. So we headed back, but it had gotten so crowded that police on horses came to control the crowds. To me the horses seemed so huge and the crowd so uncontrollable that I thought we'd never get through. After a lot of pushing and shoving we all got on the escalator, and just as we did we saw a huge portrait of Lenin made out of colored lights, shining over Moscow.

Leona. The balmy spring afternoons were made for walking and a close Russian friend took me to see the church where her mother's funeral service was held. We went to nearby Donskoi Monastery, now a museum, next to the beautiful old cemetery where Tolstoy's grandmother is buried. In the cemetery a clutch of old women, all dressed in black, argued whether or not Stalin had been good for Russia. When we were tired we went back to her apartment and ate strawberries with champagne. We finished the whole bottle, and our conversation became more confiding and intimate as we neared the bottom. She began to talk in faster Russian, forgetting that I couldn't keep up. I would have let it go but the conversation was too interesting so I stopped her and made her say things over slowly, in more simple language. She told me she was no complainer. She never criticized the government; she learned when she was still a teenager that to try to change things is hitting your head against the wall. Therefore, since she and her husband were good Soviet citizens, why should she be afraid to visit foreigners? She thought perhaps I hadn't noticed that she and Grisha never came directly to our apartment, but always asked us to pick them up at a meeting place. They always made sure we took them to the Metro in our car. "The government ought to encourage people like us to show you our country," she said, "instead of making us fearful that the militsioner will find out we're visiting you and report us." Then to stress the point she told me the secret she had refrained from letting me know the whole time we had been friends: "Grisha is a member of the Party."

I was surprised but not deeply shocked as I was to be a few days later when taking a walk through the unlistening birch woods with another Russian friend who had lived through World War II. He mused over the Kremlin's repressive measures against its dissidents and regretted his country's backwardness in technology and in its standard of living. "I know it sounds terrible," he said, "and I guess I couldn't feel this way if I were a Jew, but sometimes I wonder if it wouldn't have been better for us if the Germans had won the war." The expression on my face was incredulous. "Yes, I know they were brutal," he went on, "but that sort of thing stops when the fighting is over. A couple of years under Nazi occupation and life would go on peacefully from day to day. They, at least, would have brought us into the twentieth century. They, at least, believed in science and modernization. Under them we wouldn't have been held back by this ideological gibberish." He didn't convince me, yet I was haunted by his bitterness.

> Here in Moscow, spring is in the air. We
> can hear the ice cracking and each one of us
> wonders if this year it will be me.
> — Letter from a British journalist

On the night before May Day the slow rumble of tank treads carrying block-long, olive-green rockets sends an ominous shudder through the city's streets. The sound of war serves the regime well: for the generation that can remember World War II, this touch of nostalgia makes them appreciate how far they have come in security and well-being, a counting of blessings that is reiterated day after day in newspapers and public displays. For the generation that cannot remember war, that is too much in a hurry for consumer goods and democratic freedoms, the playacting of May Day is a reminder of past suffering. It is a warning, too, that power lies in the barrel of a gun.

I have never been closer to war than a TV set or a movie screen; when I heard the tanks a block away I ran like a child to see them in their steel reality. I was gripped with awe — an ICBM, beautiful in its abstract immensity, like a mutation left over from some brutish, mindless prehistory that has now dragged itself out of a green slime and has come lumbering in slow motion down a city street, lost, bewildered at being an anachronism. It was different from the ballistic shininess of American military displays — I could see where it had been seamed and riveted — and its huge green virile crudity sent a shiver through my legs so that nothing could have made me look away.

The first year I was in Moscow, Soviet policy clearly excluded wives of journalists from entering Red Square for the May Day parade, but offspring were invited even if you had five. The second year Jerry was away but the office received a ticket for me to attend with Stanley Cloud, another *Time* correspondent who had come the previous autumn. The Clouds' and my children were admitted, but when we arrived at the barricade Nancy Cloud found that her husband's ticket didn't admit her and she waited out the parade alone in front of the Kremlin wall.

Once inside the square, we didn't have seats but a place to stand with a good view, next to the diplomatic corps. How glad I was that I had worn something better than an old raincoat, because the wives of the ambassadors and chargés had made the occasion into a spring fashion parade. The United States was represented by the wives of the ambassador and minister, Peggy Beam and Harriet Klosson, both looking fresh in outfits of red, navy and white. For the Americans it was more than a chance to wear their new suits; it was a confrontation of consumer goods versus guns. Their chic and colorfulness stood out like flares in the crowd.

On my left were the heads of the Press Department of the Ministry of Foreign Affairs. Mr. Simonov, the deputy, was friendly as usual, even reaching over precariously to shake my hand. But Mr. Zamyatin, who knew me as well, and who had recently been promoted to head of the TASS news agency, pointedly snubbed me, thus avoiding the necessity of introducing me to Mr. Chernyakov, standing next to him, his successor as head of the Press Department. Nor did he accept congratulations for his new job from Stanley Cloud. He pointedly made himself busy with other dignitaries. At that moment we didn't know if it meant the Clouds or us, but one had to be deaf not to hear a deep rumble in the floes of shifting ice that come down the Moscow River in the spring.

Beneath the din of the May Day parade, the fireworks, the cheerful noise of streets filled with strollers who had come out to watch the city in its annual greening, a nervous speculation haunted the foreign enclaves of Moscow. Provocations and expulsions are the rites of spring in the Soviet Union. Officials of the Ministry of Foreign Affairs usually time the expulsion of foreign journalists who have a winter's record of stories considered hostile to the regime, to coincide with the end of the school year.

There is no appeal to expulsion, only the angry hope that the State Department will exercise the right of reciprocity. The foreign journalist's attitude toward being summarily told to leave the Soviet Union is an ambivalent mixture of dread and relief. On the one hand, an expulsion is a badge of honor, recognition that the correspondent has told the terrible truth in spite of threats. His expulsion may be welcomed by his family, who will be glad to get back into the free world of Captain Crunch, lettuce and cucumbers all winter long. The most smiling face at the farewell parties is usually the wife of the expelled journalist. But the expelled man never gets away without gray regrets. Gray because the Soviets always manage to besmirch the man with half-believable charges of currency violations, drunken driving, or womanizing. A whispering campaign charges him with incompetence — neglect of other stories to devote all his attention to the dissidents — or personal family hangups. Of Tony Shub, for example, it was said that he brought the expulsion on himself to live up to the honor of his Menshevik father, who had been expelled fifty years earlier.

It may seem like an hour of glory, but the individual cannot avoid some sense of rejection in being the only one picked from the whole foreign community to be told he is no longer wanted and must be out of the country within forty-eight hours, by the day after tomorrow. I've never known an expelled man to say thanks.

Late in May we were given our first tip, from a Russian whom we knew was assigned to feed us a regulated flow of information, that Stanley Cloud's temporary visa, due to run out the middle of June, would not be renewed. His family had been in Moscow barely six months. His young children were just settling into school and their last packing boxes had just been emptied. Stanley had invested a lot of time in preparing to come to Russia and he spoke Russian very well. He had hardly had a chance to build up the kind of scrapbook of stories that would finger him for expulsion. The Russians were getting rid of him because they wanted to strike back at *Time* for a recent cover story on Brezhnev that displeased them, and they reasoned that an "administrative expulsion," simply not renewing his visa, would not count against them in the seesaw with the State Department of having an equal number of Soviet correspondents thrown out of the United States, for any American they tossed out of Moscow.

As soon as the word went its rounds that the Clouds would leave by the end of the week, Ed Stevens made the friendly gesture of offering to give a farewell party for them. The Foreign Ministry could not have chosen a more ideal time for its intransigence, because the Stevens garden, manicured to stark orderliness by the grumping old gardener, was in glorious full bloom. The night of the garden party was favored by a rare mildness in the air, one of those evenings when nature turns even the scowls of doctrinaire Communists to openhearted friendliness.

Short notice for a party often creates an extraordinary guest list: on this evening there was no hint to the logic, respect for custom, or returns for what favors in the identity of the guests. Certainly, the friends of Stanley and Nancy Cloud were in the minority.

There were, of course, Mr. and Mrs. Strogin, a pair of familiar Soviet faces at mixed Soviet-foreign parties. He was a ranking editor of the *New Times,* the Kremlin's ideologically well-disciplined version of a weekly news magazine which is translated into English, French and German. He was distinguishable by his red complexion and by his oversized canines with noticeably nothing between. His lack of front teeth proved later in the evening to be a clue to what was between his ears. Remembering that Mr. and Mrs. Strogin had also been present

at the farewell party for Tony Shub when he was expelled a year
earlier, I began to wonder if attending such events was a part of his
occupation.

Mrs. Strogin spoke English well and worked as a translator at
TASS. A trim blonde in her late forties who always looked fresh from
the hairdresser, her sharply chiseled features were hardened by deep,
bitter lines and a wary, tired look in her eyes. She wore a permanent
smile that wavered between forced friendliness and sarcasm. We often
came upon each other at cocktail parties and spent time chatting about
nothing at all, sparring to make the other come out with some reveal-
ing, significant observation that each of us carefully restrained. She
dragged along with him from cocktail party to national day celebration, as we other wives did, saying little and keeping our eyes and
ears open.

At the Shubs' party the year before, I had been thrown together
with Mr. Strogin in an awkward moment when we had nothing to say
to each other. In desperation I asked a question about Maxim Gorky.
This triggered a lecture; he admonished me to remember that Gorky
was not really a Revolutionary writer because he hadn't written anything after the Revolution. Shub interrupted to disagree. He would
send Mr. Strogin articles by Gorky written in the twenties. No wonder
the Russians didn't like Shub.

I had come to the Shubs alone because Jerry was out of town.
Upon discovering that we both lived in the southwest corner of Moscow, Mrs. Strogin insisted on taking me all the way home in her taxi,
lest my Russian be unequal to the task, while her husband, overtired
and drunk, intermittently woke up and started yelling, "Where are you
taking me? We've passed our house. Why are you so stupid?"

Now, a year after Shub was expelled, twenty or thirty people
sipped gin-and-tonics in farewell to the Clouds, seated on American
garden chairs amidst the tulips and peonies of the Stevenses' backyard
garden. I knew most of the guests, but one woman, the wife of Mike
Davidoff, correspondent for the *Daily World,* the organ of the American Communist party, surprised me by her unusual desire to make
conversation. She held my drink when I left for the ladies' room, and
chided me possessively because I stopped to talk with someone else on
the way back. Mrs. Davidoff was an attractive, sophisticated American
of about forty-five who usually gave me a perfunctory hello and then

the back of her head. She and her husband, Communists since his early union-organizing days of the thirties, felt that by snubbing Americans in Moscow, their political motherland, they were paying back some of the hurts they had endured as political outcasts in the country of their birth.

Mrs. Davidoff's beautiful features were beginning to soften and crease under the pressure of middle age and life in Moscow. She was always well dressed; by Moscow standards, her copies of Chanel suits were high fashion. She appeared brisk and authoritative, and when she spoke she always made it seem that she represented not only the American Communist Party but the American working class. Beneath her exterior of femininity was an ideological hard core that had weathered the tortured history of the American Party. Now she was faced with the tougher challenge of holding onto her idealistic core in the everyday reality of dull, gritty, repressive bureaucratic socialism.

Six months earlier Mike Davidoff had been the loud and jocular life of another party at which he kept his audience of foreign Communists laughing with anti-American jokes directed at us, the outsiders. One of his colleagues, in Moscow too long to hold any more illusions, referred to him privately as a "doggie," or dogmatist. He contrasted the doggies to those like himself who know by now that there are no pure Communists, only survivors.

On this evening in early June I noticed that the doggie was lapping at Jerry's heels as unmistakably as his wife was trying to hold onto me. Did he have something to tell, or an assigned story to plant? She and I chatted and sipped. I was torn between relaxation in response to her softened tone, and caution when I recalled the barbed sarcasm she had shot at American liberals, capitalist imperialism and the "socially regressive" regimes of Western Europe and the United States in past encounters.

To complicate matters, Mrs. Strogin made repeated attempts to enter our conversation, and was rebuffed by Mrs. Davidoff as decisively as she had cut me off in the past. "Come," Mrs. Davidoff said to me as she rose from her chair, "I'm getting restless sitting so long in one place," looking disdainfully at Mrs. Strogin. "Our husbands seem to be having a good conversation. Let's join them." Jerry and her husband stood at the portable malacca-cane bar that had been set in a corner of the garden next to the door leading into the house. As we moved toward them, Mrs. Strogin followed us. There was only one garden chair near the bar so we three women played the game of offering it to each other. Finally Mrs. Davidoff pulled up a chair for herself, I sat in the other, and Mrs. Strogin was left dancing on her feet. Mrs. Davidoff made it clear she was annoyed with the other woman's presence, but I couldn't judge why. Did it mean "Can't you see we are assigned to them this evening?" Or was it "Can't you see we want to relax with another American couple who may be ideologically unsuitable but share our language and sense of humor — we're tired of being foreigners" or did she simply dislike the Russian woman? In any case, Mrs. Strogin's expression was one of thumbing her nose at Mrs. Davidoff. There was no way of getting rid of her.

Meanwhile, the two men's conversation had reached a point of intimacy. Davidoff, the labor organizer turned journalist, paunchy but still good-looking in his mid-fifties, with a full head of dramatic wavy hair, was at this point boasting to Jerry that the Communist Party in the United States was going forward with renewed vitality. He predicted a new and successful thrust for membership in the collapse of the movements of the sixties, as expectation dimmed for any change in the present system.

His wife said with undisguised pride, "Our son has stayed with the Communist Party in America and will probably emerge as an important leader in the new phase." She made sure to point out that in any family, capitalist or Communist, it was "an unexpected pleasure for a son to want to follow in his father's footsteps."

Davidoff went on to recount, in a tone more analytical and rational than we had ever heard from him or any Communist before, the mistakes the Party had made in America and what they had learned from them. He said they hadn't prepared a strategy to deal with the reaction in the States to the Communist victory in China, and the McCarthy period had caught them without defenses. It had crushed the Party outwardly and forced loyal Communists to hide their allegiance. "But," he said with a snicker, "don't think that everyone who joined in the thirties left it. Some of your friends you never think of as Communists have never left the Party," and waved the back of his hand in the direction of an American journalist who was at that moment passing by on his way to get another drink. "Many of those unsuspected Communists will regroup as the Party gains strength." He never noticed that Mrs. Strogin had disappeared.

It was hardly boredom that drove her away. As the American Communist waxed eloquent on the future of the Party and its strategy in America, she stood listening with bulging, unbelieving eyes, her jaw slack with consternation. As he waved his hand in the direction of his covert American comrade, her patience gave out and she scurried off in search of her husband. She hadn't kept her eyes and ears open through all those endless cocktails in vain.

Jerry went on listening, showing interest but no surprise at the candor of the American Communist. The older man's face indicated a relaxed pleasure in instructing us. He said, "You know, Schecter, you're not such a bad fellow." We all four laughed. "I bet we and our friends and you and your friends could still get together. I don't think the idea of a united front is dead yet." Jerry laughed and questioned him about what policies he thought could be a meeting ground. He and his wife offered up some timeworn left-wing ideas. I questioned how they would convince the whole American public to give up the profit motive when it was a necessary part of their existence. They both laughed and said they didn't know if they could join a front with me because I was too far left for them. I then asked where they stood on a negative income tax, but they were unwilling to admit they had never heard the term, so they joked again, "We feel like right-wingers next to you."

In the midst of this banter, we had all ignored the arrival of Mr. Strogin, the florid-faced *New Times* editor. He stomped up to us, led by his wife, who had called him as an angry citizen might call a policeman to confront a quartet of gamblers so intent on their dice that they never bothered to look up. She stood behind him, arms folded, tensed, waiting for the action to begin. With his menacing canines showing through parted lips, he stood impatiently, waiting for a chance to interrupt. Baffled by the interplay of our conversation, his bulk seemed to expand with frustration like a blowfish under attack. Finally, apropos of nothing, he demanded angrily, "And what about Cambodia?"

Whoever was left at the party was drawn electrically to the spot; they all stood waiting. Both Davidoff and Jerry looked at the interloper incredulously. Then Jerry said, "If you want to read me your magazine and you want me to read you back mine, why don't we meet during office hours?" The crowd that had gathered broke into laughter. There was nothing more to say.

Davidoff by this time perceived what had happened to him. He stood alone in the crowd of people saying goodnight to each other, his face haggard and unsmiling, looking at no one. Jerry whispered to him, "At least you know who your control is now." He only shrugged.

At first we didn't discern the changing mood in Moscow. During the previous year there had been isolated incidents of official anti-Israeli policy but the spring of 1970 bore the old-fashioned marks of Stalin's anti-Semitic campaigns. Even Jews who aspired to membership in the Party, who always praised or explained the government's actions, who had abandoned their Jewish upbringing to be better Soviet citizens, who told the most scathing jokes to illustrate the conniving qualities of Jews, suddenly recognized the symptoms of an anti-Semitic campaign and knew it was directed against them as much as the most religious reader of the Talmud.

"Ironically," a Soviet Jewish friend told me, "we enjoyed our longest period of ease during the purges of the 1930's and during the war. The Russians had other enemies to worry about then. Many Jews were killed in the purges, but there was no public anti-Semitic campaign. The trouble didn't start right after the war — it wasn't until the late forties and early fifties, when the economy didn't pick up as fast as it should have, that Stalin looked around for a scapegoat. That was when he said that Jewish doctors were trying to poison him. Some of our best Russian friends believed it. There was real hysteria against the Jews then."

Jerry. By the spring of 1970 the dissident movement had taken a new turn. Jewish emigration from the Soviet Union became a major issue. The Soviet press harshly attacked Zionism and "the crimes of Israeli aggression." The *Time* office became a way station for Jews seeking to leave the Soviet Union. Poets, architects and scholars making the rounds of foreign correspondents to plead their cases would ring the bell and ask to see me. One young engineer spoke English without an accent and dressed in a tweed jacket, a button-down shirt and a striped tie. The pose was part of his master plan to leave Moscow. By speaking English like a foreigner and dressing like a foreigner he would not be stopped by Soviet policemen when he went to the Dutch Embassy. Because Israel and the Soviet Union had broken diplomatic relations during the Six-Day War in June 1967 the Dutch were handling Israeli diplomatic affairs and visa applications from Jews seeking to emigrate.

His claim coincided with a story that was being told in Moscow about a group of American tourists whose baggage had been misplaced by Intourist. After days of searching without results, Intourist was forced to supply the whole group with new clothes. Intourist gave them all vouchers to outfit themselves at Glavny Universalny Magazin (GUM), the main department store. Later they went to the American Embassy to register their complaint but they couldn't get past the Russian guards in their new clothes because the guards thought they were Russians seeking political asylum.

When the engineer came to my office the militsioner let him pass, thinking he was a foreign visitor. His desire to leave the Soviet Union, he said, was based on his own feelings of Jewish identity and his inability to practice his religion in Moscow. He had begun studying Hebrew on his own after the Six-Day War and found life in the Soviet Union was barren for him. "As a Jew I have no real place here," he told me. "I'm still young and I want to build my future and be part of a culture that I can feel is my own." He carefully explained that he had applied to the Dutch Embassy for a visa and asked me to publicize his case only if he were arrested. "My friends will let you know what happens to me. I just wanted to meet you so you would know me if you have to write about me," he said.

In those days the Soviet authorities were permitting about two hundred Jews a month to leave the Soviet Union. According to the 1970 census there are three million Jews in the Soviet Union. The movement grew slowly, stemming from the stunning Israeli victory against the Arabs in the Six-Day War. The Israeli triumph kindled new interest among Soviet Jews, which created a political problem because the Arabs were the Soviet Union's official allies. Soviet arms and technicians poured into the Middle East. By 1970 the arms shipments were at full scale and MiG-23's were being sent to Syria and Egypt.

Young Jews had begun studying Hebrew clandestinely and once a year they would appear at synagogues in Moscow and Leningrad to celebrate Simchas Torah by dancing and singing in the streets. Songs like "Krugom Adni Yevrei" (There Are Jews Everywhere) carried with them the mocking response to latent anti-Semitism: all the heroes are Jews; Hemingway, the chess master Tigran Petrosian, even Stalin was of Jewish origin, the song says. Khrushchev ate matzohs in his office and the chorus responds, "Jews, Jews, there are Jews everywhere."

Always the Jews felt alone and isolated, singled out on their internal passports as of Jewish nationality and unable to assimilate into Soviet life.

The process of anti-Semitism in the Soviet Union is in many ways subtle and difficult to characterize. There is little open persecution in daily life yet Jews are carefully limited in how far they can advance in the Party and professions. Communist Party membership, access to leadership positions in the press, the government and the military are restricted. Jews flourish in academic life, in the film industry and television; medicine, law, and the sciences are open to Jews, and the estimate is that Jews have three times more university graduates than other nationalities in the Soviet Union do. Life is not unbearable for Jews but it is circumscribed and there is always the threat of an outburst of anti-Semitism.

For some Jews the dying-out of Jewish religion and culture in the Soviet Union was the impetus for their emigration. The number of synagogues decreased from four hundred in 1962 to sixty-two in 1970. Those that remained were carefully controlled by the government. One joke we heard was about the search for a new chief rabbi, who had to know both the Hebrew liturgy and Marxism-Leninism. The first graduate was rejected because he did not know the liturgy. The second was skilled in the Torah but he did not know his Marxist dialectics. Finally a candidate for chief rabbi was found who knew both the Torah and Leninism. His only problem was that he was not Jewish.

The synagogue in Moscow was filled for the Jewish high holy days of Rosh Hashonah and Yom Kippur, but otherwise functioned for only a handful of old people who met for the weekly sabbath services. The young people poured into the streets only for Simchas Torah but many met among themselves and quietly organized to find ways to leave the Soviet Union. The move to emigrate ranged from the Baltic States, Latvia, Lithuania and Estonia, to the major cities of Leningrad, Kiev and Moscow to Georgia. The estimate among Western diplomats was that only 10 percent of those who wanted to leave were being given permission to emigrate.

One night at home I received a call from Kharkov from a young man who asked me to help him get action on his visa application. He said he was sending me his biography and supporting documents. I was certain that the call was being monitored and wondered whether he was really in need of help or if I was being provoked so that the Soviet authorities could say I was not working as a journalist but trying to help Jews to emigrate from the Soviet Union and hence had become a Zionist tool. In the prevailing atmosphere, no action was taken at face value. The young man's package finally arrived a month later, torn and hastily retied. It had obviously been opened and carefully examined before being forwarded to me. I turned the details of his case over to the Dutch Embassy.

Once permission to leave was requested from OVIR, the office in charge of emigration, the harassment began. Pensions were cut off, people were fired from their jobs, and they were attacked by "outraged citizens" for being anti-Soviet. The decision to emigrate could not be taken lightly, for once the decision was made there was no turning back. In some cases the harassment consisted of drafting young people into the army or charging them with parasitism once they had been fired from their jobs. The movement grew as the Soviet authorities sought to repress it.

The Soviet government tried hard to turn back the tide by labeling those Jews who sought to leave as disloyal to the Soviet Union. In early March a press conference was called at Dom Druzhby (House of Friendship) and the most prominent Jews in the Soviet Union stood up to "brand with infamy the aggression of Israeli ruling quarters against the Arab peoples." Heading the group was a deputy chairman of the Council of Ministers, V. E. Dymshits, the most prominent Jew in the Soviet Union. He was joined on the platform by three Jewish army generals, the editor Aleksandr Chakovsky, prominent Jewish academicians, a movie actress and the famed satirist Arkady Raikin, known for his irreverent mimicking of Nikita Khrushchev and for poking fun at the foibles of socialist reality. The most famous ballerina in the Soviet Union, Maya Plisetskaya, signed the petition as did the pianist Leonid Kogan, but they refused to appear at the press conference.

The statement sought to disassociate Soviet Jews from "international Zionism" and charged that Israeli aggression "has become a component part of the imperialist, neocolonialist plot directed against the people and progressive regimes of the Middle East, the plot in which the interests of oil monopolies and international Zionist organizations are closely intertwined." Aaron Vergelis, editor of the Jewish literary magazine *Sovetish Geimland (Soviet Homeland)* stressed the contribution of Jews to Soviet life. A poem addressed to Golda Meir by L. Shkolnik, a Jewish worker in a shoe factory, was read to the assembled Soviet and foreign correspondents:

> *You don't have to save me, madam,*
> *We go different ways;*
> *No Gods will help you,*
> *Because your thoughts and soul*
> *are black.*

The conference was unprecedented and indicated the depths of concern and inability of Soviet officials to deal with the problem. Mounting international criticism of Soviet treatment of Jews who tried to emigrate had stung the Politburo and it counterattacked with the press conference. The Jews had been put in an impossible position: they must either sign the petition distributed at the conference or face charges of disloyalty and treason. The petition statement they were coerced to sign read: "Being Soviet patriots and internationalists, we scorn the ludicrous claims of the rulers of Israel and their Zionist accomplices in other countries to speak on behalf of all Jews. Jewish working people, just as progressive people of all other countries and people of the world, do not have and cannot have anything in common with the Zionist racists." The conference extolled the virtues of life in the Soviet Union for Jews and noted that 340,000 Jews had been awarded orders and medals of the Soviet Union and seventy-one Jews had become Heroes of Soviet labor.

The press conference was followed by a full-fledged press campaign throughout the Soviet Union. Letters to the editor in the Ukraine blamed Ukrainian nationalism on Zionism, and Viktor Mayevsky, a *Pravda* commentator, charged that decisions by Israeli courts defining Jewishness, were similar to the Munich race laws of Nazi Germany. Mayevsky added that Israel and the United States "try in every way to divert the attention of the international public from their black deeds and switch attention to the so-called 'Jewish question' in the Soviet Union." The transparent nature of the press conference and the crudity of the attacks revealed their true propaganda purpose.

The following week an extraordinary statement was circulating in

Moscow signed by thirty-nine young Jews, most of them professionals and workers. The letter, addressed to Leonid Zamyatin, chief of the Press Department of the Ministry of Foreign Affairs, complained that the signers had not been invited to the press conference to express their views.

"We believe," they wrote, "that now Jews will answer the anti-Israel campaign not by renunciation, but on the contrary, by fortifying their pride in their people, by exclaiming 'next year in Jerusalem.' " Foreign correspondents reported the letter, which denied that Israel is a racist state and contradicted the theme of the press conference. "It is the very preservation of national originality of Jews which is the problem in the Soviet Union, and no reference to completely equal and joyful labor together can divert our attention from the problem."

Izvestia quickly labeled the letter "another provocation by Zionists" and singled out the names of the foreign correspondents whose newspapers printed the contents of the letter. The warning of expulsion was blatant. "Until now," *Izvestia* said, "we regarded those Western correspondents as representatives of papers, news agencies or broadcasting corporations of the United States and Britain. Now we also know that they represent international Zionism too. But they were not accredited in our country in this capacity — and this should be remembered."

Leona. One of the Jewish leaders who came to see Jerry brought him the works of a poet from Riga who wrote in Yiddish. I had not read anything in Yiddish in fifteen years but I could make out enough of it to understand the deep sorrow the poems expressed. He wrote that to leave his home, the mother soil from which he grew, was for him like "tearing off his skin." But to remain would be to lose his religion, the continuity that had been maintained through the efforts and sacrifice of two thousand years. It was becoming harder in each generation to impart a Jewish education; the Yiddish theater, the religious schools were gone and if his children held on they would know less of their religion than he did and their children would lose even more of their heritage. To stay meant gradual obliteration of their Jewishness; they had nothing to lose by coming out openly to try to go to Israel. Perhaps they would be arrested and sent to labor camps, but some would survive and carry on.

It was in labor camps, in fact, that some of the present dreaming and plotting had begun. In the long months and years of imprisonment friendships and promises were made.

Jerry. "On the 15th of June in Smolny Airport [the airport for Leningrad] a group of criminals attempting to seize a scheduled airplane were arrested. An investigation is being carried out." The news was carried on an inside page of *Leningradskaya Pravda* on June 16, 1970. There were no further details in the first public report of an attempted hijacking of an airplane in the Soviet Union. As I phoned to colleagues and then made the rounds of my sources, the story began to unfold. Nine men and three women were arrested at 9:30 A.M. at Smolny Airport as they moved to board a twelve-passenger AN-10 aircraft that was scheduled to fly to Karelia near the Soviet-Finnish border. The group of twelve included four Jews who sought to leave the Soviet Union for Israel. The KGB had infiltrated an informer into the group and the hijackers were surrounded before they could even board the plane. At the same time as these arrests were made, searches and arrests were made in the homes of eight Jews in Leningrad who had applied to emigrate to Israel. Searches were also carried out in apartments of Jews in Riga, Kharkov and Moscow who likewise had applied to emigrate to Israel. Those arrested were told that the KGB was investigating a crime of high treason. Under the criminal law of the Russian Federation, "flight abroad" is a treasonable offense with punishments ranging from ten years' imprisonment to death. Silva Zalmonson and her husband Eduard Kuznetsov were sentenced to fifteen years and death respectively. The death penalty was rescinded after public protests and secret negotiations between the U.S. and Soviet governments. Silva Zalmonson was freed in September 1974 and permitted to emigrate to Israel after four years in jail. Eduard Kuznetsov is serving a fifteen-year sentence in a labor camp.

The hijacking attempt made headlines around the world and underscored the plight of Jews who were trying to leave. The hijackers had been found with a hunting knife and a rope. The threat of the death penalty for the hijackers, the Leningrad arrests, and the searches of Jews throughout the Soviet Union who had applied for emigration mobilized efforts to bring their case to the world.

In Moscow an informal committee was formed among Jews trying to leave, a committee of correspondence, which was in touch by mail with three thousand Jews throughout the Soviet Union. A Russian friend promised to put me in touch with the leaders of the group, and the week after the hijacking it was arranged. Leona and I were to meet the leader and my Russian friend Fedya, who would interpret for us.

I drove to the usual meeting place to pick up Fedya in front of the Malaya Bronnaya Theater off Gorky Street but Fedya was not there. We came back a half hour later and still he had not arrived. There was no way to telephone him and I knew he usually kept our appointments. Had he been arrested, I wondered. We drove around Moscow for another fifteen minutes and then returned to the theater. He was there and apologized for being late. Because of his lateness we had missed the Jewish leader and Fedya said he would take us to his apartment. It was nearly midnight as we drove along Leningradskoye Chaussée and then turned off on the outskirts of the city to a new apartment house development. The endless rows of buildings and fresh construction all looked alike. Fedya told us to sit in the car as he walked the final two blocks to find Vitaly, an architect. We decided it was safer to walk and talk on the street than to meet in Vitaly's apartment. I liked the architect immediately. He was an activist with a sense of purpose. He seemed to understand the needs of the people he was responsible for and did not want to take unnecessary risks. He said he was seeing me because the hijacking had changed the character of the efforts to emigrate.

"We feel that an anti-Semitic drive is beginning to build up. When you live here long enough you know the signs," he explained. He said that the hijacking was a real attempt to flee from the Soviet Union, and had been planned in a labor camp. In the soft June evening we walked quietly along the pathway between the apartment houses. He told me of the letters he had received from Jews throughout the Soviet Union. They were preparing a letter to U Thant, secretary general of the United Nations, who was soon due to visit the Soviet Union. "The letter," said Vitaly, "will explain our position. We have no national life in the Soviet Union. There is not a single Yiddish school or Yiddish textbook. Other nationalities maintain their own languages and literature, but the Jewish autonomous region in Birobidzhan is an impossible place to live. It is an area for exile, not normal life. As a result of government policy the young generation of Jews does not know its mother tongue. We ask only one thing from the Soviet government — let the Jews go to Israel." He had gathered seventy-five names and addresses for the letter. When I asked if these Jews were not afraid of reprisal he replied: "We have nothing more to lose. Once we decide to leave the Soviet Union we have to face whatever comes. We are counting on support from the outside. This government does respond to international public opinion. Our lives here are without meaning."

He told me about a young engineer from Kharkov, Aaron S. Bogdanovski, who was invited by relatives in Israel to join them. In September 1969 Bogdanovski was told that his permission to leave the Soviet Union had been granted and he should prepare to leave. After selling most of his personal household goods he journeyed to Moscow where the permission to leave was revoked. Despite eight visits to the Ministry of the Interior he was told that his case was under consideration and he would have to wait six months. Without a job, he was relying on friends and seeking to attract attention to his case. Vitaly showed me an appeal from Bogdanovsky trying to renounce his Soviet citizenship saying, "I, a Jew from Kharkov, am ready at any moment to go to Israel, even on foot, leaving all my belongings behind."

As the pressures on the Jews increased, they became more determined to leave. The government's ineptness and indecision strengthened their resolve. Vitaly and his group became adept at issuing petitions and appeals and trying to keep their cases in the news. The example of the Jews seemed to spur others to action.

One evening, minutes after I had returned home from the office, the doorbell rang. Standing in the doorway was a carefully but shabbily dressed Russian man who appeared to be in his early sixties. His blue eyes alternated between a distant look and a furtive intensity as they darted past me into the apartment, then back at the stairway and the elevator door. His face was agitated and I could see he was afraid of being followed.

"Please come in. Come in," I offered.

He thanked me profusely and politely, so much so that I found it embarrassing. Then he stopped to remove his shoes. "That's not necessary," I said, but he insisted and carried his shoes in one hand as I showed him into the sitting room of our apartment and turned on a loud record. His nervousness seemed to increase once he was inside and I tried to calm him down by offering him a cup of tea. He refused politely.

"I came from around the back side of the house through the woods so that the policeman would not see me. Then I walked up the stairs so nobody would find me," he explained, never raising his voice above a whisper.

Why had he come to see me? I asked. He had heard my name from one of the other correspondents and said he wanted me to publish his writings. "I am a secret Christian," he explained. "I want people in America to know that there are Christians in the Soviet Union and that they are opposed to the Soviet invasion of Czechoslovakia."

Did he belong to a group, I asked. He could not answer me, he said. He had come to Moscow from Tula, a hundred miles away, where he lived as a pensioner. He did not want to involve others. It was enough that he had taken the risk to come to visit a foreign correspondent, he said. I reassured him that his material was safe with me, but I also explained that just because he had brought me his writings did not mean that I could arrange to publish them. I was not a publisher, but a foreign correspondent. He took from his breast pocket three faded-blue notebooks which he carefully handed to me. I glanced through them quickly and saw references to religious faith and a strong denunciation of the invasion of Czechoslovakia. One section dealt at length with the self-immolation of a young philosophy student, Jan Palach, who had burned himself to death in protest against the invasion. There were people who did not think that Palach's sacrifice had been in vain, he wrote. His ideas were a diffuse Christian humanism based on a strong belief in God. Sympathy for his desire to have his ideas published welled up within me as I read on. He kept repeating, "How important it is to have people in America read my writings. You are the only chance for me."

In the minutes that it had taken for me to invite him into the house and hear his story my own thoughts and emotions raced through a gamut of possibilities. Was the old man sent to involve me in a provocation? The spring had been full of such moments. Only a few nights before, when I got into my car outside of Ed Stevens's house on Releyev Street a man thrust a bundle of papers into my hands and fled into the darkness. The next morning I studied them and found a series of complaints about how a hospital in Kazakhstan was being corrupted by the supervisory staff. There was a long litany of abuses and persecutions of people. Why me, I wondered. Was it the new mood or was I the subject of special attentions from the KGB? Should I deal

with this kind of material in a meaningful way? In front of the
Gastronom Leona had been approached by a man who said he was an
Armenian who wanted help in getting to the Red Cross so he could
plead his case to leave the Soviet Union. Our lives were constantly
being assaulted by people taking risks of desperation and counting on
us for help, yet we could only listen with sympathy and write their
stories. As in the case of the old man sitting next to me, each one
thought his case and ideas paramount but I had to pick and choose.
How to explain that his feelings of frustration with the invasion of
Czechoslovakia and his ideas about God were not news. I promised to
try and use some of his ideas in a story on religion in the Soviet Union
and asked him if there were any others in his group. He said he could
not tell me. His eyes had a faraway look. He seemed relieved to have
delivered the notebooks even though I could not promise their publication. We shook hands warmly and he seemed less tense when he put
his shoes on outside the door and began the long descent down from
the sixteenth floor.

Leona. Early in May of 1970, while giving the children lunch one
day, Lyuba began a tirade against the New York police. She had read
in *Pravda* that members of the Jewish Defense League had beaten up
Russians at the Soviet trade office with lead pipes and that the police
had stood by. She became vehement against the Jewish gangsters and
the U.S. government, which had obviously sanctioned the violence.
Stevo instinctively fought back, telling her that what she had read was
wrong; the police would never allow anyone to beat up foreign representatives and certainly the government wouldn't allow it. But he had
no information to counter hers; he had never heard of the Jewish
Defense League or its activities.

Lyuba's attitude was a strange combination of *Pravda* news stories,
the anti-Semitism she had been taught as a child, and a liking for the
Jews she had worked for at the Israeli Embassy before the Soviet Union
broke off diplomatic relations with Israel in 1967. When my electric
mixer stopped working, she lent me her American mixer, already
converted to Moscow current. When the Israelis left they gave away all
of the Embassy's appliances and housewares to the Russian staff, in a
gesture to demonstrate they were genuine socialists. Later, when I
mentioned Lyuba's mixer to an Israeli diplomat in Washington he

smiled wryly. "I'm glad our intentions weren't totally lost," he said. "Someone understood."

The rest of May and all of June, until we left Moscow on the first of July, Lyuba frequently brought up at lunch what she had read about Jews in *Pravda* that morning. She was a barometer of the rising pressure. The first argument with Stevo about the JDL was not the last; in addition she became concerned with Jews who openly asked for exit visas to leave for Israel.

"What do they have to complain about?" she asked. "They have jobs and food to eat, the same as any other Soviet citizen."

From day to day a residue of ill feeling between Lyuba and the children remained. What began as a small argument, perhaps a misunderstanding, was repeated so often that the air was not cleared of it before the next workday began. An issue that had nothing to do with them personally built up into visible hostility. The children were relieved to get away from her when we left for France.

When we came out of the Soviet Union we had looked forward to the wedding of our friend and former Moscow house guest, Marc Leland, in Paris the first week in July. In view of what the children would need to wear during its three days of wedding festivities, they were barefoot and in rags. We spent a week in Paris shopping for shoes, pants, jackets, socks, shirts — there was nothing in Moscow we could buy beforehand. During that week we decided we would not return to live in Moscow another year. Good friends took the children to start their vacation in Spain while Jerry and I went back to pack up the apartment and ship our household to the United States.

Russian packers from UpDK came to the apartment to estimate how much excelsior, paper and twine they would need. While the foreman was there, he picked up an ikon, put it down again, and shrugged. "It's eighteenth century, not very valuable, you can take it." He looked around at the paintings on the walls, which were mostly Japanese and Southeast Asian. He thought the "map of Ghana" was Japanese and took no notice of it.

The Russian packers should have taken a few lessons from the Japanese. I watched them pack crystal goblets in layers of excelsior and objected that they were not secure. "We always do it this way and it works well. We never get complaints." Sixteen pieces arrived in smithereens. Some miraculously got through. They helped themselves to whatever brightly colored clothes lay at the tops of boxes, and pocketed whatever silver pieces were not packed away out of sight.

When the packers were nearly finished a large truck holding room-size containers drew up to the building and began loading crates from our apartment. The trucking foreman was a tall, large-bellied man with one leg much shorter than the other, which caused him to limp with a deep dip on the short side. He was the same truck foreman who had moved us in. Seeing him again made the whole effort seem like a movie played backward.

Is that what these two years have amounted to? I asked myself. Have we ended where we began, packing up what we unpacked such a short time ago? With the addition of a few pans and pictures is this the same household we brought from Tokyo and will arrange inside new walls when we find a place to live in Washington? Are we the same people we were when we left the last resting place? Is our whole life as silly as a film played and reversed, in which wine being poured into a glass moves back into the bottle?

No. We came to try and understand the Soviet system and the well-springs of Communist power, and in the process of that self-education we changed. We absorbed the lessons Moscow teaches. We came trying to perceive what Communists heralded as the future. What we saw in Moscow was the living past. The Soviet Union, unlike Japan and America, doesn't change. It is a stagnant society, which for a newsman, once he has witnessed it, becomes a dead end.

By the time we left Moscow we felt we had lost our innocence. All of us had been forced to make moral choices we would have shrunk from elsewhere. We made friends with people we didn't trust, distrusted our real friends at times, made compromises we rationalized as the pursuit of learning. Less so than before we could not throw a first stone.

We had lost the naïveté of the wide-eyed traveler. The Soviet Union as a system had less to teach us in a positive sense than we had expected; from Russians we learned more than we had expected about depth of personal commitment and the complex demands of friendship. The intensity of these human relationships was unique in our experience. After two years we felt we had emotionally been to the end of the world. It was time to go home.

We could see it in the children. They had acquired the veneer of little Russians, reticent to speak freely and openly with people we didn't know well. They were careful and guarded, secretive about mentioning a friend's name when repeating some bit of information he had given us. Trust became reserved, finally, only for the family.

In their school life the children added to their knowledge but not to their intellectual development. In Soviet classrooms they never had the opportunity to ask questions, argue a position, test their powers of logic through to a conclusion. That kind of individual growth and learning had to wait until they returned to American classrooms. Yet the very rigidity of Russian schooling provided a comforting, predictable framework for the younger children. The demands on them were clearly marked out; there were norms to fulfill and no more was asked. They had to learn to memorize, a faculty almost lost in American schools, to organize their work, to endure the repetitive, patient study that goes into learning a foreign language. Coping with Russian school taught them never to feel insecure in an exotic situation — with effort they could survive and even excel.

They learned to rely heavily on their instincts, to judge character and intentions. They learned that communication is not only language but the perception of another person's honesty.

In striving not to be shut into a foreign ghetto they had to make choices and take chances that led to personal hurts and rich rewards. They grew older and wiser than their years. Too much silence, discipline and conformity were asked. As Americans they believed there was a better world and they wanted to become part of it.

Looking at America from Moscow made us want to move on to where the action was, where the society, for all its faults, was changing, groping, experimenting; where historical prejudices against blacks, women and other minorities were being budged. The real social revolutions, to which the Marxists lay claim, were occurring not in the Soviet Union but in America. We felt drawn home to take part in them.

The worst moment of the packing was the first, when Lyuba and I together rolled up the rugs to clear the floor. It bore down on both of us as an act of ending. I clasped my stomach, cramped in a spasmic pain, and Lyuba wept. "The worst part is that the children won't be back again before you leave. When you left with them I thought we'd see each other again after the summer. We shouldn't have . . ." She didn't finish and I looked at her questioningly, waiting for the end of the sentence. She went off to some chore where she could cry alone.

I knew what she couldn't say. She didn't care about the Jews; not enough, anyway, to have fought with the children and left them with harsh feelings to remember her by.

Index